JUSTICE ABANDONED

JUSTICE ABANDONED

*How the Supreme Court Ignored the Constitution
and Enabled Mass Incarceration*

RACHEL ELISE BARKOW

HARVARD UNIVERSITY PRESS
Cambridge, Massachusetts
London, England
2025

Copyright © 2025 by the President and Fellows of Harvard College
All rights reserved
Printed in the United States of America

First printing

Publication of this book has been supported through the generous provisions of the
Maurice and Lula Bradley Smith Memorial Fund.

Library of Congress Cataloging-in-Publication Data
Names: Barkow, Rachel E., author.
Title: Justice abandoned : how the Supreme Court ignored the Constitution and enabled mass incarceration / Rachel Elise Barkow.
Description: First. | Cambridge : Harvard University Press, 2025. | Includes bibliographical references and index.
Identifiers: LCCN 2024022348 (print) | LCCN 2024022349 (ebook) | ISBN 9780674294226 (cloth) | ISBN 9780674298927 (pdf) | ISBN 9780674298934 (epub)
Subjects: LCSH: Mass incarceration—United States. | Imprisonment—United States. | Arrest—United States. | Plea bargaining—United States. | Sentences (Criminal procedure)—United States. | Prisons—Overcrowding—Law and legislation—United States. | Stop and frisk (Law enforcement)—Law and legislation—United States. | Racism in criminal justice administration—United States. | United States. Supreme Court.
Classification: LCC KF9728 .B37 2025 (print) | LCC KF9728 (ebook) | DDC 345.73/0773—dc23/eng/20240712
LC record available at https://lccn.loc.gov/2024022348
LC ebook record available at https://lccn.loc.gov/2024022349

For Nate and Tony

CONTENTS

Introduction   1

1. Lowering the Bar for Pretrial Detention   12
   United States v. Salerno

2. Normalizing Coercive Plea Bargaining   47
   Bordenkircher v. Hayes

3. Upholding Disproportionate Sentences   82
   Harmelin v. Michigan

4. Tolerating Overcrowded Prisons   122
   Rhodes v. Chapman

5. Greenlighting Stop-and-Frisk   163
   Terry v. Ohio

6. Overlooking Pervasive Racial Bias   199
   McCleskey v. Kemp

Conclusion   236

Notes   *245*
Acknowledgments   *303*
Index   *305*

INTRODUCTION

> They who can give up essential liberty to obtain a little temporary safety deserve neither liberty nor safety.
> —BENJAMIN FRANKLIN

American identity is inextricably linked with a commitment to liberty. Our founding documents are awash with paeans to freedom. How, then, did the "sweet land of liberty" end up becoming home to the world's largest number of people behind bars? America has less than 5 percent of the world's population but almost a quarter of the world's prisoners. We keep nearly two million people behind bars, a rate that is five to ten times higher than that of other industrialized countries. More than four hundred thousand people—roughly equivalent to the population of Miami—are languishing in jails and have not yet even been convicted of a crime because they are awaiting their trials.[1] Those serving sentences after conviction often receive long sentences that cannot be justified by deterrence or any rational conception of what would be their just deserts for their crimes. These incarcerated people are typically held in squalid, overcrowded conditions, and they are disproportionately people of color.

It hasn't always been like this in America. For most of the country's existence, our punishment practices and imprisonment rates were comparable to other Western democracies. We set out on a different path beginning in the 1970s.[2] Many scholars and commentators, including me, have described the politics and cultural dynamics that drove these changes over the past fifty years.[3] The increase in violent crime in the 1960s set in motion critical political forces that propelled mass incarceration and ultimately took on a life of their own, divorced from actual crime rates and effective crime-fighting policies. Tough-on-crime politics have been a winning strategy for more than five decades in a media culture that creates the impression that violence and danger are ever present and that incarceration is the answer. Pressure mounts for more aggressive policing, less due process, more detention of people accused of crimes, and longer sentences served under ever-harsher conditions. Implicit and sometimes even explicit racial bias underlies many of the dynamics.

The politics of mass incarceration present an intractable problem that is not easily solved. Those of us who have identified possible political arguments or institutional changes to shift Americans' thinking about punishment and its effectiveness must concede that these strategies will take decades if not generations to reduce America's incarcerated population to levels comparable to other Western democracies and our own previous rates from fifty years ago. This is why many people have turned to more revolutionary tactics, including prison abolition or the rejection of capitalism. It is easy to see why people seek such dramatic, if unrealistic, changes. The politics of mass incarceration are deeply embedded in a history of slavery, racism, job displacement from industrialization, a lack of investment in a social safety net, and a host of other path dependencies that are not possible to change in any straightforward way.

But changing America's political landscape is not the only path for tackling mass incarceration. That is because it was not just the politics that started shifting five decades ago and paved the way for America's turn to large-scale incarceration and excessive punishment. There was another, equally important, transformation that occurred at the same time and also bears responsibility for the mass incarceration we see today.

The Supreme Court, starting in the 1960s, decided a series of cases that eviscerated the constitutional rights that were supposed to guard against government oppression through criminal punishment. Reasonable people can disagree over the proper methodology for interpreting the Constitution, but these cases are remarkable because they fail under all the leading approaches to constitutional interpretation. They contradict the original and plain meaning of the Constitution's text, they flout precedent that existed at the time they were decided, and they fly in the face of any theory of a living Constitution that is based on expanding notions of liberty and equality to changing circumstances. These cases can be defended only under a constitutional theory grounded in pathological deference to the government and its claims that liberty must be sacrificed for public safety. That, however, is less a constitutional theory of interpretation than it is pure politics.

Had the Court been faithful to the Constitution instead of its own notions of expediency and what it thought was best for public safety, we would not have the carceral landscape that dominates America today. Unpacking these cases is therefore a critical step in fully understanding mass incarceration in America. Doing so also provides a strategy for combatting it, because one way to curb mass incarceration is to reinvigorate the constitutional protections that should have been in full force throughout this time.

Our constitutional republic is designed to put the brakes on government excess when it infringes on liberty. That is, after all, the central story of our country's founding and the reason we fought a revolution to free ourselves from British rule. That is why George Washington's First Inaugural Address focused on "the preservation of the sacred fire of liberty, and the destiny of the Republican model of Government."[4] It is behind Patrick Henry's warning to the Virginia Convention on the ratification of the Constitution to "guard with jealous attention the public liberty" and to "suspect everyone who approaches that jewel."[5] Sam Adams spoke for a revolutionary generation when he wrote that "the liberties of our country, the freedom of our civil constitution, are worth defending against all hazards: And it is our duty to defend them against all attacks."[6]

The Framers did not miss the danger of government excess when it came to the state's authority in criminal matters.[7] Having seen the cruel operation of the Bloody Code in England and gross abuses by the kings in power, the Framers of our Constitution were well aware of the state's use and abuse of criminal laws and provided for a wealth of protections to protect and preserve individual liberty.[8] They went out of their way to make it difficult for the state to impose punishment. Under the Constitution, all three branches must agree before criminal power can be exercised. The legislature must criminalize the conduct, the executive must decide to enforce the law, and the judiciary, typically a jury, must convict. The Constitution is also replete with other provisions that check governmental abuse in criminal matters.[9] The Constitution covers everything from investigation to punishment.

And no wonder. Government power is most threatening in this context because it can strip away liberty and even take someone's life. The various constitutional provisions protecting liberty and setting up barriers before the government can punish someone all reflect the Framers' view that stopping governmental abuse of punishment power far outweighed any concerns with efficiency in response to crime. They intended to make it hard for the government to criminally punish people because they feared that making it too easy would be a far graver threat to core individual rights and safety. It is therefore not a flaw with the Constitution's design that has allowed mass incarceration to flourish. The Constitution anticipated the overreach of political actors under the guise of imposing criminal punishment. While many believe the Constitution should evolve as society changes, the threat to individual liberty from the government's power to punish has not diminished over time. We should be just as committed as the Framers were to making sure the government stays in check.

The problem is the Constitution cannot protect itself. The Supreme Court has to provide the necessary protection against government overreach when it conflicts with constitutional safeguards. Far from pushing back, however, the Supreme Court has lent the government a helping hand and paved the way for mass incarceration to thrive. Any story of mass incarceration in America is incomplete if it does not include the Supreme Court's pivotal role.

This book explores the Supreme Court's facilitation of mass incarceration by looking closely at six key decisions that, had they come out differently, could have placed an important brake on America's accelerating use of jails and prisons. While many more cases have undermined defendants' rights and increased government power than the six cases featured here, my focus is on these cases both because they form the foundation on which mass incarceration rests and because they were wrongly decided under traditionally accepted methods of constitutional interpretation that rely on text, the history at the time of the Constitution's framing, the subsequent history and precedent after the framing, and living constitutional theories that aim to expand the protection of liberty and a commitment to equality.

Most tragically of all, these cases were a fool's bargain from the outset. While the Supreme Court likely thought it was forging sensible compromises in the name of public safety when it decided these cases, thus justifying the outcomes under pragmatic or prudential theories of constitutional interpretation, empirical research shows that none of them has made us any safer.[10] On the contrary, these decisions allowed the government to avoid far more effective strategies for tackling the root causes of most criminal activity. Engaging in massive policing and detention, largely targeted at communities of color, is a superficially cheaper and quicker alternative, but it is not an effective one. We have traded liberty for the appearance of security, but not the real thing. Given his quote that opens this introduction, Benjamin Franklin would say America got just what it deserved.

It is not too late to right these wrongs. The Court that opted for the path of mass incarceration can now choose to take a different course. We can eliminate injustice simply by following the law. The Constitution stands at the ready. We just need a Supreme Court willing to do its job.

It all starts by recognizing where the Court went astray from the Constitution. Each of the following chapters explores one of the Court's crucial wrong turns. The format of these chapters is the same. They begin by explaining what the law would look like if the Court had been faithful to the Constitution's text, the original understanding of its drafters and ratifiers, and the Court's precedents, before turning to the case where the Court veered off course. The first part of each chapter will therefore appeal to those who follow these standard modalities of constitutional interpretation and make the case for overturning these decisions on those grounds. Each chapter then analyzes what happened in the aftermath of the decision and explains the relationship between the case and the rise of mass incarceration. In all six contexts, the Court's approach resulted in the dramatic curtailment of liberty and increased inequality. The aftermath section should therefore convince those who embrace more dynamic models of constitutional interpretation that, even under a flexible approach that embraces a living Constitution and focuses on pragmatic or prudential arguments, these cases were wrongly decided because they failed to expand the Constitution's core values to changing times, and instead led to disastrous outcomes for anyone concerned with liberty and equality, all while failing to make us any safer.

Chapter 1 begins by discussing *United States v. Salerno,* a critical decision lowering the bar for pretrial detention and a key factor leading to the almost half a million people who find themselves incarcerated before being convicted of anything. This is one quarter of the "mass" of mass incarceration, and if the Court had been faithful to the Constitution, only a fraction of these people could be detained. The Framers abhorred pretrial detention and heralded the presumption of innocence. The modern Supreme Court seems to have reversed these priorities. In *Salerno,* the Court, for the first time in the country's history, condoned the detention of people charged with a crime before their trials simply because they were deemed "dangerous." It is a decision contrary to due process and the Eighth Amendment, and it makes a mockery of the presumption of innocence. It is, however, a vivid example of how the Court let its own worries about crime overtake its constitutional obligations.

Most people who are incarcerated have been convicted, so Chapter 2 turns to the key decision behind the explosion in convictions in the past fifty years in America. It has been driven almost exclusively by the rise in plea bargaining and the penalties prosecutors impose on people who choose to exercise their trial rights. The government unlawfully intimidates people to give up their right to a jury trial by threatening greater punishment if they do not, but the Court has refused to protect the jury trial from this government coercion. This conflicts with the protection the Court gives other constitutional rights, where it has made clear that the government cannot impose unconstitutional conditions or penalties when someone seeks to claim a constitutional right. The Court's only reason for treating the right to a jury trial differently is a concern with judicial efficiency, not any constitutionally relevant distinction between the jury trial right and other constitutional rights that are protected from being coerced away. Chapter 2 thus explores the seminal and ultimately tragic case of *Bordenkircher v. Hayes* and its key role in the rise of mass incarceration. It is another example of how the Court set aside the Constitution because it believed it was more important to allow the government to mass-produce criminal cases to meet what it saw as public safety demands. Plea bargaining may bring efficiency benefits to the courts, but those gains come at the cost of the Constitution's jury guarantee.

Once the Court accepted coercive plea bargaining, the floodgates for incarceration opened wide. Plea bargaining not only increased admissions but also resulted in longer sentence lengths, the other key variable for mass incarceration to flourish, because prosecutors pushed for ever-harsher laws and mandatory minimums to increase their bargaining leverage. The Constitution directly confronts the dangers of excessively long sentences in the Eighth Amendment's Cruel and Unusual Punishment Clause, but the Court has almost completely abdicated its responsibility to police it, as Chapter 3 explains. The doctrinal test for whether a sentence amounts to cruel and unusual punishment has its roots in a concurring opinion by Justice Kennedy in *Harmelin v. Michigan* that a majority of the Court has embraced. That framework makes it virtually impossible for any sentence to be declared cruel and unusual because of the deference it gives the government. No matter how excessive a sentence of incarceration is in relation to a defendant's blameworthiness, the Court will accept it as long as the state can claim that it believes it brings a benefit by incapacitating the person. This standard is the reason no individualized challenge to a sentence of incarceration as violating the Eighth Amendment has succeeded before the Court in more than fifty years despite the fact that the tough-on-crime era has produced thousands upon thousands of sentences that bear no relationship to any conception of someone's just deserts.

These first three cases alone could have changed the entire landscape of punishment in America had they come out differently. If the Court were faithful to the Constitution, we would not have massive pretrial detention on the basis of predictions of dangerousness. We would not have coercive plea bargains, which would dramatically lower the number of convictions and require prosecutors to focus on the most serious crimes worthy of the time for a trial instead of mass processing minor offenses because it is essentially costless to them to do so. And we would have limits on how much punishment people could receive for their crimes, thus preventing a huge proportion of the excessive sentences that have been handed down over the past five decades and that are continually meted out in courtrooms across America. These are literally game-changing cases, and all of them were wrongly decided under all the traditional methods of constitutional interpretation. They were justified only if one believes the government should win when it claims it needs something for the sake of public safety and administrative convenience. Unfortunately, we have had enough justices on the Court who have believed just that.

While the first three chapters explore the cases that most directly facilitated mass incarceration, the last three chapters analyze cases that have an indirect but still critical role in allowing mass incarceration to metastasize. Mass incarceration costs money, and at some point the price tag will be too high for the government to continue to pursue it as a strategy. The Court, however, essentially put in place a massive clearance sale on the constitutional price of incarceration by failing to police overcrowding and the conditions of confinement in any meaningful way. Chapter 4 explores the Court's tolerance of double bunking and all the mental and physical harm that flows from it by describing the case of *Rhodes v. Chapman*. *Rhodes* is not the only key case in this area, but it is emblematic of the Court's failure to police prison conditions, and that failure has been an indispensable aspect of mass incarceration's success. If jurisdictions had to provide adequate space and constitutional conditions, incarceration would cost far more, and inevitably jurisdictions would use it less. Instead, the Court did everything in its power to lower the price instead of enforcing the Eighth Amendment's limits.

Mass incarceration depends on the police because every person in jail or prison got there after being arrested. In that sense, anything that expands the power of the police will feed mass incarceration to some extent. There is a multitude of Supreme Court cases that wrongly expanded police power, and properly exploring the relationship between the Court, policing, and mass incarceration requires the exploration of several cases, not just one. Put another way, the problems with policing are the result of a series of bad decisions. Chapter 5, however, focuses on the most consequential policing case for mass incarceration, *Terry v. Ohio*, because it is the case that ushers in the era of mass policing. The Court in *Terry* authorized the police to stop and frisk individuals based merely on suspicion, diverging from the nation's long-standing tradition of requiring probable cause for police seizures and searches. It was a key ingredient to mass incarceration because it led to a new policing model of programmatic stop-and-frisk that resulted in millions of forcible police encounters. While most of those encounters turn up no evidence of crimes, even the small percentage that do has resulted in hundreds of thousands of people occupying the country's jails and prisons, mostly for minor offenses like trespassing, disorderly conduct, and drug possession. Moreover, *Terry* reflects what was to become the dominant Court approach in the decades that followed in other policing cases: a Court capitulating to law enforcement demands instead of holding the constitutional line. The outcome in *Terry* must have seemed like a sensible balancing of interests to the Court, but instead it ushered in an era of aggressive policing that has fed mass incarceration and decimated the perceived legitimacy of the police in communities of color. It has, like all the other cases discussed, harmed instead of helped public safety.

Finally, mass incarceration is about more than just the rate of imprisonment and the overall size of the incarcerated population. It also refers to the fact that the brunt of the hardship disproportionately falls on communities of color. David Garland, the leading sociologist of punishment, explains that "imprisonment becomes mass imprisonment when it ceases to be the incarceration of individual offenders and becomes the systematic imprisonment of whole groups of the population," which, in the case of American incarceration, means young Black males from largely urban communities. At its peak, mass incarceration resulted in one in every three Black men between the ages of twenty and twenty-nine being either incarcerated or under criminal supervision.[11] Thus, as Garland notes, "every family, every household, every individual in these neighbourhoods has direct personal knowledge of the prison—through a spouse, a child, a parent, a neighbour, a friend. Imprisonment ceases to be the fate of a few criminal individuals and becomes a shaping institution for whole sectors of the population."[12] Mass incarceration would never succeed in America if its misery was not disproportionately experienced by minority groups with relatively less political power. In the key case of *McCleskey v. Kemp*, explored in Chapter 6, the Court made it almost impossible to succeed on claims of racial discrimination in the enforcement of criminal law. The case is an outgrowth of earlier cases decided by the Court, but it was not an inevitable progression to decide *McCleskey* as the Court did. The result is that racial bias permeates every aspect of the criminal punishment pipeline, from policing to charging, from plea bargaining to sentencing, and the Constitution's command for equal protection has become an empty platitude.

Taken together, these six cases serve as the foundation for mass incarceration, each one deviating from constitutional principles that should have prevented the scale of imprisonment that ultimately materialized. To be sure, long before the Court gave its imprimatur, judges were detaining people they believed to be dangerous, prosecutors were engaged in coercive plea negotiations, long sentences existed, prison conditions were dismal, the police were stopping and frisking people without probable cause, and racial bias characterized the operation of criminal law. The Supreme Court's approval, however, gave license for these practices to be employed on a massive scale. Before the Court's rubber stamp, these were often sub rosa practices or only occasionally used because of their questionable legality. When these practices remained in the shadows, their numbers stayed in check. It was not until the Court gave its explicit blessing to detention on the basis of predicted dangerousness, to coercive plea bargaining, to prison and jail overcrowding, and to police stops and searches without probable cause that their use exploded. While sentence lengths were already growing ever longer by the time the Court abandoned its Eighth Amendment oversight, and racial discrimination has characterized the operation of criminal law from the nation's founding, the Court's failure to take a stand against those developments meant that mass incarceration flourished.

What the Court says matters greatly, and there is a direct through line between the Court's pronouncement that a practice is constitutional and its explosive use throughout the country. The Court has thus played a pivotal role in establishing mass incarceration in America, and the central goal of this book is to expose its culpability. We might like to think of the Court as above the political fray, guarding long-term constitutional values against short-term panics. As the following chapters show, however, the Court fell prey to the same tough-on-crime frenzy as the public. The Supreme Court has been a key contributor to the rise of mass incarceration, and this book explores its role.

But the book aims to be more than an autopsy of what the Court got wrong and the relationship between key Supreme Court cases and mass incarceration. It is also a blueprint for shifting course. While respect for precedent is an important part of common-law decision-making and steadiness in governance, sometimes stability requires admitting error and putting the country on a better course. These cases were wrong under the major metrics by which we typically judge constitutional decisions. They conflict with the original meaning of the Constitution's text, they contradict historical tradition, and they are at odds with core notions of individual liberty and a commitment to equality that remain cornerstones of dynamic or living constitutional interpretation theories. Instead, what these cases have in common is an unquestioning deference to whatever the government argued was necessary for the efficient pursuit of public safety. And because the government got it wrong, and the compromises in these cases do not make us safer, even the most pragmatic approaches to constitutional interpretation should see these cases as abject failures.

Litigants should therefore urge the Court to overturn these cases, or at least limit their reach, because they were wrongly decided. While the current Court is a conservative one, it contains enough justices who are committed to originalism and willing to overturn cases that it is not unthinkable to imagine a doctrinal shift even with the current crop of justices staying in place. The justices who decided these cases did not focus on originalist arguments; nor did they have the empirical evidence that undercuts the government's public safety claims. It is much easier for justices today to resist the government's public safety claims in light of their inconsistency with the Constitution's original meaning and their failed track record on the ground.

Moreover, over the longer term, the personnel of the Court will change, and advocates who care about mass incarceration should pay close attention to nominations and urge the appointment of justices who will not simply reflexively rule in the government's favor in criminal matters. The social movement to reduce mass incarceration should not ignore the Court's potential as a driver for change because, while it currently props up mass incarceration, it can aid in its demise. As those who oppose mass incarceration and support racial justice gain political power, it is important to channel that power in the most productive ways to resist backlash and reversal. The Court is an ideal target for these advocates because putting justices on the Court who share those commitments can produce generational change that is not vulnerable to shifting political winds. While advocates should target state supreme court and lower federal court appointments as well, Supreme Court nominations are the most important because the Supreme Court sets the bar nationally. Lower federal courts have to follow its edicts, and while state supreme courts can go further than the US Supreme Court in protecting rights, they cannot fall below the federal threshold. This is critical because the political landscape in most states is nowhere near a point that electing state high court judges committed to reducing mass incarceration is feasible. Change is, however, achievable on the Supreme Court precisely because the appointments process is not based on a direct election and because the cases discussed here fail under so many different constitutional approaches, including the originalist methodology that appeals to Republicans and the more progressive theories of interpretation that Democrats favor. These cases are the relatively rare ones where both theories should lead to a conclusion that they should be overruled.

It is hard to imagine many other areas where the Court's failings have been more disastrous than in the cases that have failed to protect cornerstone principles of liberty and turned America into the planet's premier penitentiary operator. These cases undermine America's core values, dismiss the value of human dignity, and destroy lives and communities. And they do so without making us any safer. It is time to recommit to the Constitution's safeguards of liberty, and overturning these cases is the place to start. The Constitution provides checks on mass incarceration—it just needs a Court willing to fulfill its promise.

CHAPTER ONE

LOWERING THE BAR FOR PRETRIAL DETENTION

United States v. Salerno

> Throughout the world today there are men, women, and children interned indefinitely, awaiting trials which may never come or which may be a mockery of the word, because their governments believe them to be "dangerous." Our Constitution, whose construction began two centuries ago, can shelter us forever from the evils of such unchecked power.
>
> —JUSTICE THURGOOD MARSHALL

It would be hard to explain the presumption of innocence to Tyrone Tomlin. He purchased a soda from a discount store, and the clerk handed it back to him in a paper bag, along with a straw. Tomlin came outside and rejoined the group of friends he had been talking to outside the store in the Crown Heights neighborhood of Brooklyn, where Tomlin had lived his whole life. Two officers from the New York Police Department's narcotics squad called the group over. One of the officers inspected Tomlin's bag and questioned him about an object in his other hand. Despite Tomlin explaining that the object was just a straw for his soda, the officer arrested him, alleging that the straw was drug paraphernalia. In the arrest documentation, the officer claimed his training and experience led him to conclude straws were a "commonly used method of packaging heroin residue." The prosecutor told Tomlin if he pleaded guilty to a misdemeanor charge of possession of a controlled substance, he would get a thirty-day sentence. Tomlin refused, telling his defense lawyer, "It's a regular straw!" He was confident he would be cleared once they tested the straw. But at his arraignment, the prosecutor requested bail, and the judge set it at $1,500.

Unable to pay the $1,500 bail, Tomlin was sent to Rikers Island, one of the country's most horrific jails. All this happened without a trial, a test of the straw, or any deliberation on the necessity of his detention. Tomlin's description of Rikers echoed what so many others have said: "That place is miserable. It's dangerous. It's every man for himself. You could get abused; you could be raped; you could be extorted." A group of men brutally attacked him in the shower. It wasn't until three weeks after his arrival at Rikers that the prosecutor finally reviewed the lab report of the straw, which confirmed it was clean. The prosecutor then asked the judge to dismiss the case. Without expressing an ounce of regret that this innocent man lost his freedom for three weeks and was severely beaten while in custody, the judge told Tomlin, "This is your lucky day; you're going home." Tomlin still suffers from blurred vision in his left eye due to the assault.

Tomlin's story would likely resonate with Adriana, a young mother of a toddler, who had her own horrific experience with pretrial detention. She left a shelter for survivors of domestic violence, where she had been staying, to buy diapers for her daughter. A friend at the shelter agreed to babysit while Adriana went to the nearby store. A staff member noticed Adriana leaving without her baby and reported her to the police. When Adriana returned with the diapers, the police arrested her and charged her with endangering the welfare of a child. At her arraignment, the prosecutor objected to the defense's request for Adriana's release on her own recognizance. The judge sided with the prosecution and set bail at $1,500. Adriana's public defender asked the judge to "state the reason for setting bail in this case." The judge's response: "Thank you, counsel." No explanation, no consideration of why detention was necessary. Adriana spent two weeks on Rikers Island. She lost her bed at the shelter, and her baby was placed in foster care. After agreeing to a deal with prosecutors to attend a life-skills class, she was finally released. The judge told her, "Congratulations on being in a place where a lot of people care about you." She was still fighting to get her daughter back five months after her arrest.[1]

Even a short stay in jail can cause lasting damage, as the cases of Tyrone Tomlin and Adriana show. But often, pretrial detention drags on much longer. Take Victor Jimenez, who was arrested in August 2016 on charges of illegal possession of a firearm and selling drugs. Opting to exercise his right to a jury trial, he was acquitted of all charges in January 2018. Jimenez nevertheless spent 503 days in jail because he was detained while awaiting his trial and verdict.[2] He spent that time in a Los Angeles County jail infamous for violent gangs, savage abuse of detained individuals by corrections officers, massive overcrowding, and grossly unsanitary conditions.[3]

Kalief Browder was sixteen years old when he was arrested for allegedly stealing a backpack. He rejected prosecutors' plea deal offers and continued to assert his innocence. He was detained for three years on Rikers Island, spending roughly two of those years in solitary confinement. During this time, he suffered repeated abuse at the hands of corrections officers and fellow detainees. He made multiple attempts to take his own life while incarcerated. Eventually, prosecutors dismissed the case against him. But Browder never recovered from the trauma of his incarceration. His mental health continued to deteriorate after he was released, and he died by suicide.[4]

These stories are the tip of a tragic iceberg. On any given day in America, we have almost half a million stories like these, of people locked away in jails awaiting trial. Like Tyrone Tomlin, Victor Jimenez, and Kalief Browder, many of these individuals are detained and ultimately not convicted. Before the rise of plea bargaining inflated conviction rates, studies showed that a quarter of people detained pretrial were not ultimately convicted.[5] Even when people were convicted, they often would not face incarceration were it not for pretrial detention.[6] Additionally, many defendants detained pretrial are sentenced to the time they served in jail, which masks excess time that would never have been imposed in the first place were it not for pretrial detention.[7] These people are not compensated for their lost liberty. They are casualties in a failed war on crime that has become a war on liberty.

People locked away before their trials find themselves living in deplorable facilities. Our nation's jails are often overcrowded, lack proper heating and air conditioning, and contain mold and asbestos. They are teeming with disease. Physical and sexual violence are common, and health care in jails is notoriously bad. Suicides and other deaths are all too frequent.[8] Crushing boredom is pervasive because there is often no programming or activities.

These periods of detention are devastating to people's lives. They lose their jobs, their housing, custody of their kids. They are less likely to receive treatment for mental health and addiction problems. It should not surprise anyone that detention itself causes crime. Locking people away upends their lives in the worst of ways.[9] While media reports may lead people to think that pretrial detention is the answer to preventing crimes, it is just the opposite. We are leading people to desperate situations and criminal behavior by overusing incarceration before trial.

One might think that the category of people who are ultimately sentenced to additional terms of incarceration beyond the period they were locked away pretrial are not worse off because the time they served pretrial counts toward their sentence. But they, too, suffer injustices from their pretrial detention. The detention itself makes it more likely they will be convicted. People are more likely to plead guilty to shorten the time they will spend in jail, either because it means they will be released based on time already served or because they prefer to go to a prison that may have better conditions. Convictions are also more likely because detention makes it harder for people to help with their own defense. They are limited in how often they can meet with counsel, and they cannot help search for evidence and witnesses. Sometimes defendants know witnesses only by sight or a nickname, making it hard for counsel to locate them without the defendant's help.[10] The job loss that comes with detention means fewer resources to hire a lawyer, investigators, or expert witnesses or to procure lab analysis to help their case. The harsh conditions of confinement may "damage [a detained person's] appearance or mental alertness at trial."[11] It is no wonder people detained pretrial are more likely to be convicted as compared to people charged with the same crimes and with similar records who are released. People detained pretrial get longer sentences, too.[12] People released pretrial can show the judge what they will do if not incarcerated, whereas those detained pretrial show up in jail uniforms, and the judge may have a harder time seeing them adjusting successfully.[13] And these negative effects do not fall equally across society. People of color are detained pretrial at higher rates.[14]

People seem to take the reality of broad pretrial detention for granted in America. If the public questions anything about it, the question usually pertains to why someone is released pretrial at all. This is largely because media reports focus on cases where someone who has been released pretrial commits a heinous crime while awaiting trial. These stories are then inevitably met with calls to find out why the person was free in the first place. The prevailing public sentiment seems to be that people should be locked up after arrest.

It was not like this for most of American history. We used to release almost everyone charged with a crime pending their trial. The shift began at the end of the 1960s. From 1970 to 2015, there was a 433 percent increase in people detained pretrial.[15] We went from a presumption of release to the opposite. Now it is more likely you are going to be detained than retain your freedom if you are charged with a crime. A whopping 60 percent of all defendants face pretrial detention.[16] In the federal system, a staggering 75 percent of defendants are detained.[17]

Like many roads to hell, this one was paved with good intentions. In the 1960s, reformers aimed to address the problem of indigent individuals being detained pretrial simply because they could not afford even modest bail. They were also concerned that people were being detained as a form of punishment or because they were viewed as dangerous, neither of which were permissible grounds for detention until the Supreme Court changed a legal landscape more than two hundred years old. These reformers relied on studies showing that people could be released on their own recognizance and would still appear for their trials. These findings ultimately led to the passage of the federal Bail Reform Act in 1966, which required noncapital defendants to be released on their own recognizance unless the judge found they presented too great a risk of flight.[18] The drafters of the law explained that it "does not deal with preventive detention of the accused because of the possibility that his liberty might endanger the public" for the very good reason that "under American criminal jurisprudence pretrial bail may not be used as a device to protect society from the possible commission of additional crimes by the accused."[19]

Successfully implementing the 1966 law proved difficult. Courts struggled to establish and enforce terms of release, and crimes committed by those on release drew negative publicity.[20] As crime rates exploded toward the end of the 1960s and the nation experienced widespread civil disorder, political pressure to limit pretrial release mounted. Despite the reminder from the Bail Reform Act's drafters that American law does not permit the detention of people pretrial for dangerousness, the public instinct is to lock away anyone who presents a danger because the public overestimates the benefit of pretrial detention on community safety and essentially values the defendant's liberty interest at zero.

This was the climate in the late 1960s. With crime rates spiking, politicians saw the advantage of taking a tough-on-crime position. A few states responded by changing their laws to allow judges explicitly to consider dangerousness as a factor in pretrial release decisions.[21] Richard Nixon proposed pretrial detention of "dangerous hard core recidivists" in the District of Columbia as part of a federal crime-fighting package he put forward within days of taking office.[22] The DC law proved a model for many states, with almost half the states following that approach within eight years.[23] By the

1980s, the clamor for preventive detention for dangerousness had a "broad base of support" that was "a reflection of the deep public concern" about people committing crimes on release pretrial.[24] Thus, in 1984, Congress passed a federal law authorizing the detention of people viewed as dangerous, and "dangerous" came to be viewed so broadly that it encompassed just about anyone who was charged with any kind of crime. States then copied the federal approach. Nearly half authorize preventive detention based on the commission of certain charges, and almost all authorize judges to consider a defendant's threat to public safety in setting bail.

This strategy, like so many of our approaches to crime, is ineffective. The overwhelming majority of people awaiting trial do not commit new crimes, let alone crimes one could fairly label as dangerous. They want to beat the charges they face, and they tend to be on their best behavior. It is the rare case where someone commits a new crime. That is why detaining large numbers of people pretrial does not make a dent in crime rates.[25] In fact, evidence shows widespread pretrial detention is likely to increase crime because of the disruptive effect it has on the people detained, who are often living on the margins and then spiral as a result of the effects of confinement. This is especially so given that so many of the people detained pretrial are there for minor offenses.[26] Pretrial detention offers little more than optics when it comes to crime prevention.

Still, optics often matter more than reality when it comes to politics. State and federal officials have increasingly used pretrial detention as one of their tough-on-crime battle calls, which explains why we have almost five hundred thousand people locked away pretrial—roughly a quarter of all those incarcerated. Although there have been some efforts at bail reform and reducing the population of people detained pretrial, the results have thus far been modest and have produced a backlash in many places that casts doubt on how much success is really possible in the political realm.

The real check on pretrial detention should not be coming from politics but from the Supreme Court enforcing the Constitution. We would not be living in a world of mass pretrial incarceration without the Supreme Court ignoring constitutional protections against this very dynamic and authorizing the incarceration of people based on a prediction of dangerousness.

The Constitutional Framework

The Framers were well aware of the risks of having the government detain people before a fair trial because they were familiar with the abusive pretrial detention practices in England, where monarchs would imprison political critics and set excessive bail to deny individuals their freedom before trial. The Framers also took note of the English reforms in response to these abuses and ensured America had equally strong, if not stronger, safeguards. As a result, unlike prevailing public sentiment, the Constitution does not prioritize some vague feeling of community safety over the tangible liberty interests of the accused. It views the balance differently and guards against the populist panic that would too easily dispense with individual rights and permit detention before an adjudication of guilt.

The incarceration of almost half a million people before conviction flies in the face of both the Constitution's text and history and basic concepts of liberty that animate our constitutional republic. This should be an area where the Court's originalists, its libertarians, and its liberals all come together and protect the presumption of innocence and safeguard freedom. There should be a unanimous outcry on the Court rejecting massive pretrial detention. Sadly, what has happened instead is that there has been an overwhelming majority on the Supreme Court willing to capitulate to the government and condone sweeping detention before trial. The Court has yet to revisit and reject this erroneous precedent.

Before examining the Court's wrong turn, it is helpful to see what the right path would look like under the Constitution. The two relevant provisions of the Constitution that limit pretrial detention for dangerousness are the Due Process Clause, which states that no one should be "deprived of life, liberty, or property, without due process of law,"[27] and the Excessive Bail Clause of the Eighth Amendment, which declares that "excessive bail shall not be required."[28]

Pretrial confinement is "the ultimate deprivation of liberty" covered by the Due Process Clause.[29] The issue is when and after what process that liberty can be curtailed. If a person is accused of a crime and confinement will be the consequence of conviction, the Constitution provides various protections, including the right to a jury trial with proof of guilt beyond a reasonable doubt. Thus, in the early nineteenth century, both state and federal courts unanimously ruled that the Constitution required pretrial release on bail in all noncapital criminal cases to preserve the presumption of innocence and ensure that the constitutional process was followed before any punishment or detention occurred.[30] For example, in *Stack v. Boyle*, the Supreme Court declared that federal law had "unequivocally" preserved bail for all noncapital offenses since the Judiciary Act of 1789, noting that "unless this right to bail before trial is preserved, the presumption of innocence, secured only after centuries of struggle, would lose its meaning."[31] The Framers "understood the right to bail as central to the baseline of liberty they sought to protect with the Due Process Clause."[32] Though it may sound odd to the average person in the United States today, the Framers understood that "to deny bail to a person who is later determined to be innocent was thought to be far worse than the smaller risk posed to the public by releasing the accused."[33]

Pretrial detention was deemed acceptable only for the purpose of maintaining the integrity of the constitutional process for adjudicating guilt. Thus, it was permitted in capital cases because defendants were believed to have a large incentive to flee given the penalty they faced.[34] Pretrial detention was not permitted in capital crimes because they were inherently more dangerous. Defamation was a capital offense, as was "performing marriages contrary to law," and for sons over sixteen years old to fail to "obey the voice of his father or his mother."[35] One analysis of founding-era bail practices noted that "it is doubtful that very many people, even in the eighteenth century, thought that persons charged with [the capital crimes of] larceny of goods valued at over $50 or forging United States currency were too dangerous to release into the community."[36] Moreover, many dangerous crimes, such as robbery, were noncapital offenses and bailable. The capital offense line was entirely about the penalty and the incentive it was thought to create for defendants to leave the jurisdiction. The detention of capital defendants, in other words, was deemed necessary to address the flight risk they posed and to make sure that a trial could still occur.

The same rationale of protecting the judicial process supports "a brief period of detention to take the administrative steps incident to arrest" until a judicial officer can make a probable cause determination.[37] Similarly, detention may be necessary where the defendant poses a threat to evidence or witnesses. Detention in all these instances is based on the idea that "reasonable steps may be taken to ensure that the trial will take place."[38]

Detention for perceived dangerousness erodes rather than upholds the trial right. If the presumption of innocence means anything at all, it has to mean that people cannot be detained simply based on accusations; they must remain free until their guilt has been proven beyond a reasonable doubt at trial: "The Due Process Clause reflects the constitutional imperative that incarceration to protect society from criminals may be accomplished only as punishment of those convicted for past crimes and not as regulation of those feared likely to commit future crimes."[39] The Supreme Court, for most of its history, agreed, making clear that neither imprisonment nor punishment was permitted without a trial.[40] Due process requires that "a defendant should not lose liberty until the government produced evidence to convince the factfinder of her guilt."[41]

The Excessive Bail Clause is another constitutional anchor that should prevent pretrial detention for improper reasons, including detention based on dangerousness. It traces its lineage to the English Bill of Rights of 1689, which was passed after the Petition of Right of 1628 and the Habeas Corpus Act of 1679, which collectively protect individuals from abusive pretrial detention. The Framers were well aware of the history of abusive pretrial detention practices in England. They likewise paid attention to the remedies for this particular form of abuse because "relief against abusive pretrial imprisonment was one of those fundamental aspects of liberty which was of most concern during the formative era of English law."[42]

This tradition "crossed the Atlantic with the colonists."[43] Early colonial laws expressly referred to English bail laws, though early colonial practice was even more protective of access to bail.[44] The Eighth Amendment reflected this same concern with protecting pretrial liberty.[45] Bail could not be excessive, meaning bail could not be set in an amount greater than necessary to ensure the trial itself could occur.

This history shows that there were limits on what counted as an acceptable ground for denying bail. The function of bail was not to prevent crimes but to make sure the accused showed up for trial proceedings and to protect "the innocent against the injustice of any imprisonment in the event of an acquittal of the charge."[46] There is no case or law from England or America at the time of the framing that shows dangerousness was a valid basis for denying bail. As Judge Jon Newman of the Second Circuit summarized it, "the conclusions reasonably to be drawn from the historical materials [are] that the Framers of the Eighth Amendment did not regard bail as an absolute right in all cases, but that they also did not contemplate the denial of bail on grounds of dangerousness."[47] For an originalist, "the absence of historical support for the practice [of denying bail for dangerousness] in the Anglo-American tradition" should be the end of the matter. A denial of bail for dangerousness, in other words, would be "excessive" for purposes of the Eighth Amendment.

Thus, the best reading of the presumption of innocence, the Excessive Bail Clause, and the history and reasoning behind both is that pretrial detention in pending criminal cases should not be based on dangerousness. No case law from the English bail system "suggests that fear of danger to the community before trial motivated the distinctions typically made between bailable and non-bailable offenses."[48] As Don Verrilli, a former solicitor general, has observed, "the development of a pervasive right to bail reflects a profound historical judgment that pretrial liberty, at least for defendants who pose no risk of flight, is a requisite of fair criminal procedure" and necessary to protect the right to a fair trial and presumption of innocence.[49]

The case becomes even more compelling when one examines the history subsequent to the framing. With only two exceptions, every state that entered the union after 1789 had a right to bail in their original state constitution. Even as states amended and redrafted their constitutions, the right-to-bail clauses for noncapital cases survived.[50] In the 1960s, forty-eight states protected the right to bail in noncapital cases; forty-one of them did so through constitutional provisions.[51] Thus, there was an almost two-hundred-year period where the overwhelming majority of people charged with crimes were released pending trial,[52] including people charged with serious crimes.[53] Dangerousness was never an authorized basis for detention, though there were undoubtedly some judges who set high bail amounts ostensibly because of flight risk but in reality based on a concern with dangerousness. That sub rosa practice, however, was an extralegal one, and it was one of the reasons reformers in the 1960s pursued bail reform.[54] As a constitutional matter, it was clearly impermissible. As one commentator summed up the constitutional case, "any theory of interpretation that gives special weight to long-standing traditions and the rights of unpopular minorities" should guard against pretrial detention and preserve the right to bail.[55]

To be sure, this history does not mean that pretrial detention is always off limits. But the circumstances should be extremely narrow given the history that led to the Excessive Bail Clause and the presumption of innocence in the Due Process Clause. Moreover, whether one is an originalist or not, the dangers of government abuse that prompted our constitutional framework are ever present and must continue to be guarded against. It is acceptable to use pretrial detention to preserve the constitutional procedures for adjudicating guilt. It is not acceptable to use it as an end run around those very protections.

One acceptable reason for pretrial detention is to ensure that defendants who are flight risks appear at trial. This is the central reason for detention that emerges from the English and early American history. Detention is permitted to allow the trial itself to take place. Even when detention is for flight risk, however, courts need to make sure people are not being detained solely because they lack the ability to pay bail. When defendants are indigent, courts must first make a finding that no other condition, aside from money bail, would assure the defendant's appearance at trial before permitting detention because a defendant lacks the funds to post bail. Similarly, when it is deemed necessary to set a bail amount, courts must make sure the amount is no greater than what is necessary to guarantee appearance. Detention should be based on flight risk, not wealth.[56]

A second acceptable reason for pretrial detention is when defendants might interfere with the proceedings, such as by posing a risk of destroying evidence or threatening or intimidating witnesses or jurors. As with detention for flight risk, detention to avoid tampering with evidence or witnesses is justified to preserve the trial itself. Thus, for example, in a domestic violence case where there is a valid concern that a defendant will harm the complaining witness, detention could be permissible.

Detention based on a prediction of dangerousness, however, has nothing to do with preserving the integrity and viability of the trial. That does not mean dangerousness can never be the basis for any detention. But it does mean that it cannot be part of the *criminal* process, which has distinct detention procedures. Criminal cases are about the crime charged, and any related detention is to preserve the ability to process those cases through a trial. Beyond ensuring the ability to hold the trial, no detention should occur as part of the criminal process; doing so would mean imposing punishment without constitutionally mandated procedures.

While the state cannot detain someone for dangerousness as part of the criminal process, it can still pursue civil commitment, whether someone is charged with a crime or not. Typically, civil commitment proceedings require the state to show, by clear and convincing evidence, that a mental illness or disability renders someone a danger to themselves or others. Although proof of mental illness is the usual standard, states could also consider other forms of "proof of serious difficulty in controlling behavior."[57] Whether they misperceive the nature of their actions or cannot control themselves, the idea is that the threat of punishment does not keep them in check, so this civil alternative is necessary.[58]

If the civil commitment standard cannot be met, the state needs to explore other ways to guard against what it perceives as a threat by someone who is awaiting trial. Conditions of release could include restraining orders or restrictions on where an individual can go, or the state could use forms of surveillance to monitor those awaiting trial. If a defendant violates a condition of release, including by committing a new crime, the government can seek to punish the violation as contempt and seek detention on that basis.[59] The state can also impose enhanced penalties for crimes committed while someone is on pretrial release as an added deterrent. What it cannot do is lock someone away on the belief that a crime has already occurred without first proving that through the constitutionally required procedures.

None of this is to deny that many judges can and have surreptitiously factored in dangerousness when setting bail amounts, setting them so high that they result in detention, even when detention should only be based on flight risk or a threat to the proceedings. New York, for example, does not permit dangerousness to be a ground for detention, but it is widely understood that judges there nevertheless set bail with that factor in mind. But recognizing that some misuse of bail occurs is a far cry from openly asking judges to detain someone based on dangerousness or explicitly allowing bail itself to be set based on dangerousness as a factor. Before the Supreme Court expressly condoned using dangerousness as a standard, pretrial detention rates were exponentially lower than they are now. The stated legal standard still matters, and eliminating dangerousness as a reason for pretrial detention would make an enormous difference. Moreover, if the problem is that judges flout the law, the solution is not to make it easier for them to do so. It is to do a better job keeping them in check and making sure bail is not excessive, which means making sure it is set in relation to flight risk and with close attention to a defendant's ability to pay so that detention is not about indigency.

One can certainly understand why the government would prefer to have broad authority to detain people pretrial. Surveillance, civil commitment, and proving flight risk or witness tampering are much harder than charging someone with a crime where detention is presumed or where courts willingly accept dangerousness arguments based on a charged offense. But the Constitution is set up to protect our liberty, not to make it easier for the government to curtail it. "All guarantees of liberty entail risk, and under our Constitution those guarantees may not be abolished whenever government prefers that a risk not be taken."[60] This is for good reason, because otherwise far too many people who pose no risk at all will lose their liberty just because of the fearful politics of the majority.

Unfortunately, the Supreme Court has lost sight of the Constitution's bedrock protection of the presumption of innocence and liberty. A majority of the justices have been just as susceptible as most of the public to fearmongering around crime. Far from keeping the government within the constitutional guardrails, the Supreme Court has set almost no limits on pretrial detention.

Salerno v. United States and the Court's Wrong Turn into Dangerous Territory

The key case that paved the way for the massive number of people in pretrial detention today was *Salerno v. United States* and its approval of fundamental changes to the federal bail laws. In 1984, Congress authorized preventive detention on grounds of dangerousness for defendants charged with federal crimes and awaiting trials.[61] To understand the case, it is helpful to first trace the shift in federal law before turning to the Supreme Court's approval of it.

The Legislative Shift to Dangerousness as a Ground for Detention

The momentum for using dangerousness as a ground for pretrial detention started with the hysteria around crime that began at the end of the 1960s and continued in the following decades. President Richard Nixon first proposed legislation "whereby dangerous hard core recidivists could be held in temporary pretrial detention when they have been charged with crimes and when their continued pretrial release presents a clear danger to the community."[62] The proposal was such a dramatic shift in the nation's history that his attorney general, John Mitchell, who would later be convicted for his role in the Watergate scandal and serve nineteen months in prison, took the unusual step of writing a law review article to defend the proposal's constitutionality. Mitchell's main argument was that bail was unavailable in certain cases at the time of the Eighth Amendment's drafting; therefore, "it is reasonable to conclude that anticipated danger to other persons or the community was a substantial motivating factor for those decisions."[63] That is hardly top-notch originalist analysis. One does not just assume reasons for decisions. You have to look for evidence. As one court that did analyze the evidence noted, "no materials thus far examined bear out the claim" that dangerousness was a valid basis for denying bail.[64] Instead, the evidence shows that the reason some cases were not bailable is because they were capital offenses, and the risk of flight in those cases was deemed to be too great. As for the presumption of innocence, Mitchell similarly stated without support or argument that "there is no basis for thinking that the presumption of innocence has any application to proceedings prior to trial."[65]

Larry Tribe, one of the country's leading experts on constitutional law, wrote a devastating reply to Mitchell's article and the proposal, pointing out both its constitutional shortcomings and the "dubious ability of pretrial detention to contribute to the control of crime." Passing the proposed law might "create the impression that the Administration was taking substantial steps to restore safety to our communities," but it was deluded thinking given the small number of people who commit crimes pretrial. This would, in Tribe's words, be the "false impression of progress." It would also "operate as a dangerous palliative by relieving public pressure for the less dramatic and more expensive types of reform that alone might restore peace to urban life." This "psychological comfort for the silent majority" would come at a cost of "heightened insecurity of the many minorities, both racial and political."[66]

Tribe noted that "no tenable concept of due process could condone a balance that gives so little weight to the accused's interest in pretrial liberty." It was a "calculated sacrifice of innocent individuals" for the end of reducing crime, and it would do a poor job at that. The proposal failed to sufficiently account for the hardships of pretrial detention, including its devastating effect on the ability of a person to prepare a defense for trial and the economic and social hardships of detention, including job loss and damage to personal relationships. Dangerousness would not serve as a limiting principle because "once the Government shows that the accused may well be guilty of the pending charge and has previously been charged with a similar crime, it has made a plausible case for suspecting possible danger."[67]

Unfortunately, and despite these fundamental flaws, Nixon's vision came to pass, first in a more limited form with respect to cases in the District of Columbia and eventually in the broader form with respect to all federal cases. The DC Act passed in 1970 and marked the first time a statute expressly authorized that competent adults could be detained pretrial upon a finding that they were a danger to the community.[68] When he introduced it, Nixon hoped it would be seen as a "model anticrime package," and sadly it was. A dozen states followed this model in the 1970s, and more followed after the law withstood a constitutional challenge in the Court of Appeals for the District of Columbia in 1981.[69]

At the federal level, the Bail Reform Act of 1984 mirrored key elements of the DC law, except where it made it even worse. Both acts allow for detention based on dangerousness. The Bail Reform Act does not define danger, but Congress clearly viewed drug trafficking as sufficiently dangerous to merit detention, and subsequent court cases have even allowed detention of people viewed as posing an economic danger.[70] In some cases, prosecutors do not even bear the burden of showing dangerousness to secure detention. Instead of the presumption of release for those accused of crimes that characterized American law for two hundred years, the Bail Reform Act creates presumptions of detention in certain cases, including where a defendant is charged with a drug crime with a statutory maximum of ten years or more or any firearms case where the firearm was used in furtherance of a drug crime.[71] For those specific charges, the burden shifts to defendants to prove that they are not a flight risk or a danger to the community. This was the height of the war on drugs, so Congress focused on drug cases as the most dangerous because it was caught up in the hysteria of the times. That panic turned two hundred years of history on its head.

As it turns out, the presumptions were way off the mark and do a terrible job predicting risk, as subsequent empirical studies have shown.[72] Even though the legislative history indicates Congress thought the number of people covered by its terms would be "small" and "limited," the law has been sweeping.[73] Indeed, because federal drug penalties are so high and a statutory maximum of ten years or more is commonplace—as law professor and former federal prosecutor Dan Richman notes, "it is hard to find a federal narcotics charge that does *not* expose a defendant to more than ten years"[74]—this statutory provision has become "an almost de facto detention order for almost half of all federal cases."[75]

Another key difference between the DC law and the federal law that made the latter far broader is that the Bail Reform Act allows a limitless period of detention. The DC law had a limit of sixty days' detention, with an option to extend that period to ninety days for good cause.[76] After that time, the person had to be brought to trial or bail had to be set. The Bail Reform Act, in contrast, provides no cap on how long detention may last. Only the Speedy Trial Act provides an upper limit, but the Speedy Trial Act provides broad grounds for delays, which are commonplace.[77] Many members of the Senate that passed the Bail Reform Act, however, seemed unaware that detention could be longer than ninety days. For example, Senator Thurman erroneously said, "90 days is the worst case limit," and Senator Laxalt called ninety days the "upper bound."[78] This led one court of appeals judge to posit that "it may well be that the Senate did not fully appreciate just how long pretrial detention might last."[79]

Just how off the mark were they in their estimates? The *average* period of pretrial detention for a federal defendant is 255 days. That is eight and a half months, a longer period than the six-month sentence that triggers the right to a jury trial. In some federal districts, the average is more than 400 days—more than a year of incarceration for people presumed innocent who have had no trial. Even the district with the lowest average of 111 days is imposing detention periods higher than what Congress thought would be the maximum.[80]

The Bail Reform Act is broader than the DC law in another fundamental respect. The DC law required prosecutors to present evidence of a "substantial probability" that defendants committed their charged crimes, which is absent in the Bail Reform Act because prosecutors told Congress that the requirement in the DC law had made it too hard to get people detained.[81] In fact, the law in DC was used sparingly, with prosecutors seeking detention under the law roughly sixty times in the first five years after it was enacted.[82] Prosecutors wanted broader powers in the Bail Reform Act, specifically asking for and receiving the authority to get defendants imprisoned on a standard that was less burdensome than the standard used to get preliminary injunctions in civil cases.[83]

The sweep of the Bail Reform Act and its extensions from the DC law were all based on a faulty assumption. According to Congress, the act was in response to "the alarming problem of crimes committed by persons on release."[84] A General Accounting Office study in 1987, however, looked at a random sample of thousands of pre–Bail Reform Act cases and found that only 1.8 percent of all federal defendants who were released pretrial were rearrested. In the debate over the Bail Reform Act, Congress referred to higher rates of between 7 and 20 percent, but it was referencing studies that looked at defendants in local jurisdictions, not federal cases. More fundamentally, the 1.8 percent included not just rearrests on felonies but arrests for misdemeanors as well. Indeed, 56 percent of the rearrests were for misdemeanors, the most common of which was illegal operation of a motor vehicle. Crimes like illegal operation of a motor vehicle hardly meet the threshold of dangerousness that Congress was so keen on preventing when passing the Bail Reform Act. And it should be emphasized that all these numbers inflate any sense of danger because these are merely arrests, not convictions.

The massive number of people detained under the Bail Reform Act for months and months and all the harm they suffer serve only to lower the rearrest rate of those released pretrial from the 1.8 percent level before the Bail Reform Act was passed to a rate of 0.8 percent after it passed.[85] You do not need more than a back-of-the-envelope cost-benefit calculation to see that the act's harms far outweigh its benefits.

To summarize, the fundamental shift that authorized pretrial detention based on dangerousness was the brainchild of people in the Nixon administration who offered the thinnest constitutional analysis in favor of it and who were themselves ultimately convicted of crimes. Their idea eventually made its way into a law passed by Congress that was designed to solve a problem that never existed at the federal level. The lawmakers misunderstood the practical effects of their proposed solution, believing the law would be limited in scope and that detention would be limited in time when in fact it opened the floodgates to lengthy terms of incarceration for the bulk of people charged with a federal crime.

The Supreme Court's Approval of the Bail Reform Act

The background of the Bail Reform Act is embarrassing enough as a policy matter, but the background of the Supreme Court case that upheld it is even worse. The case that tested the constitutionality of the Bail Reform Act arrived at the Court under dubious circumstances. The government had brought a twenty-nine-count indictment against Anthony Salerno and Vincent Cafaro under the Racketeer Influenced and Corrupt Organizations Act, better known as the RICO Act. The alleged racketeering activity included conspiracy to commit murder, gambling, extortion, and fraud, all alleged to have been committed as part of their respective roles in the Genovese crime family. Salerno, known as "Fat Tony" to his associates, was the boss of the family, and Cafaro, "Fish," was a lieutenant. The government clearly thought this was the ideal vehicle for showing why pretrial detention was needed in some cases based on the danger defendants presented. They had a mafia don who ranked at the top of *Fortune* magazine's fall 1986 list of the "50 Biggest Mafia Bosses" and one of his top henchmen, and the allegation was not that they were a risk of flight but that they presented a danger to the community. The district judge, Judge John Walker, agreed, noting that the defendants had a "a strong incentive" to "continue business as usual," which, given the nature of their mafia activities, "involves threats, beatings, and murder."[86] The Second Circuit reversed. The government successfully petitioned the Supreme Court to review the case, undoubtedly thrilled to get what it saw as the perfect vehicle for its arguments given the defendants' long and notorious criminal careers.

The pretrial detention issue, however, was moot by the time the case reached the Supreme Court, so the government engaged in questionable behavior to get around what should have been a jurisdictional bar. After the Court granted the petition for certiorari and agreed to take the case but before the justices heard arguments in the case, Salerno was tried, convicted, and sentenced to one hundred years' imprisonment in another case involving his criminal activities as part of the "Commission" that resolved disputes among the major crime families. That should have mooted Salerno's case because Salerno's detention at that point should have been pursuant to a lawful conviction. Indeed, the relevant law states that his detention was required after his conviction unless "the judicial officer finds by clear and convincing evidence that the person is not likely to flee or pose a danger to any other person or the community."[87] The sentencing judge, however, with the government's consent, did not order his detention pending appeal because he said Salerno was "presently being detained pretrial" and ordered that his bail status "shall remain the same."[88] So the government was simultaneously arguing he was not dangerous for purposes of beginning to serve his one-hundred-year sentence, but he was dangerous for purposes of keeping its Supreme Court case alive.

The circumstances surrounding Cafaro were even more outrageous, or, as Justice Marshall put it in his dissent, "disturbing."[89] After the government filed its petition for certiorari with the Court but before it was granted, Cafaro signed up with the government as a cooperator. Cafaro was then released, with the claimed reason that he was going to receive medical care and treatment. The government conditioned his release on a one-million-dollar personal recognizance bond. The government never disclosed any of this to the Court. It did not tell the Court it had enlisted Cafaro as a cooperator or that his release was conditioned upon the exercise of the million-dollar bond. Instead, the government informed the Court only that Cafaro's release was temporary and that he was still subject to the pretrial detention order, thus continuing to make the case justiciable and not moot. In essence, the government was insinuating that Cafaro still posed a danger to the community, despite secretly collaborating with him and securing his release under conditions it did not fully disclose. The government was thus doing everything it could to keep members of the mob as the test cases for pretrial detention for dangerousness.

The Court should have found the case moot as to both defendants, but instead the Court seemed eager to use this case to bless preventive detention. Justice Stevens noted his "uneasy feeling about the case" in his dissent, along with his impression that "the Government is much more interested in litigating a 'test case' than in resolving an actual controversy concerning respondents' threat to the safety of the community."[90] The Court, however, ignored the inconvenient facts of Salerno not serving his sentence after conviction and of Cafaro's release on bond, both of which undercut the government's claims of danger, just as the Court would ignore bedrock constitutional principles when deciding the merits of the case.

Chief Justice Rehnquist, who wrote part of the DC legislation authorizing pretrial detention for dangerousness when he worked in the Office of Legal Counsel in the Nixon administration and was Attorney General Mitchell's "right-hand man," assigned the opinion to himself.[91] It was hardly surprising that he would find no problems with the Bail Reform Act given that it was modeled to a large extent on the legislation he crafted. His opinion for the Court was relatively cursory and spent no time on the presumption of innocence in the Due Process Clause, on originalist arguments around pretrial detention, or on the meaning of the Excessive Bail Clause. The Court "destroy[ed] two-hundred years of American and almost a millennium of Anglo-American tradition" without giving much thought to history.[92] Instead, the Court breezily dismissed the Due Process Clause claim by concluding that the detention was a regulatory matter, not punishment. If the preventive detention was punishment, everyone (including the majority and the government) agreed it would be unconstitutional. The Court therefore had to conclude it was not punishment to permit it.

The Court reached the incredible conclusion that detention in a cage is not punishment because it believed Congress was detaining people to "prevent danger to the community . . . a legitimate regulatory goal." There are two glaring problems with the Court's brief treatment of the due process claim and its cursory dismissal of the argument that pretrial detention is punishment. First, one of the central goals of punishment is to prevent danger by incapacitating people. Indeed, this is often the dominant reason for incarceration in America today. People are warehoused for long periods so that they do not pose a threat to people outside the prisons in which they are kept. The Court, however, seems to be saying that unless Congress is using detention for the retributive function of punishment, then it is not punishment for purposes of the Due Process Clause. This is an artificially cramped view of what punishment is. Punishment is imposed for retributive and utilitarian reasons, and one of those utilitarian reasons is incapacitation. The Court itself has recognized as much: "It would be archaic to limit the definition of 'punishment' to 'retribution.' Punishment serves several purposes; retributive, rehabilitative, deterrent—and preventive. One of the reasons society imprisons those convicted of crimes is to keep them from inflicting future harm, but that does not make imprisonment any the less punishment."[93] More fundamentally, there is nothing in the history of the Due Process Clause or the English law from which it derives that suggests the Framers were only worried about detention when it was used for retributive reasons. Neither English law nor the Framers made such a distinction. Pretrial detention was sharply curtailed, whether deemed punishment or not, because it infringed on liberty and was too readily subjected to abuse by the government. That is why, for example, when the right to bail was first expressed in the colonies in the Massachusetts Body of Liberties of 1641, the law stated that no one "shall be restrained or imprisoned . . . before the law hath sentenced him thereto."[94] The "restraint or imprisoned" language focuses on the liberty infringement, not on the underlying rationale for it. The Supreme Court, too, has previously recognized that due process concerns with imprisonment are distinctly important, whether or not the imprisonment is imposed as punishment. In *Hudson v. Parker*, for example, the Court noted that bail statutes in America were "framed upon the theory that a person . . . accused of crime shall not, until he has been finally adjudged guilty in the court of last resort, be absolutely compelled to undergo *imprisonment or* punishment, but may be admitted to bail."[95] Justice Jackson likewise observed that the right to bail was critical because without it, "even those wrongly accused are punished by a period of imprisonment while awaiting trial."[96] He made no mention of the intent behind the detention as being critical.

People are suffering consequences for their alleged crimes when they are detained pretrial. Unless the detention is to preserve the trial—the cornerstone of the due process framework—it should be deemed unlawful no matter why the government wanted to pursue it because no consequences should follow an allegation of criminal behavior unless a defendant gets the constitutionally mandated process for adjudicating guilt. Thus, pretrial detention is permissible when the defendant poses a flight risk or threatens witnesses or evidence. It should not, however, be used to serve any of the purposes of punishment, including incapacitation. The Supreme Court invented out of whole cloth the punishment/regulatory divide for purposes of unlawful detention analysis.

The second major flaw with the Court's approach is that the Court concluded detention under the Bail Reform Act was not punishment because Congress did not say it was punishment.[97] One does not need a law degree to see the flaw with that reasoning. If all Congress needs to do to avoid due process issues with detention is avoid saying "this is punishment," then the Due Process Clause is not worth the paper it is printed on.

Because the Court concluded the detention was regulatory, it went on to consider whether the restrictions imposed by the act were "excessive in relation" to the regulatory purpose and found "the conditions of confinement envisioned by the Act 'appear to reflect the regulatory purposes relied upon by the' Government."[98] The Court relied on the fact that detainees would be placed in a "facility separate, to the extent practicable, from persons awaiting or serving sentences or being held in custody pending appeal."[99] The act said nothing about what the conditions should be like. The separation requirement was not even mandated. It is just something that should be done "to the extent practicable."

The reality is that federal detention centers contain people serving sentences as well as those awaiting trial. The facilities are thus serving as punishment spaces, and there is nothing about the treatment of those who reside there pretrial that sets them apart from those serving sentences. The facilities, themselves, moreover, are indistinguishable from prisons. People are put behind bars and locked doors, all movements are controlled, and access to visitors and the outside world is curtailed. If anything, conditions are worse because the population is so transient that little to no programming is offered. Putting a different sign over the building that says "detention center" instead of "prison" does not change the fundamental nature of the space or its infringement on liberty.

Moreover, although the Court claimed Congress was merely pursuing a regulatory purpose, the legislative history of the Bail Reform Act revealed its punitive side. The proponents of detention viewed the people they hoped to incarcerate as guilty and deserving of incarceration. Congressman Romano Mazzoli, a member of the House subcommittee considering the bill, reflected the overall tenor of the arguments when he expressed his disregard for procedural protections for defendants: "I appreciate this interesting discussion and all this esoterica, but the streets are full of dangerous people just out there raping and mugging and pillaging, and I have to say with all respect that I think we are here putting more roadblocks into the path of law enforcement people, tying hands even tighter, and the criminal follows no guidelines. The criminal decides when he is going to strike and he doesn't ask for guidelines and with respect, I think we have to be very careful."[100] Attorney General Mitchell noted, without any evidence or support, that a person charged with the kinds of crimes that qualified as dangerous "is rarely apprehended on his first criminal venture."[101] The idea seems to be these people are guilty of many things and pretrial detention is an appropriate punitive response.

In the end, though, it should not matter what Congress or the originators of the law said it was doing. What should matter is the operation of the law itself and its effect on the people subject to its dictates. No one experiencing pretrial detention conceives of it as anything other than punishment. Society views it that way as well, which explains the outrage whenever someone released before trial commits a crime. The vast majority of the public believes detention should begin immediately because they have already prejudged the merits of the case. The editorial board of the *New York Post*, for example, criticized bail reform efforts because, in their words, they "help no-one except sociopathic scum."[102] A Louisiana news station similarly reflected this common view, noting that "some believe right now it is too easy for some of these violent offenders to be bailed out and released back onto the streets," again conflating being charged with a crime with being guilty of it and suggesting detention is the appropriate punitive response.[103]

The presumption of innocence is a meaningless platitude if all the state has to do to incarcerate someone is charge them with a crime and then say that their detention is not punishment but regulatory. As the ACLU noted in its amicus brief to the Court in *Salerno*, "preventive detention ... seeks to serve only the same public interest in safety served by the criminal justice system itself, but without the constitutional safeguards built into the criminal justice system. It is thus a constitutional subterfuge."[104]

For an originalist or for anyone who cares about liberty, the majority opinion is a travesty. The Court never considered the relevant history around pretrial detention. It brushed aside the core substantive due process argument grounded in liberty by saying that the "general rule" against pretrial detention has recognized exceptions. But there has never been an exception for pretrial detention on the basis of dangerousness, and the presumption of innocence and Eighth Amendment should have precluded it. That should have been the end of the case. To hold otherwise undermines the trial right and all the protections that go along with it. As the New Jersey State Supreme Court has observed, "there is an indissoluble connection between

[the] presumption [of innocence] and the right to liberty before conviction."[105] The Supreme Court should have recognized that the total deprivation of liberty through incarceration to prevent future crime exceeds what is permitted by the Due Process Clause.

Because the Court ignored all of that, it went on to evaluate pretrial detention for dangerousness "in precisely the same manner that [it] evaluated the laws" in other contexts that also involved detention. The Court thus applied a balancing test weighing the government's interest against the individual's liberty interest and assessing whether the risk of erroneous detention is too great.[106] It should have never come to that point, but even assuming the balancing test applied, the Court got the balance wrong. The liberty interest at stake is, of course, the most fundamental because it involves physical detention. The risk of error, moreover, is exceedingly high. Predictions of dangerousness are notoriously poor, and the criteria used to predict dangerousness in the Bail Reform Act have no empirical support. The crime with which a defendant is charged does not predict whether a defendant will commit a new crime upon release.[107] And while the government's interest in preventing future harm is a worthwhile one, it has other means of doing so, including surveillance.

Certainly, the government's interest in a criminal case is far less weighty than its use of detention during times of war and insurrection, which is the lead parallel relied upon by Chief Justice Rehnquist in his opinion. This mirrored the Solicitor General's argument in the case, because its brief also begins its argument in support of detaining "dangerous" people with this example. The Solicitor General's brief starts by noting the president can deport dangerous aliens during times of war and then notes that American citizens can also be detained and relocated during wartime, citing *Korematsu v. United States*.[108]

It is hard to imagine a more offensive citation in support of pretrial detention than *Korematsu* and its acceptance of internment camps to hold people of Japanese descent during World War II. The *Korematsu* decision has been "excoriated as one of the two or three worst moments in American constitutional history."[109] The Supreme Court itself eventually recognized that *Korematsu* was a low mark in the Court's history in, ironically enough, the case upholding Trump's so-called Muslim ban, which barred people from entering the United States from certain predominantly Muslim countries. In 2018 (more than thirty years after the Solicitor General heralded *Korematsu* as supporting its claim for preventive detention in the Bail Reform Act), the

Court admitted that "*Korematsu* was gravely wrong the day it was decided, has been overruled in the court of history, and—to be clear—'has no place in law under the Constitution.'"[110] Someday, an apologetic Court should write similar words about *Salerno* and its acceptance of pretrial detention. It is certainly telling that the logic of *Salerno* rests on the same discredited claims of exigency and safety overriding fundamental liberty interests that condoned internment camps on American soil.[111]

The other main basis of support for accepting preventive detention as a regulatory measure was the Court's decision from a few years earlier in *Schall v. Martin*.[112] The issue in *Schall* was the constitutionality of a New York law that authorized the pretrial detention of juveniles based on a finding that there was a "serious risk" that they would "commit an act which if committed by an adult would constitute a crime."[113] The Supreme Court voted 6–3 to uphold the law, and just as in *Salerno*, Rehnquist wrote the majority opinion.[114]

Like *Salerno*, *Schall* undervalued the liberty interest at stake and rested on a cursory due process analysis that failed to consider how the New York law operated in practice. The Court recognized that a child has a constitutionally protected liberty interest but said it was not like an adult's because children "are always in some form of custody."[115] The idea that parental supervision is akin to lockup in a juvenile detention facility such that both are just forms of custody is, to say the least, a stretch. The Court, however, accepted the state's argument that detention was pursuant to its parens patriae interest in protecting the child's welfare. It bought the idea that the state was acting benevolently to help the child avoid the consequences that would follow from committing a crime while released. By the time the Court decided *Schall*, preventive detention had been "virtually the universal practice in the juvenile justice system."[116] According to the Court's superficial analysis of the issue, the state was not imposing punishment but was acting in the child's interest. Clearly a probing inquiry into whether something is actually punishment is not something Rehnquist was interested in doing in either case.

Justice Marshall's dissent in *Schall* offered a withering criticism of the majority's analysis. He pointed out that these juvenile detention hearings were typically five to fifteen minutes long and provided one telling example:

COURT OFFICER: Will you identify yourself.
TYRONE PARSON: Tyrone Parson, Age 15.
THE COURT: Miss Brown, how many times has Tyrone been known to the Court?

MISS BROWN: Seven times.
THE COURT: Remand the respondent.[117]

One could be forgiven for asking how that hearing had anything to do with the child's best interest. Parson's arrest had been for encouraging others to play three-card monte. He was detained for five days and then released because the government realized "the offense alleged did not come within the provisions of the penal law."[118]

To further prove his point that the state was actually imposing punishment in these cases, Justice Marshall also noted that many of the children detained pretrial were released even after being found guilty because the judge concluded that the detention itself was sufficient punishment—a similar result in the adult context where many people end up with time served as their sentence, and all the time was pretrial detention. Both cases, in other words, involve the kind of punitive detention that should not take place without due process and a finding of guilt beyond a reasonable doubt. The majority of the Court found otherwise only by refusing to acknowledge reality.

Schall itself was an abomination, but even assuming *Schall* was correctly decided, it is still a far different regime than what the Court condoned in *Salerno*. While children and adults both have liberty interests, the state has greater authority with respect to children because of the parens patriae authority. At the time of *Schall*, every state plus DC had authorized some form of preventive detention in cases of juveniles accused of crime. The Court's jurisprudence rests on the idea that "juveniles are presumptively unformed beings—frequently immature and thus unlikely to be constrained by the normal deterrent effect of law or to conform their behavior to the dictates of the penal law." A similar rationale allows individuals with certain mental illnesses to be involuntary committed for dangerousness.[119] None of this is relevant for analyzing the detention of competent adults. That alone should critically distinguish *Schall*.

There is still more, however. The law in *Schall* was far more limited than the Bail Reform Act. The maximum amount of detention that any child could receive was seventeen days. In contrast, as noted, there is no maximum amount of detention an individual can receive under the Bail Reform Act. The conditions of confinement in the two contexts were also different. While Chief Justice Rehnquist tried to claim that both reflected a regulatory, nonpunitive nature, the argument was far more persuasive in the context of juvenile detention. The *Schall* opinion noted that nonsecure juvenile detention facilities were more like halfway houses without locks, bars, or guards. It admitted that secure detention was "more restrictive" but pointed out the ways in which it differed from traditional jails and prisons. The institution provided "street clothes" to the kids, and the children were placed in dorms according to their age, size, and behavior. In addition, the institution hired social workers to provide educational and recreational programming. This Pollyanna description of secured juvenile facilities glosses over quite a bit. As Justice Marshall noted in dissent, the secure juvenile detention facilities "closely resemble[d] a jail," and the children there were vulnerable to assaults, including sexual assaults.[120] But it is nevertheless true that, as bad as the New York juvenile facilities were and are, a case can at least be made that they try to meet the needs of children in ways that are different from clearly punitive adult settings. No such claim can be made about federal detention facilities, which look exactly like federal prisons in all the key ways. These facilities do contain the "locks, bars, [and] security officers" that the Court found notably absent in the juvenile facilities.[121]

Schall was the key case relied on by the majority in *Salerno* to establish dangerousness as a ground for preventive detention, and it was distinguishable in every critical respect. Precedent, in other words, provided no life raft for an opinion that was already sunk as a matter of the Constitution's original meaning and its respect for the presumption of innocence. And that was just the Due Process Clause analysis.

The Court's analysis of the Eighth Amendment claim was, if anything, even more problematic. The first hint that the majority was not going to take the original meaning of the Excessive Bail Clause seriously is that it started off by saying the clause "merely" provides "excessive bail shall not be required." There is nothing *mere* about this clause and the long history it stands on. The Court, however, spent no time investigating the history of this provision. Instead, it looked at the text without any context and declared that it "says nothing about whether bail shall be available at all." Because bail had been refused in capital cases and in other cases where a defendant is a flight risk or poses a threat to the judicial process, the Court concluded that there was no absolute right to bail. The Court dismissed its own previous proclamation—that unless the "right to bail before trial is preserved, the presumption of innocence, secured only after centuries of struggle, would lose its meaning"—as dicta, because it was made in a case where the claim was that bail was excessive.[122] It did not explain why this sentiment would be any less true if detention were permitted based on a finding of dangerousness pretrial. The Court didn't even spend two full pages on the Eighth Amendment.

Just as he had in *Schall*, Justice Marshall filed a withering dissent in *Salerno*. He did not spend much time on the originalist case for his argument, but he did begin by noting how unprecedented the case was. The Court was seeing for "the first time a statute in which Congress declares that a person innocent of any crime may be jailed indefinitely, pending the trial of allegations which are legally presumed to be untrue, if the Government shows to the satisfaction of the judge that the accused is likely to commit crimes, unrelated to the pending charges, at any time in the future."[123] He noted this kind of law was "consistent with the usages of tyranny and the excesses of what bitter experience teaches us to call the police state" and found it inconceivable that the majority could bless what has "long been thought incompatible with the fundamental human rights protected by our Constitution."[124] The dissent decimated the majority's attempt to label the law as "regulatory" instead of punitive as "an exercise in obfuscation" and its brief treatment of the Eighth Amendment as "mere sophistry."[125]

The dissent went to the core of both legal issues by highlighting what the majority ignored: the presumption of innocence. It pointed out that the government cannot continue to detain someone on grounds of dangerousness if they had been held pretrial and subsequently acquitted because doing so would "allow the Government to imprison someone for uncommitted crimes based upon 'proof' not beyond a reasonable doubt." The dissent went on to explain that "our fundamental principles of justice declare that the defendant is as innocent on the day before his trial as he is on the morning after his acquittal."[126]

Salerno should be overruled as clearly inconsistent with the presumption of innocence protected by the Due Process Clause and the limits on pretrial detention in the Excessive Bail Clause. The current Supreme Court has shown a willingness—indeed, an eagerness—to revisit what it sees as faulty lines of authority. It is hard to find many cases worse than this one. There is no greater liberty interest than being free of total state control in a locked facility. Pretrial detention undermines core constitutional values, and the Supreme Court can and should correct the misguided path it began when it got caught up in the tough-on-crime panic and delegated its constitutional responsibilities to the whims of prosecutors.

Salerno should be overruled because it is flatly inconsistent with any theory of constitutional interpretation. That should be reason enough, but the case against *Salerno* grows stronger when one considers how it needlessly permitted hundreds of thousands of people to be jailed without a trial in the name of public safety that never materialized. What followed in *Salerno*'s wake is the definition of tragedy: untold human suffering based on a false belief it would be to the public's benefit.

The Aftermath of *Salerno*

In the wake of *Salerno*, states increasingly modeled their laws along the lines of the federal approach and authorized detention on the basis of dangerousness.[127] Eighty percent of state constitutions had a right-to-bail clause in their constitutions in 1978. That number dropped to 48 percent by 1998.[128] Forty-eight states and the District of Columbia enacted laws allowing detention of defendants deemed to be dangerous.[129] Detention for dangerousness has thus become the norm, with New York and its disallowance of dangerousness as an approved factor the exception.[130] Judges have set ever higher bail amounts as the focus shifted toward safety and away from release.[131] Between 1970 and 2015, there was a 433 percent increase in the number of people held pretrial.[132] In the past four decades, society has grown accustomed to seeing mass numbers of people locked away before trial.

As bad as the decision in *Salerno* is, it was not foreordained that pretrial detention would explode the way it has. One could have still held out hope that the Court would later keep government excesses in check. After all, the Court in *Salerno* took pains to emphasize that the case involved a facial challenge, which meant the law could only be found unconstitutional if there was no set of facts under which the statute could be validly applied. The door was still open for as-applied challenges where a defendant could show that a particular detention order was excessive given the liberty interest at stake. The Court even dropped a footnote in the case to note that it was "intimat[ing] no view as to the point at which detention in a particular case might become excessively prolonged, and therefore punitive, in relation to Congress's regulatory goal."[133] The Court further stated that the Bail Reform Act focused on a "specific category of extremely serious offenses," suggesting that broad application in less serious cases might draw closer scrutiny.[134]

Despite these suggestions, the Court has done nothing to rein in excessive detention, even though today's reality is far different than the predictions of how the Bail Reform Act and other laws authorizing pretrial detention based on dangerousness would play out. When John Mitchell initially advocated for the idea of a federal law authorizing preventive detention, he argued it would be "quite narrow," estimating it would only lead to detention in roughly 10 percent of federal cases.[135] The majority opinion in *Salerno* also described the authorized pretrial detention in the Bail Reform Act as "the carefully limited exception."[136]

What actually happened? In 1983, the year before the Bail Reform Act was enacted, fewer than 24 percent of people were detained pending their federal trials. The year after it was enacted, the rate climbed to 29 percent and has been climbing ever since. Today, a whopping 75 percent of federal defendants are detained pretrial.[137] One reason for this huge rise is the statutory presumption of detention for certain offenses, particularly drug cases. Currently, 93 percent of all federal drug cases trigger the statutory presumption of detention,[138] and judges rarely find that presumption is rebutted. As noted in a 2022 report on federal pretrial detention practices, a "culture of detention" has emerged in federal courts, where jailing people has become the norm.[139]

Congress and the Supreme Court also expected the Speedy Trial Act to keep the length of detention in check, with the Court noting the act's "stringent time limitations."[140] But the exceptions to the Speedy Trial Act swallow its time limits. Defense motions pause the Speedy Trial Act clock. That puts defendants in the tough bind of deciding whether to pursue the legal avenues of relief to which they are entitled even though it means they will spend more time in jail. There are ample grounds for the government to stop the clock as well. Given these exceptions, it is no wonder the average detention period has climbed from roughly two months in 1985, just after the Bail Reform Act's enactment, to nearly a year today.[141]

It has been a steady, steep climb since *Salerno,* with the number of people and the length of their detention growing constantly. That is how incursions on liberty work. The unthinkable—detaining someone without a trial just based on an accusation—starts to feel normal and then expected, and before you know it, people cannot even remember a time when the world was different.

The Supreme Court is supposed to guard against the erosion of liberty and, as noted, held out the promise that it would. However, when it became clear that the Bail Reform Act would authorize long periods of incarceration and apply to huge numbers of people—indeed most of the federal defendant population being held on average for almost nine months pretrial and averaging more than a year in some districts—the Court did nothing. It turned away petitions for certiorari that asked the Court to specify "the point at which detention in a particular case might become excessively prolonged" and therefore amount to punishment.[142] It also declined cases that raised questions about when conditions of detention could cross the line into punishment. For example, it refused to take a case where the defendant awaiting trial was held for three and a half years in a prison's death row, surrounded by people awaiting execution, three of whom were executed while he was there.[143] In fact, the Court has not agreed to take a case involving the Bail Reform Act since the 1980s despite the explosion in federal pretrial detention, the now commonplace long periods of confinement, and the increasing dangers of confinement, including during the pandemic.

The lower courts, federal and state, have taken this cue to mean nothing is amiss. They routinely approve lengthy periods of pretrial detention and excessive bail amounts, and they rubber-stamp findings of dangerousness with little to no scrutiny. Federal judges often grant requests based on dangerousness without first finding that an offense qualifies under the Bail Reform Act. The Federal Criminal Justice Clinic at the University of Chicago observed hundreds of federal court proceedings and found that prosecutors failed to provide a legal basis under the Bail Reform Act for their detention requests in 81 percent of the cases, yet judges granted those requests 99 percent of the time.[144]

Too often state and federal appellate judges have no direct experience with the day-to-day operation of the lower criminal courts, or, if they do, it is from the perspective of a prosecutor. There is nothing in the Supreme Court's case law that forces them to do otherwise because the Court has basically abandoned this area of law. They therefore do nothing to stop the excess of pretrial detention.

Professor Tribe anticipated the political dynamics that would lead to pretrial detention expanding once dangerousness and crime prevention became the touchstone for depriving people of liberty before trial:

> Once the government has instituted a system of imprisonment openly calculated to prevent crimes committed by persons awaiting trial, the system will appear to be malfunctioning only when it releases persons who prove to be worse risks than anticipated. The pretrial misconduct of these persons will seem to validate, and will indeed augment, the fear and insecurity that the system is calculated to appease. But when the system detains persons who could safely have been released, its errors will be invisible.[145]

The errors with overdetention might be invisible to the public, but "all experience with the scientific study of prediction shows that this back side of the moon is where most of the errors will in fact occur."[146] No one—not judges, not prosecutors, not mental health professionals—is very good at predicting whether someone will be violent in the future.

Sadly, what can be predicted with stunning accuracy is who bears the burden of these inaccurate predictions of violence. The people detained pretrial are disproportionately poor people of color.[147] A study of pretrial detention in New York City, for example, found that Black defendants were 10 percent more likely to be detained than similarly situated white defendants.[148] A study of counties in Florida, Illinois, Texas, and California concluded that Black defendants were subject to higher bail amounts than white defendants for the same crimes.[149] Hispanic defendants are also disproportionately affected.[150] This holds true at the federal level as well. Court watchers in federal court noted that prosecutors sought pretrial detention without offering a valid legal basis under the Bail Reform Act more than twice as often when the defendant was a person of color than when the defendant was white.[151]

There is, moreover, an entrenched lobby to guard against questioning the detention state we have become. Police and prosecutors are on the front lines lobbying for pretrial detention, just as they urged the Court in *Salerno* to endorse preventive detention.[152] In states around the country, there has been a concerted effort to tackle the enormous pretrial population with bail reform, and prosecutors and the police have been the most vocal critics, arguing without evidence that doing so will increase crime. The private bail bonds industry has spent a fortune blocking efforts to reduce cash bail and supporting candidates who align with their views.[153] Political candidates at the state level received more than $3.1 million from the bail industry from 2002 to 2011.[154] The return on these investments has been substantial. The bail industry has successfully protected their profits by funding efforts to roll back or stop reform measures.[155]

In individual cases, too, prosecutors push for detention. In the federal system, prosecutors sought detention in 77 percent of their cases in 2019, and in some circuits the rate was as high as 87 percent.[156] Pretrial release rates are higher in states, often because they offer bail in all noncapital cases, but 38 percent of defendants are still detained before trial.[157] It is hardly surprising that prosecutors seek detention so often. They have everything to gain and nothing to lose by it. The longer people spend in pretrial detention, the more likely they are to plead and the harder it is for their attorneys to mount an effective defense. And if there is a rare case of someone released pretrial committing a dangerous crime, the prosecutor might get some of the blame for not seeking detention.[158] Given these political dynamics, it is no wonder that the rate of pretrial incarceration has increased at a far greater rate than even the high rates of incarceration after sentencing.[159]

While the political side of pretrial detention's expansion was entirely predictable, what was not preordained was the Court's utter lack of interest in keeping the state in check. *Salerno* claimed that "in our society liberty is the norm, and detention prior to trial . . . is the carefully limited exception."[160] When detention came to be the norm, however, the Court failed to do anything about it.

What has followed is a torrent of misery. People lose their jobs, their children, and even their lives because of pretrial detention. But the tragic stories of unnecessary and unconstitutional preventive detention cannot compete in the news cycles with the cases of people on release committing crimes. Most members of the public do not anticipate being detained, but they do fear being a victim of crime. So the stories of detention's downsides take a back seat to the stories of crime.

This is exactly the dynamic the Constitution is supposed to be stopping. The Framers knew the government would have every incentive to try to cut corners in its quest to take away the liberty of people it views as threats. They also knew majorities in the public could easily turn against the rights of minorities. That is why the Bill of Rights spends so much time spelling out limits on policing, prosecution, and punishment. This was a core threat, and the Constitution met it.

If the Court did its job, we would not have people presumed innocent locked up because they were viewed as dangerous. Any statute authorizing pretrial detention for dangerousness would be struck down. That would not stop judges from trying to achieve the same outcome with the bail amounts they set. Indeed, the American Bar Association (ABA) endorsed authorizing preventive detention for community safety reasons because it believed judges were already making bail decisions on this basis, and the ABA thought it was better to do it "openly" and "not masked behind manipulations of bail amounts."[161] Supporters of the Bail Reform Act similarly argued that it was a positive development because it would bring this practice out of the shadows and "allow the courts to address the issue of pretrial criminality honestly and effectively."[162] We now know how things actually turned out. We have laws authorizing detention on the basis of dangerousness, *and* "money bail is still being used as a back-door means to manage dangerousness."[163]

In this current landscape, some advocates have sought to eliminate cash bail by endorsing, or at least accepting, the use of risk instruments that predict dangerousness to detain people believed to pose the greatest risk. In a regime in which predictions of danger govern the pretrial detention inquiry, they reason that the best approach is to use risk instruments because they are more accurate than individual assessments of dangerousness by judges, and their use can lower the number of people detained pretrial. That has, in fact, been the result in places like New Jersey and the District of Columbia. They have dramatically reduced their pretrial populations by shifting to pretrial risk instruments instead of the imposition of cash bail based on individualized assessments of risk by judges. But liberty should not be based on a choice between a flawed cash bail regime that incarcerates people too poor to pay and an unconstitutional regime of pretrial detention on the basis of dangerousness. New Jersey still incarcerates almost one-fifth of the people charged with crimes pretrial using its risk instrument, and racial disparities in pretrial detention are still stark. The risk instruments used in jurisdictions like New Jersey offer, in the words of some commentators, "a Faustian tradeoff: a new approach to pretrial justice that comes with a chance (and a hope) of reduced incarceration, but that also ratifies recent erosions of the fundamental rights of the accused."[164]

This Faustian bargain is only necessary because the Supreme Court has allowed it. If dangerousness was not a permissible basis for pretrial detention in criminal cases, as the Constitution demands, we would see a precipitous drop in jail populations. This would not inevitably mean an uptick in crime or harm, because most people detained pose no risk at all. Moreover, if a state thinks a person truly presents a danger to others, there is a civil commitment procedure that can be used. Preventive detention would be harder, leading it to be used appropriately sparingly. While judges might try to mask dangerousness findings in their setting of cash bail, were it still to exist, the solution is not to condone the use of dangerousness. It is to do a better job policing bail determinations to make sure the amounts being set are not excessive given the proper purposes of pretrial detention. Bail should only guard against flight risk, and it should not be excessive.

As Justice Robert Jackson observed, if bail is set to keep defendants in jail, "it is contrary to the whole policy and philosophy of bail."[165] The idea is to make sure defendants appear at trial, and nearly everyone released pretrial returns to court. At the federal level, the return rate is 99 percent. And most people released pretrial do not commit new crimes. Again, the rates of compliance hover over 98 percent. This is true in districts with high release rates and low release rates. These high compliance rates have been virtually unchanged since the 1980s. State courts also report appearance rates around 90 percent.[166] The best way to increase appearance rates is with simple text reminders and transportation subsidies because the main reason people do not show up to court is forgetting or lacking a means to get there.[167] In many cases, no bail is needed. Studies show that money bail does not increase the odds that a defendant will appear in court as compared to alternative nonfinancial conditions of release.[168] Yet jurisdictions continue to require ever larger sums of bail from mostly indigent defendants as the price of their pretrial freedom.[169] If courts did their job, no one would be detained because of an inability to pay unless no other measure would assure an appearance at trial. The number of people in that category should be quite small.

We live in an alternative reality of massive pretrial detention and all the tragedy it brings because the Supreme Court fell victim to the same sense of panic as the rest of America in the 1980s and thought pretrial detention would protect us from dangerous criminals. As a policy matter, the broad use of pretrial detention is a proven failure. Police and prosecutors told the Supreme Court in an amicus brief in *Salerno* that, in their "considered view, no single measure in criminal justice today holds greater promise for cutting the rates of crime in America than pretrial preventive detention of dangerous offenders and recidivists."[170] They were proven wrong. The massive preventive detention that followed in *Salerno*'s wake has done as much to exacerbate crime as prevent it. Even short periods of detention increase the likelihood that someone will reoffend—and it is no wonder, given that detention typically means a loss of employment, housing, custody of children, and any semblance of regularity in someone's life.[171] The negative effects of pretrial detention last for years, hampering people's ability to find employment and housing long after their release. The effects of pretrial detention on children cause lasting damage as well, as parents who lose custody of their children and have them placed in foster care because of pretrial detention have a much harder time getting them back.[172]

We are thus imposing needless and incalculable costs on people facing trial—and on taxpayers. Federal pretrial detention costs alone are estimated to run taxpayers roughly one billion dollars per year—costs that are eight times higher than those associated with supervising people released pretrial.[173]

The senseless mass of people suffering in pretrial detention is an affront to the Constitution's commitment to liberty and due process. The Supreme Court should have been the body to protect those constitutional values. Its failure to do so paved the way to massive detention without trial. Justice Marshall ominously warned in his dissent in *Salerno* that the opinion was "a decision which will go forth without authority, and come back without respect."[174] Sadly, *Salerno* has not received the negative publicity it so richly deserves. But it is a constitutional abomination that has been a major driver of mass incarceration, and it should be overturned.

CHAPTER TWO

NORMALIZING COERCIVE PLEA BARGAINING

Bordenkircher v. Hayes

> However convenient these may appear at first (as doubtless all arbitrary powers, well executed, are the most convenient), yet let it be again remembered that delays and little inconveniences in the forms of justice, are the price that all free nations must pay for their liberty in more substantial matters; that these inroads upon this sacred bulwark of the nation are fundamentally opposite to the spirit of our Constitution; and that, though begun in trifles, the precedent may gradually increase and spread, to the utter disuse of juries in questions of the most momentous concern.
>
> —WILLIAM BLACKSTONE

If you received your knowledge about how criminal cases are processed in America from watching television or movies, you might think most cases get resolved in courtrooms. You might believe the norm is to have trials where prosecutors must prove their cases beyond a reasonable doubt, and juries stand between the accused and the awesome power of the government to make sure punishment is appropriate.

The reality could not be farther from this image. Most defendants who have been convicted pleaded guilty without any trial or process. Criminal cases in America are like cheap goods produced en masse in assembly-line fashion. How could this be, you might wonder, given that every defendant has a right to a jury trial when facing punishment greater than six months? Prosecutors have put so high a price on the exercise of that right that most defendants plead guilty to avoid the risk of a much longer sentence if they are convicted at trial.

Consider what happened to Clarence Aaron. He grew up in poverty and was a hardworking student-athlete who earned a scholarship to attend Southern University. He worked while in college to help support his family and cover school expenses. He had never been in trouble with the law until he decided to introduce a former high school football teammate to a current college classmate who had a brother who sold drugs. Clarence was present for one of the drug transactions and again at a subsequent attempted drug sale, and he received $1,500 for his efforts. Months later, the federal government discovered the drug conspiracy, and Clarence was among those charged. Clarence's more culpable codefendants, who played a far greater role in the conspiracy, pleaded guilty and received sentences that averaged eight years. Clarence exercised his right to go to trial. He was found guilty and sentenced to life without parole, a mandatory punishment given the charges against him under the federal guidelines. The prosecutor justified this result, explaining that the codefendants were "perhaps guiltier or more culpable," but Aaron "suffered . . . the consequences of the arrogance of thinking that you're going to beat this, that I'm too good to take a deal."[1]

Prosecutors all too often hold this view and have no qualms about filing far more serious charges against people who refuse to accept their plea deals and choose to exercise their constitutional right to a jury trial. That is how Weldon Angelos found himself serving a mandatory minimum sentence of fifty-five years after rejecting prosecutors' offer to plead guilty for a fifteen-year sentence. Angelos, a first-time offender, had sold marijuana to a police informant on three separate occasions. The informant testified that a handgun was present, though not used or brandished, during two of those encounters. After Angelos rejected the plea offer, prosecutors introduced additional charges that required the judge to impose the fifty-five-year sentence once Angelos was found guilty. The judge, bound by the statutory requirements of the charges, handed down the sentence but condemned it as "unjust, cruel, and even irrational." The prosecutors, who had requested an even longer sentence of sixty-one and a half years, viewed it as an appropriate penalty for Angelos's decision to go to trial.[2]

We live in a world of prosecutors controlling the entirety of the criminal justice process pursuant to overly punitive laws that were passed with the goal of letting them do just that. It is the inverse of what the Framers intended when they enshrined the jury trial in the Constitution as a bulwark against government abuse of power. The jury is designed to protect liberty "not only by getting the facts right but also by getting the people right." Jurors represent their communities and are "our best assurance that law and justice accurately reflect the morals, values, and common sense of the people asked to obey the law."[3] Prosecutors bypass this check by threatening defendants with punishments orders of magnitude greater than anyone thinks appropriate for their conduct if they exercise their jury trial right. That is why more than 95 percent of criminal convictions are the result of pleas, not trials. It is a system of institutional blackmail, and you cannot have mass incarceration without it. There is no realistic way to generate the same number of convictions and people in prison with trials given the state's limited resources.

The Supreme Court paved the way for the jury's demise and mass incarceration's triumph in *Bordenkircher v. Hayes*.[4] The case left no doubt that the prosecutor was threatening the defendant with a life sentence just to get him to plead guilty. The prosecutor candidly admitted it, and the Supreme Court said that was fine. This decision led to more aggressive prosecution practices in plea negotiations, massive increases in pleas, and, in turn, a huge rise in prison admissions. You cannot get mass incarceration without mass case processing, and you cannot get mass case processing without destroying the constitutional right to a jury.[5]

Tragically, it was precisely the efficiency of plea bargaining that led the Supreme Court to condone it. At the beginning of the 1970s, when the Court first took up the question of plea bargaining, it worried that, "if every criminal charge were subjected to a full-scale trial, the States and the Federal Government would need to multiply by many times the number of judges and court facilities."[6] The Court brazenly showed its hand and admitted that it cared more about the costs of jury trials than the reasons they were so important. America was experiencing a rise in crime and a corresponding increase in the number of criminal cases in the courts. The Court had also made trials more complicated, resource intensive, and time-consuming because it provided criminal defendants with more procedural rights. If the Court required jurisdictions to provide jury trials in all criminal cases unless defendants opted to plead guilty without any pressure from prosecutors, jurisdictions would effectively collapse under the weight of the resource burden. Inevitably cases would be dismissed, and the Court would be attacked for producing chaos.

That is why, when the Court officially approved of plea bargaining as a practice, it emphasized its necessity in keeping the administration of criminal law and punishment functioning effectively. It appeared, as Blackstone warned us it would in the quote at the outset of this chapter, convenient. The Constitution, however, is not a document about government efficiency and convenience. Quite the opposite. The Constitution deliberately separates powers and imposes multiple checks on the government before it can proceed in criminal cases. It is designed to be inefficient because the government should not be able to impose punishment unless it gets all relevant branches to agree, and in the judicial branch, that means agreement from the jury. That "inconvenience" is indeed a fair price to pay for liberty, but the Court was willing to sell it short.

The Supreme Court could not see past the need for plea bargaining to properly evaluate its constitutionality. Jury trials make life harder for judges, and plea bargaining eases their burdens. It is no wonder plea bargaining won and the Constitution lost when the Supreme Court had to confront efficiency versus individual rights in that context. That crucial decision did more to pave the way for mass incarceration than any other Supreme Court decision.

The Constitutional Framework

Understanding the constitutional problem with plea bargaining requires the consideration of two areas of law. The first is the right to trial by jury, and the second is known as the doctrine of unconstitutional conditions. That is because the problem with plea bargaining is that prosecutors coerce defendants to give up their jury trial rights by threatening sentences orders of magnitude longer if a defendant opts for a trial instead of pleading guilty. Leniency is conditioned on giving up the jury trial right.

The Right to Trial by Jury

The Framers were obsessed with curbing government overreach in criminal matters. The original Constitution, even before the addition of the Bill of Rights, provided numerous protections in criminal cases to make it difficult for the state to take away someone's liberty. The Framers knew all too well that the tyranny of the majority could seek to override individual rights. One line of defense therefore focused on keeping legislatures from singling out people for punishment. Thus, the Constitution prohibits bills of attainder identifying specific people as targets of legislation and ex post facto laws that could accomplish the same thing by tailoring laws to fit conduct after it occurs.

The Framers also knew, however, that the legislature might try to achieve the same ends by working in concert with the executive branch. The executive, after all, has ample ability to single out people in its enforcement of the laws. The Constitution therefore establishes the judiciary as a bulwark against attacks on individuals. Typically, most people think of judges performing this task because they are the professional members of the judiciary. And it is certainly true that the Constitution created a federal judiciary designed to protect individual rights. That is why federal judges have life tenure and salary protections. The greater independence is designed to give them some insulation from political pressures so that they can keep other constitutional limits in check. For example, if Congress tries to pass a law in violation of the Ex Post Facto Clause, judges are the ones who will strike it down. "The Federal Judiciary was therefore designed by the Framers to stand independent of the Executive and Legislature—to maintain the checks and balances of the constitutional structure, and also to guarantee that the process of adjudication itself remained impartial."[7]

But the Framers did not trust judges alone to perform the judicial task of protecting against executive overreach in the pursuit of individual criminal cases. Judges, after all, still form part of the government and could be too partial to government interests. Article III of the Constitution therefore establishes not only judges but also juries as key actors in the judicial branch. As Judge Learned Hand observed, juries have advantages over judges:

> The individual can forfeit his liberty—to say nothing of his life—only at the hands of those who, unlike any official, are in no wise accountable, directly or indirectly, for what they do, and who at once separate and melt anonymously in the community from which they came. Moreover, since if they acquit their verdict is final, no one is likely to suffer of whose conduct they do not morally disapprove; and this introduces a slack into the enforcement of law, tempering its rigor by mollifying influence of current ethical conventions. A trial by jury, however small, preserves both these fundamental elements and a trial by judge preserves neither, at least to anything like the same degree.[8]

The founding generation saw the criminal jury as a key element of the separation of powers, providing a needed "slack into the enforcement of law."

"The criminal jury reliably stood between the individual and the government, protecting the accused against overzealous prosecutions, corrupt judges, and even tyrannical laws."[9] This is why the original Constitution ensured jury trials for all crimes, making it a fundamental component of Article III and the foundational design of the government, even before the addition of the Bill of Rights.[10] The state constitutions that existed before the federal constitution reflect this same value, as they also all contained the right to trial by jury.[11]

These constitutional protections grew out of the Framers' awareness of the jury's valuable role as a safeguard against government abuse of power. The historian John Reid has documented the importance of juries in colonial America. They frequently used their acquittal power to oppose British laws they viewed as unconstitutional. They also convicted customs officials who used violence. Gouverneur Morris, a key member of the Constitutional Convention and a member of the Constitution's drafting committee, noted that one highly publicized colonial case was particularly influential in "impressing thousands of Americans with the importance of the right to jury as a bulwark against official oppression" and helped to "revolutionize[] America." John Peter Zenger published criticisms against the royal governor of New York in 1734, and the governor sought to punish Zenger as a result. After three grand juries refused to indict him, the governor proceeded on an information, which is a charging document that is presented to a magistrate instead of a grand jury. The case then went before a trial jury, and although the governing law at the time stated that truth was no defense to libel, Zenger's defense lawyer told the jurors that they "ha[d] the right, beyond all dispute, to determine both the law and the fact" and could therefore decide to acquit if they thought the publication was truthful. The jury returned a general verdict of acquittal, and an account of the trial circulated widely in pamphlet form throughout the colonies.

When Britain sought to limit the power of juries, it helped spark the American Revolution. Deprivation of the jury right became a key complaint in the colonies. The First Continental Congress attacked acts that stripped the colonists of their right to trial by jury and noted that they were entitled "to the great and inestimable privilege of being tried by their peers of the vicinage." The Second Continental Congress likewise listed the Crown's interference with the jury trial right as one of the colonists' objections. The deprivation of the jury trial was at the top of the list of grievances in the Declaration of Independence.[12]

The jury was valued for far more than its fact-finding responsibilities, though that is undoubtedly a key aspect of its authority. As Judge Hand observed and the Zenger trial demonstrated, juries have always had an unreviewable power to acquit. This gives the jury the ability to check government overreach, even if the letter of the law applies to the facts. The unanimity requirement further enhances the checking function of the jury because it requires all members of the jury to agree before the government can impose punishment, bringing a variety of views to bear on the state's actions. Each juror becomes a safeguard of liberty and must be convinced. The Framers worried about the danger of government overreach in criminal matters, and the jury was a key check against it.

The jury's importance was so well established and universally recognized that it was one of the few subjects that sparked a consensus view among the Framers. Alexander Hamilton wrote in Federalist No. 83 that "the friends and adversaries of the plan of the convention, if they agree in nothing else, concur at least in the value they set upon the trial by jury." The extent of their disagreement was about whether the jury was, in the Federalist view, "a valuable safeguard to liberty" or, as the Anti-Federalists saw it, "the very palladium of free government."[13] Thomas Jefferson went as far as saying that, "were I called upon to decide whether the people had best be omitted in the Legislative or Judiciary department, I would say it is better to leave them out of the Legislative."[14] The people serve different roles in each context. As voters, people see crime as a general threat and support legislation that might be broader or harsher than they would approve if they were assessing the facts of individual cases. As jurors, the people from the community make precisely those individualized evaluations to make sure no one loses their liberty when it would be unjust. "On many occasions," the Supreme Court has observed, "fully known to the Founders of this country, jurors—plain people—have manfully stood up in defense of liberty against the importunities of judges and despite prevailing hysteria and prejudices."[15] It is impossible to overstate how important the Framers believed the jury is to checking the government when it seeks to deprive individuals of their liberty.

Given their historical pedigree and firm footing in the constitutional architecture, jury trials were the norm in early American history. Courts discouraged defendants from pleading guilty, and guilty pleas were relatively rare. No one suggested trials were too costly, time-consuming, or inefficient. The commonsense views of jurors were deemed critical before any punishment could be imposed. The jury "gives protection against laws which the ordinary man may regard as harsh and oppressive" and serves as "insurance that the criminal law will conform to the ordinary man's idea of what is fair and just."[16]

Over time, however, guilty pleas became more common, and some judges were more lenient in their sentences when defendants pleaded guilty. Defendants, however, could not be sure whether they would get such a benefit from a judge. There was no promise or bargain associated with the plea. Just a hope that it might lead to a more favorable sentence.

Eventually, prosecutors and sometimes even judges started to explicitly bargain with defendants and offer a more lenient charge or sentence if a defendant pleaded guilty. No one thought this was sanctioned, but the pressure to deal with rising caseloads made it too tempting. The legal historian George Fisher found evidence of prosecutors dropping charges against defendants who did not contest the remaining charges going back to the early 1800s.[17] By the end of the 1800s, plea bargaining was already quite common, with some studies finding that 40 percent of the convictions were the result of guilty pleas. Despite its relative frequency, plea bargaining largely operated in the shadows until the twentieth century because "the idea that the jury right could become the subject of an agreement between the prosecutor and the defendant was abhorrent to nineteenth-century judges."[18]

The reality of plea bargaining as a common practice did not come to light until the 1920s when it was discovered by a number of commissions studying criminal justice practices. By that point, guilty plea rates were even higher, with a number of jurisdictions reporting plea rates in the 70 to 80 percent range. Though it was commonplace, it was still not accepted as appropriate. Critics of plea bargaining in the early twentieth century worried that it let defendants avoid proper punishment and that prosecutors might be corruptly discharging their duties. As one commentator put it, it was "already pervasive when it was discovered, but it was far from normal."[19]

Despite the negative reaction to the discovery of widespread plea bargaining, it continued unabated. The pressure to reach a resolution in a case without conducting a trial came from a combination of factors, including expanding caseloads and increasingly complicated, and therefore time-consuming, trials. Views of plea bargaining gradually grew more positive among some members of the legal profession as they increasingly appreciated its ability to move cases quickly and efficiently. By 1934, a team of researchers led by the then dean of Yale Law School, Charles Clark, noted that "it is doubtful if the system could operate" without plea bargaining.[20] By the 1960s, when close to 90 percent of convictions were the result of pleas in many places, there seemed to be a growing consensus that plea bargaining had become necessary, and it was time to bring it out of the shadows.[21] The

Katzenbach Commission, charged by President Johnson with studying crime and the administration of criminal justice in America, praised plea bargaining in its 1967 report for bringing "a degree of certainty and flexibility" into the system.[22] That same year, the American Bar Association issued a report endorsing plea bargaining and highlighting its ability to limit delay and conserve resources.[23] But even supporters of plea bargaining worried about whether it could be too coercive. The Katzenbach Commission was concerned about the "real dangers that excessive rewards will be offered to induce pleas or that prosecutors will threaten to seek a harsh sentence if the defendant does not plead guilty."[24]

Critically, the potential coercion in plea bargaining is not just a policy concern but a constitutional one because of the burden it places on the exercise of the jury trial right.

The Doctrine of Unconstitutional Conditions

The Court has recognized "in a variety of contexts that the government may not deny a benefit to a person because he exercises a constitutional right." This concept is known as the doctrine of unconstitutional conditions, and, in the words of the Supreme Court, it "vindicates the Constitution's enumerated rights by preventing the government from coercing people into giving them up."[25] The Court requires the government to show that it has a compelling state interest in withholding benefits or imposing penalties because someone exercises a constitutional right and that doing so is the least restrictive alternative for achieving that interest.[26]

Plea bargaining has been called the "most natural setting" for the unconstitutional conditions doctrine to apply.[27] The state is conditioning a benefit it has the power to give (leniency) on the defendant's willingness to give up a constitutional right (the jury trial).[28] If a prosecutor told defendants that they would get a $20,000 bonus for pleading guilty but nothing for going to trial, the Court would likely have no problem seeing the unconstitutional conditions problem. A price would be put on the trial right. It should not matter if that price is in dollars or prison time. Allowing plea bargaining is to condone "just what the Framers expected the jury to prevent, the aggrandizement of state power."[29]

Given the jury's critical importance to the Constitution's design, one would think the Supreme Court would be vigilant in protecting it from being undermined by the government. When prosecutors tell defendants that they will bring lesser charges or recommend a lighter sentence if they plead guilty instead of going to trial, or that they will pursue more severe charges or sentences if defendants opt to go to trial, prosecutors are placing an unconstitutional condition on the very mechanism designed to check them. "Under the doctrine of unconstitutional conditions, courts would presume that the right to a jury trial is not subject to bargaining" because that "would allow the government to extend its power beyond constitutional limits, undermine the public interest rights protect, and would likely entail undue coercion."[30]

This analysis holds even if the government is under no obligation to provide the benefit in the first instance, so it is no counterargument to say that pleas involve sentencing breaks or benefits. The Supreme Court has noted that "virtually all of our unconstitutional cases involve a gratuitous government benefit of some kind," and it has "repeatedly rejected the argument that if the government need not confer a benefit at all, it can withhold the benefit because someone refuses to give up constitutional rights."[31] The Court has held that forcing someone to choose between a constitutional right and some privilege it wants from the government is "in reality . . . no choice, except a choice between the rock and the whirlpool—an option to forego a privilege which may be vital to his livelihood or submit to a requirement which may constitute an intolerable burden. . . . If the state may compel the surrender of one constitutional right as a condition of its favor, it may, in like manner, compel a surrender of all. It is inconceivable that guarantees embedded in the Constitution of the United States may thus be manipulated out of existence."[32]

It is precisely that kind of manipulation that has taken jury trials out of existence. Despite the jury's key checking function—or, sadly, perhaps because of it—the Supreme Court has never analyzed plea bargaining as an unconstitutional conditions problem even though it is indistinguishable from the other constitutional rights it has protected from being traded away.[33] The right to a trial by jury is no less fundamental than the First Amendment rights of speech, religion, and association that have been protected from unconstitutional conditions being attached to them. Nor is it less important than the taking of private property for public use without paying just compensation. Just as those rights have received the Court's protection, so, too, should the jury trial right.[34] If anything, the jury trial right has an even firmer constitutional pedigree, having been included in the very structural design of the government before the Bill of Rights was added. The legal historian Bill Nelson has shown that, "for Americans after the Revolution, as well as before, the right to trial by jury was probably the most valued of all civil rights."[35]

But whereas the Court has plainly seen the coercion in other government dealings involving conditions on constitutional rights, it has been blind to the coercion in plea negotiations.[36] Instead, it has seen plea bargaining as akin to voluntary contract negotiations. When the right at issue is the right to a jury trial, "coercion is replaced by choice; freedom means the power to bargain, and the public's interest lies in foregoing rights, not keeping them intact," all of which "turns the doctrine of unconstitutional conditions on its head."[37]

In fact, there is no reason based in the Constitution for treating plea bargaining differently than other constitutional rights for purposes of the unconstitutional conditions doctrine. The Court treats plea bargaining differently not because of a legitimate constitutional distinction between rights but because of the higher value it places on the administrative efficiency plea bargaining brings. Notably, it is not just any kind of efficiency but the efficient operation of the courts. The Supreme Court is part of the judicial branch, and it shares its interest in effective judicial administration. That institutional self-interest has trumped any concern for the importance of the jury in the constitutional order. This is consistent with other contexts where the Court has taken a more relaxed approach to enforcing the separation of powers when judicial power has been limited or reduced. The Court has shown "receptivity to claims that a proposed change in government will yield efficiency gains for the judiciary."[38]

It is not just that the Court places premium value on the convenience of the courts. It is also that it does not give as much respect to the jury or to trials as other constitutional guarantees. Beginning in the late nineteenth century and continuing through today, legal elites have viewed the jury's role in American governance as less important than the Framers viewed it. Whereas the Framers saw the benefit of placing ordinary citizens between a person accused of a crime and the government, respect for the jury eroded over time as more faith was placed in the government instead. By the end of the nineteenth century, the Supreme Court decided that juries had the power but not the right to decide questions of law through their ability to give a verdict of acquittal.[39] That is, juries could disagree with a law and acquit on that basis, but because the Court did not view this as a right, they allowed judges to give jurors strict instructions that they had to follow the judge's view of the law. So, if a jury was going to acquit based on disagreement with a law, it would have to defy a judge's instructions. Similarly, after being "squarely on record as declaring that a criminal defendant could not waive jury trial," the Court shifted gears in 1930 and decided a jury trial could be waived if both parties agreed in favor of a bench trial.[40] The jury trial stopped being seen as an important, nonwaivable structural check.

With the rise of the administrative state, the jury's unreviewable discretion to acquit has looked increasingly out of place. Expert agencies face judicial scrutiny to make sure their decisions are consistent with the law, yet jurors drawn from the population at large can acquit a defendant with no explanation or oversight. Legal elites thus started to question why laypeople hold such a powerful role in the process.[41] Why, they asked, should "the fate of both society and a defendant [be] left to the arbitrary and capricious notions of at most twelve individuals."[42] Critics viewed the jury as too easily swayed by emotion or prejudice and doubted jurors' ability to understand complex cases and legal standards.[43] For judges and many academics, the criminal jury became "difficult to square with demands for rationality, equal justice, and public accountability," which became the defining hallmarks of the twentieth-century vision of the rule of law.[44]

The public, for its part, has retained a more favorable view of juries. Unlike most government institutions, which have plummeted in favorability polls, the jury is relatively well regarded by the American people. More than three-quarters of the public believes "the jury system is the most fair way to determine the guilt or innocence of a person accused of a crime." Almost 70 percent believe "juries are the most important part of our judicial system."[45] Two-thirds of all adults agree that serving on a jury "is part of what it means to be a good citizen," though younger people are less likely to hold that view.[46]

Judges and prosecutors do not seem to share this perspective, at least insofar as they place a greater value on easing their workload than on protecting the jury. For these insiders, plea bargaining was a welcome solution to the problem of crime and resource constraints. Its approval, though, required seeing the jury trial right as somehow different from other constitutional rights subject to the doctrine of unconstitutional conditions. The result is that plea bargaining has become, in the words of one commentator, "a black hole, disassociated with the remainder of the constitutional universe."[47] And along with it, we have lost the jury's critical role in our democracy and the scrutiny of government conduct that trials bring.

If the Court applied the doctrine of unconstitutional conditions to plea negotiations that put a price on jury trials, we would not have the unfettered approval of plea bargaining that exists today. Instead, the Court would have to follow one of two possible doctrinal paths to be consistent with the rest of its unconstitutional conditions jurisprudence. The first path would lead to the more stringent conclusion that no conditions can be placed on a defendant's exercise of the jury trial right, and therefore no bargaining is acceptable. The second path would accept that the government has a sufficiently compelling interest in plea bargaining, but courts would have to police the terms of the bargain to make sure they are not unduly coercive.

There is strong support in case law for the first path and the more stringent view that prosecutors cannot offer any reduced charges or promise to seek lower sentences of incarceration in exchange for a guilty plea because any inducement chills the exercise of the jury trial right.[48] "There are rights of constitutional stature," the Court has observed, "whose exercise a State may not condition by the exaction of a price."[49] The jury trial is a prime candidate for this kind of absolute protection given its check on the other branches of government.[50] The jury trial right is at least on par with other rights that the Court has said cannot be the subject of barter. The trial exists precisely to check the government, and the public value of the jury is too important to allow it to be undermined. Plea bargaining "forfeits the benefits of formal, public adjudication; it eliminates the protection for individuals provided by the adversary system and substitutes administrative for judicial determinations of guilt; it removes the check on law enforcement authorities afforded by exclusionary rules; and it distorts sentencing decisions by introducing noncorrectional criteria."[51] Allowing the government to avoid that check by placing any price on its exercise would therefore run afoul of the Constitution. While it might seem extreme or even impossible to imagine a ban on plea bargaining given how much the operation of criminal law and punishment today depends on it, it is important to remember that "the Constitution makes no provision for the suspension of these fundamental guarantees for reasons of convenience or economy."[52]

Moreover, while this version of the unconstitutional conditions doctrine's applicability to plea bargaining would likely mean a substantial reduction in guilty pleas, it would not mean their end. Even under this stringent view prohibiting plea bargaining, judges could still properly decide on their own to give some leniency in a sentence for a plea without running afoul of the unconstitutional conditions doctrine. Many defendants would recognize that the potential for a judicial discount, even if it is not an explicit promise, would still make it worth their while to forgo a jury trial. Some defendants would also still plead guilty because they would want to avoid the embarrassment or trauma of a trial. Additionally, prosecutors who want to exercise leniency because laws are too harsh in a particular case could still do so "gratuitously," just not as part of an attempt to extract a guilty plea.[53] This was the regime that existed for most of the country's history, where plea discounts operated in the shadows and the rates of guilty pleas were high but nowhere near the rates they are with plea bargaining condoned as legitimate. This more extreme view, however, seems in tension with the Court's decision almost a century ago that the parties can agree to a bench trial instead of a jury. Moreover, while plea bargaining can be coercive, that is not always the case, so a complete ban seems excessive.

Plea bargaining thus seems better analyzed under a second take on the unconstitutional conditions doctrine that is less extreme. Under this second framework that exists in the case law for some rights, prosecutors could continue to offer some benefits in exchange for guilty pleas and relinquishment of the jury trial right as long as those offers were furthering a compelling governmental interest. Specifically, the Court has said that if a condition "has no other purpose or effect than to chill the assertion of constitutional rights by penalizing those who choose to exercise them, then it would be patently unconstitutional."[54] The key question for plea bargaining, then, is whether it has a purpose or effect other than causing defendants to relinquish their trial rights that is a compelling governmental interest.

When the ABA's Project on Minimum Standards for Criminal Justice related its Standards Relating to Pleading Guilty, it offered several possible rationales for the practice. One possible justification is that a guilty plea serves one of the purposes of punishment, thus allowing for a discount in the remainder of the punishment that needs to be imposed. Perhaps a jurisdiction wants to recognize an admission of wrongdoing as a sign that the defendant is taking responsibility for wrongful actions and will therefore be easier to rehabilitate. Obviously, a defendant might not really be sorry and just want a sentencing break, but it would be hard for a court to rule that a jurisdiction cannot take a different view about contrition. A lesser sentence might also be appropriate because there are good reasons to avoid a public trial given the trauma it could cause witnesses or survivors of crime, such as in sexual assault cases.[55] The strongest argument for the discount for guilty pleas is that the government has a compelling interest in saving the costs of trials if a plea bargain can produce similarly fair and accurate results. The problem with this argument is that the Supreme Court has rejected cost savings as a compelling interest in other contexts.[56] That makes sense, because otherwise the government could always claim it has an interest in saving money by preventing some right from being exercised. That said, the cost argument in this context might be deemed unique because giving a jury trial to every criminal defendant would effectively destroy the operation of criminal administration due to the extreme resource investment needed.[57]

Even if one of these reasons is properly recognized as a compelling government interest, that would not mean bargains would not receive oversight. Whatever the reason the government believes justifies the sentencing discount, the benefit given to the defendant would need to be commensurate with the value identified. The government's offer cannot be designed to coerce a defendant into giving up the constitutional right to trial or create "an intolerably high risk of erroneous punishment."[58] Using this framework would therefore require courts to oversee the substance of plea bargains to make sure they are not coercive and are the least restrictive way of achieving the relevant interest.

While this admittedly may sound tough to pin down, it is no more difficult than the kinds of lines the Court has to draw in the other contexts in which it reviews unconstitutional conditions claims along these lines. Those other areas also offer some guidance on how it could be done. For example, the analytical framework from the land-use permitting context transfers well to the plea bargaining context. When someone applies for a land-use permit, the government will sometimes ask for a public right-of-way or take a piece of real property as a condition of granting the development permit. If the government simply took the property outright, outside the permitting approval process, it would be a taking, and the government would need to provide just compensation under the Fifth Amendment. Because the government has broad regulatory powers in requiring and granting permits, "applicants are especially vulnerable to the type of coercion that the unconstitutional conditions doctrine protects because the government often has broad discretion to deny a permit that is worth far more than property it would like to take." At the same time, the Court recognizes that many proposed land uses do impose costs on the public that conditions on the approval appropriately offset. The Court therefore balances these competing concerns by allowing conditions on permit approvals as long as there is a "nexus and rough proportionality between the property that the government demands and the social costs of the applicant's proposal."[59]

The Court could use a similar balancing of interests when it reviews plea bargains. It could recognize that there are public benefits when a defendant pleads guilty, so some concession by the government can account for that. At the same time, criminal defendants—far more than property owners—are "especially vulnerable to the type of coercion that the unconstitutional conditions doctrine protects" because they place such a high value on their liberty and will relinquish their jury trial right when the risk of additional punishment is too high. The nexus and rough proportionately requirements would make sure that prosecutors do not abuse their leverage or make unreasonable demands and therefore coerce defendants into relinquishing their constitutional rights.

Under this approach, plea bargains would not be dismissed out of hand, but instead judges would have to consider the terms of the specific bargain just as they consider the nature of the condition placed on any other constitutional right as part of the unconstitutional conditions framework.[60] As John Langbein has noted, the "sentencing differential is what makes plea bargaining coercive," so courts would have to police those differentials, so they are not too great.[61] Keeping the sentencing differential in check is particularly important in making sure plea bargaining is an accurate substitute for trials because if the difference is too great, even innocent people will plead. This kind of inquiry admittedly lacks the benefit of a bright-line guidepost, but courts engage in open-ended balancing inquiries all the time. Courts do this, for example, when they decide whether a government spending condition goes too far even though "whether federal spending legislation crosses the line from enticement to coercion is often difficult to determine."[62] Courts have to police similarly difficult lines in a host of other constitutional areas outside unconstitutional conditions cases, including inquiries into whether fines or punitive damages are excessive. While this kind of judging lacks the clarity of a bright-line rule, there are some contexts where gray areas are the accepted price for needed oversight. The jury trial right is no less sacrosanct than the property rights at issue in land-use cases, and criminal defendants are even more vulnerable than people seeking land-use permits because their liberty is at stake. The fact that the Court seems to see property interests as meriting greater protection is "indefensible and ironic," given the Court's view that the jury is fundamental to our system of justice.[63]

Moreover, while sentencing discounts are the most difficult lines to police, other plea bargain terms are more easily dismissed under the nexus and proportionately framework. Some prosecutors, for example, have insisted that defendants agree in advance as part of a plea to never ask for compassionate release despite the fact that the circumstances giving rise to compassionate release are often unknowable at the time of a plea. Prosecutors in these contexts are asking defendants to waive the right to seek relief from a court in the future should they later develop a terminal illness or have a child who loses all other caregivers and has only the defendant as a possible option. Other prosecutors have required defendants to waive their right to appeal or to request to seal their conviction at any point in the future. Prosecutors also often insist that defendants waive any pretrial hearings, effectively shielding police misconduct from any oversight and forcing defendants to plea without knowing whether evidence will be excluded at trial.[64] A defendant cannot make a knowing plea without being aware of what evidence is going to be permitted at trial, and requiring defendants to waive pretrial hearings does not further the interest associated with trial costs.

Indeed, none of those waivers has anything to do with the government's claimed public interest in avoiding a trial. The government is using its leverage over punishment to extract extraneous concessions. There is no basis for the government to require defendants to waive rights beyond those associated with the trial itself, so these kinds of terms fail the nexus test. While full-scale trials may impose huge costs that create a compelling government interest to mitigate, the same cannot be said of motions practice or appeals, which can easily be handled by courts with their existing resources.

The nexus and proportionality framework should also require any plea terms to focus only on a defendant's case and not those of third parties. Prosecutors will sometimes promise in plea negotiations that they will not charge someone else, often a defendant's loved one, if a defendant pleads guilty. Using emotional leverage has no place in the state's negotiation with the defendant, and a nexus analysis should easily rule this kind of bargain unconstitutional.

The nexus framework would allow courts to see how improper these plea terms are, and there would no line-drawing difficulties with most of them. Courts now fail to give these terms scrutiny because the unconstitutional conditions model is erroneously thought inapposite to plea bargaining.

The unconstitutional conditions framework was well established when the Supreme Court confronted the constitutionality of plea bargaining.[65] While it could yield two possible outcomes given the Court's approach to other rights—either an outright prohibition of any prosecutorial offer or threat or more oversight over the terms of the deals offered—it would cabin what prosecutors could do.

The Court, however, chose a third path that has no basis in law. There was no reason for the Court to treat the jury trial right as some kind of second-class constitutional protection that required no analysis under the unconstitutional conditions doctrine. Or, to put it more accurately, there was no *legal* reason for doing so. The Court's path is explained by its desire to reach a preferred policy outcome, in this case, preserving the efficiency of plea bargaining.

Bordenkircher v. Hayes and the Acceptance of Coercive Plea Bargains

The Supreme Court did not rule on the constitutionality of plea bargaining until the 1970s. While it had previously viewed plea bargaining with suspicion and expressed concerns about its coercive nature, it had no occasion to rule on it directly. By the time the Court squarely confronted the constitutionality of plea bargaining, it was so entrenched as a practice that the Court seemed unable or unwilling to see it as an unconstitutional condition on the jury trial right. It never even analyzed plea bargaining that way. Instead, the Court gradually just accepted plea bargaining as inevitable and then ultimately took inevitability to mean it was constitutional.

In 1970, the Court took the first step toward accepting plea bargaining in dicta. In *Brady v. United States,* the Court concluded that a system that tolerated guilty pleas would necessarily have to accept plea bargaining. Robert Brady was charged under a statute that would impose the death penalty if he had a jury trial and was convicted, but he could avoid that punishment if he pleaded guilty.[66] The Court refused to find the statutory scheme coercive because it did not see how it could make that decision without calling into question all guilty pleas. The Court did not see daylight between the hope of judicial leniency in exchange for a guilty plea and the government making clear a defendant would definitely get a lighter sentence with a guilty plea and face a longer one if the case went to trial.

It is, however, a far different situation for a defendant to plead guilty and hope that a more lenient outcome might result than one in which the government, through its deliberate actions, offers leniency to someone who relinquishes a constitutional right. The entire framework of the unconstitutional conditions doctrine rests on just such distinctions. The inquiry under that framework focuses on whether the government seeks to coerce the abandonment of a constitutional right through explicit conditions. In a case where a defendant hopes that a judge might be more lenient, there is no such coercion as long as the judge is not explicitly bargaining with defendants and telling them that they will get lower sentences if they relinquish their jury trial rights. As long as defendants are just hoping to get a break in their individual cases because the judge will consider their guilty pleas as one factor in their favor, there is no unconstitutional conditions problem.

In Brady's case and in plea bargaining scenarios where prosecutors make it clear that there will be a penalty for going to trial and leniency for pleading guilty, there is an explicit and concrete cost to exercising a constitutional right. It is the classic unconstitutional conditions framework, but the Court failed to see it is as such.

Instead, the Court grouped all guilty pleas together and seemed to worry about doing anything that would call any of them into question given that they had become critical to the administration of criminal law and punishment in America. The Court observed "that at present well over three-fourths of the criminal convictions in this country rest on pleas of guilty, a great many of them no doubt motivated at least in part by the hope or assurance of a lesser penalty than might be imposed if there were a guilty verdict after a trial." The Court was so blinded by its concern with maintaining guilty pleas and not calling them into doubt that it failed to see that hope is much different than a certain price.

Far from seeing the jury trial as a core constitutional right to protect, the Court seemed to view jury trials as an impediment to the efficient operation of the judicial branch. The same year that *Brady* was decided, Chief Justice Burger gave a speech on the state of the judiciary at the annual meeting of the American Bar Association. It was the first such speech given by a chief justice and televised on all three major networks. Burger emphasized in the speech how important guilty pleas were for the effective operation of the judicial branch. He noted that a reduction in the guilty plea rate from 90 percent to 80 percent would "require[] the assignment of twice the judicial manpower and facilities," and a reduction to 70 percent would "treble this demand." When the guilty plea rate dropped to 65 percent in the District of Columbia, "it was little short of disaster" given the strain on existing judicial resources.[67] It is hardly surprising that the Court in *Brady* was reluctant to do anything that would call into question guilty pleas or diminish their frequency given that it threatened "disaster."

One year later, Chief Justice Burger essentially repeated this speech, only this time it was part of his opinion for the Court in *Santobello*. Rudolph Santobello had been charged with two first-degree felony gambling counts and originally pleaded not guilty. After negotiations with the prosecution, he agreed to plead guilty to a single, second-degree gambling count in exchange for prosecutors dropping the more serious charges and agreeing not to make a sentencing recommendation to the judge. A different prosecutor took over the case by the time of Santobello's sentencing, and that prosecutor recommended to the judge that Santobello receive the maximum sentence of one year under the statute, which the judge imposed. Santobello then sought to withdraw his guilty plea and pursue his appeal. The Supreme Court held that, "when a plea rests in any significant degree on a promise or agreement of the prosecutor, so that it can be said to be part of the inducement or consideration, such promise must be fulfilled." In getting to that result, Chief Justice Burger first sang the praises of the benefits of plea bargaining with echoes of his ABA speech. He wrote for the Court: "The disposition of charges after plea discussions by agreement between the prosecutor and the accused, sometimes loosely called 'plea bargaining,' is an essential component of the administration of justice. Properly administered, it is to be encouraged. If every criminal charge were subjected to a full-scale trial, the States and the Federal Government would need to multiply by many times the number of judges and court facilities." In Chief Justice Burger's estimation, plea bargaining was not just essential but also "a highly desirable" part of the criminal justice process "for many reasons." He praised the fact that it "leads to a prompt and largely final disposition of most cases." He claimed it "avoid[ed] much of the corrosive impact of enforced idleness during pre-trial confinement" for those in pretrial detention. He argued, without elaboration, that it somehow "protects the public from those accused persons who are prone to continue criminal conduct even while on pretrial release." And, perhaps most incredibly of all, he stated that, "by shortening the time between charge and disposition, it enhances whatever may be the rehabilitative prospects of the guilty."[68]

A few years later, the Court reiterated the notion that plea bargaining was part of the fabric of the administration of criminal law, stating, "Whatever might be the situation in an ideal world, the fact is that the guilty plea and the often concomitant plea bargain are important components of this country's criminal justice system."[69] It is disturbing that the Court seemed to conflate the constitutional right to a jury with some kind of unreachable "ideal world." At this point, however, the Court had not yet addressed the constitutionality of coercive plea bargaining practices head-on. No case had yet required the Court to confront an actual threat by a prosecutor to bring more serious charges if a defendant did not plead guilty. *Brady* specifically clarified that it was not deciding the constitutionality of "the situation where the prosecutor or judge, or both, deliberately employ their charging and sentencing powers to induce a particular defendant to tender a plea of guilty."[70] Pleas must be voluntary, so the Court still had room to use the voluntariness framework to strike down any plea bargain in which the prosecutor coerced the plea by threatening more severe punishment if the defendant went to trial.[71]

The first case where the Court confronted an explicit threat by a prosecutor to bring more serious charges if a defendant exercised his jury trial right was *Bordenkircher v. Hayes*. Paul Lewis Hayes, a twenty-nine-year-old Black man, stole a check from a local business in Lexington, Kentucky. He forged the signature on the check to pay for $88.30 worth of merchandise at a Pic Pac grocery store. He was initially charged with uttering a forged instrument and faced a punishment of two to ten years in prison. During plea negotiations, the prosecutor, Glen Bagby, offered to recommend a sentence of five years to the judge if Hayes agreed to plead guilty. If Hayes decided to exercise his constitutional right to a jury trial, Bagby threatened to amend the charges to include a count of violating the Kentucky Habitual Criminal Act, Kentucky's version of a three-strikes law that was in effect when Hayes committed his crime. The Kentucky legislature later concluded the law swept too broadly, and under the revised version, Hayes would not have qualified. Unfortunately for Hayes, though, he had two prior felony convictions that triggered the recidivism enhancement in the act as it existed when he was charged. If Bagby added the habitual offender count, it would mean a mandatory life sentence if Hayes was convicted. Surprisingly, given the likelihood of a conviction, Hayes rejected Bagby's offer. Unsurprisingly, Hayes was convicted.

It is worth pausing at this point to think about the case from Bagby's perspective. He clearly thought a five-year sentence was appropriate, or he would not have offered it. Presumably, Bagby believed that was the right punishment, and it was not one on the lower end of the statutory range for the check forgery; given the small amount of the check itself, this was presumably because of Hayes's prior record. Hayes was on probation for a robbery conviction when he committed the check forgery, and he had another conviction for "detaining a female" when he was seventeen that involved an allegation that he and an adult man were involved in the sexual assault of a woman. Those charges, however, were not sufficiently severe to justify seeking a life sentence under the Habitual Criminal Act. Neither of those convictions resulted in prison time. Hayes spent five years in a reformatory for the "detaining a female" offense, and he received probation for the robbery. Hayes would thus be getting life imprisonment even though he had never served time in prison before and the trigger this time was a check for $88.30. Bagby threatened the count that carried the life sentence not because he thought that sentence was appropriate but because he did not want Hayes to exercise his jury trial right on the check forgery charge. The Habitual Criminal Act was a tool Bagby used to get the sentence he thought appropriate without having to work for it in a trial. Bagby admitted as much when he cross-examined Hayes at his trial, asking Hayes, "Isn't it a fact that I told you . . . if you did not intend to plead guilty to five years for this charge and . . . save the court the inconvenience and necessity of a trial and taking up this time that I intended to return to the grand jury and ask them to indict you based upon these prior felony convictions?"[72]

In Bagby's view, the price of Hayes refusing his offer and insisting on "the inconvenience and necessity of a trial" was a life sentence. It was not what he thought was the right punishment for Hayes's check forgery, or he never would have offered the five-year sentence—that gap is just too big. Prosecutors were not even seeking mandatory life sentences under the habitual offender law for people who had far more serious priors than Hayes. Hayes personally knew of people with six prior felony convictions who did not get charged under that act.[73] Bagby just wanted to use the recidivist law as a threat, so he would not have to deal with the burden of taking the case to trial, as he readily admitted in his question to Hayes at trial. Bagby was likely shocked when Hayes refused the offer, but he could not let Hayes call his bluff, or defense lawyers would learn that Bagby's threats in plea negotiations were empty.

Bagby's methods were hardly unique. One of the amicus briefs filed with the Court was from a group of incarcerated people in Texas similarly situated to Hayes. There were more than four dozen people mentioned. They included Jimmy Harris, who, like Hayes, received a life sentence for forgery. Harris turned down a Texas prosecutor's offer of eight years if he pleaded guilty to forgery and was then reindicted under a Texas habitual offender law comparable to the one in Kentucky. Mitchell Ray Rodgers was serving a life sentence for heroin possession in Texas after he turned down a plea offer of sixteen years.[74] The attorney general of Texas all but admitted that district attorneys in Texas were relying on these threats to get guilty pleas, noting in an amicus brief that "a holding that a prosecutor may never seek the maximum punishment after a defendant has rejected his offer would . . . destroy the plea bargaining process." And without plea bargaining, the Texas attorney general warned, "the criminal justice system, already stymied by an overly burdensome case load, would collapse under the pressure of trial on each case."[75] Whereas prosecutors saw these threats as necessities, a brief filed on behalf of public defenders in California viewed them as "prosecutorial extortion."[76]

In a 5–4 decision, the Court refused to say this violated the Constitution. Justice Stewart wrote the brief opinion for the majority. The opinion began by observing that the Court had already "open[ly] acknowledg[ed] this previously clandestine practice" of plea bargaining in prior decisions. It did admit, however, that none of those decisions dealt with a challenge to the substance of a plea offer itself. Justice Stewart dismissed the idea that Bagby was acting vindictively and in violation of due process. The Court acknowledged that it had previously condemned efforts by the state to impose additional punishment on defendants who exercised their rights to appeal, noting that "to punish a person because he has done what the law plainly allows him to do is a due process violation of the most basic sort." Why, then, was Bagby's threat and subsequent indictment not squarely within those cases? He was, after all, punishing Hayes for exercising his jury trial right, something the "law plainly allows him to do." The Court gave only the conclusory response that that analysis did not apply to "the 'give-and-take' of plea bargaining" because it "flows from 'the mutuality of advantage' to defendants and prosecutors."[77] "Defendants advised by competent counsel," continued the opinion, are "presumptively capable of intelligent choice in response to prosecutorial persuasion and unlikely to be driven to false self-condemnation." Hayes was, in the Court's description, simply faced "with the unpleasant alternatives of forgoing trial or facing charges on which he was plainly subject to prosecution."[78]

Before dismantling the Court's claims on the merits, it is worth first paying attention to the Court's choice of language because it provides a window into how far off the mark it was in understanding the dynamics of plea bargaining. The description of the threat of a life sentence as "prosecutorial persuasion" and the couching of a life sentence for a defendant who exercises his jury trial right as an "unpleasant alternative" are almost comical understatements. It is as if the Court was just a helpless witness incapable of having a say on how the alternatives could be framed. Imagine the Court offering a similar analysis to conditions placed on other government benefits that threatened constitutional rights. The Court would never say that requiring someone to forgo practicing their religion to receive government benefits is just "persuasion" or an "unpleasant alternative." The entire point of the unconstitutional conditions framework is to avoid just these kinds of coercive offers. Plea bargaining, however, was treated as just another set of choices for defendants.

The Court's failure to see the coercion in the prosecutor's offer led it to make three demonstrably false assumptions. The Court's first assumption was that there is "give-and-take" and "mutuality" in plea negotiations. The reality is that the prosecutor holds all the cards. Armed with a range of laws to potentially charge in most situations, the prosecutor has a wide range of threats to make against a defendant to extract a plea. Even an innocent defendant can never be sure that a jury will see the case from the defendant's point of view, so there is always a risk in going to trial. If exercising the jury trial right means risking punishment orders of magnitude more severe, the prosecutor's leverage in these negotiations cannot be matched by the defendant. Plea bargaining, as the legal scholar Al Alschuler colorfully puts it, "benefits both parties only in the sense that a gunman's demand for your money or your life benefits you as well as the gunman."[79] Hayes's case makes this crystal clear. As plea bargaining expert Carissa Byrne Hessick notes, "all Hayes had was the right to require the prosecutor to prove his case to a jury beyond a reasonable doubt—something that was probably inconvenient but otherwise didn't really affect the prosecutor." Bagby, on the other hand, "had Hayes's freedom *for the rest of his life* as leverage."[80] Not exactly mutuality. Moreover, for those defendants being detained pretrial, the prosecutor often uses the detention as leverage, offering time served if a defendant pleads guilty. In many misdemeanor cases, pretrial detention would last longer than any sentence the person would ultimately receive, so it is easy to see how even an innocent person would agree to plead under those terms.

The second false assumption in the Court's opinion was that the right to counsel somehow provides protection against coercion by the state and allows a defendant to make a "choice." Professor Alschuler again provides a vivid analogy, pointing out that "the presence of counsel has little relevance to the question of voluntariness. A guilty plea entered at gunpoint is no less involuntary because an attorney is present to explain how the gun works."[81] Counsel can only explain the impossible situation the prosecutor is putting the defendant in. In Hayes's case, for example, she could make clear that the life sentence really is mandatory upon conviction. That, however, does not make the prosecutor's threat any less coercive. The lawyer helps only to get the message across.

Third, the Court was also wrong to claim that allowing these kinds of threats would not lead to "false self condemnation." The Court had made a similar assumption in *Brady*, noting in that case that it "would have serious doubts about this case if the encouragement of guilty pleas by offers of leniency substantially increased the likelihood that defendants, advised by competent counsel, would falsely condemn themselves."[82] It is hard to say whether the Court was naive or willfully blind to the risk that innocent people were pleading guilty to avoid the risk that they would be falsely convicted and receive huge punishments after trial. Either way, the Court's assumption has been proven wrong with empirical evidence. Of the people exonerated by DNA evidence—that is, scientifically proven innocent—15 percent were the result of guilty pleas.[83] These people knew they were innocent, but they pleaded guilty because the prosecutor was threatening too much additional punishment if they exercised their jury right. If the jury got it wrong and they were convicted, the risk was just too great. These DNA cases, moreover, are just the tip of the iceberg of wrongful convictions after guilty pleas. There are certainly cases without DNA evidence where individuals faced the same horrible choice and opted to take the certain, lesser punishment rather than risk the far greater punishment being threatened. There is also reason to believe that some prosecutors might be particularly aggressive in trying to get guilty pleas in weak cases.[84] Defendants have a greater temptation to go to trial on weaker cases, so prosecutors will need to do even more to overcome their will.[85] False self-condemnation is not unlikely; it is commonplace. And it is a direct result of the Court's failure in *Bordenkircher* to protect the jury trial right.

In the end, the Court accepted Bagby's behavior because it viewed it as inextricably part of plea bargaining, and it believed it already accepted plea bargaining in *Brady*. "It follows that, by tolerating and encouraging the negotiation of pleas, this Court has necessarily accepted as constitutionally legitimate the simple reality that the prosecutor's interest at the bargaining table is to persuade the defendant to forgo his right to plead not guilty."[86] The Court in *Bordenkircher* seemed to be saying that it already acknowledged plea bargains as a reality in the operation of criminal law, so that necessarily meant that prosecutors could be permitted to use those negotiations to try to get defendants to plead guilty. Indeed, the Court later said that "the outcome in *Bordenkircher* was mandated by this Court's acceptance of plea negotiation as a legitimate process."[87] Recall, though, that *Brady* specifically clarified that was not deciding the constitutionality of "the situation where the prosecutor or judge, or both, deliberately employ their charging and sentencing powers to induce a particular defendant to tender a plea of guilty."[88] The Court in *Bordenkircher* seemed to think it was a foregone conclusion that once you allow guilty pleas and you allow prosecutors to negotiate, you have to accept whatever happens in those negotiations. It seems to have assumed that *Brady* already found a sufficient government interest in guilty pleas. That, though, flies in the face of the approach the Court takes in other unconstitutional conditions cases where it has recognized the government interest at stake as compelling but has still placed nexus and proportionality limits on the terms of the agreement.

The Court in *Bordenkircher* did not use that framework, however, and thus it offered only two possible substantive limits on plea bargaining. First, the prosecutor needs probable cause to believe a defendant committed any offense that the prosecutor threatens to charge. This does not act as much of a limit. The Supreme Court itself has said probable cause to indict is "not a high bar." It requires less than the preponderance of evidence in civil cases. It requires a mere "fair probability" that justifies a reasonable person, not a legal expert, to act.[89] Second, the Court dropped a footnote clarifying that it was not resolving the question whether there were "constitutional implications of a prosecutor's offer during plea bargaining of adverse or lenient treatment of some person *other* than the accused."[90] As it turned out, this limit amounted to nothing because the Court has never followed up on it to strike down pleas on this basis.

So probable cause is the only guardrail. William Ortman, a legal scholar who has studied probable cause in-depth, has persuasively argued that this standard is too weak for a plea bargaining regime because the entire point of probable cause is based on the idea of a trial jury finding guilt beyond a reasonable doubt.[91] This low bar can operate only because another check is in place. But plea bargaining has dissolved that check, thus increasing the risk of innocent people being convicted.

The Court in *Bordenkircher*, however, seemed uninterested in setting up checks on plea bargaining. It vaguely suggested that "there are undoubtedly constitutional limits upon its exercise." But if the limit did not cover seeking a life sentence on a crime a prosecutor thought merited five years in order to obtain a guilty plea, it is hard to see exactly what the limits would be.

Even the dissenters were not willing to fully protect jury trial rights. Justice Blackmun's dissenting opinion, joined by Justices Brennan and Marshall, saw this case as one of vindictive prosecution. They objected to Bagby filing more serious charges only after Hayes elected to exercise his jury trial right and noted that Bagby himself admitted that "the sole reason for the new indictment was to discourage the respondent from exercising his right to a trial." Even if Bagby had not been so candid, however, they believed that the subsequent indictment's more serious charges would create "a strong inference of vindictiveness."[92] While that would have given Hayes relief—and was the argument relied upon by his lawyers—it would not have made much of a difference for most defendants because prosecutors could simply charge excessively at the outset and then "bargain" down. The majority was correct to note that, "[a]s a practical matter," the "case would be no different if the grand jury had indicted Hayes as a recidivist from the outset, and the prosecutor had offered to drop that charge as part of the plea bargain."[93] Justice Blackmun's dissent admitted that its approach might "prompt the aggressive prosecutor to bring the greater charge initially in every case" and bargain from there, but he noted that this was preferable to what the prosecutor did in the *Bordenkircher* case because it would at least "hold the prosecution to the charge it was originally content to bring and to justify in the eyes of its public."[94]

Justice Powell filed a separate dissent. He originally voted with the majority in the case but changed his mind as he came to see the case as "terribly unjust."[95] He started his dissent by noting he "agreed with much of the Court's opinion." Justice Powell pointed out that, in most cases, it would not be possible to know why a prosecutor brings a superseding indictment for a more serious offense, and an inquiry into motive would be fruitless. But he viewed this case as different because Bagby openly admitted he brought the more serious charge because of Hayes's "insistence on exercising his constitutional rights." He ended by noting that plea bargaining is "essential to the functioning of the criminal-justice system" and that "only in the most exceptional case should a court conclude that the scales of the bargaining are so unevenly balanced as to arouse suspicion."[96] This was that exceptional case in his view because Bagby admitted he threatened the more serious charge to get a guilty plea and then brought it to penalize the exercise of the jury trial right. So, under Powell's take, only when prosecutors state explicitly that they are engaged in "a strategy calculated solely to deter the exercise of constitutional rights" would the plea bargain be ruled unconstitutional. Needless to say, even if that had been a majority view, little would change because most prosecutors would figure out that they should not openly admit that their goal is to penalize defendants who opt to go to trial.

What was missing from all the opinions in *Bordenkircher* was an analysis of the case as an unconstitutional condition on the jury right. The Court viewed the plea negotiations as another form of contract negotiations and gave insufficient attention to the importance of the jury trial right and "the ways in which contracts involving constitutional rights merit special scrutiny." "If the promise of public employment or the threat of being denied a building permit rise to the level of undue coercion and impermissibly deter the exercise of First Amendment and Fifth Amendment property rights," as the unconstitutional conditions doctrine holds they do, "the threat of additional criminal prosecutions" and increased punishment should likewise be seen as unduly coercive and an impermissible infringement of the jury trial right.[97] Indeed, in the words of one set of observers, it is impossible "to reconcile the Court's approach to plea bargaining with its continued commitment to the modern unconstitutional conditions doctrine."[98]

The Court's acceptance of plea bargaining is an affront to the value of juries and trials. It cannot be reconciled with the doctrine of unconstitutional conditions. It was simply not a decision grounded in law. It was, if anything, just a naked judgment that, in the words of law professor Josh Bowers, "plea bargaining is simply too big to fail."[99]

The Aftermath of *Bordenkircher*

In the first twelve years after *Bordenkircher*, the number of felony prosecutions and the number of people incarcerated more than doubled because of the "more aggressive use of plea bargaining" that followed in *Bordenkircher*'s wake. The percentage of convictions obtained by guilty pleas rose from 80 percent in the middle of the 1970s to more than 90 percent at the end of the 1980s and is now more than 95 percent. The Court's greenlighting of plea bargaining—indeed, its full-throated defense of it in cases like *Brady, Santobello,* and *Bordenkircher*—made it clear to prosecutors that they had free rein to threaten harsher punishments to gain guilty pleas. Bagby's behavior has "become the norm, not the exception."[100] As Angela Davis, a leading expert on prosecution practices notes, prosecutors now routinely "charge more and greater offenses than they can prove beyond a reasonable doubt" because "this tactic offers the prosecutor more leverage during plea negotiations."[101] The *average* difference between a defendant's sentence after trial and a defendant's sentence after a plea in federal felony cases is now seven years, and the average gap is nine years in drug cases.[102] In a world in which the Court refuses to recognize prosecutorial coercion as an unconstitutional condition on jury trial rights, it is open season for just that kind of behavior by prosecutors.

It is not just longer sentences that prosecutors have achieved. They have grown more aggressive in their requests to have defendants waive other rights as part of a plea deal. For example, asking a defendant to waive the right to appeal was a "rare or nonexistent" practice before the Court condoned plea bargaining. Gradually, appeal waivers became more commonplace, such that two-thirds of all plea agreements in a federal sample from 2003 required defendants to waive their appeal rights. Prosecutors have grown bolder still, insisting that defendants waive their right to receive exculpatory impeachment evidence and to make ineffective assistance of counsel claims as part of their agreement. Accepting waivers of the jury trial thus had a snowball effect. "As plea bargaining becomes normal, one may see no reason not to make it more effective."[103]

The steep decline in trials, appeals, and other legal challenges means the loss of critical oversight of government conduct. A 2023 ABA report calls jury trials "rare legal artifacts in most U.S. jurisdictions—and even nonexistent in others."[104] When cases are resolved by plea, it is hard to know what really happened because the plea bargaining process, unlike a trial, does not spend much time trying to get at the truth. Juries, unlike prosecutors, are impartial actors. Prosecutors work with the police on a repeat basis and do not closely scrutinize their work with the same fresh set of eyes. Prosecutors may have also investigated the same case they are charging and therefore have developed a bias against the defendant as a result. Prosecutors also develop an insensitivity over time to the enormity of what is at stake for a defendant. They throw out long sentences in plea negotiations on a daily basis and lose the perspective of just how life altering those years are. As the English writer G. K. Chesterton observed, prosecutors "have got used to it. Strictly they do not see the prisoner in the dock; all they see is the usual man in the usual place. They do not see the awful court of judgment; they only see their own workshop."[105]

The plea process, unlike a trial, thus offers a distorted perspective because it is based not on finding the truth but on getting to the prosecutor's preferred result. That preference is securing a conviction without having to go to trial. This process leads to innocent defendants pleading guilty because the punishment they face if they lose at trial is just too great. We also know that people who have committed crimes will plead guilty to entirely different crimes under the terms of the deals they are offered if that is what gets them a more favorable sentence. Judge Gerard Lynch has vividly described how minimal court oversight of pleas is:

> The judicial "process" consists of the simultaneous filing of a criminal charge by a prosecutor (often by means of a prosecutor's "information" rather than an indictment, with the defendant waiving the submission of evidence and charge to a grand jury) and admission of guilty by the defendant. The charging document may be quite skeletal, the defendant's account of his guilty actions brief, and the judicial inquiry concerned more with whether the defendant is of sound mind and understands the consequences of what he is doing than with the accuracy of the facts to which he is attesting.

Judges are under no obligation to decide if a defendant really is guilty, and they lack the information to make that decision even if they wanted to.[106]

Pleas also make it difficult to check police abuses. It is not just that prosecutors are more likely to defer to the police because they have to work with them on a repeated basis, though that is certainly problematic. It is also the lack of judicial oversight. While evidence obtained in violation of the Fourth Amendment will be excluded at trial, these kinds of abuses are routinely overlooked in the plea negotiation process.[107] Prosecutors often require defendants to accept a plea offer before any pretrial litigation challenging police misconduct, so there are no consequences for the police abuses. On the contrary, the police see their behavior rewarded with a conviction.

We are, sadly, a long way from the careful separation of powers designed by the Framers with the jury as a key judicial check. Instead, prosecutors now combine executive and adjudicative powers because they make the final decision about what happens in a defendant's case. Justice Frankfurter cautioned that "a democratic society, in which respect for the dignity of all men is central, naturally guards against the misuse of the law enforcement process" and that "safeguards must be provided against the dangers of the overzealous as well as the despotic." It is necessary to have checks because "the awful instruments of the criminal law cannot be entrusted to a single functionary."[108] Unfortunately, prosecutors now hold all the cards, and they present all the "dangers of the overzealous" that Justice Frankfurter feared.

It is not just the adjudicative function that has been tainted by plea bargaining. It has warped the legislative process as well. Prosecutors are the dominant actors in criminal lawmaking now. They brazenly ask legislators to create new crimes, so they have a broader menu to choose from in making charging decisions.[109] They also request laws with mandatory minimums and longer sentences, not because those punishments are the proportionate penalty for a given offense but because they give prosecutors leverage to get pleas and cooperation. Even the Supreme Court acknowledges this is now the world we live in, as it concedes that defendants who go "to trial and lose receive longer sentences than even Congress or the prosecutor might think appropriate, because the longer sentences exist on the books largely for bargaining purposes."[110] "The legally authorized sentence is harsher than the sentence prosecutors want to impose" in "a large fraction of cases."[111] The harsher statutory sentence is, however, good for bargaining.

Mandatory sentences are particularly valuable to prosecutors because they leave no doubt about what will happen if a defendant opts to go to trial and is convicted. A judge would be unable to sentence below that threshold, just as the trial judge in *Bordenkircher* had no choice but to give the life sentence. Thus, prosecutors urge legislators to pass more mandatory minimums and fight tooth and nail to keep in place the ones that exist.[112] For example, the US Attorney for the District of Columbia testified against a reduction in mandatory minimums for the possession of crack cocaine because prosecutors use them as a "hammer" to get defendants to cooperate with prosecutors.[113] At another legislative hearing, the chief of the Narcotics and Dangerous Drug Section of the Criminal Division of the Department of Justice called mandatory minimum sentences "an indispensable tool for prosecutors" to obtain pleas and cooperation.[114]

Legislators have embraced the plea bargaining model and pass legislation to foster its use. They pass overinclusive laws with few elements, so prosecutors can more easily claim probable cause to charge, and they include mandatory minimums and severe sentences, so prosecutors have the leverage they need to extract guilty pleas. Legislators get tough-on-crime credibility, and prosecutors get the tools they need for plea bargaining.[115] No one—not legislators, not prosecutors—expects the maximum punishment or anything close to it to be imposed in the ordinary case. Stephanos Bibas made an apt comparison in his study of plea bargaining dynamics: "It is like the sticker price for cars; only an ignorant, ill-advised consumer would view full price as the norm and anything less as a bargain."[116] Pleas are not bringing discounts; trials are being penalized. As Professor Alschuler notes, "sane societies ... do not sentence 95% of all offenders to less than they deserve."[117]

Plea bargaining thus means harsher sentences across the board because prosecutors are now getting longer sentences without the check of a trial, and people who do go to trial are getting longer sentences when they are convicted. And more people are getting these longer sentences because plea bargaining allows the mass production of cases.[118] This is the formula for mass incarceration: more convictions and longer sentences.

Resources that should have been spent on the required constitutional process of jury trials have been funneled into massive prison spending instead.[119] Legislators embrace this model because they view it as a steeply discounted way to deal with—or appear to deal with—crime. Instead of investing in root cause solutions or paying for constitutionally mandated procedures, legislators increase prosecutorial leverage, so they can exact pleas and save on court costs. They openly admit they pass laws to enhance prosecutorial power. Senator Charles Grassley opposed reductions in mandatory minimums for drug crimes because he was worried it would undermine prosecutors' leverage. He said an "intended goal" of these laws is "to put pressure on defendants to cooperate in exchange for a lower sentence."[120]

Prosecutors love mandatory minimum laws because of the leverage it gives them in plea bargaining, but like so many aspects of plea bargaining, their use of these laws in plea negotiations results in glaring racial disparities. Black defendants are less likely than similarly situated white defendants to receive plea offers that will avoid mandatory minimum sentences in drug and gun cases. It is not just negotiations around mandatory minimums that produce racial bias in plea bargaining. An ABA task force investigating plea bargaining recently found "across all charges . . . evidence of significant racial disparities in prosecutorial decisions to drop or reduce charges." Hayes's treatment as a Black defendant was sadly not unusual. Black and white defendants with similar conduct and criminal records are being treated differently in plea negotiations, and there is effectively no oversight to correct it.

Plea bargaining is also an affront to traditional notions of proportional punishment based on culpability. Instead of punishment corresponding to relative culpability, the key determining factor is whether a person pleaded guilty. This is all too easy to see in cases with multiple defendants. There are countless examples where more culpable defendants pleaded guilty and received lower sentences than other people involved in the same crime who were less culpable but exercised their jury trial right. Consider the bank robber who brandished a gun at a teller, pleaded guilty, and received a maximum sentence of forty-three years, while his getaway driver went to trial and got ninety-nine years.[121] Then there was the leader and mastermind of a conspiracy to rob an alleged stash house who pleaded guilty and received a sentence three and a half years shorter than a low-level participant he had recruited.[122] It is, sadly, not uncommon in drug cases to have people higher up in a drug conspiracy receiving shorter sentences than lower-level participants because they have more information to trade and thus receive more generous plea offers.[123] In all these contexts, people are being sentenced based on their guilty plea and their value to a prosecutor and not based on any concept of proportional desert.

For its part, the Court now candidly views "the negotiation of a plea bargain, rather than the unfolding of a trial," as "the critical point for a defendant."[124] Yet it has done little to police this process. It has clung to a naive belief—belied by mounds of evidence of actual prosecutorial practice—"that the great majority of prosecutors will be faithful to their duty" and not abuse their bargaining power.[125] Even though it expressed reservations in *Bordenkircher* about plea bargains that involve an offer by prosecutors to treat a third person leniently or a threat to treat them more harshly depending on whether the defendant pleads guilty, it has shown an unwillingness to police even this aspect of plea bargaining. Lower courts have regularly upheld bargains involving third parties, and the Court has been uninterested in reviewing these cases.[126] For example, the Court refused to hear a case where the defendant, Jonathan Pollard, pleaded guilty after prosecutors made clear that their willingness to plea bargain with the defendant's wife, Anne, who had also been charged and was seriously ill, depended on Jonathan's guilty plea. The Court denied cert even though there was a circuit split, with some lower courts finding "familial coercion" renders a plea involuntary and others, such as the DC Circuit in Pollard's case, finding it to be an irrelevant factor absent a showing of prosecutorial bad faith.[127] The Court also refused to hear Bryan Spilmon's case. Spilmon was a dentist who pleaded guilty to Medicaid fraud, and he argued that he pleaded guilty because the government threatened to seek incarceration for his wife if he did not. His petition also highlighted a circuit split among the lower courts in addressing plea agreements that involve third parties.[128]

Plea bargains affect third parties in another troubling way. Defendants face enormous pressure to cooperate with the government to get better deals. The result is that they are all too willing to implicate others to catch a break. Sometimes that means outright lying. In a whopping 60 percent of the cases in which a defendant was wrongfully convicted and later exonerated, someone had falsely accused the defendant. "Most often, witnesses lie because they receive some benefit for testifying against the defendant," and typically that benefit comes in the form of a desirable plea bargain.[129] Perhaps even more common is a defendant willing to embellish or color facts to make a case against someone else who is guilty easier for a prosecutor to bring. It is hard to sort truth from fiction when the incentives for lying are so high.

The Court, however, has largely stood on the sidelines when it comes to any regulation of plea bargaining, with the sole exception of stepping in when necessary to make sure the plea process is as efficient as possible. That explains why *Santobello* required prosecutors to keep their promises. It is also the rationale behind the Court's cases recognizing that a failure to inform a defendant about a plea offer or the giving of erroneous advice about the consequences of a plea versus going to trial is the basis of an ineffective assistance of counsel claim that requires either a resentencing or giving the defendant another chance to accept the original plea offer.[130] In those cases, the Court wanted to make sure that lawyers made defendants aware of plea offers and gave constitutionally adequate advice about what it would mean if they pleaded guilty versus opted for trial because that makes it more likely a lawyer can convince a client to take a good deal. Enforcing procedural rules like these "serve[s] primarily to keep the guilty-plea apparatus humming along smoothly."[131]

What the Court has completely avoided, however, is any oversight of the substance of the bargain itself. "The size and nature of the club which the prosecution can wield, remains in a constitutional blind spot."[132] Even if the Court is not prepared to treat conditions on the exercise of the trial right like it does other constitutional rights for purposes of the doctrine of unconstitutional conditions, it could still do more to police pleas to make sure they are truly knowing. A main source of uncertainty is what is likely to happen if a defendant goes to trial.[133] Defendants cannot assess their risk at trial without knowing the evidence prosecutors have against them. Even innocent defendants need to know what kind of case is being mounted against them to assess whether a jury might be misled and convict them. The Supreme Court has held that prosecutors need to turn over all exculpatory evidence to defendants before trial, but in a world of plea bargaining, that is often too late. The Court should hold, as some state courts have under their state constitutions, that exculpatory evidence must be turned over before a defendant must make a decision about whether to accept a plea offer.[134]

The Court, however, seems uninterested in any substantive oversight of plea bargaining much less the kind of oversight the Constitution demands of it. By leaving plea bargaining to operate unchecked, the Court has thus paved the way for mass incarceration to flourish. Trials are costly, and if the government had to use constitutionally mandated procedures to criminally punish someone, it would have to use punishment less. Policymakers might therefore consider other strategies for addressing social problems. Turning to the root causes of conduct that lead to social harm becomes more attractive when the deceptively easy fix of criminal punishment becomes more expensive. Perhaps governments would make the kind of community investments that reduce crime because they would become more fiscally attractive as compared to the cost of providing jury trials for everyone entitled to one under the Constitution. Maybe they would turn more often to violence intervention programs, public health models, or civil enforcement strategies. If they still wanted to use the crime model, punishments that fall below the jury trial threshold of six months would become more desirable. Requiring the constitutional process might not be as administratively convenient, but it would actually make government more rational.

There is a reason the Framers made criminal punishment hard for the state to obtain. It should require a significant state investment because the price of stripping away liberty should be high. When it can be obtained on the cheap, the temptation will be too great to overuse punishment—which is, of course, exactly what has happened in America. Plea bargaining has facilitated both of the drivers of mass incarceration: admissions and sentence length. It makes convictions easier, meaning more people are admitted to prison. It has also spurred the increase in sentence length. Prosecutors have been a driving force in asking legislators to pass mandatory minimums and sentencing increases because of the leverage it gives them in plea bargaining. Prosecutors are using that leverage to demand ever longer prison terms.

It is no exaggeration to say that, without plea bargaining, mass incarceration could not occur. The mass numbers of cases require mass processing, and you cannot have that without plea bargaining. It is the rotten core of mass incarceration, and it exists only because the Supreme Court has allowed the government to coerce people into giving up one of the most sacred of constitutional rights.

CHAPTER THREE

UPHOLDING DISPROPORTIONATE SENTENCES

Harmelin v. Michigan

Let the punishment match the offense.
—MARCUS TULLIUS CICERO

The stories sound like plot lines in modern-day versions of *Les Misérables*. Homeless and hungry, Michael Riggs stole a bottle of vitamins from a grocery store. When he was caught, he apologized profusely and asked if he could work to pay for what he stole. He would scrub floors or clean. Instead, he was arrested and initially offered a five-year sentence if he pleaded guilty. His public defender did not realize his prior conviction for robbery would trigger California's three-strikes law if the prosecutor opted to pursue that approach, so she recommended that he wait for a better offer. It never came, and instead Riggs received a twenty-five-years-to-life sentence.[1]

Jerry DeWayne Williams, a warehouseman from Compton, was intoxicated and hanging out with a friend when each man asked a group of young people eating an extra-large pepperoni pizza if they could have a slice. When the kids said no, Williams and his friend each took a slice nonetheless. Williams's friend was never prosecuted—understandable given the "crime" was taking a slice of pizza. Williams, however, was charged under California's three-strikes law because he had prior qualifying convictions. That slice of pizza resulted in a sentence of twenty-five years to life.

When he was twenty-three years old, Duane Silva stole a video recorder and a coin collection from his neighbors. Silva has an IQ of 70, and his only prior offenses were setting fire to trash barrels and to the glove compartment of a car. He, too, was charged under California's three-strikes law and received a thirty-years-to-life sentence.[2]

While California has handed down some of the most unjust sentences, it is not alone. Egregiously long sentences have been handed down across the country. In Louisiana in 1996, Timothy Jackson received a life sentence as a fourth felony offender in Louisiana for shoplifting a jacket worth $159. Jackson was addicted to drugs when he stole the coat and had a sixth-grade education.[3] Lance Saltzman's life-without-parole sentence under Florida's Prison Release Reoffender Law was for stealing and reselling the gun his stepfather previously used to shoot his mother. Like Jackson, Saltzman was struggling with drug addiction and also had cognitive impairment from the traumatic brain injury he suffered as a child.[4] Another Florida man, Todd Hannigan, was sentenced to fifteen years for possessing thirty-one Vicodin tablets in a public park. At trial, Hannigan presented evidence that he took the Vicodin from his mother for the purpose of taking his own life.[5]

People prosecuted in federal court fare no better. Stephanie George received a life sentence for the minor and nonviolent role she played in helping her boyfriend distribute crack cocaine. At her sentencing, the trial judge noted that her "role has basically been as a girlfriend and bag holder and money holder but not actively involved in the drug dealing." The judge had no choice but to give the life sentence, however, because it was mandatory under the law.[6]

Every day in America, judges hand down draconian sentences like these. Oftentimes, the judges' hands are tied because the sentences are mandatory penalties established by legislation. The legislation is often the result of some crime panic, and not much thought is given to how these laws will apply in individual cases. Politicians take action with the worst possible cases in mind and are not bothered with the details of how the law will play out across a range of possible factual scenarios. To the extent they do care, they leave it to prosecutors to use their discretion.

Prosecutors, for their part, use these laws just as the prosecutor did in *Bordenkircher*—as a hammer to induce pleas. For the poor souls who want to exercise their constitutional rights, there is no relief. Just as the judge in *Bordenkircher* had no choice but to hand down the life sentence once the prosecutor brought the charges and the jury convicted, judges in these cases often have no discretion to make sure the punishment fits the crime.

When these cases go to trial, the jury has no idea what is at stake because courts have held that they cannot be instructed about the potential punishment in noncapital cases. When they convict, they likely have no clue that they are paving the way for sentences this harsh. Indeed, when they find out, they are horrified.

We should all be horrified. More than that, we should be furious. The Constitution should be preventing injustices like these. The Framers knew full well the danger that existed from unduly severe laws. The Constitution takes aim at this threat in multiple ways. Article II gives the president, right alongside the commander-in-chief powers, the clemency power to check excessive sentences in federal cases because, as Alexander Hamilton noted in the Federalist Papers, otherwise "justice would wear a countenance too sanguinary and cruel."[7] Article III has the jury guarantee, which should act as a community check against excessive sanctions.[8] When the Bill of Rights was added, the Framers made sure to include a specific ban on disproportionate sentences, banning excessive fines and cruel and unusual punishments. The Eighth Amendment is incorporated through the Fourteenth Amendment to apply to state punishments. How, then, can these disproportionate sentences stand?

Clemency does not act as a meaningful check because the same tough-on-crime politics that produce these harsh sentences lead presidents and governors, who have similar clemency powers under state constitutions, to avoid second-guessing sentences because they do not want to appear too soft on crime. The jury could provide a check, but as we saw in Chapter 2, plea bargaining has taken the jury out of the picture in almost every case.

That leaves the Eighth Amendment, which should be the ultimate safeguard. It explicitly targets disproportionate sentences, which should result in limits on punishments like these, even in a world of plea bargaining. Why is the Eighth Amendment failing? How are these sentences, the cornerstones of mass incarceration, allowed to stand? The answer should be a familiar one by now. The Supreme Court has shirked its constitutional duty.

The Court has been so worried that robust Eighth Amendment review would give unelected judges too much discretion to override sentencing legislation that it has established a test for excessive sentences that is virtually impossible to meet in noncapital cases. Under this test, almost no one can successfully challenge their sentence. Notably, this is in contrast to the active role the Court has played overseeing capital sentences for proportionality. While the Court may declare that "death is different," in fact there is no constitutional basis for treating capital and noncapital cases differently for purposes of applying the Eighth Amendment, which by its terms applies equally to all types of sentences. While *outcomes* may differ given the severity of a death sentence and what is necessary for it to be deemed a proportional sentence, the *test* for evaluating a sentence for proportionality should be the same.[9]

In recent years, the Court has grudgingly admitted that some aspects of the Court's review of capital sentences under the Eighth Amendment must also apply to noncapital cases. It has, for example, concluded that the test for deciding if a noncapital punishment is categorically cruel and unusual is the same as the test for capital sentences. But there remain huge differences in the two contexts that cannot be justified as a matter of the Eighth Amendment's text, history, or purpose.

The starkly different approaches in capital and noncapital sentence review demonstrate the importance of Court oversight. Capital sentences face stringent review by the Supreme Court to make sure they comply with the Eighth Amendment, and as a result, they have declined sharply. The threshold for getting noncapital sentences reviewed is effectively impossible to meet, and the result is that just about every noncapital sentence given to an adult has been deemed acceptable, whether it is fifty years to life for stealing a few videotapes, a life sentence for shoplifting a jacket, or twenty-five years to life for a slice of pizza. Normalizing and accepting disproportionate sentences is how you become the most punitive nation on the planet, with more people incarcerated per capita than any other country. We used to be comparable to other Western democracies, but we veered off course five decades ago and are now an outlier. Our incarceration rate more than quadrupled between the mid-1970s and the mid-2000s, and a major driver of that surge was the increase in time served by those incarcerated.[10] Legislatures know there is no limit on how harsh they can be because courts have accepted whatever harsh punishments they have enacted. Prosecutors, in turn, use these severe sentences as cudgels to extract pleas. This is how you churn millions of people into prisons and fuel mass incarceration.

This is not happening because the Constitution overlooks sentencing severity. It is happening because the Court is overlooking the Constitution.

The Constitutional Framework

The case for constitutional review of sentences for proportionality is rock solid and based on the Constitution's text, original meaning, and precedent—

at least until the Court shifted course abruptly in 1980. The Eighth Amendment provides that "excessive bail shall not be required, nor excessive fines imposed, nor cruel and unusual punishments inflicted." It therefore imposes a proportionality requirement in three contexts: bail, fines, and punishment. Just as bail and fines cannot be excessive and "exceed the bounds of justice," neither can other punishments, including sentences of incarceration.[11]

The language in the Constitution was modeled after the English Bill of Rights of 1689, which used almost identical wording, albeit with different spelling conventions: "excessive Baile ought not to be required nor excessive Fines imposed nor cruell and unusuall Punishments inflicted." The latter provision addressing punishment in the English Bill of Rights was a reaction to unprecedented sentences handed down by judges during the reign of King James II, but its content reflected the more enduring value of proportional punishment in English law and practice.[12] Henry De Bracton noted in his comprehensive work on English law that "it is the duty of the judge to impose a sentence no more and no less severe than the case demands" and made clear that proportionality was required in all forms of punishment, "pecuniary as well as corporal."[13] Proportionality was required by the Magna Carta and established in English court decisions holding that "imprisonment ought always to be according to the quality of the offence."[14] "By 1400, the English common law had embraced the principle, not always followed in practice, that punishment should not be excessive in severity or length."[15] The use of the phrase "cruel and unusual" in the English Bill of Rights reflects this historical lineage against excessively harsh punishment. John Stinneford is a legal scholar who has conducted exhaustive inquiries into the origins of the terms "cruel" and "unusual," and his research shows that the English Bill of Rights prohibited punishments that were significantly harsher than punishments that had previously been imposed as a matter of long-standing practice for particular offenses.[16]

The prohibition on cruel and unusual punishments in the English Bill of Rights covered two versions of excess, or two ways in which something could improperly depart from tradition. First, a punishment could be cruel and unusual in an absolute sense and therefore be unacceptable in any context. This captures the notion of particular modes of punishment being off the table because they constitute some new barbaric method or because a jurisdiction tries to reintroduce a violent punishment that had already fallen out of usage. Second, a punishment could be acceptable in some contexts but too harsh for the criminal conduct at issue. For example, a life sentence for murder could be justified, but a life sentence for parking in a no-parking zone would be excessively harsh and contrary to long-standing practice.[17] The language "cruel and unusual" captures the idea that punishment must be proportionate and not grossly excessive given the blameworthiness of offenders.

"Cruel and unusual punishment" was thus a legal term of art focused on outlawing disproportionate punishments when the Framing generation borrowed the wording.[18] As it was forming a state government, Virginia prepared a Declaration of Rights that included limits on cruel and unusual punishment drawn from the English Bill of Rights. The drafters of the US Constitution then followed the same path.[19] "Drafters of all three provisions considered themselves to be restating a longstanding common law prohibition that was common to both England and the United States."[20] While much of the discussion focused on particular modes of punishment that were torturous, the Framers expressed broader worries about legislative abuse of power to punish that went beyond concerns with the methods of punishment and focused on excessive punishment as well.

The Bill of Rights in the US Constitution was designed to provide at least as much protection as the English Bill of Rights. At the Virginia Convention on the Constitution's ratification, George Mason advocated the adoption of a bill of rights, and Patrick Henry agreed it was necessary because, without it, Congress would have too much power over punishment. As he put it, "when we come to punishments, no latitude ought to be left, nor dependence put on the virtue of representatives." He quoted the Virginia Declaration of Rights language and said these limits were needed because, in their absence, "you depart from the genius of your country." Without constitutional limits, Congress would "punish with still more relentless severity," and "they will tell you that there is such a necessity of strengthening the arm of government."[21] The Eighth Amendment, in other words, was specifically designed to guard against excessive punishments because the Framers knew legislators would have an incentive to authorize them if they could operate unchecked.

This understanding of "cruel and unusual" as requiring an analysis of proportionality finds ample support in framing-era usage. The term "cruel and unusual" meant excessive in state statutes that used the phrase, and this was also how state courts interpreted analogous cruel and unusual punishment prohibitions in state constitutions.[22]

A requirement of proportional punishment also comports with universal moral intuitions about just punishment. As one commentator has noted, "we should not lightly conclude that the only constitutional limitation on punishment was understood . . . not to include a limitation so central to commonly held convictions about just punishment." There should thus be "clear evidence that the proportionality principle was rejected by the framing generation" to overcome this kind of bedrock moral sensibility.[23] Not only is that evidence missing, but all signs point to a reading of the Cruel and Unusual Punishment Clause as banning disproportionate sentences as well as certain modes of punishment.

This reading is also consistent with the Court's subsequent treatment of the clause, at least for most of its history. The Supreme Court did not have many occasions to consider excessive sentences because the Eighth Amendment originally applied only to the federal government, and there were not many federal criminal cases for most of the nation's early history. It took seventy-six years for the first case involving a claim of excessive punishment to make its way to the Supreme Court, and the Court refused to decide the Eighth Amendment issue because it was a state case, and the Court did not at that point believe the Eighth Amendment applied to the states.[24]

The second Eighth Amendment case raising an excessive sentence claim, *O'Neill v. Vermont*, arrived at the Supreme Court in 1892. John O'Neill operated a liquor distribution business out of Whitehall, New York. He was charged with selling liquor in Vermont "without authority" because he filled mail and telegraph orders in New York for alcohol that was delivered to Vermont over a period of three years. The state charged him with separate violations for each order, and he was convicted of 307 separate offenses. The fine and fees associated with the costs of prosecution totaled more than $6,600, an astronomical sum at the time, and if he could not pay, he was to "be confined at hard labor in the house of correction at Rutland for the term of 19,914 days," a sentence of more than fifty-four years. The Supreme Court of Vermont rejected his challenge to the sentence, finding that it cannot be said to be "excessive or oppressive" because it is the result of the fact "he has committed a great many such offenses."

A majority of the Supreme Court refused to consider the sentence on the merits because it repeated its earlier view that the Eighth Amendment did not apply to the states. Justice Field dissented, concluding that the Eighth Amendment protects individuals against both federal and state excessive punishments and that this particular punishment was cruel and unusual. This view was shared by Justices Harlan and Brewster.[25] Justice Field noted that the prohibition on cruel and unusual punishments "is usually applied to punishments which inflict torture" but explained that it also applies "against all punishments which by their excessive length or severity are greatly disproportioned to the offenses charged." He reached this conclusion based on the text of the Eighth Amendment, finding that "the whole inhibition is against that which is excessive either in the bail required, or fine imposed, or punishment inflicted." In other words, he read each section in pari materia with the others, the most natural reading of the text.

Justice Field then concluded that "the punishment imposed was one exceeding in severity—considering the offenses of which the defendant was convicted—anything which I have been able to find in the record of our courts for the present century." Justice Field added that, "had [O'Neill] been found guilty of burglary or highway robbery, he would have received less punishment." The penalty, he noted, was "six times as great as any court in Vermont could have imposed for manslaughter." In other words, Justice Field looked at how similarly situated people had been sentenced and compared the sentence for this crime to the sentences for other, more serious crimes. He wrote, "It is hard to believe that any man of right feeling and heart can refrain from shuddering" at a sentence of fifty-four years' hard labor, "away from one's home and relatives, and thereby prevented from giving assistance to them or receiving comfort from them." He rejected the argument of the Vermont Supreme Court that the punishment was justified "because the defendant committed a great many offenses." As Justice Field explained, "an imprisonment at hard labor for a few days or weeks for a minor offense may be within the direction of a human government; but, if the minor offenses are numerous, no authority exists to convert the imprisonment into one of perpetual confinement at hard labor."[26]

Justice Field's view that the Eighth Amendment covered excessive sentences and not merely modes of punishment prevailed before a majority of the Court two decades later in *Weems v. United States*. Weems was a Coast Guard official in the Philippines who had been convicted of making a false entry in a government cash log. Specifically, Weems noted wages had been paid to lighthouse employees that were not, in fact, paid. Weems was sentenced to fifteen years *cadena temporal,* a form of incarceration that would require him to have "a chain at the ankle and wrist" and to perform "hard and painful labor." He would also lose parental and property rights and be subject to surveillance even after release. Weems challenged the punishment as cruel and unusual. The Court, in an opinion by Justice McKenna, first noted that "what constitutes a cruel and unusual punishment has not been exactly decided." The Court then set out to define cruel and unusual punishment.

In reviewing the constitutional debate over the term, the Court noted the origins of the clause in the English Bill of Rights. It then rejected an observation by Justice Joseph Story in his treatise on the Constitution that it was adopted to warn the government against engaging in "such violent proceedings as had taken place in England in the arbitrary reigns of some of the Stuarts." Justice McKenna's opinion responded by agreeing that the constitutional debates did refer to those abuses but then observed that the Framers "surely . . . intended more than to register a fear of the forms of abuse that went out of practice with the Stuarts" because "their jealousy of power had a saner justification than that." The Framers were, after all, "practical and sagacious" men, "and it must have come to them that there could be exercises of cruelty by laws other than those which inflicted bodily pain or mutilation." The Court asked rhetorically, "With power in a legislature great, if not unlimited, to give criminal character to the actions of men, with power unlimited to fix terms of imprisonment with what accompaniments they might, what more potent instrument of cruelty could be put into the hands of power?" The clause, in other words, was designed to cabin abuses more broadly than just limiting certain modes of punishment and included limits on "terms of imprisonment." The Court then concluded that the punishment given to Weems was cruel and unusual both because of its "degree and kind." In assessing the punishment's disproportionality, the Court engaged in a comparative analysis and noted that degrees of homicide, inciting rebellion, and conspiring to destroy the government by force were not punished as severely as the far less serious conduct engaged in by Weems.[27]

Justice White, joined by Justice Holmes, dissented in *Weems* because he disagreed with the Court's "interpret[ing] the inhibition against cruel and unusual punishment as imposing upon Congress the duty of proportioning punishment according to the nature of the crime, and cast[ing] upon the judiciary the duty of determining whether punishments have been properly apportioned in a particular statute." Justice White thought it was "not questioned by anyone" that the English prohibition against cruel and unusual punishments covered "atrocious, sanguinary, and inhuman punishments" and did not speak to disproportionate punishments. When states used identical language as the English Bill of Rights in their constitutions, he argued, they intended to incorporate "the same well-understood meaning" the wording had "in the mother country."[28] While Justice White was correct that one should assume the same meaning traveled with these terms of art, he was wrong about the English meaning, as more detailed histories than his cursory review have revealed.[29] Justice White was blind to a contrary interpretation because it was unfathomable to him that the legislature would be limited in doing what "it deemed necessary for the prevention of crime, provided, only, resort was not had to the infliction of bodily punishments of a cruel and barbarous character."[30] Most critically, Justice White was writing a dissent. His view did not prevail.

Until the drug war panic of the 1980s and 1990s led some justices to resurrect the flawed interpretation of the Eighth Amendment from Justice White's dissent in *Weems*, the Supreme Court consistently recognized that the Eighth Amendment's Cruel and Unusual Punishment Clause prohibited excessive sentences, just as it prohibits excessive fines and excessive bail. In the 1958 case of *Trop v. Dulles*, the Court held that forfeiture of citizenship was a cruel and unusual punishment for wartime desertion. All nine justices began the Eighth Amendment analysis by asking whether denaturalization was excessive in relation to the gravity of the crime; thus they all agreed that this kind of proportionality inquiry was appropriate. Their disagreement was over whether denaturalization violated "the evolving standards of decency that mark the progress of a maturing society," which is what the five-justice majority said was the proper standard for assessing Eighth Amendment cruel and unusual punishment claims.[31]

In 1962, in *Robinson v. California*, the Court again engaged in a proportionality analysis and concluded that a ninety-day sentence was cruel and unusual for the crime of being "addicted to the use of narcotics." This marked the first time a majority of the Court applied the Eighth Amendment to a state punishment. Justice Stewart, writing for the Court, explained that "imprisonment for ninety days is not, in the abstract, a punishment which is either cruel or unusual." In other words, it was not an unconstitutional mode of punishment. But a punishment could be cruel and unusual in a particular case because it is grossly excessive. "Even one day in prison would be cruel and unusual punishment for the 'crime' of having a common cold."[32] Justice Douglas's concurrence amplified this point, noting that "a punishment out of all proportion to the offense may bring it within the ban against 'cruel and unusual punishment.'"[33]

The Court's review of capital sentences for proportionality under the Eighth Amendment has been particularly robust since the late 1970s. It has not ruled that capital punishment is an unconstitutional mode of punishment that is banned altogether, but it has found it to be an unconstitutionally excessive punishment in multiple circumstances. Specifically, the Court has concluded that it violates the Eighth Amendment's Cruel and Unusual Punishment Clause to impose the death penalty for the rape of an adult or a child or for felony murder when defendants do not personally kill someone, attempt to kill someone, or intend that a killing take place.[34] The death penalty is also unconstitutionally disproportionate regardless of the offense when it is imposed on an individual with intellectual disabilities or on a juvenile.[35] It is also unconstitutional to execute someone who meets the test for legal insanity.[36]

This is, then, another doctrinal area where all the traditional tools of constitutional interpretation point in the same direction: the Cruel and Unusual Punishment Clause bans excessively severe punishments. It is the most natural textual reading, given the surrounding provisions that prohibit excessive bail and fines. It is also consistent with the original meaning of the term, given its origins. It is derived from the English Bill of Rights, which reflected the well-established prohibition on disproportionate punishments. The Framers had every intention of preserving all traditional rights of British subjects, so there is no reason to doubt they wanted to give this phrase the same robust meaning it had in England. Moreover, the phrase "cruel and unusual" was a term of art used at the time of the framing in varying contexts to refer to punishments that were too harsh. Subsequent history reinforces this original meaning, as the Court has consistently interpreted the clause as disallowing excessively severe punishments and not just improper modes of punishment.

Where the methods of constitutional interpretation diverge is not in whether the Eighth Amendment requires review of sentences for proportionality but in how to identify a disproportionate sentence. An originalist would focus on whether the punishment has long been used in the context to which it is being put without having fallen out of favor. It would be improperly cruel and unusual if it is both unsupported by long usage and extremely harsh. Someone who adopts a more dynamic theory of constitutional interpretation would prefer the test from *Trop v. Dulles* and consider how society itself has evolved in thinking about the punishment. Under that standard, the relevant benchmark would be a comparative analysis of how other jurisdictions treat the crime at issue and how the sentence compares to other forms of punishments. This is the approach that has dominated in capital cases, but there is no reason to limit it to that context. "Evolving standards of decency suggest that both capital and noncapital sentences alike can become cruel and unusual."[37]

Whichever of these two approaches one prefers, however, it is clear that proportionality is a key requirement for sentences of incarceration under any traditional method of interpreting the Eighth Amendment and that excessively harsh sentences should be struck down. The Supreme Court has chosen a third path that has no basis in the Constitution but is instead grounded in uncritical deference to legislative judgments.

Harmelin v. Michigan and the Court's Disproportionate Deference to Legislatures

While the Supreme Court long recognized a prohibition on disproportionate punishments in the Eighth Amendment, it did not have many occasions to consider specific applications of the Cruel and Unusual Punishment Clause. It was not until its decision in *Robinson* in 1962 that it ruled the Eighth Amendment applied to state punishments by incorporation through the Fourteenth Amendment. Because the footprint of federal criminal law was minimal for most of the country's history, there were thus few cases to raise the issue.

The Court opened its doors to reviewing state punishments just as the tough-on-crime decades were about to get underway, and states were beginning to experiment with harsh new recidivist laws, expansive use of life without parole sentences, and draconian drug sentences. The federal government, too, was expanding its reach over criminal law and enacting similarly severe punishments. This was also the same era when the Court was beginning its intensive oversight of capital sentences.

One might have thought that the stars were therefore aligned for the Court to use the Eighth Amendment to keep disproportionate terms of incarceration in check. But as we have now seen with pretrial detention and plea bargaining, the Court itself was under the same tough-on-crime spell as legislators, prosecutors, and voters. As a result, the Court dramatically pulled back on oversight of noncapital sentences without any grounding for doing so in the Eighth Amendment. As mass incarceration took off and jurisdictions embraced excessively harsh sentences that put people away for decades—

often even for life—for relatively minor offenses, the Supreme Court struck down a grand total of one sentence for being cruel and unusual.[38]

The Run-Up to *Harmelin*

The initial weakening of the Eighth Amendment came in 1980 when the Court upheld a mandatory life sentence for a man who committed a total of three property crimes totaling less than $230. In 1973, William Rummel accepted a payment of $120.75 in exchange for promising to fix an air conditioner, which he never did. He was charged with felony theft under false pretenses. Because he had two previous convictions—one in 1964 for the fraudulent use of a credit card to obtain $80 worth of goods and services and another in 1969 for passing a forged check for $28.36—his criminal record triggered a mandatory life sentence under a Texas recidivist statute. Justice Rehnquist wrote an opinion for the Court upholding the sentence and characterizing the Eighth Amendment as virtually inapplicable in noncapital cases of imprisonment. As was typical of his approach, Justice Rehnquist did not spend time closely analyzing text or history. Instead, he reasoned backward from his desired result. In this case, Justice Rehnquist began by noting that the Court "has on occasion stated that the Eighth Amendment prohibits imposition of a sentence that is grossly disproportionate to the severity of the crime." He noted that "this proposition has appeared most frequently in opinions dealing with the death penalty" and then dismissed the applicability of those cases to Rummel's punishment because "a sentence of death differs in kind from any sentence of imprisonment."

The majority distinguished *Weems* because "its finding of disproportionality cannot be wrenched from the extreme facts of the case," which included "the triviality of the charged offense, the impressive length of the minimum term of imprisonment, and the extraordinary nature of the 'accessories' included within the punishment of *cadena temporal*," the latter referring to the chains and hard labor aspect of the punishment. Thus, the Court reasoned, "given the unique nature of the punishments considered in *Weems* and in the death penalty cases, one could argue without fear of contradiction by any decision of this Court that for crimes concededly classified and classifiable as felonies, that is punishable by significant terms of imprisonment in a state penitentiary, the length of sentence actually imposed is purely a matter of legislative prerogative."[39] Justice Rehnquist dropped a footnote holding out the possibility of finding a punishment to be disproportionate in extreme circumstances, such as the hypothetical raised by the dissenting opinion of a life sentence for an overtime parking violation. But aside from the footnote, Justice Rehnquist's opinion was content to relegate the Eighth Amendment to a virtual nullity in noncapital cases.

Justice Powell wrote a dissenting opinion for himself and Justices Brennan, Marshall, and Stevens. He rejected the majority's suggestion that oversight for proportionality "may be less applicable when a noncapital sentence is challenged." He noted that this distinction was unsupported by the Eighth Amendment, its history, and Court precedent. "Both barbarous forms of punishment and grossly excessive punishments are cruel and unusual." He noted that a proper proportionality analysis looks at the nature of the offense, how the same crime is punished in other jurisdictions, and how the sentence imposed compares with other sentences in the same jurisdiction. The dissent concluded that "objective criteria clearly establish that a mandatory life sentence for defrauding persons of about $230 crosses any rationally drawn line separating punishment that lawfully may be imposed from that which is proscribed by the Eighth Amendment."[40]

Two years later, in 1982, a majority of the Court gave *Rummel* the broadest possible reading and summarily reversed a case in which the lower courts struck down on Eighth Amendment grounds a forty-year sentence and $20,000 fine for possession with intent to distribute nine ounces of marijuana. Without full briefing or oral argument, the Court issued a per curiam opinion in *Hutto v. Davis* that said its decision in *Rummel* to treat challenges to prison terms differently was based on its concern that Eighth Amendment determinations "should neither be nor appear to be merely the subjective views of individual Justices" and its conclusion that "the excessiveness of one prison term as compared to another is invariably a subjective determination." The per curiam opinion therefore cautioned that any successful challenge to a term of imprisonment should be "exceedingly rare," using the example it previously provided in *Rummel* of a life sentence for overtime parking as the kind of case that crosses the line. It chastised the court of appeals for upholding the district court's decision to strike down Davis's sentence on Eighth Amendment grounds, finding it to be "an intrusion into the basic line-drawing process" belonging to legislatures and a rebuke "consciously or unconsciously" of the Court's decision in *Rummel*.[41]

A little more than a year after the *Davis* decision and three years after *Rummel*, the Court reversed course and reaffirmed the availability of proportionality review under the Cruel and Unusual Punishment Clause for a term of imprisonment. *Solem v. Helm* was another 5–4 decision with similar facts to *Rummel*. Jerry Helm was a thirty-six-year-old man with a long history of alcohol problems who wrote a "no account" check for one hundred dollars. Because he had six previous felony convictions (three for third-degree burglary, one for theft by false pretenses, one for grand larceny, and one for drunk driving), the judge gave him a life sentence without the possibility of parole. This time, there were five votes to strike down the sentence as unconstitutional, with Justice Blackmun shifting his vote from *Rummel* and ruling for the defendant, though without writing separately to explain why. Justice Powell wrote the majority opinion in *Solem* and repeated many of the points from his dissent in *Rummel*.

Justice Powell made the case for proportionality review of sentences of incarceration under the Eighth Amendment using all the traditional tools of constitutional interpretation. He made the textual argument that the Eighth Amendment imposes "parallel limitations on bail, fines, and other punishments" and noted it would be anomalous to subject the lesser punishment of a fine to proportionality review but not do the same for prison sentences. He recounted the "deeply rooted and frequently repeated" commitment to proportionality in the common law and the English Bill of Rights. The Eighth Amendment mirrored its language and incorporated that same commitment, as "one of the consistent themes of the era was that Americans had all the rights of English subjects." Justice Powell also noted the Court's consistent interpretation of the Eighth Amendment to prohibit disproportionate sentences.[42]

He then explained the framework for this proportionality review, whether for a capital or noncapital case. The Court should compare the sentence imposed to the gravity of the offense, to sentences imposed on other criminals in the same jurisdiction, and to sentences imposed for the same crime in other jurisdictions.[43] He disputed the dissent's accusation that this three-pronged test is inherently subjective because of the widespread agreement about the relative severity of crimes. And he noted that line drawing is often necessary in constitutional interpretation. Applying this test to the facts of the case, the majority rejected the sentence given Helms because no one else had been given a life-without-parole sentence in South Dakota for a comparable crime, and in the only other state where it would have even been possible (Nevada), there was no evidence anyone in a similar situation ever received a life-without-parole sentence there, either. Finally, the majority opinion distinguished *Rummel* because the defendant there had the possibility of parole.

Chief Justice Burger wrote the dissent for himself and Justices White, Rehnquist, and O'Connor. All of them had been in the majority of *Rummel* except Justice O'Connor, who was not yet on the Court. The dissent argued the majority's view was "completely at odds with the reasoning" of *Rummel* and noted that the author of the *Rummel* dissent was "of course, Justice Powell." In addition to expressing anger at what it viewed to be a lack of commitment to stare decisis, the dissent focused its concerns on the subjectivity inherent in the majority's commitment to proportionality. It said that the majority's approach "means that a sentence is unconstitutional if it is more severe than five justices think appropriate." The dissent further argued that past Court cases applying proportionality did not involve sentences of imprisonment and noted that distinction mattered because in the other contexts "a line could be drawn," whereas "drawing lines between different sentences of imprisonment would thrust the Court inevitably 'into the basic line-drawing process that is pre-eminently the province of the legislature' and produce judgments that were no more than the visceral reactions of individual Justices."[44] The dissent's objection, then, was not about the text or original meaning of the Eighth Amendment but a "prudential" concern that proportionality review of terms of incarceration would give judges too much discretion to overturn legislative judgments. It read the per curiam opinion in *Hutto* as rejecting not the district court's analysis of the various objective factors it considered but the fact the court "even embark[ed] on a determination whether the sentence was 'disproportionate' to the crime." In other words, no sentence of incarceration could be reviewed by the courts, save the lone example it repeated from *Rummel* of a life sentence for a parking violation.

Just as Chief Justice Burger worried about what a rejection of plea bargaining could mean to the courts' workload in *Santobello*, he worried in his *Solem* dissent that appellate review of sentences would "'administer the coup de grace to the courts of appeals as we know them.'"[45] For Burger and the justices who agreed with him, the workload of judges was the human cost worth focusing on in these cases, not the millions of people who would spend time incarcerated.

The majority approach in *Solem*, in contrast, focused on the people being punished and was consistent with the Eighth Amendment's text and history and the Court's pre-*Rummel* cases. Unfortunately, the dissent's concern with too much judicial discretion, not the Constitution's commands, would ultimately drive the doctrine.

Harmelin

These closely divided decisions coming on the heels of one another showed that the Court's Eighth Amendment doctrine was not exactly stable in the 1980s. It was upended yet again in 1991 when the Court decided the case of *Harmelin v. Michigan*, a decision that would produce a concurrence by Justice Kennedy that would ultimately provide the test challenging individual noncapital sentences under the Eighth Amendment that is still in use today. In 1986, Ronald Allen Harmelin was pulled over for failing to come to a complete stop at a red light while driving in Oak Park, Michigan. The police discovered 672 grams of cocaine in the trunk of his 1977 Ford. Possessing that quantity of drugs triggered a mandatory life-without-parole sentence when he was convicted because of a law passed by the Michigan Legislature in 1978. Harmelin was forty-five years old and had never before been arrested. Harmelin made two arguments before the Court. First, he argued his sentence was unconstitutionally disproportionate to his crime. Second, he argued that the mandatory nature of the sentence violated the Eighth Amendment because it prevented the judge from taking into account his individualized circumstances.

The Court voted 5–4 and rejected both arguments. The five Justices who formed the majority (Chief Justice Rehnquist and Justices O'Connor, Scalia, Kennedy, and Souter) did not agree on how to address the proportionality argument even though they all ultimately rejected it in Harmelin's case. Chief Justice Rehnquist assigned the opinion to Justice Scalia, who wrote that the Eighth Amendment bans only modes of punishment and does not prohibit excessive punishments. In his view, no term of incarceration, no matter how long and no matter how minor the offense, could be challenged. Justice Scalia's opinion thus reflected the view Rehnquist expressed for the Court in *Rummel*, minus the footnote about life sentences for parking. As he put it, "*Solem* was simply wrong; the Eighth Amendment contains no proportionality guarantee."[46] Only Chief Justice Rehnquist joined that part of the opinion. Justice Kennedy wrote a concurring opinion, joined by Justices O'Connor and Souter, accepting a narrow proportionality principle ostensibly on the basis of stare decisis but ultimately setting out a different test for proportionality than the one established in *Solem* and used in the Court's capital cases. The new test elaborated by Justice Kennedy makes it virtually impossible for any state punishment to fail. His support of proportionality was thus more cosmetic than real, but the test from his concurrence has become the test that individuals challenging their sentences have to pass. The dissent in *Harmelin* was faithful to *Solem*, but there were no longer enough votes on the Court for it to prevail.

JUSTICE SCALIA'S FLAWED ORIGINALISM

Before turning to Justice Kennedy's test, which has come to define Eighth Amendment challenges, it is worth pausing to reflect on Justice Scalia's opinion. While one might have expected Rehnquist to write off the Eighth Amendment in noncapital cases in *Rummel*, because Rehnquist was not known as either a committed textualist or originalist and therefore did not spend time on those arguments, it is more puzzling to see Justice Scalia adopt that view. How could the Court's most prominent textualist and originalist decide there is no proportionality review in light of the Eighth Amendment's language and original meaning? It may be because there was no briefing on this issue, so Justice Scalia lacked guidance from the parties or legal historians who might have filed briefs had they known a relitigation of history was on the table. But it may also be because Justice Scalia's distaste for constitutional balancing tests blinded him from acknowledging a test for proportionality that requires just that. It is likely not a coincidence that Justice Scalia concluded both that the Framers did not intend to prohibit excessively disproportionate punishments and that "there was good reason for that choice."[47]

Whatever the reason, Justice Scalia's opinion had fatal shortcomings. The textual analysis was largely relegated to a footnote responding to the dissent's arguments. Justice Scalia dismissed the idea that the first two clauses addressing excessive bail and fines should be read consistently with the third clause by saying that a "difference in meaning is assumed" because the Framers used different wording in the last clause. He further suggested that it was not irrational for the drafters of this language to care more about overseeing fines than other punishments because, according to Justice Scalia, the state profits from fines and therefore it was reasonable to think it needed to be more closely scrutinized in that context. And with that, he was done with the textual analysis of how the Cruel and Unusual Punishment Clause fits into the larger structure of the Eighth Amendment.

As explained above, the three clauses should be read in parallel with each other. The phrase "cruel and unusual" was employed instead of "excessive" for punishments because it had a settled meaning that captured the two forms of excess the Framers meant to include. It referred both to gross disproportionality and the lack of support in custom that the drafters intended to convey. Justice Scalia suggests the Framers could have used more precise wording if they meant to cover proportionality, but "cruel and unusual" was just such a phrase for the time. It was Justice Scalia's approach that "eschew[ed] any historical analysis of the founding generation's actual understanding of the word 'unusual' and relies solely on abstract logic."[48] There was a long and established tradition in English law requiring proportionality in punishment, and the US Constitution's Bill of Rights aimed to preserve "the rights of Englishmen."

Justice Scalia thought otherwise because so many disproportionate sentences were handed out in England at the end of the eighteenth century. That these punishments existed in the Bloody Code did not mean they were not cruel and unusual to those who drafted the Bill of Rights. In fact, Parliament's actions during this time were cruel and unusual—it is just that there was nothing that could be done about it because there was no basis for challenging Parliament's laws. The American Bill of Rights, in contrast, was designed to remedy that precise flaw and protect rights against legislative infringement. In the context of the Eighth Amendment, that meant disallowing the legislature from authorizing excessively disproportionate punishments that went against the long tradition of how crimes had been treated.[49]

Moreover, as Justice White noted in dissent, Justice Scalia's demand for a clearer expression to cover proportionality is hardly the standard the Court uses in interpreting the rest of the Constitution, replete as it is with phrases like "due process" and "unreasonable searches and seizures." It is filled with terms of art, and nowhere else has the Court insisted on language that is based on how "plain-talking Americans would have expressed themselves."[50]

Justice Scalia's attempt to explain why fines should be more closely scrutinized also finds no support in history. Among the most prominent abuses that motivated the English Bill of Rights were deprivations of liberty to silence enemies of the Crown. The state certainly "stands to benefit" when it can abuse its authority to take away liberty, and in fact, that was a constant concern in the framing debate and explains why the state's criminal powers were so highly regulated.

Justice Scalia did not spend time on the origins of the terminology of "cruel" and "unusual" and how those terms were used in England and then in the United States. If he had, he would have seen the error in his analysis. Instead, he took a narrower approach that asked what motivated the English to place a restriction like that in their Bill of Rights, and he zeroed in on one historical event. He believed the impetus for the "cruel and unusual" language in the English Bill of Rights was the punishment handed down in the case of an Anglican clergyman by the name of Titus Oates. Oates falsely accused fifteen Catholics of being involved in a plot to kill the king, testified against them at their trials, and was thus ultimately responsible for their wrongful executions. When his falsehood came to light, however, Oates was charged and convicted of perjury, not murder. He could therefore not be sentenced to death because that was not an authorized punishment for perjury. Instead, in 1685 he was sentenced to life imprisonment, to be pilloried four times each year for life, to pay a large fine, and to lose his clerical status. He was also ordered to be dragged across the City of London, whipped all the while, first "from Aldgate to Newgate" and then two days later from "Newgate to Tyburn." Oates managed to survive the whipping, and several years into his sentence, he petitioned Parliament, which had just adopted the Bill of Rights, to suspend judgment against him on the ground that he received a cruel and unusual punishment. Though Oates lost his appeal, the discussion in the House of Commons about Oates's case, cited by Justice Scalia, showed that the English drafters did, in fact, have Oates's case as one of the abuses in mind when they drafted the prohibition on cruel and unusual punishment in the English Bill of Rights. In referring to Oates's sentence, members of Parliament said things like it was without "Precedents" and it was "contrary to Law and ancient practice." Justice Scalia's takeaway from the discussion of the Oates case and the response to it was that the English Bill of Rights prohibition on cruel and unusual punishments barred judges from issuing illegal punishments that were outside the common law tradition. It did not, in Justice Scalia's estimation, prohibit disproportionate punishments.

In fact, the Oates case supports reading the prohibition of cruel and unusual punishments to ban disproportionately severe sentences. All of Oates's punishments had been traditionally used. "They were not considered inherently cruel by the standards of the seventeenth century." They crossed the line in his case because they were "grossly disproportionate" and "exceeded the scope of any punishment previously permitted" for the specific crime Oates had been convicted of, which was perjury.[51] England whipped people for crimes until 1948, and life sentences have survived to this day. The problem with Oates's sentence was that it was disproportionate given the offense of perjury, and it was that mismatch that violated the Bill of Rights in the views of those lords who dissented.[52] A proper originalist take on the Oates case and the Eighth Amendment would therefore recognize that disproportionate punishments are disallowed.

Justice Scalia's opinion reads like a textbook example of confirmation bias. He thought it made no sense to have unelected judges reviewing punishments for proportionality, and he assumed the Framers must have agreed. He then cherry-picked all the evidence that supported this view but missed the forest for the trees. The evidence is overwhelming that both the drafters of the English Bill of Rights and the US Bill of Rights feared government abuses of power in imposing punishments and sought to protect the individual's right against it. It was not just the ability to get excessive fines that would benefit the state. The ability to use the punishment power and take away liberty was just as advantageous—as the kings of England had demonstrated.

The Eighth Amendment presents an intellectual dilemma for someone like Justice Scalia, with libertarian tendencies and deep concerns about the abuse of state power, but who also harbors a deep repugnance toward judicial overreach and activism. Proportionality review necessarily gives courts greater leeway because it is not amenable to many bright lines, and certainly not the same convenient bright line Justice Scalia devised of focusing only on modes of punishment and ignoring the length of any sentence.

It is hard to read Justice Scalia's opinion in *Harmelin* and not think about his anger over the Court's capital cases. He issued a series of stinging dissents in that context accusing his colleagues in capital cases of making a "mockery" of the judicial role and derisively proclaiming the Court as the "sole arbiter of our Nation's moral standards."[53] When the Court found the execution of the intellectually disabled to be cruel and unusual, he wrote that "seldom has an opinion of this Court rested so obviously upon nothing but the personal views of its members."[54] His critique in *Harmelin* that the objective factors at the root of proportionality review give judges too much power is basically just a recap of his complaints in the capital cases. It is no wonder, then, that Justice Scalia was eager to simply say "death is different" to keep proportionality review cabined to that context. That was also how he disposed of Harmelin's second challenge, arguing that the mandatory nature of his life sentence violated the Eighth Amendment.

The problem with this strategy for Justice Scalia, however, was that, while the Court's concern with mandatory sentencing to that point was limited to capital cases, its concern with proportionality was not. That is why three justices joined the part of his opinion that addressed the mandatory nature of Harmelin's sentence but did not agree with his analysis of the proportionality claim. A majority of the Court was not willing to write off proportionality review entirely, though they came close.

THE KENNEDY CONCURRENCE AND TODAY'S EIGHTH AMENDMENT TEST

Justice Kennedy's concurrence began by noting that "*stare decisis* counsels our adherence to the narrow proportionality principle that has existed in our Eighth Amendment for 80 years." Justice Kennedy did not bother to relitigate the originalist case for that proportionality principle or focus on the text of the Eighth Amendment. Instead, he saw proportionality as settled in the Court's cases.

As it turns out, however, Justice Kennedy's restatement of the proportionality test was more of a rewrite than an application, and his new approach makes proportionality review an almost pro forma fiction where sentences get upheld no matter how egregiously long they are. In practice, there is almost no space between his test and Justice Scalia's approach. Justice White aptly described the respective approaches of Justice Scalia and Justice Kennedy in *Harmelin*: "While Justice Scalia seeks to deliver a swift death sentence to *Solem*, Justice Kennedy prefers to eviscerate it, leaving only an empty shell."[55]

Justice Kennedy claimed that the "precise contours" of the proportionality principle were unclear given the divergence between *Rummel* and *Davis*, on the one hand, and *Solem* on the other. Justice Kennedy therefore felt free to stake out his own version, but he ended up on the *Rummel/Davis* side of the divide. He offered four "common principles" of proportionality review that he claimed to elicit from a "close analysis" of the Court's prior decisions. They actually came from the brief of the Solicitor General (SG).[56] They were "the primacy of the legislature, the variety of legitimate penological schemes, the nature of our federal system, and the requirement that proportionality review be guided by objective factors."[57] Together, these factors establish that only "extreme sentences" will be considered grossly disproportionate.

In what would become the standard for analyzing future Eighth Amendment claims, Justice Kennedy then argued that the proportionality test had a threshold inquiry to see if there was an inference of gross disproportionality when comparing the punishment to the crime and emphasized that only in rare cases would that threshold be satisfied. If it was not, neither an intrajurisdictional comparison of how other crimes are sentenced nor an interjurisdictional comparison of how the same crime is sentenced in other jurisdictions would be conducted. The flaw with this new framing of *Solem* is that the comparative analysis is needed to shed light on the threshold gross proportionality inquiry. "Because the Court will not look to comparable sentences elsewhere before making this threshold determination, it is likely that the Court will fail to appreciate just how excessive a particular sentence is."[58]

The application of this threshold test to the facts in *Harmelin* is a prime illustration of how high a bar Justice Kennedy erected. Life without parole is the harshest sentence available in Michigan because the state has no death penalty. Only narcotics crimes involving more than 650 grams and first-degree murder received a mandatory life without parole sentence in Michigan when Harmelin was convicted. No other jurisdiction permitted life without parole for a first-time drug offender except Alabama, and its quantity threshold was 10 kilograms or more of cocaine, or roughly 22 pounds, compared to Michigan's triggering threshold of less than 1.5 pounds. Justice Kennedy did not consider these comparisons because he reserved his inquiry to his threshold comparison of the gravity of the offense and the punishment imposed to see if the state had a penological goal that justified it.

In conducting his review of the state's penological goals, Justice Kennedy parroted the usual justifications for the war on drugs, many of which came from amicus briefs. The National District Attorneys Association, for example, wrote that they were "in the front lines of dealing" with "the narcotics trafficking problem of the 1990s" and supported Michigan's sentencing regime as "not only constitutionally sound but good public policy as well."[59] The SG at the time, Kenneth Starr, filed a brief on behalf of the United States in support of Harmelin's sentence that reads like a manifesto for the war on drugs. It cites the federal government's interest "in the nationwide effort to rid our society of the scourge of drug abuse and the violence that follows in its wake." The SG brief argued that drug trafficking is "not a victimless crime, but is in fact equivalent to a violent assault both on the users of the drugs and on others who suffer the consequences of their use." Far from being an outlier, the SG argued that Michigan's severe sentence "may well be *more* in accord with the public consensus concerning the gravity of drug-related offenses than are the laws of other jurisdictions that have not been recently amended to reflect changes in public attitudes toward drug trafficking."[60]

Justice Kennedy drew liberally from the briefs supporting Michigan. He agreed with the SG's position that the Eighth Amendment does not require a commitment to any one penological theory and that states can support their sentences using any of them. He rejected Harmelin's argument that his possession offense was victimless and nonviolent as "false to the point of absurdity" because of the "grave harm to society" drugs cause. He argued there is a "direct nexus between illegal drugs and crimes of violence," referring to studies of people committing homicides, assault, and robbery who tested positive for illegal drugs in their system that were cited in an amicus brief filed jointly on behalf of various victims' rights and pro-law-enforcement groups. That same amicus brief referred to Harmelin on the previous page as a "courier of death" who was a "savvy shark swimming in the ocean of illegal drugs."[61] After Justice Kennedy reiterated the harms cataloged in the amicus briefs, he argued that the "legislature could with reason conclude that the threat posed to the individual and society by possession of this large an amount of cocaine—in terms of violence, crime, and social displacement—is momentous enough to warrant the deterrence and retribution of a life sentence without parole."[62]

He rejected the challenge to the mandatory nature of the punishment by noting that only in capital cases had the Court required individualized sentencing. He then added—without any support—that Michigan's law was a "recent enactment calibrated with care, clarity, and much deliberation to address a most serious contemporary social problem." Finally, he noted that prosecutorial discretion and executive clemency could provide any individualization that was needed.[63]

It is hard to believe anyone could describe the Michigan legislation as the product of care and deliberation. The goal was to target kingpins, but anyone familiar with the drug trade knows that kingpins rarely have possession of large quantities of drugs. That risk falls to low-level mules who transport the drugs and who often have no information to trade for a sentencing break, so they get hit with the harshest sentences. A mandatory life-without-parole sentence based on quantity alone ignores these dynamics. And it is not as if the legislators who passed this weren't warned about this dynamic. Opponents of the bill predicted that the major traffickers would use addicts to transport their drugs, so they would not personally risk the long prison terms at stake. There was also no evidence that this kind of sentence would deter drug trafficking because, given the nature of the drug trade, it is easy to replace someone sent to prison with someone else.[64]

The claim that prosecutorial discretion and executive clemency could provide any needed individualization shows no appreciation for the function of either of those offices. Prosecutors focus on making cases and getting convictions; thus, they use sentences like the one given to Harmelin as hammers to get guilty pleas and cooperation. They are interested parties, not neutral arbiters, in these cases. Governors and presidents are even less reliable sources of individualization. Clemency is a purely political process, and the same panics that produce excessive sentences lead executives to steer away from granting any relief. As Harmelin's lawyer accurately observed in her brief, "[g]iven the climate of hysteria over the war on drugs, it is reasonable to assume that no elected official would risk taking this action, no matter how right the cause."[65]

Harmelin's sentence survived review, not because it was proportional in any sense of the word but because the Supreme Court decimated the proportionality test. A study in contrast is provided by the Michigan State Supreme Court, which struck down the same law under the state constitution just a year after the Supreme Court decided *Harmelin*. In *Michigan v. Bullock*, the state's highest court explained that the history of the Michigan constitution plainly prohibited grossly disproportionate sentences and then applied a test for proportionality that looked like the one from *Solem*.[66] It noted that the state's most severe penalty applied to mere possession without any intent to sell or distribute, so it could, for example, apply to a teenage courier. The majority agreed with Justice Kennedy's opinion that the collateral effects of the drug trade are "terrible indeed" but pointed out that a conviction under the law does not require proof that a defendant "committed, aided, intended, or even contemplated any loss of life or other violent crime, or even any crime against property." "It would," the majority noted, "be profoundly unfair to impute full personal responsibility and moral guilt to defendants for any and all collateral acts, unintended by them, which might have been later committed by others in connection with the seized cocaine." Michigan's highest court thus concluded that, "even under Justice Kennedy's restrictive view of *Solem*" that focused only on the first prong, the sentence was grossly disproportionate. Justice Kennedy reached a different conclusion only because he allowed the state to justify the punishment based on broader concerns with drug trafficking that had nothing to do with the defendant's own culpable state of mind or conduct.

The Michigan court then applied the next two prongs. It highlighted that only first-degree murder yielded the same sentence, and more serious crimes like second-degree murder, rape, and mutilation received lesser punishments. Moreover, no other state in the country imposed a penalty as severe. Thus, "the only fair conclusion that can be reached regarding the penalty at issue is that it constitutes an unduly disproportionate response to the serious problems posed by drugs in our society."[67] The Michigan State Supreme Court's remedy was to eliminate the no-parole aspect of the law and thereby make anyone convicted under the law eligible for parole after serving ten years.

The Aftermath of *Harmelin*

Justice Kennedy's stripped-down version of proportionality review from *Harmelin* became the dominant test under the Eighth Amendment for non-capital sentences.[68] Predictably, it is basically impossible for any given sentence to fail that test no matter how disproportionate it is. The Court's application of that test shows how meaningless it is, and the ultimate result of this toothless approach to the Eighth Amendment is that the United States is awash in excessively harsh punishments that keep millions of people in prisons for decades.

Harmelin's Cruel Indifference to Excessive Punishment as Applied: California's Three-Strikes Law

A pair of cases involving California's three-strikes law decided on the same day in 2003 illustrate just how deferential to state legislative decisions the Court is and the kinds of excessive punishments that become constitutionally acceptable as a result. So-called three-strikes laws swept the nation in the early 1990s, with twenty-four states and the federal government enacting versions of such laws between 1993 and 1995.[69] Jurisdictions have long had habitual offender laws that imposed harsher punishments on people with prior convictions; the new versions tended to impose particularly severe punishments on people with two prior convictions, thus the three-strikes reference. The first such law passed via ballot initiative, with financial support from the National Rifle Association, in the state of Washington in 1993 and imposed a life-without-parole sentence on someone convicted of a third violent offense.[70]

California's three-strikes law followed. Mike Reynolds, whose daughter was killed by two people with long criminal records, started the effort to get a three-strikes law placed on the ballot as an initiative. He was struggling to get the requisite number of signatures when a horrific crime changed the political dynamic. In October 1993, Richard Allen Davis kidnapped, raped, and killed twelve-year-old Polly Klaas. Davis had a long record of violence, including past convictions for kidnapping and sexual assault. He had served only about half his sixteen-year sentence for his most recent crime of kidnapping and assault when he was released on parole. He was still on parole when he abducted Klaas. As voters became aware of Davis's criminal history, support for the three-strikes ballot initiative skyrocketed. The law was intended to "keep murderers, rapists, and child molesters behind bars." When it imposed mandatory twenty-five-year minimum sentences for people with two prior convictions, Davis was the type of person they had in mind. Marc Klaas, Polly's father, supported a version of the law that would have required the third strike to be a serious or violent felony. He explained, "I've had my car broken into and my radio stolen and I've had my daughter murdered, and I know the difference." The political dynamic, however, took on a life of its own. Reynolds's three-strikes proposal allowed any felony to qualify as a third strike and did not exclude offenses no matter how long ago they took place. As state legislators considered three-strikes legislation, Reynolds told lawmakers that any amendment to his proposal would be unacceptable. Legislators, for their part, were terrified of looking like they were insensitive to victims of violent crime, so they agreed to pass whatever bill the governor wanted. The California governor at the time, Pete Wilson, supported Reynolds's version instead of other proposed bills that had the support of California prosecutors and would have been limited to violent or serious third strikes. The bill easily passed, as did an identical three-strikes ballot initiative that Reynolds continued to campaign for that made it much harder to later amend the three-strikes law.[71]

The sweep of California's initiative was bad enough, but to make matters worse, California allows some of its misdemeanors to be treated as felonies. These are known as wobblers, and it is up to the prosecutor whether to charge them as misdemeanors or as felonies, with courts having the discretion to reduce a wobbler charged as a felony back down to a misdemeanor. If the prosecutor and judge both agree a misdemeanor should be treated as a felony, and the individual has two prior qualifying strikes, that misdemeanor turns into a life sentence with no chance for parole for at least twenty-five years if a person is convicted.

The consequences of this legally sloppy regime were predictably awful. Half the people serving sentences under California's three-strikes law had committed nonviolent crimes. It was also disproportionately applied to people of color, with African Americans making up 45 percent of the people serving life sentences under the law.[72]

The Supreme Court took up the issue of the constitutionality of California's three-strikes law in two companion cases. Gary Ewing brought one of them. Ewing stole three golf clubs that were worth a total of $1,197 from the El Segundo Golf Club. The offense qualified as grand theft under California law given the amount, and if Ewing had had no criminal record, he would have faced a maximum sentence of three years. Because Ewing had previously been convicted of three burglaries and a robbery, including one incident where he brandished a knife at the victim, he fell under the three-strikes law if the golf club theft, a wobbler, was treated as a felony. That was, in fact, how the prosecutor elected to charge it because the district attorney at the time, Gil Garcetti, "took a hard line on three strikes cases."[73] The judge rejected both Ewing's request to treat the golf club thefts as a misdemeanor and his argument not to count one of his prior strikes in furtherance of justice, as California case law would have permitted.[74] Ewing, by this point, was battling AIDS and in a weakened state, and he had already lost his vision in one eye because of the disease. He hardly posed a threat of future criminality. But because Ewing remained subject to California's three-strikes law, he received a life sentence when he was convicted of stealing the golf clubs, and he would not be eligible for parole for twenty-five years. His minimum sentence was thus eight times longer than the maximum he faced if he had no record. Moreover, even after twenty-five years, parole would hardly be a given. The California Board of Prison Terms, which must approve any request for parole, recommended parole in less than 1 percent of the two thousand life-imprisonment cases it had considered by the time Ewing was sentenced.[75]

Justice O'Connor delivered the opinion affirming Ewing's sentence, and it was joined by Chief Justice Rehnquist and Justice Kennedy. The other two votes to uphold Ewing's sentence came from Justices Scalia and Thomas, both of whom refused to acknowledge any proportionality principle in the Cruel and Unusual Punishment Clause.[76] Justice O'Connor began her opinion noting that Justice Kennedy's framework from *Harmelin* provided the governing test. In applying that test and comparing the gravity of the offense to Ewing's sentence, she noted that states can justify their sentences on the basis of "incapacitation, deterrence, retribution, or rehabilitation" because *Harmelin* made clear that "the Eighth Amendment does not mandate adoption of any one penological theory."[77] California could thus defend its three-strikes law on the basis of its view that "protecting the public safety requires incapacitating criminals who have already been convicted of at least one serious or violent crime."[78] She added that California's interest in deterrence also supported the sentence under the law.

Allowing states to justify a sentence using incapacitation or deterrence without any concern for proportionality effectively nullifies the Cruel and Unusual Punishment Clause. Under this view, "the word 'cruel' has no meaning, as the most barbaric forms of punishment will always further some penological goal."[79] Indeed, as Justice Stevens observed at oral argument, the incapacitation theory would seem to allow a life sentence for people who rack up a multitude of speeding tickets if the state believes they are too dangerous.[80]

The Court's willingness to permit any purpose of punishment to justify a sentence is also inconsistent with the rest of the Court's Eighth Amendment case law. The Court has struck down death sentences in contexts where they could deter or incapacitate but in which they were still held to be excessive under a retributive justice rationale. It has similarly rejected certain conditions of confinement as cruel and unusual whether or not they have deterrent value. Put another way, in these other contexts, "multiple purposes of punishment may be pursued so long as no sentence is undeservedly harsh is imposed."[81] The Court, however, treated terms of incarceration as outside this framework.

Justices Stevens, Souter, Ginsburg, and Breyer dissented, with all of them signing on to two dissenting opinions, one authored by Justice Stevens and the other by Justice Breyer. Justice Stevens wrote a short dissent to point out that the Eighth Amendment "broadly prohibit[s] excessive sanctions" and "directs judges to exercise their wise judgment in assessing the proportionality of all forms of punishment."[82] Justice Breyer wrote the longer dissenting opinion laying out the reasons why Ewing's sentence was unconstitutional. Justice Breyer deemed the decision important enough that he took the relatively unusual step of reading part of his dissent from the bench on the day the opinion was announced. He noted that California "reserves the sentence that it here imposes upon (former-burglar-now-golf-club-thief) Ewing for nonrecidivist, first-degree murderers." As Ewing noted in his brief, "a first-time offender who blew up the pro shop in an effort to kill the pro shop clerk or who kidnapped the clerk to rob him would be eligible for parole in California nearly two decades before Mr. Ewing."[83] As for interjurisdictional comparisons, there was but a single case in the entire country comparable to Ewing's out of a prison population that at the time approached two million people.[84]

The sentence handed down in the companion case decided the same day, *Lockyer v. Andrade,* was even more indefensible. Leandro Andrade, a nine-year army veteran and father of three, received a fifty-years-to-life sentence after he shoplifted nine videotapes worth a grand total of $153.54 on two separate occasions, two weeks apart, from two different Kmarts. The items were recovered, so Kmart did not ultimately suffer any loss. Given the dollar value of the tapes stolen on each occasion, Andrade was charged with two separate counts of petty theft. Petty theft is ordinarily punishable up to six months, so under normal circumstances, Andrade would be facing a maximum of one year in total for the two incidents. If a defendant has certain qualifying prior theft-related convictions, however, California law allows the thefts to be treated as felonies punishable by up to three years. Andrade had previously committed residential burglaries that allowed prosecutors to charge each of the two shoplifting incidents as petty theft with a prior and therefore treat them as felonies. Once the thefts qualified as felonies, they could then be charged as a third strike. When he was convicted, each theft charge triggered a separate application of the three-strikes law, and under California law, they had to be sentenced consecutively. He thus received two sentences of twenty-five years to life that had to be served consecutively. Andrade's prior residential burglaries converted what would have been a one-year maximum into a life sentence where he would not even be eligible for parole for fifty years, when he would be eighty-seven years old.

It is hard to imagine a reasonable basis for making any sentence fifty times greater because of prior convictions. By way of comparison, courts typically reject punitive damage awards in civil cases that are more than ten times the economic damages.[85] In Andrade's case, it is even more outrageous because his offenses became less serious over time. Indeed, had they been committed in the reverse order, with the petty thefts coming first and then escalating to residential burglary, he would not have qualified under the three-strikes law. Moreover, Andrade's prior theft convictions occurred twelve years before he was arrested for shoplifting. California could not point to a single person in the United States outside the state of California who had received a life sentence without the possibility of parole for fifty years for a shoplifting charge.[86] While the state court rejected Andrade's claim that his sentence was cruel and unusual, Andrade ultimately succeeded with his habeas claim. The Ninth Circuit found that the sentence violated clearly established federal law. If the Cruel and Unusual Punishment Clause bars grossly disproportionate sentences, it is hard to see how the ruling could be otherwise. And yet five justices affirmed Andrade's sentence, with Justice O'Connor writing the majority opinion.

Justice O'Connor concluded that the Ninth Circuit should not have granted habeas because the state court did not violate clearly established law. The law was not clearly established, according to Justice O'Connor, because the Court's precedents interpreting the Cruel and Unusual Punishment Clause were not "a model of clarity."[87] The majority thus seemed to endorse the view that, because the Court has been so inconsistent in its approach, no court could be faulted for rejecting a claim that a sentence is cruel and unusual no matter what the facts. This analysis bears a strong resemblance to the Court's qualified immunity jurisprudence where police officers cannot be liable for violating someone's constitutional rights unless there was a previous case involving identical facts.[88] The Court has repeatedly overturned lower court decisions for applying an overly broad interpretation of qualified immunity that "define[s] clearly established law at a high level of generality."[89] Requiring such specificity means those challenging government action almost never win.[90]

As Justice Souter said in dissent, if Andrade's "sentence is not grossly disproportionate, the principle has no meaning." Unfortunately, if there is one takeaway from the Court's cases, it is sadly that the principle does, indeed, have no meaning. The fact the case was on habeas review should not have mattered because Andrade's sentence was "on all fours with those of *Solem*." They were both repeat offenders who committed minor thefts, and Andrade's fifty-year minimum was effectively life without parole given that he was thirty-seven years old when sentenced. Justice Souter also noted that the state's incapacitation theory made no sense because "Andrade did not somehow become twice as dangerous to society when he stole the second handful of videotapes." Even if the first sentence of twenty-five years to life was defensible, adding an additional twenty-five years was, according to Justice Souter, irrational.[91]

The Court's track record reviewing sentences under the Cruel and Unusual Punishment Clause since 1980 is appalling. Only *Solem*'s sentence was struck down, and since then, the Court has done everything to limit *Solem* to its precise facts. If someone can get a fifty-year sentence for stealing videotapes, truly there is nothing left to the proportionality test. Just as *Salerno* ignored constitutional limits on pretrial detention in the name of preventing danger, the Court has ignored the limits of the Cruel and Unusual Punishment Clause for the same reason. It is not a coincidence that the key cases focused on the danger represented by defendants as opposed to what they actually did, whether it was Harmelin's drug possession or the minor offenses committed by Ewing and Andrade because they were recidivists. In all three cases, prosecutors, states, and the Solicitor General informed the Court that the threat of danger—whether from drugs or recidivism—required incapacitation.

Their language was hardly subtle. The California District Attorneys Association, for example, filed briefs in both Ewing's and Andrade's cases and painted each of them as irreparably dangerous. They described Ewing, who never laid a hand on anyone, as having a background that is "a trail of mud" and a character that "is a patchwork of greed, sloth, and obstinacy." They claimed "his prospects are an abyss," and "bloodshed by him is surely a matter of time."[92] Andrade's theft of children's videos from a Kmart was portrayed as just one step away from violence, as "confrontations between shoplifters and those trying to stop them can escalate to deadly confrontations." Stores must hire security "to combat such pestilence." Even though Andrade never harmed anyone, the district attorneys referred to him in their brief as "a scoundrel who has had his chances" and "a danger to California and so we have incapacitated him." In their vision, "'Three Strikers' have *earned* their long sentences because they are the most thick-skulled and predictably wicked of felons." They chillingly ask, "What remains but to remove them from us for long periods of time?"[93]

Even more disturbing than a group of prosecutors with this vision of their fellow citizens is a Supreme Court that shares it. At oral argument in Ewing's case, Chief Justice Rehnquist asked why the state couldn't say "where a person has a string of convictions like this man has, that it's time to get him off the street." The justices seemed to recognize how harsh they appeared and tried to address it by dismissing Ewing's lawyer's focus on the three golf clubs "like we're some judges out of Victor Hugo," and instead emphasizing the recidivism aspect of the case. They asked, "Why can't California decide that enough is enough, that someone with a long string like this simply deserves to be put away?" Unsaid is that he would be "put away" for the rest of his life unless a parole board, twenty-five years later, gave him relief.[94] *Rummel* planted the seeds for this view when it argued that recidivists could be sentenced more harshly because "by repeated criminal acts [they] have shown that they are simply incapable of conforming to the norms of society."[95] While *Solem* seemed to roll that back by emphasizing that "a criminal sentence must be proportionate to the crime for which the defendant has been convicted,"[96] *Ewing* and *Andrade* doubled down on the *Rummel* view and used the *Harmelin* test to condone life sentences without any chance of parole for decades for shoplifters. It is hard to see what, if any, protections remain for repeat offenders.

The Court's approach to reviewing individual sentences in noncapital cases under the Eighth Amendment stands in sharp contrast to its review of capital cases. In the capital context, the Court follows the *Trop v. Dulles* "evolving standards of decency" test and is sensitive to those facts and circumstances that make people and acts less culpable. The Court disallows mandatory death sentences because "the fundamental respect for humanity underlying the Eighth Amendment requires consideration of the character and record of the individual offender and the circumstances of the particular offense."[97] It has recognized that those with intellectual disabilities "do not act with the level of moral culpability that characterizes the most serious adult criminal conduct" and thus made them ineligible for capital punishment.[98] It has likewise disallowed the death penalty for juveniles because "their own vulnerability and comparative lack of control over their immediate surroundings mean juveniles have a greater claim than adults to be forgiven for failing to escape negative influences in their whole environment."[99] The Court has concluded death is a disproportionate punishment given the reduced culpability of people in these categories.

The Court has taken only a small step toward collapsing its capital and noncapital sentencing lines of authority. In a 2010 case, *Graham v. Florida*, the Court disallowed life without parole (LWOP) sentences for juveniles in nonhomicide cases, using the framework of its capital cases.[100] The Court reasoned that "categorical" challenges to punishments—those that seek to rule out a punishment for an entire category of cases—should be analyzed under the proportionality framework from the capital cases that engages in intra- and interjurisdictional comparisons without requiring any threshold inquiry. Thus far, however, the Court has used this approach in only two limited contexts that both involve juveniles: LWOP for juveniles in nonhomicide cases and mandatory LWOP for juveniles in homicide cases.[101] It has refused to hear cases seeking to extend *Graham* to situations where juveniles convicted of nonhomicides received a sentence that would exceed their life expectancy[102] or where the defendant is a youthful offender but not a juvenile.[103] There are thus no signals the Court is prepared to go further and reject mandatory minimum punishments and require individualized determinations of culpability in all cases, not just capital ones, even though mandatory sentences often lead to disproportionate outcomes.

Most litigants, moreover, cannot craft a colorable argument challenging their sentences in categorical terms to apply to an entire group or type of crime, so they remain stuck with the test laid out by Justice Kennedy in his *Harmelin* concurrence. That means no intra- and interjurisdictional comparison takes place until a litigant can show gross disproportionality. That, in turn, is an almost impossible task given Justice O'Connor's elaboration in *Ewing* that any theory of punishment, including incapacitation or deterrence, can justify a sentence and undercut any claim of gross disproportionality. Unsurprisingly, just about everyone loses their Eighth Amendment challenge alleging an excessive punishment, and lengthy sentences go unchecked.

The Court's Unfounded Fears of Judicial Oversight

When the Court accepted plea bargaining in spite of its clear conflict with the doctrine of unconstitutional conditions, it was motivated by efficiency concerns and freeing courts from the burden of too many trials if there were insufficient guilty pleas. The Court's Eighth Amendment jurisprudence is also motivated to a large extent by judicial self-interest. The Court does not want to be inundated with petitions to review sentences for proportionality and turned into a "constitutional sentencing commission," as Michael Chertoff put it when he represented the view of the United States at oral argument in *Ewing*.[104] Chief Justice Burger made this point explicitly in his *Solem* dissent when he worried that the majority's approach "will flood the appellate courts with cases."[105] A majority of justices have been concerned far more with the workload of judges than with the cruel effects of coercive plea bargaining and excessive punishment on people on the receiving end.

It is not just the volume of cases that worries the Court but the inability to control lower court discretion. The Court does not trust the lower courts to make fact-specific decisions about when a plea bargain is too coercive or a punishment is too excessive without bright lines to guide them. In *Rummel*, the Court worried that "the lines to be drawn are indeed 'subjective,' and therefore properly within the province of legislatures, not courts."[106] In its quest for administrative efficiency and control over the lower courts, the Supreme Court has failed to fulfill its constitutional obligation, and millions of people have been subject to excessively harsh punishment as a result. These long sentences are a necessary ingredient in the disastrous recipe of mass incarceration.

Justice Kennedy recognized that the Court's abdication means excessively harsh sentences will be imposed. He gave a speech to the American Bar Association in 2003—after his votes in *Harmelin*, *Ewing*, and *Andrade*—urging lawyers to seek reform of mandatory minimum and three-strikes laws. "Courts may conclude the legislature is permitted to choose long sentences," he said, "but that does not mean long sentences are wise or just." He went on to say that "[a] court decision does not excuse the political branches or the public from the responsibility for unjust laws."[107] Justice Kennedy was clearly taking no responsibility for the existence of such laws, even though it was his duty under the Eighth Amendment to police them and declare unconstitutional those laws that imposed cruel and unusual punishments. He turned his back on that obligation because he thought it was too hard to draw lines.

It is not up to the Court, however, to avoid enforcing constitutional guarantees just because there may be many cases affected or because the Court does not like the open-ended way in which the Constitution protects the right. The Framers recognized that oversight of punishments (and bail and fines) could require courts to make judgment calls, but it was well worth the price of liberty. Moreover, the Court itself has recognized this obligation in contexts that do not involve incarceration. It has, as noted, taken far more care in reviewing death sentences for proportionality. But both capital and noncapital cases are reviewed under the same Cruel and Unusual Punishment Clause. The text of that clause does not vary based on whether a sentence is capital or not. Nor is there anything in the history of the clause that supports variation.[108] The Court's unwillingness to police noncapital sentences is thus not grounded in the Constitution but is rather a matter of its own preferences and concerns with administrative convenience. Several dozen people each year, at most, receive capital sentences, but millions receive noncapital sentences. The Court has thus carved out capital cases for greater scrutiny because it views the task as more manageable. It is also possible that the Court feels more personally responsible for capital decisions because it typically gets a stay application on the eve of any given execution and is therefore a key part of the process of imposing death sentences.[109] The Eighth Amendment, however, does not allow the Court to pick and choose which cases will get constitutional protection. They all should, whether capital cases or noncapital cases.

The Court has also taken more care to police fines under the Excessive Fines Clause than it has sentences of incarceration, and here, too, there is no basis for differential treatment. The Court has stated that "the touchstone of the constitutional inquiry under the Excessive Fines Clause is the principle of proportionality."[110] The Court's approach to this inquiry in *United States v. Bajakajian* shows how much more scrutiny the Court gives monetary penalties even though the proportionality question is the same. Justice Thomas wrote the opinion in *Bajakajian* striking down the fine in that case as grossly excessive, even though he has refused to engage in that same kind of oversight when individuals are imprisoned. The majority in *Bajakajian* did not accept the fine as long it served any basis of punishment, including deterrence, as it has done with prison sentences. Instead, the Court required the fine to be retributively just in light of the harm caused and the offender's culpability. That inquiry is no more susceptible to bright lines in the context of a fine than a prison sentence, but the Court did its duty. The Court has also policed forfeitures under the Excessive Fines Clause to make sure they are not disproportionate, leading the constitutional law scholar David Pozen to wryly observe that "the owner's property receives more Eighth Amendment protection than the owner herself."[111]

The Court has also accepted the difficult line-drawing task of making sure companies do not pay excessive amounts of punitive damages in violation of the Due Process Clause because, in the Court's words, it is a "deeply rooted" principle "that punishment should fit the crime." It thus analyzes punitive damages to make sure that they are reasonable in light of "the degree of reprehensibility of the defendant's conduct." It approvingly cited *Solem* for "the accepted view that some wrongs are more blameworthy than others." Whereas Justices O'Connor and Kennedy were skeptical of drawing these same lines in the context of criminal punishment, they joined a five-justice majority striking down a punitive damages award against BMW as "grossly excessive."[112] A few years later, both of them were again in the majority striking down a punitive damages award against State Farm Insurance as disproportionate to the wrong committed. Chief Justice Rehnquist also signed on to Justice Kennedy's majority opinion in the State Farm case even though it engaged in the same kind of proportionality analysis he condemned in the context of Cruel and Unusual Punishment Clause review. Justice Kennedy's opinion for the Court in that case said it was "neither close nor difficult" to rule the $145 million award excessive even though the factors he used were the same factors that could be used to assess whether a prison sentence is excessive for a crime. He looked at whether the harm was physical or economic, whether the conduct showed a reckless disregard for the safety of others, whether the victim was financially vulnerable, whether the defendant was a recidivist, and whether "the harm was the result of intentional malice, trickery, or deceit, or mere accident."[113] These benchmarks—the degree of harm caused, the defendant's mens rea, the defendant's past behavior, and the nature of the victim—are all susceptible to analysis in criminal punishment cases as well. Moreover, while Justice Kennedy was willing to condone a life sentence in *Harmelin* because of the overall harm caused by drug trafficking instead of looking at the defendant's individual responsibility, in *State Farm*, he condemned issuing punitive damages "to punish and deter conduct that bore no relation" to the harm in the specific case. "A defendant should be punished for the conduct that harmed the plaintiff, not for being an unsavory individual or business."[114] The Court compared the punitive damage award to civil and criminal sanctions for similar misconduct and looked at the ratio between the punitive damage award and the compensatory damage award to determine if it was too large even though that hardly admits of a bright-line analysis. If the Court is willing to engage in that kind of analysis, it is hard to see why it will not consider the ratio between a recidivist bump and the sentence a defendant would receive without one to determine if the enhanced penalty is grossly excessively.

Yet the same justices who closely look at punitive damage awards refuse to engage in the same analysis of terms of incarceration.[115] The framework for assessing punitive damage awards is the kind of open-ended multifactor test that "gives lower courts leeway to strike down punitive damage awards as they see fit," whereas the Court has foreclosed this very same approach when someone is sentenced to prison.[116] As expected, lower courts rarely find sentences unconstitutional under the *Harmelin* framework, but they have frequently overturned punitive damage awards.[117]

Individual liberty should not be treated as less deserving of protection than financial interests. Justice Stevens has noted the anomaly of "suggest[ing] that the Eighth Amendment makes proportionality review applicable in the context of bail and fines but not in the context of other forms of punishment, such as imprisonment."[118] It is telling that some of the same justices who expressed concerns with administrability have had no problem putting those concerns aside when property interests are concerned. Justice Kennedy did not urge BMW to seek relief through the political process even though, as a major corporation with huge financial resources, it would be far more likely to achieve relief through that process than an individual defendant seeking to curb prison sentences, particularly given that curbing excess punitive damages is already a cause some politicians champion.[119] Justice Kennedy instead recognized it was the Court's role to protect the company's rights against excessive punishment and not rely on the legislative process to provide limits. When individual liberty interests are at stake, however, as opposed to the financial interests of a corporation, he flouted his constitutional duties. When he gave the speech asking the lawyers at the ABA to seek to reform sentences through the political process or executive clemency, he was completely ignoring the main channel in our constitutional republic that already exists for keeping punishments in check. That is exactly what the Eighth Amendment is supposed to do. It has fallen short only because the Court has ignored its role in keeping punishments proportional.

Even if administrability concerns could override valid constitutional limits, there are administrable ways to enforce the Eighth Amendment's proportionality limitations. Using long-standing prior usage as a benchmark, for example, is a relatively easy test to administer. A court would first ask whether a given punishment for a crime is contrary to long usage, and if it is, the next step would be to consider if the harshness of the punishment is significantly greater than the severity of the punishment practices that were traditionally authorized.[120] The Court's failure to enforce the Eighth Amendment for decades, however, means that there are now some punishments that have longevity only because they were not struck down when they should have been. A time horizon that predates *Rummel* may be appropriate because the Court's own failure to enforce the Constitution has muddied the analysis otherwise.

Comparative analysis also makes proportionality review feasible. Indeed, that inquiry makes the analysis more objective than the threshold inquiry from *Harmelin,* which has no guideposts. Looking at how a given punishment compares to the sanction in other jurisdictions can help identify outliers, as can an intrajurisdictional comparison of how other crimes are treated. More serious offenses should receive more serious punishments, and there is broad agreement on how offenses compare with each other in terms of seriousness and culpability.[121] Here, too, there are some limits to the utility of the analysis. Because this has been an area with so little oversight, unduly harsh sentences may not be outliers because other jurisdictions may copy severe sentences if they are not struck down. Moreover, the Court's willingness to condone coercive plea bargaining means that legislation is not the "most reliable objective evidence of contemporary values"[122] because the reality is that many legislative enactments do not reflect what policymakers think are acceptable punishments. Because the Court has condoned prosecutors threatening much longer sentences as leverage and prosecutors have asked legislators to give them that tool, statutory ceilings often reflect longer sentences than even the people who voted for them think should be given. They expect the actual sentence to be bargained down from that end point. A much lower sentence than what one sees in a statute is typically the more accurate reflection of contemporary values. Still, there is value in making comparative assessments of authorized and imposed punishments, and it is one reason why the Kennedy approach in *Harmelin* is flawed. It is helpful to see how a sentence compares to others to make the proportionality determination even if the comparison is less helpful than it could be because of the Court's dereliction of duty in making sure punishments are proportionate.

The Court's failure to impose any meaningful proportionality review, even with its limitations, has meant that, in the twenty-year period between *Solem* and *Ewing*, when incarceration rates exploded and America binged on harsh and excessive sentences, only 11 cases of the more than 2,500 that cited *Solem* resulted in a sentence being deemed unconstitutional.[123] Cruel sentences start to seem normal given what the Court has already condoned. Its acceptance of life sentences for the most minor of offenses just because a person has a criminal record—no matter how long ago the prior offenses and even if none of them involved harm to anyone—has meant that life sentences have proliferated in America. According to the Sentencing Project, one out of every seven incarcerated people is serving a life sentence, and that ratio rises to one out of every five for Black men who are incarcerated.[124] Only 38 percent of these life sentences were for first-degree murder. Nationwide, more than 8 percent of the life sentences were for nonviolent offenses, and in some jurisdictions, like Nevada and Delaware, almost a third of the life sentences are for nonviolent crimes.[125]

The Court's acceptance of the argument that drug offenses fuel violence, even when the person was just a low-level participant who did not harm anyone, has allowed insane mandatory minimum sentences to proliferate in narcotics cases.[126] This is how Hamedah Hasan, a mother and grandmother, ended up serving a twenty-seven-year sentence for her minor role running errands and transferring money for her cousin's operation selling crack cocaine despite having no criminal record.[127] This is the same panic behind Paul Carter's life sentence under the Louisiana Habitual Offender Law after being arrested with a residual amount of heroin that was so small it was unweighable.[128]

The sentences for just about every type of crime have increased dramatically after the 1980s.[129] Getting on the right path now will thus be difficult given what the Court has already permitted. It is, however, still possible. Judges assessing proportionality can compare a sentence to the gravity of an offense given what we know about relatively culpability. As in the punitive damages context, courts can compare types of harm, a defendant's mens rea, victim attributes known to a defendant, and relevant criminal history. State courts, for example, engage in these kinds of inquiries under state constitutional provisions requiring proportionality review of sentences, and they have struck sentences down using proportionality review, so their analyses can also be guides.[130]

The death penalty context also offers helpful guideposts because the Court has to consider whether capital punishment is grossly out of proportion given the severity of the crime or the culpability of the person committing it. For example, the Court has rejected the death penalty for those with intellectual disabilities because intellectual disability is relevant to culpability. Intellectual disability is also relevant to the culpability of an individual for noncapital crimes, and it should therefore be deemed cruel and unusual for a jurisdiction to disallow a judge from taking that factor into account when sentencing someone. Indeed, all mandatory punishments suffer from the flaw of disallowing relevant culpability factors from being considered. That is why, in the capital context, the Court has rejected all mandatory death sentences. Just as "the fundamental respect for humanity underlying the Eighth Amendment requires consideration of the character and record of the individual offender and the circumstances of the particular offense as a constitutionally indispensable part of the process of inflicting the penalty of death," so, too, should it require individualized consideration in all sentencing proceedings.[131] The fundamental respect for humanity does not disappear in noncapital cases when people are locked in cells. In both capital and noncapital sentencing, judges need to be able to consider a broad range of factors beyond the crime of conviction to make sure the punishment is proportionate. The Court in *Harmelin* dismissed the Court's analysis from the capital context by saying simply that there was a "qualitative difference" in capital cases. But the Court's reasons for rejecting mandatory punishment in capital cases applies equally to noncapital cases. It has simply chosen not to be vigilant in policing Eighth Amendment concerns in noncapital cases.[132]

The Eighth Amendment does not have to be a dead letter in the context of noncapital punishment. It could still fulfill its intended purpose. That will only happen, however, with a Court that enforces it. The Court has thus far refused to perform its function in this context, and that has been a crucial factor that has allowed mass incarceration. It is not just increased admissions to prisons that drive incarceration rates. It is also how long someone stays there. And because the Court has failed to police sentence lengths, people now stay incarcerated for previously unthinkable amounts of time given their underlying criminal conduct. Our incarceration rates have been blown out of proportion because our sentences are disproportionate. The Constitution is supposed to guard against this very dynamic, but it cannot enforce itself. It was the Court's job to fulfill the Eighth Amendment's promise, and it has tragically failed to live up to its obligation.

CHAPTER FOUR

TOLERATING OVERCROWDED PRISONS

Rhodes v. Chapman

> The true measure of our commitment to justice, the character of our society, our commitment to the rule of law, fairness, and equality cannot be measured by how we treat the rich, the powerful, the privileged, and the respected among us. The true measure of our character is how we treat the poor, the disfavored, the accused, the incarcerated, and the condemned.
>
> —BRYAN STEVENSON

When civil rights lawyers and federal courts finally started to consider the conditions in America's prisons in the 1960s and 1970s, they were horrified by what they discovered.

One lawyer described crowded conditions in Alabama's Holman Maximum Security Facility and Atmore Prison Farm: "Everywhere we went we were engulfed in a sea of humanity of men who endured unrelenting idleness, a constant fear of being raped or stabbed and virtually no hope that these conditions or their lives would ever improve." Conditions were even worse at Alabama's Draper Correctional Center where, in "one second floor dormitory," they found "dozens upon dozens of old, helpless men, many in wheelchairs, incontinent or bedridden, unable to care for themselves and jammed into squalid, dilapidated living quarters which could only be described as a human death trap." Still more disturbing was the segregation unit at Draper, known as the "doghouse." While two cells stood empty, "each of the other four-foot by eight-foot cells contained either five or six prisoners." People were sent to this unit for offenses as minor as showing up late to work and "talking back." Writing in 1987, an observer noted that "what we saw in Alabama in 1975 . . . has been seen in prison system after prison all over the country."[1]

Successful challenges to prison conditions were mounted across America, and remedial orders tackled some of the worst abuses. Yet much of what prisons were like in Alabama in 1975 remains true today of prisons in Alabama and in many other places in America. Prisons are still overcrowded. They are disproportionately occupied by people of color. Relations between staff and those who are incarcerated are strained. Incarcerated people are warehoused with little to no programming and live in fear for their safety and their health.

Consider, for example, what a detailed investigation of Alabama's 13 state prisons for men found between 2016 and 2019 when the Department of Justice sued the state. Its complaint details a "pervasive and systemic" pattern of violence in all the prisons, with high rates of homicide and assault. Prison officials "fail to protect prisoners from homicide even when [those] officials have advance warning that certain prisoners are in danger from violence at the hands of other prisoners." Sexual abuse and violence are also prevalent. The violence does not just occur at the hands of other incarcerated people. Security staff at the prisons frequently use excessive force. Some of the incarcerated people have died from the force, and those who survive are often placed in segregation "until any injuries can heal unobserved and undocumented." Unsafe and unsanitary conditions exist throughout its prisons. Conditions at Draper and Holman, two of the facilities that were subject to lawsuits in the 1970s, were so unsafe and unsanitary that the Alabama Department of Corrections announced their closure after the Department of Justice visited them. (Holman still houses people on death row and people classified as low-risk in some of its dormitories.)

The Department of Justice notes that overcrowding is a big reason for the violence. Alabama's facilities operate well above their design capacity. Prisons designed to hold 9,462 men have more than 14,000 occupants. Occupancy rates of 140 percent are common among its prisons, and some top 201 percent and 257 percent occupancy. Even its death row had a 282 percent occupancy rate. The density of the population increases tensions and makes supervision more difficult. Security staffing is at a "dangerously low level," with fewer than half of the positions filled. Most of the men in these facilities receive no programming, and "the idle time combined with lack of adequate supervision" increases the opportunities for violence.[2] Governor Kay Ivey conceded in 2019 that its prisons had a problem with "violence, poor living conditions and mental illness" and further noted that they were all "exacerbated by a crowded inmate population, correctional and health care staffing challenges, and aging prison structure—each piece compounding the others."[3] A plan by the Alabama legislature to build new prisons will not remedy the overcrowding, however, because the new facilities house even fewer people than the existing ones.[4]

Conditions like these do not just come about because malevolent officials try to create a hellish environment for those who have committed crimes, though sometimes that is the case. This is a pervasive problem with prisons and jails throughout the country, even when they are run by well-meaning wardens and officials, because of the politics of the past five decades. The core problem is that spending money on incarcerated people provides little to no political benefit. This is not a politically powerful or popular group. Incarcerated people are banned from voting in almost every state. Formerly incarcerated people with felony convictions also face voting restrictions. To the extent incarcerated people get the attention of politicians, it tends to be to single them out for mistreatment. Newt Gingrich, for example, argued that people in prison were being treated too well as part of his 1994 reelection campaign. In his book *To Renew America*, which echoed his campaign themes, he claimed that "numerous people in poor neighborhoods say that the young men in their areas refer to prison as 'vacation time.' They eat better, bulk up." He then argued that people in prison should be "doing penance," and "we should eliminate all weight and muscle-building rooms" in prisons and implement mandatory sixty-hour work and study weeks.[5] Joe Arpaio, the self-proclaimed "World's Toughest Sheriff," also emphasized his use of severe penological practices as a selling point throughout his many reelection campaigns for Maricopa County sheriff. For example, his 2016 campaign website highlighted his creation of "Tent City," an outdoor jail utilizing Korean War–era tents to house people outside in the frequently sweltering heat.[6] He forced those in his custody to wear pink underwear and socks as a form of humiliation, and he bragged about offering the cheapest meals to incarcerated people and feeding them only twice daily to cut the labor costs of meal delivery.[7] Former Milwaukee sheriff David Clarke also sought to attract voters by amassing a similarly harsh record that included cutting almost all programming for incarcerated people, waking them up with bullhorns, and using nutraloaf, a deliberately bland brick of mashed-up food that has been banned in several states,[8] as a disciplinary measure.[9]

Politicians who trade on tough-on-crime policies never bother with the details, like the fact that most people in jails are there pretrial and therefore have not been convicted of anything or that prison conditions apply to everyone, no matter their crime. All the rhetoric is designed to conjure the worst offenders and offenses voters can imagine so that harsh conditions seem deserved.[10] They ignore the criminogenic effect of these conditions and how they undermine public safety because people released from these facilities are often more damaged than when they entered.

Even when they are not being targeted for harsh treatment, people in jail and prison find themselves on the short end of funding decisions, which effectively amounts to the same thing because the lack of funds inevitably results in deplorable conditions. Texas governor Greg Abbott, for example, diverted four million dollars in state prison funding (without any decarceration measures) to instead go to election audits in an attempt to "ensure election integrity." Michele Deitch, a law professor at the University of Texas, condemned the decision because the Texas prison system is already underfunded and the severe budget cut would exacerbate already alarming understaffing and further jeopardize adequate provision of health care and food to incarcerated people.[11] States have every incentive to pack jails and prisons to the breaking point and let them deteriorate until something forces their hand.

One of those forces should be the Constitution. The Eighth Amendment disallows inhumane conditions of confinement. But just as state prison populations were exploding, resulting in overcrowded and deplorable conditions, the Supreme Court sent a signal to lower courts that it was not the business of the judiciary to second-guess state legislatures and prison officials on matters of prison administration. The lower court judges often witnessed the conditions firsthand, and they knew there was no denying the Eighth Amendment violations once they had seen them with their own eyes. The Supreme Court, in contrast, viewed prisons in the abstract and ignored the palpable human cruelty within them. Prison condition lawsuits were just more pieces of paper that made their way inside the marble building in which the justices isolate themselves. The Court seemed unable to grasp the humanity at stake.

Thus, as many lower courts were dutifully enforcing the Eighth Amendment in prison conditions cases, the Court decided to step in, not to lend a hand but to stop those efforts in their tracks. In 1981, in *Rhodes v. Chapman*, the Court overturned a district court judge who, after personally visiting an Ohio prison and holding a five-day trial, found the conditions violated the Eighth Amendment. The prison packed two people in cells barely big enough for one person, exceeding its design capacity by 38 percent and failing to give incarcerated people the minimal space every empirical study said was required to avoid physical and mental deterioration. After the Court decided *Rhodes*, it was almost impossible to bring a successful challenge on the basis of overcrowding, paving the way for decades of prisons bursting at the seams with people. Prisons routinely double bunk people facing long terms of confinement, treating them like warehoused animals in a factory farm. Just as every expert predicted, these deplorable, crowded conditions leave death and unimaginable harm in their wake. *Rhodes* sent a signal to lower courts to limit aggressive oversight of prison conditions, and with few exceptions, courts heard the message loud and clear.

The Court's unwillingness to police prison capacity and conditions has been another key driver of mass incarceration. If there are limits on how many people can be put in a given correctional facility, the state either needs to release people to make more room or turn away people it would otherwise prefer to detain until it can construct new facilities. If living conditions are held to be inhumane, states need to invest in improvements. State budgets are tight, and most states are required to keep a balanced budget.[12] If the Supreme Court held states to constitutional standards, that would create pressure on them to maximize their resources. Prisons are expensive, so inevitably it would mean they would turn to other alternatives. One of the tragic ironies of mass incarceration is that it causes untold human misery and is not even the most effective or cheapest strategy for combatting crime. States continue with this irrational approach because political incentives push them in that direction, and the Supreme Court has failed to enforce the constitutional provision that could help correct the pathology by making these officials internalize the true constitutional costs.

Lower courts grasped the situation far better than the Supreme Court. After the Supreme Court decided that the Eighth Amendment applied to the states in 1962, civil rights and public interest lawyers started focusing on prison conditions and the rights of incarcerated people. Many judges took the time to see the conditions for themselves and were horrified by what they saw. Incarcerated people who violated prison rules were whipped in Arkansas, placed in solitary confinement with no clothing and no heat in New York, and put in a concrete building with no plumbing, lights, ventilation, or furniture in Alabama. They were denied medical care.[13] Judges found unconstitutional conditions in prisons and jails in almost every state. Sometimes entire state prison systems were found to be constitutionally deficient. As Malcolm Feeley and Ed Rubin note in their detailed overview of prison condition litigation, these judges "were not fire-breathing radicals" coordinating their efforts but "middle-of-the-road, upper-middle-class Americans, largely white and male, appointed by Republicans and Democratic presidents" each making separate decisions based on the evidence before them.[14] The conditions cried out for intervention, even by judges who were not otherwise inclined to take bold steps.

The Supreme Court, however, stood apart from this judicial trend. Instead of policing prisons, the Court policed the lower courts and stopped the prisons conditions movement in its tracks. The Court sent an unmistakable signal in *Rhodes v. Chapman* that prisons were not meant to be "comfortable" and that states could cram people into tight quarters without regard for what every expert and study concluded were the minimum space requirements. According to the Court's view, prison conditions had to rise to the level of something out of a Dickens novel to be even close to the constitutional line.

It is no wonder, then, that prison populations continued to explode after the Court's decision. States were given the equivalent of a clearance sale on incarceration because they did not need to pay the full constitutional price for their decision. They could refuse to provide the minimum space necessary for physical safety and mental health and offer only the barest necessities of existence to those in its custody. This discount let them run up their prison populations and provide far less than what the Constitution requires.

The Constitutional Framework

As we saw in the previous chapter, the phrase "cruel and unusual" bars disproportionately harsh punishment. Incarceration is a mode of punishment, and the previous chapter considered how the Supreme Court has approached the question of when the *quantity* of incarceration is unconstitutional. The test the Supreme Court created to make that determination permits most sentences, no matter how long they are, which has been one reason mass incarceration has flourished in spite of what should be a robust Eighth Amendment proportionality check.

There is a second way in which the Eighth Amendment puts limits on incarceration, and that is with its *quality*. Incarceration is not a single mode of punishment but differs widely in terms of how states implement it. It would be, for example, a far different type of punishment for people to be placed in well-ventilated structures with private space, adequate nutrition, programming, and mental and physical health care than for them to be placed in a crowded tent with vermin-infested food and no attention to their health needs. While both may be thought of as incarceration, they are in fact different types of punishment. Recall that the Court's 1910 decision in *Weems v. United States* focused not only on the length of the sentence but also the imposition of *cadena temporal*, which was a form of chained hard labor during incarceration. The Court condemned both the length and the type of incarceration, noting that the sentence was "cruel in its excess of imprisonment" and "unusual in its character." The Bill of Rights, it explained, is concerned both with the "degree and kind" of punishment, and the assessment of what is cruel and unusual "is not fastened to the obsolete but may acquire meaning as public opinion becomes enlightened by a humane justice."[15]

The Court has acknowledged that "it is now settled that 'the treatment a prisoner receives in prison and the conditions under which he is confined are subject to scrutiny under the Eighth Amendment.'"[16] That is, once a state opts to use incarceration as punishment, it assumes responsibility for the "safety and general well-being" of a person in its custody.[17] The Eighth Amendment requires certain minimum standards as part of that duty. Accordingly, no matter what offense someone has committed, certain forms of incarceration would be disproportionately cruel and unusual if they fall below the standards of human decency and fail to meet basic human needs. The difficult question is identifying what those minimum standards are.

Constitutional Challenges to Prison Conditions in the Lower Courts

The Supreme Court and lower federal courts did not have many occasions to confront these questions until the 1960s. Before that time, various procedural and substantive hurdles, which were collectively later labeled the "hands-off doctrine," made it difficult to bring actions challenging conditions of confinement.[18] Margo Schlanger, a leading prison law scholar, has noted there were "some important, if scattered cases in which lower courts did indeed declare conditions of confinement unconstitutional when they (as they rarely did) had jurisdiction to decide the issue." It took a series of doctrinal shifts, though, for prison conditions lawsuits to become commonplace and eventually make their way to the Supreme Court.[19] These key legal changes included the Supreme Court's holding in *Robinson v. California* in 1962 that the Eighth Amendment applied to the states and its decision in *Cooper v. Pate* in 1964 allowing incarcerated people for the first time to sue state prison officials by bringing Section 1983 claims for civil rights violations.[20] Changes to class action rules also made it easier to bring system-wide litigation as a class action instead of in individual suits.[21]

It was not just the doctrinal landscape that placed the issue of prison conditions front and center in the 1960s and 1970s. The civil rights movement of the era brought these issues to the fore. Civil rights lawyers at the NAACP Legal Defense Fund viewed prisoners' cases as the natural next step after *Brown v. Board of Education*. The rights of incarcerated people were, according to prison law experts Claudia Angelos and Jim Jacobs, "a natural adjunct to the civil rights movement and society's increasing interest in the plight of the poor and disenfranchised."[22] Incarcerated people began to claim that they were deserving of rights, and as they secured victories in pro se matters, they were emboldened to file still more complaints.[23] Uprisings at Folsom State Prison in California and Attica in New York also energized the movement.

Early prison litigation focused on racial segregation in prisons and discrimination against Black Muslims, so the cases raised equal protection and First Amendment claims. The Supreme Court therefore did not have to break new doctrinal ground under the Eighth Amendment. For example, the Court upheld a decision finding that Alabama's segregation of incarcerated people into prison housing units by race was unconstitutional under the Equal Protection Clause.[24] In *Wolff v. McDonnell*, the Court held that incarcerated people were entitled to due process before losing good time credits, and Justice White's opinion emphasized that "there is no iron curtain drawn between the Constitution and the prisons of this country." His opinion went on to list the rights incarcerated people "enjoy," including due process and equal protection.[25] Notably, he did not mention the Eighth Amendment.[26]

The next wave of prison litigation put the Eighth Amendment front and center, with litigants using the Cruel and Unusual Punishment Clause to challenge prison conditions. This wave had the support of a new cadre of lawyers focused on prisoners' rights. The ACLU established a prisoners' rights project in its northern Virginia affiliate in 1968 and launched its National Prison Project in 1972. Its first case challenged prisons in Alabama.[27] Subsequent cases were brought against facilities throughout the country and sometimes entire state prison systems. In the five-year period between 1970 and 1975, federal judges found prison conditions in Alabama, Arkansas, Florida, Louisiana, Mississippi, and Oklahoma to be unconstitutional. In the next five-year period from 1975 to 1980, federal judges declared prisons in another twenty-eight jurisdictions unconstitutional. That does not even count the cases involving jails or those in state court.[28] Thirty-one states were under a court order to reduce prison and jail overcrowding in 1981.[29] Court decisions described conditions that "would shock the conscience of any reasonable citizen who had first-hand opportunity to view them."[30] Judges around the country found that "the squalor of prison conditions" was unconstitutional even though "such degradation was commonplace across the United States" and therefore not unusual.[31]

Constitutional Challenges to Prison Conditions in the Supreme Court

The Supreme Court eventually confronted Eighth Amendment questions about prison conditions as the enormous number of lower court cases worked their way up through the appeals process. Importantly, in terms of methodological approach, the Court did not approach these claims by asking whether a particular condition of confinement existed at the time of the framing or was unusual as compared to other jurisdictions. Even if a barbaric practice was tolerated in the past or was currently being used across jurisdictions, the Court would rule it unlawful if it violated the minimal standard of decency that all people in civilized society deserve.

The Court made clear this was the approach in *Estelle v. Gamble* in 1976. J.W. Gamble was incarcerated in Texas when he injured his back while performing prison labor. He filed a handwritten pro se petition complaining about the medical treatment he received after his injury. The district court dismissed his claim, but the Fifth Circuit reversed and remanded with instructions for the district court to reinstate the complaint. The Supreme Court took the case and made clear that people in prison have a right to adequate medical care, though it reversed the Fifth Circuit's decision as to Gamble in an 8–1 vote. It was "a low-profile case" that did not even attract amicus to file briefs. The parties themselves agreed that the state was under an obligation to provide medical care to those in its custody, but they disagreed on the standard for liability.[32] Justice Marshall wrote the opinion for himself and six others. (Justice Blackmun agreed with the reversal but did not join the Marshall opinion or write separately to explain his view.)

The Court did not consider what the provision of health care for those in custody looked like at the framing or take a survey of other state practices. If either of those inquiries was determinative, incarcerated people would be given little to no medical care. Imprisonment was not used widely as punishment at the framing. It was thirty years after the framing that the precursors to modern American prisons were founded. When the Constitution was drafted, those in government custody were typically in jails for short stays, awaiting trial.[33] The idea of providing care would thus not be central to short-term stays in small facilities. Moreover, the practice of medicine when the Constitution was drafted looked very different. "Physicians could diagnose and comfort but could rarely intervene without extraordinary pain and distress." By the 1970s, in contrast, "medicine could often bring alleviation of suffering, disease and the accompanying pain." Thus, as one medical expert noted, whereas "the provision of medical care could not have been argued to be morally mandatory when its benefits were so uncertain," by the time the Court heard Gamble's case, "in an age of successful medical technologies and interventions, the radical disjunction of practice within and outside of the walls [of prisons] was clearly unacceptable."[34]

Despite advances in medical care, it remained all too common for states to provide abysmal care to those in its custody. A survey of jails in 1972 conducted by the American Medical Association found that fewer than 50 percent had any regular sick call and 6 percent had no medical services available at all. They did not even contain a first aid kit. Prisons also provided shockingly substandard care, with the "distance from any decent and justifiable standard of medical practice" all too apparent to any observer.[35]

When the Supreme Court addressed the question of medical care in prisons, it did not look to history or common practice but to bedrock notions of human decency. Justice Marshall wrote that the Eighth Amendment not only bars "physically barbarous punishments" but that it also "embodies 'broad and idealistic concepts of dignity, civilized standards, humanity, and decency,'" quoting language from an opinion written by Justice Blackmun when he was a judge on the Eighth Circuit that condemned whipping as a form of prison punishment.[36] Justice Marshall's opinion noted that the Court has "held repugnant to the Eighth Amendment punishments which are incompatible with 'the evolving standards of decency that mark the progress of a maturing society'" or "which involve the unnecessary and wanton infliction of pain." The Court reasoned from these principles that the government has an obligation to provide medical care to those in its custody.

The focus on standards of human decency was a victory for incarcerated people, but two aspects of the opinion were less favorable to them. First, the opinion noted that it was the state's "deliberate indifference to serious medical needs" that amounted to cruel and unusual punishment, and the deliberate indifference standard is a tough one to meet. Second, the Court rejected Gamble's specific claim against the medical director of the Corrections Department because it concluded that Gamble was seen by medical personnel seventeen times over a three-month stretch and received treatment for his back injury. The medical decision not to order more diagnostic tests was, in the Court's view, "a classic example of a matter for medical judgment" and "does not represent cruel and unusual punishment."[37] Thus, while the Court's language describing the Eighth Amendment's scope indicated a significant role for courts in overseeing prison conditions, the Court's actual decision in Gamble's case was a sign that the Court had some skepticism when it came to claims about medical care.

Justice Stevens was the only justice who dissented, and he argued that the complaint should not have been dismissed at that point. He noted that "it is surely not inconceivable that an overworked, undermanned medical staff in a crowded prison is following the expedient course of routinely prescribing nothing more than pain killers when a thorough diagnosis would disclose an obvious need for remedial treatment." He also worried that the Court's "deliberate indifference" standard "improperly attaches significance to the subjective motivation of the defendant as a criterion for determining whether cruel and unusual punishment has been inflicted." A prison condition could be cruel and unusual, in his view, whether it was by design, negligence, or lack of funds. They key question should be "the character of the punishment rather than the motivation of the individual who inflicted it."[38]

An originalist reading of the Eighth Amendment supports Justice Stevens's view that the subjective intent of the punisher should be irrelevant and the standard should be an objective one. John Stinneford has canvassed the linguistic and historical evidence and found "no instance in which an eighteenth or nineteenth-century speaker claimed that a showing of cruel intent was part of the minimum factual criteria necessary to show a violation of the Cruel and Unusual Punishments Clause."[39] The clause instead refers to the effect of a punishment on its recipient. Unfortunately, the Court has built on the language from *Gamble* and now requires all litigants challenging prison conditions to show that a "prison official acted with a 'wanton' state of mind" unless the pain being inflicted was "formally meted out as *punishment* by the statute or the sentencing judge." The Court is essentially using a recklessness standard that requires showing that a prison official was aware of the risk of causing harm.[40] Justice Stevens correctly intuited in *Gamble* that the Court would make subjective intent an important part of its Eighth Amendment jurisprudence and that the Court would be all too eager to reverse lower court decisions finding violations.

Despite these limitations, *Gamble* made clear that the Eighth Amendment polices prison conditions and that the obligation of the state is to respect human decency and not simply establish that some condition existed in the past. The next major prison reform case to reach the Court, *Hutto v. Finney,* gave Justice Stevens the opportunity to write the majority opinion. The case arose out of litigation, which began in 1965, challenging prison conditions in Arkansas. After years of litigation, the district court ultimately found the entire prison system in Arkansas unconstitutional under the Eighth Amendment and issued a sweeping remedial order that essentially put the entire system under federal receivership.[41] The lower court judge described Arkansas's prisons as "a dark and evil world completely alien to the free world." Incarcerated people "slept together in large, 100-man barracks" where "rape was so common and uncontrolled that some potential victims dared not sleep; instead they would leave their beds and spend the night clinging to the bars nearest the guards' station." Incarcerated people faced brutal punishments for misconduct, including being "lashed with a wooden-handled leather strap five feet long and four inches wide" and given "electrical shocks to various sensitive parts" of their bodies. More serious infractions were punished by punitive isolation, where people were held for indeterminate periods in crowded cells eight feet by ten feet "with no furniture other than a source of water and a toilet that could only be flushed from outside the cell." They received fewer than one thousand calories per day during punitive isolation. By the time an appeal from the litigation arrived at the Supreme Court in 1978, however, the issues of disagreement between the parties were limited. Arkansas corrections officials did not disagree with the district court's decision that conditions in its prisons, including overcrowding and the conditions in its punitive isolation cells, amounted to cruel and unusual punishment. They challenged only two issues in the Supreme Court. One was an award of attorney's fees, and the other was an order disallowing any person to be held for more than thirty days in punitive isolation. The Supreme Court upheld the remedial order on both counts.

Justice Stevens's opinion reiterated the language from *Estelle v. Gamble* that the Eighth Amendment prohibits punishment "that transgress today's broad and idealistic concepts of dignity, civilized standards, humanity, and decency."[42]

The majority opinion also noted "the exercise of discretion in this case is entitled to special deference because of the trial judge's years of experience with the problem at hand." Justice Rehnquist was the lone dissenter on the question of the thirty-day limit on punitive isolation. He began by noting that "no person of ordinary feeling could fail to be moved by the Court's recitation of the conditions formerly prevailing in the Arkansas prison system."[43] Nevertheless, he dissented because he thought the district court went beyond its remedial authority. That skepticism of judicial oversight over prisons would ultimately become the dominant view on the Court. Notably, though, Justice Rehnquist focused only on the remedy and did not dispute the relevance of the Eighth Amendment to the underlying substantive claim.

These early prison condition cases thus reflect a consensus that the Court should be playing a role in making sure incarceration practices do not run afoul of the Cruel and Unusual Punishment Clause. There is a constitutional floor of human decency and dignity that the Court must police even if there is disagreement over the content of the minimum standards and how a violation should be remedied. Lawyers and judges working on prison conditions cases "interpreted *Hutto* as a green light" to challenge the totality of conditions in prisons, and lawsuits sprang up all over the country. Signals from the Supreme Court matter, and the message from *Hutto* was that prison conditions cases could be successful. *Hutto*'s green light quickly turned to red, however, as the Court shifted course and sent an unmistakable message that prison conditions cases were disfavored.

Rhodes v. Chapman and the Court's Failure to Police Prison Capacity

Prison populations exploded in the 1970s. With violent crime and social unrest increasing in the late 1960s and early 1970s, jurisdictions responded by passing longer sentences and abolishing or narrowing parole. The police stopped and arrested more people, and prosecutors used their discretion to seek pretrial detention and pursue more serious charges in cases. Plea bargaining rates skyrocketed, and cases were processed at a much faster clip. Jails and prisons filled as a result. While eventually this would also lead to a prison building boom, construction did not keep pace with the rise in populations, thus creating ever more crowded conditions in prisons and jails.

Overcrowding was often at the root of unconstitutional conditions claims in federal litigation. Of the forty jurisdictions embroiled in lawsuits over prison litigation at the end of 1981, thirty-six were facing allegations of overcrowding.[44] Overcrowding is not a matter of mere inconvenience or discomfort. It threatens the physical safety and health of everyone in a densely packed facility. It stretches resources too thin and brings an already tense environment to a boiling point, frequently leading to violence and sometimes even riots. Overcrowding is also the prison condition that state legislatures and politicians will be most inclined to ignore. They have political incentives to appear tough on crime and pass ever harsher sentences. At the same time, they have budgetary incentives to cram as many people as possible into existing facilities to avoid spending money on new ones. Prison officials have no choice but to accept the people sentenced and use the resources they are given; they lack the authority to remedy the situation even if they think the conditions are unsafe or unconstitutional. Judicial enforcement of the Eighth Amendment is thus the last line of defense. Unfortunately, as prison populations were exploding and jurisdictions failed to spend money to provide incarcerated people with requisite space, the Supreme Court adopted a policy of appeasement.

The Supreme Court first confronted the issue of overcrowding when pretrial detainees in the Metropolitan Correctional Center (MCC), a then newly built federal facility in Manhattan, brought a conditions lawsuit challenging, among other things, the fact they had to share a seventy-five-square-foot space with another person, a practice known as double bunking. The space was designed for single occupancy and contained a wash basin and uncovered toilet. The facility was double bunking some incarcerated people because the population was 16 percent over its design capacity. After visiting the facility, Southern District of New York Judge Marvin Frankel concluded that double bunking was a "fundamental denial[] of decency, privacy, personal security, and, simply, civilized humanity."[45] The Second Circuit affirmed, concluding that the only conditions permissible for those in pretrial detention were ones that "inhere in their confinement itself or which are justified by compelling necessities of jail administration."[46]

These concerns did not persuade the Supreme Court, which voted 6–3 to reverse the Second Circuit on the question of double bunking. Justice Rehnquist wrote the opinion for the Court in *Bell v. Wolfish* and rejected the "compelling necessity" test used by the lower courts to assess the jail conditions. The Second Circuit argued that the presumption of innocence required the conditions of confinement for someone detained pretrial to be justified by a compelling necessity. In rejecting that approach, Justice Rehnquist introduced the same flawed arguments he would later use in *Salerno* to justify the unprecedented detention of individuals deemed to be dangerous. He began by stating—without support—that the presumption of innocence "has no application to a determination of the rights of a pretrial detainee during confinement."[47] In his view, it is merely a doctrine that allocates the burden of proof at trial. Justice Stevens, joined by Justice Brennan in his dissent, was taken aback by this view of the presumption of innocence. Justice Stevens wrote, "I cannot believe the Court means what it seems to be saying." He noted that Justice Rehnquist "rel[ied] on nothing more than the force of assertion," and that assertion contradicted the Court's cases finding the presumption of innocence to be fundamental.[48]

While Justice Stevens may not have believed it, it was the view of the majority of the Court. Five justices joined Justice Rehnquist in the view that, once someone is properly detained pretrial, they have only the right to be free from punishment. "Absent a showing of expressed intent to punish on the part of the detention facility officials," the Court stated any condition of confinement will be permitted as long as it "is reasonably related to a legitimate government objective." This cramped view of what constitutes punishment would reemerge in *Salerno*. Here, it permitted the use of double bunking because there was no intent to punish on the part of the corrections officials in using it, and double bunking was being imposed as part of the state's management of the facility. The Court dismissed the lower courts' concerns with a person's privacy interests in having to share the same small space and toilet with another, snarkily noting there is not "some sort of 'one man, one cell' principle lurking in the Due Process Clause."

The opinion also sounded notes of caution about prison reform cases more generally, observing that some courts "have waded into" complex areas and become "increasingly enmeshed in the minutiae of prison operations," while also noting throughout the opinion that prison officials merit deference on maintaining order and security within their facilities.[49] As Justice Marshall wryly observed in his dissent, "lest the point escape the reader, the majority reiterates it 12 times in the course of the opinion."[50]

As dismissive as it was of the privacy interests in the case, the opinion contained some important caveats about the scope of its holding. It noted that the pretrial detainees were required to spend only seven to eight hours per day in their rooms during evening hours when they were likely sleeping and that most people were detained for fewer than sixty days. It explicitly left open the possibility that longer periods of detention in crowded conditions might not be permissible. It cautioned that "confining a given number of people in a given amount of space in such a matter as to cause them to endure genuine privation and hardship over an extended period of time might raise serious questions."[51]

Lower court judges, who often took the time to witness overcrowded conditions firsthand and therefore could not miss their human costs, picked up on the Court's caveats and continued to find overcrowded conditions unconstitutional after *Wolfish* was decided. These judges typically refrained from imposing release orders and tried to use other remedial means.[52] As one group of commentators observed, had *Wolfish* been the last word on overcrowding, "lower court decisions would apparently have continued on a rather uninterrupted course," distinguishing the facts in cases before them from those in *Wolfish*.[53]

The Supreme Court, however, remained aloof from the human costs of overcrowding and wretched conditions. It took up another case involving allegations of overcrowding just two years later, this time in the context of a challenge by people who had been convicted and were serving out long prison terms in double-bunked cells. State officials around the country who wanted to use double bunking and avoid challenges to overcrowding "could not have hoped for a better factual situation for the Supreme Court to consider" because, like *Wolfish*, the case involved a newly built facility unlike most prisons in the country.[54] The case involved the Southern Ohio Correctional Facility (SOCF, or what is commonly known as Lucasville), which was built in 1972 when prison populations had been on the decline. It replaced a decrepit facility in Columbus, Ohio, and was the only maximum-security prison in the state when it opened. It was designed to hold one person in each of its 1,660 cells. Almost immediately after the SOCF was built, Ohio, like other states, experienced a huge increase in its prison population. The result of this prison population boom was that sometime in 1975, prison officials began putting two people in each sixty-three-square-foot cell. By 1977, Lucasville was already 38 percent over its design capacity with approximately 2,300 people. Approximately 1,400 people were double bunked because Ohio "had no other adequate facilities in which to house them."[55]

Two of the incarcerated people at Lucasville who were double bunked filed a pro se lawsuit alleging that they were being subjected to cruel and unusual punishment. Eventually, the lawsuit became a class action with lawyers from the American Civil Liberties Union of Ohio representing the class. After a five-day trial with multiple witnesses, forty exhibits, and a personal visit to the prison by the judge, Chief Judge Timothy Sylvester Hogan of the Southern District of Ohio concluded the double-celling conditions were unconstitutional. His opinion was not exactly a model of detailed factual support for his conclusions. Because the SOCF was a new facility, it did not have the ventilation problems and decaying conditions typical of most prisons. Most of the judge's factual findings were therefore favorable to the state prison officials. He called the prison, for example, "unquestionably a top-flight, first-class facility."[56] The portion of the opinion explaining the constitutional infirmity was only two pages. His analysis boiled down to the fact that each person in a double-bunked cell had "something in the neighborhood of 30–35 feet at best" of living space, which he found insufficient to comport with the Constitution given the long terms being served by those in the facility.

The trial court referenced but did not detail testimony at trial that supported the need for more space. A number experts testified about the dangers from overcrowding and double bunking. A former Lucasville psychologist testified that the double celling in maximum security facilities was particularly problematic because the population had "a large percentage" of people who were there "because they have been unable to cope" in other prisons.[57] That group had a harder time dealing with the space constraints. Moreover, as the district court noted, "a substantial number of the [incarcerated people at Lucasville] are victims of some form of emotional or mental disorder."[58] There was evidence at trial that 75 to 80 percent of the incarcerated people had "some sort of personality disorder, including schizophrenia, paranoia, and depression."[59] Many people at Lucasville had been transferred from the Lima State Hospital for the Criminally Insane and had been "assigned cells routinely with other[s]." A psychiatrist who worked at the Lima State Hospital testified that people with schizophrenia who are put in double-bunking situations will have tendencies to see the activities of their cellmates "as threatening, even when they are not intended as such," making it more likely that the person with schizophrenia will "act out towards this individual in a mistaken feeling that he must protect himself." Experts also testified that overcrowding taxed prison resources and left many of the incarcerated people idle. The decrease in opportunities and outlets for incarcerated people to "engage in any form of activity which would allow them to sublimate their emotions, that is to disperse them into socially approved behavior," could "result in aggressive outbursts."[60]

The district court opinion did not spend time discussing this testimony but instead cited multiple studies, none of which was contradicted, that people incarcerated for long terms need at least fifty square feet of floor space. Many of the studies had higher minimum requirements. The Army, for example, complied with a study requiring fifty-five square feet. Chief Judge Hogan, himself a World War II Army veteran, noted that the Army was "not known for 'coddling.'" The experts who studied these issues explained that "overcrowding and double celling increase aggressiveness and break down normal social behavior," leading to psychological damage, as well as sexual and other forms of violence, including riots.[61]

Chief Judge Hogan noted that this risk was pronounced because incarcerated people at Lucasville spent many hours of the day in their cells with another person, with "a substantial number" spending all but four to six hours per week in their cells.[62] At trial, experts testified that this prolonged time together in cells was "particularly harmful because at SOCF double celling was done without classification or choice."[63] Chief Judge Hogan also relied on the fact that the incarcerated people at Lucasville were there for the "long term," which "can only accent the problems of close confinement and overcrowding." Additionally, he observed that, while "double celling in 60-foot cells is undoubtedly permissible as a temporary measure," the conditions at Lucasville had persisted for two years and the trend line showed no changes in the future.[64] The Sixth Circuit affirmed in an unpublished order.[65]

When the Supreme Court agreed to hear the case, other parties filed briefs to weigh in. The American Medical Association and the American Public Health Association filed a joint brief, over the objection of the state of Ohio, and explained to the Court that the minimum space requirement of sixty square feet per person was "based upon the broad consensus of epidemiological, medical and psychological findings that long term overcrowding causes and accelerates the spread of communicable disease and results in the increased occurrence of stress-induced mental disorders, tension, aggression and physical violence." The communicable diseases can be serious and fatal, such as pulmonary tuberculosis, which spreads rapidly in prisons and then ultimately becomes "a significant source of infection for the community at large" as people released from the prison spread the disease. Overcrowding leads to "increased illness complaint rates, higher death and suicide rates, and higher disciplinary infraction rates." These effects are "more pronounced where crowding is present under conditions of threats to personal security, when resources are scarce, and when the environment is 'closed' and when large amounts of time must be spent in the crowded setting." They emphasized that these conclusions are not based on "intuitive, normative, or idealistic notions" but are grounded in "empirical findings in the fields of medicine, psychology and epidemiology that sustained crowding, especially under adverse conditions in closed institutions, causes demonstrable mental and physical injury."[66] Moreover, these issues are worsened because overcrowding also renders medical and other staff members less available to incarcerated people in need. Their brief noted the many prison riots that occurred because of overcrowded conditions.

A brief filed by the state public defender of California told the Court that California's decision to institute a determinate sentencing scheme and increase sentences resulted in overcrowding in its facilities, resulting in physical and psychological damage to incarcerated people. At San Quentin, for example, twenty-six people "were admitted to the prison psychiatric ward as a direct result of the mental trauma of double celling." The warden of San Quentin, George Summer, called the practice "inhuman" because it produced "increased tension and violence, as well as psychological breakdowns."[67]

The Solicitor General of the United States filed a brief that took no position on the merits but included a copy of the Federal Standards for Prisons and Jails that had been released on December 16, 1980, while the case was pending before the Supreme Court. The preamble to those federal standards described them as designed to "promote practices that protect the basic constitutional rights of" incarcerated people while cautioning that they "should not be taken to be a statement of constitutional minima." Those standards specified that cells should be at least sixty square feet and hold one person. The SG brief to the Court made clear that, though a small percentage (5%) of the federal prison population were double bunked in spaces smaller than sixty-three square feet, it was "firm federal policy that there should be no double celling in long-term correctional facilities."[68]

Although the federal government took no position on the merits in the case, several states did. A brief filed on behalf of twenty-nine states and the government of the Virgin Islands urged the Court to erect a high bar for any incarcerated person to successfully claim unconstitutional living conditions in prison. They argued "the kind of pain prohibited [under the Eighth Amendment] is that which hurts; that which causes one to say 'ouch.'" The pain must be "sharp or acute," which would seemingly rule out chronic pain caused from living conditions. It would also rule out many mental health problems caused by prison conditions because the standard they proposed ruled out "the kind of pain that is identified as a dull ache" and did "not prohibit a sense of anxiety."[69] In other words, an incarcerated person who lives in constant fear of others because of overcrowded and dangerous prison conditions cannot bring a challenge until an actual physical assault takes place.

The Supreme Court sided with Ohio in a vote of 8–1. The opinion by Justice Powell was joined by Chief Justice Burger and Justices Stewart, White, Powell, and Rehnquist. The majority began by acknowledging the stakes. The Court was facing "for the first time" the question of what limits the Eighth Amendment places on the conditions of confinement.[70] The Court thus knew it was establishing an important precedent in a field that was rapidly occupying the lower courts. The message it sent in this all-too-brief opinion was that courts should be highly deferential to state legislatures and prison administrators. Judges, it noted, "cannot assume that state legislatures and prison officials are insensitive to the requirements of the Constitution."[71] The majority acknowledged in a footnote that "the increase of serious crime and the effect of inflation" had taxed the resources of states and communities. Instead of seeing this as a reason to be particularly attentive to prison conditions because jurisdictions may be looking to cut corners and ignore individual rights when it came to a politically unpopular and powerless group, the Court seemed to relate to the state officials and legislators and their concern with crime and budgets.[72] It is, of course, the role of the Court to focus on individual rights and not budget pressures, but its sympathies were the opposite of what the Constitution demands.

The majority acknowledged conditions could be so "deplorable" and "sordid," particularly in older prisons, that they crossed the constitutional line. At the same time, however, the Court made clear its view that it would take truly horrendous circumstances to support an Eighth Amendment violation. The Court noted that conditions can be "restrictive and even harsh" but that "the Constitution does not mandate comfortable prisons." This line would become the mantra in future cases rejecting challenges to all sorts of horrific prison conditions. The legal scholar Jonathan Simon has observed that this "sneering" rhetoric "fits right in line with the increasingly punitive and degrading 'tough on crime' rhetoric that was becoming firmly established in the electoral branches of the state and federal governments."[73] The Court, like those electoral branches, accepted without question that prisons "cannot be free of discomfort." The Court gave little deference to the district court's firsthand look at the facility and its findings, concluding that "these general considerations fall far short" in showing an Eighth Amendment violation because "there is no evidence that double celling under these circumstances either inflicts unnecessary or wanton pain or is grossly disproportionate to the severity of crimes warranting punishment." Justice Powell's opinion observed that, "at most, these considerations amount to a theory that double celling inflicts pain," but far more pain was required to show a constitutional violation, according to the Court.[74]

The majority also cast doubt on the lower court's reliance on expert assessments of space requirements, noting in a footnote that it "erred in assuming that opinions of experts as to desirable prison conditions suffice to establish contemporary standards of decency." Greater weight should be given to "the public attitude." The justices in the majority also seemed to be making their own independent assessment—even though they never saw the prison firsthand—because they noted that "the cells in the SOCF are exceptionally modern and functional; they are heated and ventilated and have hot and cold running water and a sanitary toilet. Each cell also has a radio."[75] It seemed as if the majority could not believe there could be severe psychological harm from people being forced into such proximity with others for most of the day, over decades, or that it produced a great risk of violence, even though many of the people housed in the facility had severe mental illnesses. As long as the prison was thoughtful enough to include a radio, the majority did not see the problem.

Justice Brennan filed a separate opinion, joined by Justices Blackmun and Stevens, concurring in the judgment. These concurring justices worried that the tone of the majority would cause lower courts to rethink their approach to prison conditions cases and tried to send a different message. Justice Brennan's concurrence began by "emphasiz[ing] that today's decision should in no way be construed as a retreat from careful scrutiny of prison conditions."[76] Justice Blackmun's short, separate concurrence was even more direct. He worried that the majority opinion "might be regarded, because of some of its language, as a signal to prison administrators that the federal courts now are to adopt a policy of general deference to such administrators and to state legislatures, deference not only for the purpose of determining contemporary standards of decency, but for the purpose of determining whether conditions at a particular prison are cruel and unusual." He not only joined the Brennan opinion but wrote his own separate concurrence to highlight his track record supporting the rights of people in prison and to express his hope that the courts would "remain as an available bastion" against "unconstitutional cruelty and neglect."

While these justices were not willing to uphold the lower court decision, they tried their best to signal to lower courts through their concurring opinions that they should remain open for business when it came to prison conditions lawsuits. Justice Brennan's opinion began by noting that, "although this Court has never before considered what prison conditions constitute 'cruel and unusual punishment' within the meaning of the Eighth Amendment," lower courts had ample experience with these issues. He noted that prisons in at least twenty-four states, and sometimes entire prison systems, had been declared unconstitutional by the lower courts and commended the oversight as "*indispensable* if constitutional dictates—not to mention considerations of basic humanity—are to be observed in the prisons."[77] The Brennan opinion then recounted some of the more horrific conditions found by lower courts. They included Judge Frank Johnson's findings with respect to Alabama's prisons, which were infested with bugs and vermin and declared by a health officer as "wholly unfit for human habitation." Incarcerated people had to sleep on mattresses put out on the floor of hallways or next to toilets. In one case, two hundred men shared a single toilet. Violence was rampant. Justice Brennan noted that "the Alabama example is neither aberrational nor anachronistic" and included a footnote with a long list of cases finding unconstitutional conditions in the lower courts.

The concurring opinion chastised the majority opinion for suggesting that courts in these cases had been "overeager to usurp the task of running prisons" or that they were "order[ing] creation of 'comfortable prisons,'" as the majority put it. Instead, Justice Brennan's opinion quoted a lower court decision that noted "the soul-chilling inhumanity of conditions in American prisons ha[d] been thrust upon the judicial conscience" and required judicial oversight for compliance with the Constitution. Indeed, the political environment made court oversight a necessity. While one could respect the need to defer to legislatures and prison administrators about the operation of prisons, "many conditions of confinement . . . including overcrowding, poor sanitation, and inadequate safety precautions, arise from neglect rather than policy." In a footnote, the concurrence went still further and observed that "sad experience has shown that sometimes [state legislatures and prison officials] can *in fact* be insensitive" to constitutional requirements. The concurring opinion pointed out that "oftentimes, funding for prisons has been dramatically below that required to comply with basic constitutional standards" and had lagged behind the explosive growth in prison populations in the 1970s. The political reality, the concurring justices observed, is that incarcerated people lack political power, and the public is generally apathetic to their plight. This puts "even conscientious prison officials" in a tough spot because they lack the resources to comply with constitutional requirements. "Insulated as they are from political pressures, and charged with the duty of enforcing the Constitution, courts are in the strongest position to insist that unconstitutional conditions be remedied."[78] Indeed, the concurrence commented, that is why prison officials have often welcomed court involvement.

The concurring opinion then set out some guideposts for lower courts in these cases. Courts need to "examine the totality of the circumstances" and not just consider conditions in isolation. Expert opinion, through testimony and studies, is a valuable resource for the courts evaluating conditions. Justice Brennan's opinion admitted that the standard for reviewing conditions was far from precise, given the nature of an inquiry focused on dignity, decency, and basic notions of humanity. Citing a lower court case from New Hampshire, he urged courts to conduct this inquiry by focusing on "the effect upon the imprisoned" and asking if "the cumulative impact of the conditions of incarceration threatens the physical, mental, and emotional health and well-being of the inmates and/or creates a probability of recidivism and future incarceration."[79]

One could read most of Justice Brennan's concurrence and expect it to be a dissent given everything it says about the role of the judiciary in making sure prison conditions are constitutional. After it states the standards courts should use in reviewing claims from incarcerated people, it is hard to see how these justices did not dissent. The trial court judge looked at the totality of the circumstances and relied on a consensus of experts that the amount of space given to incarcerated people in this facility because of double bunking would cause physical and mental hardship. Justice Brennan did not harbor "the slightest doubt that 63 feet of cell space is not enough for two men" and conceded that "every major study of living space in prisons has so concluded."

Why, then, did these justices vote with the majority and reverse the decision in this case? A footnote seems to provide the answer: "If it were true that any prison providing less than 63 square feet of cell space per inmate were a *per se* violation of the Eighth Amendment, then approximately two-thirds of all federal, state, and local inmates today would be unconstitutionally confined."[80] Thus, even though there was not enough living space in this prison to avoid serious physical and mental health consequences, these justices were afraid they would be putting the courts on a path to saying the same thing about most of the nation's prisons, and the resistance to such a decision would have been tremendous. States could not build prisons fast enough to make up the shortfall in space, and massive releases would lead to a backlash against the Court. These justices may have decided it was not worth using the Court's political capital in this case.[81] Lucasville, after all, was better than most. The concurrence candidly admitted that "this prison, crowded though it is, is one of the better, more humane large prisons in the Nation." They may have therefore rationalized that their energy was better spent trying to encourage lower courts to focus on prisons and jails in worse shape. By distinguishing Lucasville from those facilities, they may have believed they would have more credibility with the majority and judges around the country that they were sensitive to the pressures on state officials while also balancing constitutional rights. They also left a path for a different outcome in this case on a fuller record because they based their decision on the fact that the district court judge did not "identify any actual signs" that the double celling had yet "reached the point of causing serious injury."[82] Their message to lower courts seemed to be that it was important to create a strong record before finding unconstitutional conditions but that courts should continue taking on that important task. They rejected crowding as per se unconstitutional, but they did their best to reinforce those pursuing constitutional challenges based on the totality of the circumstances.[83]

Justice Marshall was alone in recognizing the unconstitutional conditions at Lucasville on the record before the Court. He immediately set out in his dissent to correct the misperception created by the Court's opinion about what life in the SOCF was like. The prison, he noted, "is overcrowded, unhealthful, and dangerous." He further observed that this was not because state or prison officials made a "considered policy judgment" about "the best way to run the prison" or because officials decided they needed to operate this way as a matter of discipline or security. Rather, he noted, those same officials agree that double celling people in prison is undesirable. "The *only* reason double celling was imposed," he went on, "was that more individuals were sent there than the prison was ever designed to hold."[84] The notion that the judiciary needed to defer to the state's expertise was therefore, in his view, misplaced. The case was really about inadequate funding and resources, which should not excuse a constitutional violation.

Justice Marshall further emphasized there was ample support in the record for the district court's conclusions that the conditions were cruel and unusual. The prison was far above its design capacity, and two-thirds of the people serving sentences there were serving long terms, many of which were life sentences. Moreover, there was no evidence that the double celling was a temporary phenomenon. These incarcerated people would spend most of their time each day for decades in confined and cramped spaces that, after accounting for the furniture in a cell, gave each person "an area about the size of a typical door."[85] The district court properly concluded in these circumstances, in Justice Marshall's view, that "long exposure to these conditions will '*necessarily*' involve 'excess limitations of general movement as well as physical and mental injury.'"[86] There was "no reason to set aside the concurrent conclusions of two courts that the overcrowding and double celling here in issue are sufficiently severe that they will, if left unchecked, cause deterioration in respondents' mental and physical health."[87]

Justice Marshall then turned to the Court's "unfortunate dicta that may be read as a warning to federal courts against interference with a State's operation of its prisons." He was particularly concerned about this language from the majority: "In discharging this oversight responsibility, however, courts cannot assume that state legislatures and prison officials are insensitive to the requirements of the Constitution or to the perplexing sociological problems of how best to achieve the goals of the penal function in the criminal justice system: to punish justly, to deter future crime, and to return imprisoned persons to society with an improved chance of being useful, law-abiding citizens." Justice Marshall worried that, "if taken too literally, the majority's admonition might eviscerate the federal courts' traditional role of preventing a State from imposing cruel and unusual punishment through its conditions of confinement." He found this dictum irrelevant in the current case because "no one contends that the State had those goals in mind when it permitted SOCF to become overcrowded." More generally, he worried that the Court's language "takes far too limited a view of the proper role of a federal court in an Eighth Amendment proceeding" and "far too sanguine a view of the motivations of state legislators and prison officials." The federal courts, he noted, "are required by the Constitution" to step in "when conditions are deplorable and the political process offers no redress." Those circumstances are far from rare, given "the current climate" of rising crime rates and "an alarming tendency toward a simplistic penological philosophy that if we lock the prison doors and throw away the keys, our streets will somehow be safe." In this environment, Justice Marshall noted, "it is unrealistic to expect legislators to care whether prisons are overcrowded or harmful to inmate health." In contrast to the majority, he noted that "too often, state governments truly are 'insensitive to the requirements of the Eighth Amendment,' as evidenced by the repeated need for federal intervention."[88]

The Aftermath of *Rhodes*

Justice Marshall and the concurring justices were right to worry about the effect of the Court's opinion in *Rhodes* on judicial oversight over prison conditions and therefore on prison conditions themselves. The lower courts picked up on the Supreme Court's admonition to defer to prison officials. After *Rhodes*, "plaintiffs bringing constitutional claims in federal court can expect to win only in the most extreme cases, leaving the prison environment largely free of judicial regulation."[89]

Rampant overcrowding followed in the wake of *Rhodes*. The situation in Ohio of sharp prison population increases and not enough space was hardly an outlier. Rapid prison population growth was happening throughout the country, as states and the federal government increased sentences and limited parole opportunities—trends that would continue unabated for decades. States quickly picked up on the Supreme Court's cue that it was uninterested in both overcrowding and protecting incarcerated people from physical safety threats and mental deterioration. States thus felt free to let their prison populations skyrocket because *Rhodes* "wound up providing constitutional cover for prison officials nationwide to respond to ever-increasing prison populations by jamming two people into cells built to the minimum adequate specifications for a single person."[90] They built some new prisons, but they did not keep pace with the increase in the incarcerated population. For example, between 1979 and 1984, states opened 138 new prisons and renovated others, increasing their prison space by 29 percent. During that same time frame, however, the population grew by 45 percent; thus, there was an 11 percent decrease in the average square feet of space per incarcerated person.[91] The same dynamic occurred at the federal level. From the end of 1940 to 1980, the federal prison population held steady with minimal fluctuations, at approximately 24,000 people. Starting in fiscal year 1980, it began an unabated rise. In fiscal year 1981, federal prisons were 11 percent over capacity. Five years later, they were 49 percent over capacity, and by 1990, they were a whopping 69 percent over capacity. Federal prisons were bursting at the seams even though the number of federal prisons increased from 43 in 1981 to 64 in 1990.[92] The population went from 25,000 in fiscal year 1980 to more than 205,000 in fiscal year 2015.[93] The building could not keep pace with the incarceration rate rise. Instead of seeking ways to stop the population tide from rising, which they would have been forced to do had the Supreme Court policed design capacity and insisted on adequate living space, these jurisdictions simply crammed more and more people into smaller and smaller spaces. *Rhodes* gave them a license to incarcerate at what was effectively a constitutional discount.

Prison law experts agree that *Rhodes* was a linchpin of mass incarceration. Malcolm Feeley and Ed Rubin note that the case was the turning point in judicial reform of prisons.[94] Justin Driver and Emma Kaufman believe a different outcome in *Rhodes* could have been "an impediment to the explosion in American incarceration rates that began in the 1980s."[95] Jonathan Simon views *Rhodes* as "the last chance to stop mass incarceration in its tracks" and argues that, "had *Rhodes* come out the other way, mass incarceration would likely not have happened."[96] Judith Resnik explains that "*Rhodes* is foundational to the expansion of incarceration because, by not enforcing architectural capacity rules, the opinion enabled states to prosecute more people without internalizing the costs of confinement in appropriate spaces."[97] If the Court held states to one person per cell, "the escalation of people being sent to prison and the lengthiness of sentences would have been stopped in its tracks by a hard constitutional line that states could never have afforded to overtake through prison building."[98] If the Court in *Rhodes* disallowed double celling for those serving long-term sentences, states would be forced to reform their sentencing and parole laws to stem the tide of people flowing into their facilities. Without that pressure, the floodgates remained open.

Overcrowding "tended to erode many of the gains in prison conditions" from the prison lawsuits that were successful, and deteriorating conditions helped fuel a cycle of recidivism because people exited prisons worse off than when they arrived.[99] Overcrowding taxed the prison infrastructure around the country, increasing maintenance costs, decimating staff-to-incarcerated-person ratios, and overwhelming the already limited programming. Two or three people now routinely reside in cells designed for one person. Other spaces in the prison, like classrooms, chapels, hallways, and gymnasiums, have been co-opted for bed space. Some facilities have used tent camps or trailer parks in prison yards. "Training and rehabilitation programs have been either overwhelmed with participants or restricted to small fractions of eligible [people], and prison officials have been compelled to shift from management to coping strategies."[100] *Rhodes* thus paved the way for "hyperchronic" overcrowding, which is both extreme in density and long-lasting. "Overcrowding forces all considerations other than security inside the prison to recede." Even when new prisons were built, they "lacked serious attention to health, education, or treatment" and were instead "supersized containers for prisoners of various risk levels."[101]

Although the Supreme Court has couched its extraordinary deference to prison officials as necessary because of the difficult task prison officials have in maintaining security and order, overcrowding is not one of those security choices.[102] Indeed, it is neither a decision made by prison officials nor is it beneficial for security. It thus falls well outside the bounds of the usual reasons the Court gives for deference in prison cases. Overcrowding is the consequence of legislative decisions about bail, sentencing, parole, and budgets. It is not a considered choice about prison management but the byproduct of legislators failing to think about the long-term consequences of their tough-on-crime policies and their desire to spend as little money as possible. Prison officials have no choice but to live with the consequences of those legislative choices, accept those detained pretrial or sentenced to incarceration, and find some place for them to be held in their existing facilities. They would not choose to operate under crowded conditions, as those conditions make their jobs more stressful. In fact, prison officials have often supported lawsuits challenging overcrowded conditions and have used them as leverage with their political overseers to get more resources.[103] It is not just high-level officials who dislike overcrowding. Correctional officers are more likely to keep working in facilities with single occupancy cells than those with double bunking.[104] The Court's deference in this context is thus not to prison expertise or management but to legislative malfeasance.

Once overcrowding exists, it forces prison officials to try to manage excessive populations to keep a facility safe and secure. Studies find that rule infractions, particularly assaults, increase as the amount of space per incarcerated person decreases in a prison. This is especially true with younger prison populations.[105] As prisons become tougher to manage because of those violations, prison officials adopt tougher measures in response. For example, prison officials have justified their use of solitary confinement as necessary to address threats posed by overcrowded facilities. "Hyper-isolation travel[s] with hyper-density," with the number of people in solitary increasing as prisons become more crowded.[106] Lockdowns become commonplace. Programming and the provision of needed medical and mental health care diminishes, not only because there are not enough resources for everyone but also because moving people around facilities becomes more dangerous.[107] The mind-numbing idleness increases tensions in the facility and creates more opportunities for violence.

In some cases, this vicious cycle reaches a breaking point. Lucasville, the prison at issue in *Rhodes,* is a case in point. It was the site of a deadly prison riot in 1993. On Easter Sunday that year, 450 incarcerated people in the facility took hold of the facility for eleven days. At the time the riot broke out, Lucasville housed 1,820 people in a facility originally designed for 1,540, and 840 people were sharing cells that were designed for single occupancy. The inevitable tensions from such crowded conditions were exacerbated when a new warden, hired in response to a recent violent incident in the prison, instituted draconian measures including a major curtailment of programs and more limited and tightly controlled movement outside of cells.[108] These tensions came to a head the day before the prison was going to mandate tests for tuberculosis. Some of the incarcerated people were Muslims who had religious objections to the testing and objected to the warden's refusal to make accommodations for them. Some of these individuals, with the help of other incarcerated people, forcibly overwhelmed the guards and took control of the L block of the prison. By the time security officers regained control of the facility, ten people had died, including one corrections officer. The occupation of the prison ended when the prison officials agreed to consider the prisoners' demands.[109] Many of these demands were directly related to overcrowding, including explicit requests to reduce overcrowded conditions, to address inadequate accommodations in public spaces, and to limit double celling.[110] Thirty years after the riot, however, conditions do seem to have appreciably improved in Ohio prisons. Cynthia Davis, the current warden of Lucasville, says the practice of double celling there has ended, and the prison has renewed its focus on programming.[111] However, Ohio prisons on the whole remain seriously overcrowded, with the total prison population at 43,820 in a prison system designed to incarcerate about 37,000 people.[112]

The riot at Lucasville was far from the first or last rooted in problems from overcrowding. The 1971 Attica Prison riot, one of the deadliest and most infamous prison rebellions, was also caused in large part due to conditions created as a result of overcrowding. When the riot began, Attica had a prison population of 2,250 in a facility designed to hold 1,600 people.[113] As a result, incarcerated people spent at least fourteen hours a day in their cells, did not have access to adequate medical care, and were regularly limited to one shower a week and one roll of toilet paper a month.[114] In the course of the riot and the excessively violent retaking of the prison by state troopers, 39 people—29 incarcerated people and 10 corrections officers—died, making it the deadliest prison conflict since the Civil War.[115] Overcrowded conditions were also at the root of a riot in 2009 at the California Institution for Men in Chino, California. At the time of the riot, the facility designed to hold 3,000 people had a population of 5,000, resulting in egregiously inadequate medical and mental health care. The riot lasted four hours, left more than 240 incarcerated people injured, completely destroyed one of the prison units by fire, and ended up inflicting approximately $5.2 million in damages to the prison.[116]

Overcrowding causes extraordinary harm even when it does not lead to riots. The empirical evidence presented in *Rhodes* on the mental and physical health effects of overcrowding has been more than borne out by actual experience and subsequent studies. Dense populations put pressure on every aspect of the prison, from maintaining sanitary conditions to evacuating people safely in the event of a fire or other emergency. Overcrowding takes a toll on the physical plant, leading facilities to become uninhabitable sooner than they would without such a strain on the infrastructure.[117] It facilitates the transmission of diseases, which COVID made painfully clear. The physical and mental toll of overcrowding and double bunking has also been demonstrated, as overcrowded facilities have higher rates of illness, suicide, psychiatric commitments, and violent deaths.[118] This is exacerbated, as it was in Lucasville, by the prevalence of incarcerated people with preexisting mental illnesses.

Overcrowding and the lack of adequate care create a vicious cycle of recidivism. The pervasive violence and threat of violence in overcrowded spaces leads individuals to engage in aggressive behaviors and constantly live on edge, which impedes their ability to successfully readjust when they reenter society after serving their prison terms. People with mental health needs go into prisons to be warehoused, not treated, and they live in crowded, dangerous conditions that often make them worse off than when they came in. Corrections officers focus almost exclusively on security, and that "emergency/security ethos feeds back into a corrections culture among staff that emphasizes weapons, riot suppression, and labeling of prisoners as threats without human features or vulnerabilities."[119] This makes "degrading treatment . . . a routine feature of imprisonment in America, a factor that may explain why our recidivism rates are roughly twice what they were in the 1970s."[120]

As prison conditions have grown ever more crowded and dangerous, the Supreme Court has sat on the sidelines in the decades after *Rhodes*. To the extent it has intervened, it has been to make the doctrinal landscape worse. For example, in *Wilson v. Seiter*, decided in 1991, Justice Scalia wrote an opinion for himself and four other justices (Chief Justice Rehnquist and Justices O'Connor, Kennedy, and Souter) responding to a claim of overcrowding, inadequate ventilation, excessive temperatures, and other unconstitutional conditions by announcing that the test for all unconstitutional prison conditions claims would henceforth require not only objective evidence that the deprivations or risks of harm were sufficiently serious but also proof that prison officials acted with a sufficiently culpable state of mind. While the Court endorsed that subjective standard in *Gamble* when it addressed a claim related to the provision of medical care, it did not impose such a requirement in either *Rhodes* or *Hutto*.[121] Justice White made this latter point in his separate opinion in *Wilson*, which was joined by Justices Marshall, Blackmun, and Stevens, noting that "*Rhodes* makes it crystal clear" that the test is "only the objective severity, not the subjective intent of government officials." Justice White's opinion took issue with the claim in the majority opinion that if the pain or deprivation at issue "is not formally meted out *as punishment* by the statute or the sentencing judge, some mental element must be attributed to the inflicting officer before it can qualify" as punishment under the Eighth Amendment. Justice White noted that the "conditions are themselves *part of the punishment.*" When a state elects to "use imprisonment as a form of punishment, a State must ensure that the conditions in its prisons comport with the 'contemporary standards of decency' required by the Eighth Amendment."

Justice White also explained why functionally it made no sense to shift to a subjective standard for all conditions cases. "Inhumane prison conditions often are the result of cumulative actions and inactions by numerous officials inside and outside a prison, sometimes over a long period of time." He worried, in particular, that prison officials would defend challenges to inhumane conditions by arguing that they were the result of "insufficient funding from the state legislature rather than by any deliberate indifference on the part of the prison officials."[122] Justice Marshall pointed out similar problems with a focus on punitive intent in the context of due process challenges to pretrial detention conditions in his dissent in *Bell v. Wolfish*. He noted that, "by its terms, the Due Process Clause focuses on the nature of deprivations, not on the persons inflicting them. If this concern is to be vindicated, it is the effect of conditions of confinement, not the intent behind them, that must be the focal point of constitutional analysis."[123] The Court in *Wilson* nevertheless endorsed this additional subjective hurdle in any conditions challenge, not just those involving the failure to provide adequate medical care, thus making it still harder for incarcerated people to challenge their confinement conditions.

The Court followed up a couple years later in *Farmer v. Brennan* to specify that the deliberate indifference test was not satisfied if a risk was so obvious that it should have been known (an objective mental standard) but instead requires that the relevant official be aware that there is a substantial risk to an incarcerated person's health or safety and disregard it to be liable.[124] Justice Blackmun wrote separately in *Farmer* to state his view that *Wilson* was wrong and should be overruled. Punishment, he explained, does not require "a culpable state of mind on the part of an identifiable punisher" but should instead be focused on the experiences of the person receiving it." The "punishment is simply no less cruel or unusual because its harm is unintended." He also pointed out that the focus on prison officials is misguided because, "where a legislature refuses to fund a prison adequately, the resulting barbaric conditions should not be immune from constitutional scrutiny simply because no prison official acted culpably." It should not matter whether it is the legislature or the prison official that caused the harm because "the experience of the [incarcerated person] is the same."[125] Under the new subjective framework of *Wilson* and *Farmer*, however, attention is diverted from the conditions in prisons and their effect on incarcerated people to the mindset of prison officials.

Brown v. Plata and a Glimpse of the Road Not Taken

There is little left of the Eighth Amendment under the Supreme Court's watch. But even the Supreme Court has a breaking point, and the state of California pushed that limit, finally getting the Court to take a stand for the Constitution on the horrific effects of overcrowding. The Court's decision in *Brown v. Plata* offers a hint of what the world might look like if the Court consistently upheld the Constitution in cases of gross prison overcrowding.

California's prison population grew 750 percent since the 1970s when it shifted to a determinate sentencing model of longer sentences, widespread use of mandatory minimums, much more limited use of parole, and strict policies for parole violations.[126] California's prison budget allocations did not keep up with the rise in its incarceration rates, and the result was excessive overcrowding.[127] The overcrowding was so bad that then governor Arnold Schwarzenegger issued a Prison Overcrowding State of Emergency Proclamation in 2006 because all thirty-three of the state's prisons were operating at or above their maximum capacity, and twenty-nine of the prisons were, in the words of the governor, "so overcrowded that the [California Department of Corrections and Rehabilitation (CDCR)] is required to house more than 15,000 [people] in conditions that pose substantial safety risks, namely, prison areas never designed or intended for . . . housing, including, but not limited to, common areas such as prison gymnasiums, dayrooms, and program rooms, with approximately 1,500 [people] sleeping in triple-bunks." The proclamation noted that the overcrowding in these twenty-nine facilities posed health and safety risks, including an increased risk of violence and disease transmission. The excess population also "overwhelmed the electrical systems and/or wastewater/sewer systems," resulting in blackouts, sewage spills, and environmental contamination.[128]

The conditions in California's prisons were the subject of years of litigation, and two class actions eventually reached the Supreme Court in *Brown v. Plata*. One case involved a class of incarcerated people with serious mental health problems. In 1995, after a trial that lasted over a month, a federal court found "overwhelming evidence of the systemic failure to deliver necessary care to mentally ill" people in California's prisons. The court noted that the prisons were "seriously and chronically understaffed" and that people with serious mental illnesses "languish for months, or even years, without access to necessary care."[129]

The second action involved a class of people with serious medical conditions. After they challenged the inadequate treatment they were receiving in 2001, the state conceded the Eighth Amendment violation and agreed to a remedial injunction. It was "an uncontested fact" that, on average, an incarcerated person "needlessly dies" in one of California's prisons "every six to seven days due to constitutional deficiencies" in the prisons' delivery of medical care. The court found that "the California prison medical care system is broken beyond repair" and leads to an "unconscionable degree of suffering and death." When the state failed to meet the terms of the remedial injunction, the court appointed a receiver in 2005. The receiver noted that overcrowding was impeding efforts to remedy the violations. Overcrowding made it difficult to hire and retain competent staff, resulted in "day to day operation chaos," increased the incidence and transmission of infectious diseases, and "led to rising prison violence and greater reliance on custodial staff on lockdowns," which in turn "inhibits the delivery of medical care."[130]

The state's failure to remedy the problems identified in both cases over a span of more than a decade prompted the plaintiffs to request a three-judge district court to be convened under the Prison Litigation Reform Act (PLRA) because only such a court could enter an order limiting the prison population. The plaintiffs believed an order mandating a reduction in the prison population was necessary to remedy the unconstitutional conditions associated with the delivery of medical and mental health care because overcrowding was the primary cause of the problems and all other reform efforts short of a population reduction had failed.[131] Even the California Correctional Peace Officers Association agreed a reduction order was appropriate given the danger of overcrowding to everyone inside the facility.[132] The three-judge district court panel considering both cases together agreed, concluding that "overcrowding strains inadequate medical and mental health facilities; overburdens limited clinical and custodial staff; and creates violent, unsanitary, and chaotic conditions that contribute to the constitutional violations and frustrate efforts to fashion a remedy."[133] Among other evidence at trial was the assessment of the former head of corrections in Texas, who described California's prison conditions as "inhumane" and "appalling" and noted that he had "never seen anything like it" in his "more than 35 years of prison work experience."[134]

Ample evidence supported the three-judge panel's conclusions. Overcrowding impeded the ability to provide adequate care in a number of ways. Without enough treatment beds for those with serious mental illnesses, some incarcerated people at risk for suicide were held for prolonged periods in "telephone-booth-sized cages without toilets." Others were held in administrative segregation, waiting as long as a year to receive mental health care. Many of these individuals died of suicide while awaiting treatment. The suicide rate in California's prisons was almost 80 percent higher than the national average for prison populations. A special master investigating and reviewing facilities in California found that "some measure of inadequate assessment, treatment, or intervention" was involved in 72.1 percent of the suicides; thus, they were "most probably foreseeable and/or preventable."

Similar problems existed for those with physical illnesses. The prisons had backlogs of up to seven hundred people waiting for medical care. They lacked clinical space available for treatment. Medical staff had to "operate out of converted storage rooms, closets, bathrooms, shower rooms, and visiting centers." As many as fifty sick incarcerated people would be held together in a twelve-by-twenty-foot cage for up to five hours waiting to see someone for their illnesses. People experienced prolonged illnesses and unnecessary pain because of the inadequate treatment, and as with the suicides, an expert reviewing the situation in California's prisons found the ratio of "possibly preventable or preventable" deaths was "extremely high," with a "preventable or possibly preventable death occur[ring] once every five to six days" in 2006 and 2007, the last years for which the three-judge panel had data. Overcrowding also fostered unsafe and unsanitary conditions. For example, in some facilities, as many as fifty-four people shared a single toilet. The prisons were "breeding grounds for disease." The "crowded, unsafe, and unsanitary conditions" could cause some conditions to worsen and impeded the ability to provide care.[135]

California's correctional facilities at the time of the three-judge order had almost double the number they were designed to hold, with approximately 156,000 people in prisons designed to house just under 80,000 people. This was not a new development. The prisons in California were at roughly 200 percent of their capacity for over a decade. The three-judge court ordered a reduction to 137.5 percent of the system's design capacity, which would require a reduction of between 38,000 and 46,000 people in the prison population.

Despite the deplorable conditions in California and the overwhelming evidence of their specific negative consequences, the incarcerated people challenging the conditions could capture only a narrow majority at the Supreme Court. The justices voted 5–4 to uphold the three-judge district court. Justice Kennedy wrote the majority opinion, which was joined by Justices Ginsburg, Breyer, Sotomayor, and Kagan. He began by noting that people in prison "retain the essence of human dignity inherent in all persons" and that "respect for that dignity animates the Eighth Amendment prohibition on cruel and unusual punishment." When a state incarcerates, it "takes from prisoners the means to provide for their own needs"; thus, the state assumes the obligation to care for those within its custody. "A prison that deprives prisoners of basic sustenance, including adequate medical care, is incompatible with the concept of human dignity and has no place in civilized society." While the opinion acknowledged the need for courts to defer to the expertise of prison officials, it noted that "courts nevertheless must not shrink from their obligation" to protect constitutional rights.

The majority also observed that the remedial order to reduce the prison population had not been taken lightly. Efforts to remedy the unconstitutional provision of medical care had been ongoing for nine years, and remedial efforts to improve the provision of mental health care had been ongoing for sixteen years by the time the Supreme Court heard the case. Justice Kennedy thus observed that, while "at one time, it may have been possible to hope that these violations would be cured without a reduction in overcrowding," the "long history of failed remedial orders, together with substantial evidence of overcrowding's deleterious effects on the provision of care, compels a different conclusion today." The Court also took judicial notice of the "political and fiscal reality" of California's unwillingness to "allocate the resources necessary to meet this crisis" through other steps, particularly in the midst of a budget shortfall.[136]

Whereas the Court came out the other way in *Rhodes* because it doubted the studies cited by the district court showing the harm overcrowding wreaks, here the Court had living proof for more than a decade that all those studies were correct. If this record was not enough to justify a prison population cap, it is hard to see what would.

In spite of the mounds of evidence, four justices still could not find an Eighth Amendment violation on these facts. These four conservative dissenters—three of whom are on the current Court—represent what is likely the majority sentiment on the Court today. Justice Scalia penned a dissent, joined by Justice Thomas, that is dripping with contempt for people in prison and any role for courts in maintaining minimal standards. He would require members of the class to each show they have suffered a grievous injury.[137] The dissent does not seem to recognize a substantial risk of injury as sufficient even though prior cases consistently recognize this as a viable ground for an Eighth Amendment claim.[138] The Scalia dissent's bigger beef was with the remedial order, which he called "the most radical injunction issued by a court in our Nation's history."[139] Justice Scalia seemed offended that the remedial order might incidentally benefit those outside the class because, while reducing the overcrowding problem would address the deficiencies in medical and mental health care provision, the people released might not be in the class itself. Justice Scalia posited that "many will undoubtedly be fine physical specimens who have developed intimidating muscles pumping iron in the prison gym," conjuring imagery of violent people living a life of leisure that was completely at odds with the hellscape that constituted life in California's prisons and the vulnerable people suffering as a result of its excessive population.[140] His more fundamental disagreement was with structural injunctions in general, which he believed transformed "judges into long-term administrators of complex social institutions such as schools, prisons, and police departments."[141] An injunction that releases people from prison really piqued his anger, as he warned of "the inevitable murders, robberies, and rapes to be committed."[142] Justice Scalia admitted at the end of his dissent that his view "may invite the objection that the PLRA appears to contemplate structural injunctions in general and mass prisoner-release orders in particular." The PLRA does far more than "appear to contemplate" injunctions. It lists the specific requirements for such injunctions, including prisoner release orders. The PLRA was designed to dramatically limit the ability of incarcerated people to bring lawsuits, so it was not as if Congress did not know how to place limits where it believed they were needed. All of the PLRA's onerous requirements were met in this case.

Justice Scalia's dissent thus amounts to a disagreement with the Eighth Amendment and the PLRA. Ironically, given his view that a prisoner-release order "raise[s] grave separation-of-powers concerns and veer[s] significantly from the historical role and institutional capability of the courts," it is his dissent that is an example of those very shortcomings. He may disagree with the Eighth Amendment and the PLRA as a policy matter, but it is his duty as a judge to enforce them. If Congress sets out the specific requirements for structural injunctions, it is not his place to disagree and "bend every effort to read the law in such a way as to avoid" what he believes are "outrageous result[s]" when those are the very results contemplated by the statute. That was hardly his theory of statutory interpretation in any other context. It is the job of a judge to read the PLRA and the Constitution as written. Justice Scalia, however, seemed to be trying to resurrect his own version of the "hands-off" doctrine.

Justice Alito wrote a separate dissent, joined by Chief Justice Roberts. Justice Alito's dissent did not take issue with the findings of Eighth Amendment violations or that overcrowding was a contributing factor. His dispute was with the remedial order, which he warned was "very likely to have a major and deleterious effect on public safety." As he described the order, "the equivalent of three Army divisions" were going to flow from the prisons and "lead to a grim roster of victims."[143] This fear led him to conclude that California's noncompliance over nine and sixteen years, respectively, in the two cases, which produced seventy-two judicial orders, was somehow not enough, and more needed to be tried before the release order was issued. Even though experts testified before the three-judge panel that prison populations could be reduced without adversely affecting public safety and offered numerous examples from many states and Canada,[144] Justice Alito called it a "fundamental and dangerous error" for the trial court to rely on that testimony. He argued that "a more cautious court, less bent on implementing its own criminal justice agenda, would have at least acknowledged that the consequences of this massive prisoner release cannot be ascertained in advance with any degree of certainty."[145] That Justice Alito saw the lower court as "implementing its own criminal justice agenda" instead of protecting vaunted Eighth Amendment rights is telling. Under his view, it was just too risky to enforce the Constitution and, apparently, the PLRA, as written. He would have created a new appellate standard of review that does not give deference to lower courts that rely on expert testimony about crime prevention and public safety. In Justice Alito's estimation, the three-judge panel did not give sufficient weight to public safety, as the PLRA requires, because it did not reach the same conclusion he would have reached.[146]

The perceived public safety risk to enforcing the Constitution has been the running theme throughout all of the wrong turns by the Court explored in previous chapters. It led the Court to flout the presumption of innocence and condone massive pretrial detention, to allow prosecutors to place unconstitutional conditions on the exercise of the jury trial right to churn millions of cases on minimal resources, and to turn a blind eye to disproportionately harsh sentences. As Chapter 5 shows, it also drove the Court's decision to permit the police to seize and search people on less than probable cause. The Constitution was designed to guard against the hysteria of the moment and protect enduring rights from panics over public safety. But the Constitution will not work if it is being enforced by justices who harbor those same fears and fall prey to the same anticrime frenzy as the public.

Plata offers a glimpse of what it looks like when the Court does its job and is not crippled by the fear of what happens when constitutional rights are enforced. Justice Alito ended his dissent by saying he "hope[s] that I am wrong" about his dire predictions of crime run amok from the release order and noted that, "in a few years, we will see."[147] It has now been more than a decade since *Plata* was decided, so we can, in fact, take stock and see.

Justice Alito's dire public safety predictions were proved wrong. The remedial order gave the state flexibility to determine how to reduce the prison population to 137.5 percent of its rated capacity, and the state opted for a plan that relied on county jails to take some of the incarcerated people from the prisons, known as the Public Safety Realignment Plan. Specifically, the realignment plan provided that people who were serving time for "non-violent, non-serious, non-sex offenses" and who had not previously been convicted of such offenses would serve their sentences in local county jails as opposed to state prison. In addition, instead of sending parolees who violated the terms of their parole to state prison, the plan created the option of sending those not serving life sentences to county jail for up to 180 days or of using alternatives like house arrest or drug treatment.[148] Two months after passage, California's total incarceration rate fell to its lowest level in twenty years, with no significant changes in recidivism.[149] By 2015, California was able to meet its mandate of reducing the prison population to 137.5 percent of capacity, with an average of 135.3 percent capacity in its state prisons.[150] In contrast to the public safety concerns expressed by the *Plata* dissenters, the realignment plan had little effect on crime rates. While the crime rate increased slightly in 2012, the year following implementation, that was due mostly to an increase in auto thefts, which increased by approximately 17 percent. There was no evidence of an increase in violent crime, and crime rates overall fell again in 2013 and 2014 after that initial uptick in 2012. Moreover, auto theft rates returned to pre-realignment levels, and a 2022 study calls into question whether the brief rise in auto thefts can be traced to realignment at all.[151] In other words, California complied with *Plata* without the "major and deleterious effect on public safety" predicted by Justice Alito.[152]

That is not to say that compliance with *Plata*'s remedial order and the implementation were without flaws. Politicians did the bare minimum to comply. The shift of people from prisons to jails put a strain on local facilities and communities. Moreover, the provision of health care in the state prisons remained abysmal. Real change would require sustained judicial oversight, and even that might not be sufficient in the face of political recalcitrance. The populist pressures that produce mass incarceration do not go away in the face of a court order, so it is not as if greater judicial involvement provides a magic fix overnight.

That said, *Plata* gives us a possible answer to the question, "What if the Court decided *Rhodes* differently?" Setting a prison population cap sparked California to take action, and that action reduced human misery without sacrificing public safety. It was not a panacea, but it was an improvement. Nor is California an outlier. Other states have achieved similar public safety outcomes while reducing prison populations. For example, many states tried to keep prison costs in check by establishing sentencing commissions and ordering them to promulgate sentencing guidelines that would keep prison populations within a certain percentage of existing capacity. States that have pursued this model reaped the benefits of saving money, lowering incarceration rates, and enjoying improved or undiminished public safety. These states, however, have achieved more modest gains than California in terms of prison population reduction because their legislatures set the limits based on their appetite for fiscal spending. California's limits were more sweeping because they were set by the judiciary and based on minimally decent constitutional conditions. If the Court was adequately policing minimal space requirements to protect the health and safety of incarcerated people in all cases, states would have to reduce far more dramatically their prison populations or go on a huge prison spending spree.

Most likely, states would respond to a requirement for minimally humane prison conditions by both reducing the incarcerated population and spending more money. State politicians did, after all, approve insane amounts of money for prisons in the 1980s and 1990s, and they continue to face incentives to build facilities in struggling communities.[153] Moreover, politicians do not want to be blamed if it looks like dangerous people are free because there is insufficient bed space. Avoiding anything that looks like an early release has been a central part of the political playbook for decades because it is so politically costly to do otherwise. If the Court had made clear in *Rhodes* that double bunking in confined spaces was unacceptable, building more facilities would certainly have been part of the strategy for compliance.

It is unlikely, however, that states would have spent the money to build as many prisons as would be needed to meet the minimal space requirements and keep prison populations as high as they are now. Their budgets are not unlimited, and we have seen how states shift criminal justice policies when the price gets too high. For example, many states took dramatic actions to reform criminal justice policies in the early 2000s to avoid taking money from other popular spending initiatives for criminal justice policies. In states with conservative political leadership, like Texas, South Carolina, and Mississippi, dramatic criminal justice reforms passed as cost savings measures.[154] Similarly, when courts did take the drastic step of ordering reductions because of overcrowding, states responded not only by building new facilities but also by providing for early release mechanisms and other sentencing changes to reduce the population.[155] Correctional reform litigators were explicit that this was one of their goals.[156]

But states have never had to pay the full constitutional price of incarceration because the Court's decision in *Rhodes* gave them the biggest discount of all by letting them double bunk, effectively giving them a constitutional two-for-one sale. States were thus never forced to make the hard choices litigants intended. That kind of cost constraint will never materialize through the political process. The lieutenant governor of Florida gave an interview in the 1980s where he stated the difficulty with prison funding: "[The public doesn't] want to spend all this money on prisoners, because the public, they'll tell you real quick ... 'put 'em in tents.' I mean they'd bury 'em all if it was up to the public."[157] There is not, to put it mildly, a great public concern with people in prison or the conditions they live under. The judiciary has to put that pressure on political decisions by enforcing the Eighth Amendment. If *Rhodes* had done so, states would have had to make different policy choices along the way to avoid running out of funds, just as California was forced to be creative in complying with the order in *Plata*. *Plata* was not the public safety disaster the dissenters predicted, and a different outcome in *Rhodes* would not have been either. Complying with the Constitution is consistent with public safety. It should not take the extreme conditions of California's prisons to get the Court to see overcrowding as a problem. Unconstitutional conditions exist in prisons and jails throughout the country, and they persist because the Court is failing to fulfill its constitutional obligation to enforce the Eighth Amendment.

CHAPTER FIVE

GREENLIGHTING STOP-AND-FRISK

Terry v. Ohio

> We must not pretend that the countless people who are routinely targeted by police are "isolated." They are the canaries in the coal mine whose deaths, civil and literal, warn us that no one can breathe in this atmosphere. They are the ones who recognize that unlawful police stops corrode all our civil liberties and threaten all our lives. Until their voices matter too, our justice system will continue to be anything but.
>
> —JUSTICE SONIA SOTOMAYOR

Mass incarceration is fueled by how many people the police stop and arrest because that is the beginning of the pipeline to jails and prisons. Anything that makes policing easier therefore contributes to mass incarceration, and there is no shortage of Supreme Court cases that twist the Constitution's meaning to give the police widespread authority. Overpolicing in America exists in part because of an interconnected web of Supreme Court decisions that fail to fully enforce constitutional limits on the police. At the center of that web is the Court's refusal to place any meaningful limit on what can be labeled a crime in the first place, because the police then have wide discretion to enforce those laws.[1] The Court has given the police still greater authority by allowing them to arrest people even when they are charged with misdemeanors that are punishable only by fines. A person can thus find themselves put in jail for something as minor as not wearing a seatbelt.[2] Still worse, the Court has condoned the police using stops for minor traffic offenses as pretexts for the investigation of more serious crimes for which they would otherwise lack the authority to forcibly stop someone.[3] Then there is the Court's almost comically loose standard for what counts as a consensual encounter or search, a doctrine that utterly ignores the power dynamics between police and the citizenry.[4] One could go on and on in identifying cases where the Court fails to keep constitutional guardrails in place when it comes to the police. The story of the Supreme Court, policing, and mass incarceration is therefore the story of multiple cases, not just one.[5]

That said, there are two reasons to take a closer look at one case, *Terry v. Ohio*, which marked the first time in the country's two-hundred-year history that the Supreme Court gave approval to having police officers forcibly stop and frisk people even without probable cause.[6] First, *Terry* stands out among the crowd of misguided policing cases because it ushered in a new era in proactive policing. *Terry* led departments to engage in the programmatic use of stops that resulted in millions of forcible police interactions. It unleashed a scale of policing never seen before in America, which in turn helped to fuel arrests and incarceration. Second, the circumstances that led the Court to decide *Terry* reflect what seemed to be happening in a range of cases where the Court bent constitutional rules for law enforcement demands. In the face of violence and widespread disorder, the Court in *Terry* conceded to those saying public safety demanded giving the police more leeway and thus constitutional lines needed to give way. *Terry* is a prime example of this capitulation because the Court's decision flouted the Constitution's text, original meaning, and subsequent history on the standard for seizures and searches.

The Constitution allows police officers to approach people and ask for information in a voluntary exchange. But when the police order people to stop and even briefly restrain their liberty of movement, it is a seizure. When they frisk people looking for a weapon, it is a search. The Fourth Amendment clearly requires "probable cause" for searches and seizures. Probable cause requires "facts and circumstances within [police officers'] knowledge and of which they had reasonably trustworthy information [that are] sufficient in themselves to warrant a man of reasonable caution in the belief that an offense has been or is being committed."[7] It is usually based on forensics, witnesses, informants, and outwardly culpable behavior by the target.[8] The law enforcement argument in *Terry*, however, was that officers should be able to stop and frisk people based on the suspicions they have given their expertise in the field. They asked the Court, in the words of the legal historian Sarah

Seo, to "legalize what had been unlawful under the centuries-long common law of arrests, which required probable cause for all seizures and searches of persons."[9]

The Court had never faced this question before *Terry* because it had no occasion to do so. Local police did not face any consequences for their forcible stops no matter what standard they used to justify them until 1961. That was the year the Court decided the landmark case of *Mapp v. Ohio*,[10] which required state courts to exclude evidence that the police obtained in violation of the Fourth Amendment. Moreover, it was not until the 1950s and 1960s that police departments started to use stops and frisks as part of a new vision of policing as a proactive crime-fighting enterprise.[11] Even then, departments were largely using it on a case-by-case basis as individual officers confronted suspicious activity on their beat patrols.

The *Terry* case required the Court to confront this new trend and decide whether to stop it in its tracks as violating the Constitution if based on anything less than probable cause or whether to find a way to accommodate a practice that the police claimed was an important crime-fighting tool. The Court opted for the latter and permitted stops and frisks on the basis of a new, less stringent standard: reasonable suspicion. The Court itself has emphasized that this is a lenient test that is "obviously less demanding than that for probable cause" and requires only a "minimal level" of justification that is "considerably less than proof of wrongdoing by a preponderance of the evidence."[12] This low threshold gives police enormous discretion to forcibly restrain people and frisk them for weapons based on weak claims of suspicion based on their claimed expertise that a crime might be in the offing.

After *Terry*, police departments felt emboldened to expand the use of stop-and-frisk and employ it as a programmatic tactic. By the 1990s, big city police departments across America, from New York and Chicago to Baltimore and Philadelphia, embarked on strategic campaigns to stop hundreds of thousands of people each year in the poorest neighborhoods, which are predominately minority neighborhoods.[13] In Chicago, for example, the police stopped 45,000 people in one month alone in 2015, which, given the population of roughly 2.7 million people, meant a rate of twenty stops for every 100 people.[14] Multiply that across urban cities across America, and you have millions of forced interactions with the police that likely would never have occurred had the Court continued to insist on the two-hundred-year baseline of probable cause because nothing close to that number of pedestrian stops would meet the test.

Given the weak threshold, it is no wonder that stops and frisks have abysmally low hit rates at finding weapons or contraband, and only a fraction of them result in arrests. In the period from 2004 to 2012, only 12 percent of the stops made by the New York Police Department (NYPD) ended in a summons or arrest, and only 1.5 percent of the frisks yielded weapons.[15] The patterns are comparable in Philadelphia, with only 7.5 percent of the stops resulting in arrests or citations and frisks producing weapons only 1 percent of the time. Similarly low hit rates exist nationwide, with frisks failing to yield weapons 98 to 99 percent of the time.[16] Random checkpoints have yielded higher hit rates than supposedly targeted stops and frisks.[17]

Nevertheless, because the overall number of stops and frisks is so enormous, even the small percentage resulting in arrests translates to a staggeringly high number of cases leading to jail and prison time. The vast majority are for low-level offenses like marijuana possession and disorderly conduct (which is often a trumped-up charge based on the incredulous response of the person being stopped for no reason) that churn 10 million people in and out of jails in a typical year while maintaining an average population on a typical day around 547,000.[18] Even if some cases are ultimately dropped, people typically spend time in jail, thus feeding the mass incarceration machine.

Although some theorists once posited massive stop-and-frisk campaigns would deter crime and lower crime rates because they would detect more crimes, empirical studies have shown that stop-and-frisk does not lead to lower crime rates.[19] That is how New York was able to drop from a peak of almost 700,000 stops per year to 12,000 stops per year—a decline of roughly 98 percent—and still see its crime rates fall.[20] One reason stop-and-frisk is not more effective is the way it damages people already living on the margins, creating at least as much harm as it prevents. Another reason is that this kind of aggressive policing leads people to stop seeing the police as legitimate. Communities stop cooperating with law enforcement and disengage, leading to more crimes going unreported and unsolved. A study of NYPD stop-and-frisk practices found, for example, that every time a person was stopped, they were "eight percent less likely to report a future violent crime against them to the police."[21] And this is all disproportionately felt in minority communities because that is where the police employ stop-and-frisk as a programmatic tactic.

Consider, for example, the way the police used stops in New York City. At its peak, the New York Police Department stopped more than two thousand people *each day*. More than 80 percent of the people stopped were Black or Latino even though they made up only slightly more than 50 percent of the population.[22] If you were a Black resident in New York City at that time, you had a 92 percent chance of being stopped at some point within a year.[23] Three examples give a flavor of what leads the police to stop someone and the effect those stops collectively have on communities.

Leroy Downs, a Black man who was in his mid-thirties when he was stopped, was standing in front of the chain-link fence of his own home on Staten Island, making a call to a friend on his cell phone using an earpiece. An unmarked police car drove past, stopped, reversed, and double-parked in front of Downs's house. Two officers got out of the car and, while approaching Downs, said in an aggressive tone that it looked like Downs was smoking pot. They pushed him backward against the fence. Downs, who is actually a drug counselor, informed the police of his profession and explained he was talking on the phone, not smoking marijuana. At that point, it should have been obvious to the officers that there was no marijuana smoke or smell. The officers, however, frisked him, patting his legs and torso, and then reached into his front and back pockets, removing all the contents. They took out a wallet, keys, and a bag of cookies. They searched his wallet. Finding nothing, they left. Downs has been stopped multiple times by the police.

Cornelio McDonald was a middle-aged Black man who had just finished visiting his mother in a public housing complex in Queens when he was stopped. McDonald was crossing a wide boulevard to go from his mother's home to his own, which was in a private co-op on the other side of the street. The majority of people who live on McDonald's side of the street are white, whereas the majority of people on his mother's side of the street are Black. McDonald was leaving his mother's home around one a.m. It was a cold night, so McDonald was wearing his jacket zipped up and had both hands in his pockets as he crossed the street. He also had a cell phone in his jacket pocket, keys in his right pants pocket, and his wallet in his back pocket. He was on an island between lanes getting ready to cross the second lane when an unmarked car with plainclothes officers pulled in front of him. The officers did not identify themselves as police. They rolled down the window and asked McDonald where he was coming from. McDonald replied by asking why he was being stopped. The officers, both of whom were white, stepped out of the car, identified themselves as police, and began to search McDonald. Finding nothing, the officers left. Later, one of the two officers said he stopped McDonald because of a suspicious bulge in his pocket and crime patterns. The crimes were robberies and burglaries reported somewhere in Queens by a Black male, but the officer could not be more specific about where those crimes occurred. The basis for stopping McDonald was nothing more than that he was a Black man who existed in the 109 square miles of New York City's largest borough and had something in his pocket.

David Ourlicht was twenty-five years old and attending school at St. John's University when he was stopped by police. Of mixed Black and white heritage, Ourlicht was walking to a deli near his dorm around two p.m. He had a five-subject notebook tucked into one of his external jacket pockets. As he made his way up the street, Officer Christopher Moran crossed paths with him on a scooter. When Ourlicht reached the intersection where Officer Moran had stopped, the officer asked what he was doing in the area and requested identification. Ourlicht inquired why he was being stopped. Officer Moran asked if Ourlicht went to school in the area, to which Ourlicht responded, "Why are you asking me this? What did I do?" Officer Moran then said it looked like Ourlicht had a gun on him and frisked him, finding no weapons. Ourlicht produced his student identification. At that point, backup officers arrived and searched all of Ourlicht's pockets. Despite finding nothing incriminating, Officer Moran gave Ourlicht a ticket for disorderly conduct, which was later dismissed.[24]

Standing in front of a house on the phone. Walking home from a family visit with hands in pockets. Getting food from a deli near a dorm in the middle of the day. These situations all aroused the suspicions of the police, at least when the people involved were people of color.

First-person accounts of people stopped by the police shed insight on what it feels like to endure these encounters and how they can escalate:

> "My jeans were ripped. I had bruises on my face. My whole face was swollen. I was sent to the precinct for disorderly conduct. I got out two days later. The charges were dismissed. . . . I felt like I couldn't defend myself, didn't know what to do. No witnesses there to see what was going on. I just wish someone was there to witness it. I felt like no one would believe me."

> "I get nervous. I get paranoid 'cause you never what's going to happen, and I don't feel safe, like especially in Queens, 'cause they just pull you from no matter, any reason. And they won't tell you anything."

> "They done mess your whole life up and this is what they do. . . . They arrest you and build up all these little, petty things . . . and after a certain time . . . you can't get [a] job."[25]

These stops alienate communities who rightly see themselves as being targeted and harassed without probable cause—indeed, often without any cause other than their skin color.

The Supreme Court had ample warning this would be the effect of a decision in *Terry* that abandoned probable cause. The NAACP Legal Defense Fund filed a brief that described in devastating detail the "ill effects of stop and frisk practices," particularly in communities of color, and how the practice, even then at the much smaller scale on which it was taking place, helped spark many of the riots and protests then engulfing the country:

> In Cincinnati, a Negro man protesting the death sentence of another Negro is arrested. In Boston, police advance with truncheons on women sitting-in at the welfare department. In Tampa, a cop shoots a Negro burglary suspect in the back after he had refused to halt. Each incident triggered violence. Stores were burned and looted, people injured. Rioting ended in Boston not because the police had dispersed crowds, but because the cops went away.... Some minor incident begins it all, often the arrest of a Negro by a policeman.[26]

Two blue-ribbon commissions had documented the racial tensions created by the aggressive and disproportionate use of the emerging practice of stops and frisks of Black people.[27] The Court was thus fully aware of the racial consequences of authorizing stop-and-frisk practices.[28] The mass use of stop-and-frisk after *Terry* predictably worsened the relationship between the police and communities of color. One can readily see the through line between *Terry* and the police violence and resulting racial justice protests of today.

It is hard to shake the feeling that the Court ignored the racially disparate harms of stop-and-frisk, abandoned probable cause, and adopted a new standard because it fell victim to the panic of the times and the claims of law enforcement that this was necessary to maintain order on the streets. It was the middle of a presidential election, and the Court itself was a central part of two of the candidates' platforms. Richard Nixon and George C. Wallace were both highly critical of the Court and some of its criminal procedure decisions. They accused the Court of "coddling criminals and handcuffing the police."[29] The public was receptive to these arguments. Polls showed a negative reaction to the Court's decision in *Miranda* placing limits on police interrogation practices and requiring the police to warn suspects in police custody of their right to remain silent. Two-thirds of the respondents to a survey about the case thought the Court made a mistake.[30] The Court's decision in *Mapp* was also wildly unpopular because it meant some guilty people would go free.[31] Indeed, other than *Brown v. Board of Education,* no other decisions of the Warren Court "more rankled southerners and other conservatives" than *Mapp* and *Miranda*. "Impeach Earl Warren" signs could be seen all across America.

At the same time, crime and violence dominated the news. The homicide rate was rising. By the time the case got to the Supreme Court, one of John Terry's codefendants at his trial had been shot and killed because he was in a shootout with the owner of a drugstore he was robbing. After the case was argued, but before it was decided, Martin Luther King Jr. was assassinated. Senator Robert Kennedy was murdered five days before the Court's decision. Massive protests against the Vietnam War and urban riots were commonplace, with significant unrest following King's killing. Many American cities were in flames, including the District of Columbia, where the Supreme Court was deliberating about what to do in *Terry*. Racial tensions were red-hot. Many African Americans were protesting precisely because of mistreatment by largely white police forces. Many white people resented the civil rights protests and advances and placed much of the blame on the Supreme Court, which was at the center of desegregation fights.[32]

The Supreme Court may have thought relaxing the standard for stops and frisks was the only way to respond to a country literally on fire and to allow the police to do what it believed was an important job of order maintenance.[33] The Constitution, however, appropriately takes the long view and does not just focus on the headlines of the day. It gets the balance right about how best to ensure public safety. The police should not be able to use force to stop or frisk someone except when there is probable cause of criminal activity. This does not mean the police cannot engage people without probable cause. It just means they cannot use force. It is a sensible approach that appropriately limits the government's use of brute force. It also directs the state to devise other strategies for battling crime and engaging in order maintenance. The Supreme Court relieved communities of thinking about alternatives and making investments outside of policing because it made the mass deployment of stop-and-frisk a readily available option. The Framers knew better. If you let the state treat every problem as one to be dealt with by brute force, it will be all too tempting to govern by fiat. Limiting policing, by contrast, forces the democratic process to build up the state in other, more productive ways.

Terry rested on the idea that constitutional rights had to be sacrificed for the benefit of law enforcement. The tragic truth is that the massive increase in police discretion *Terry* authorized in violation of the Constitution has been a critical cog in the churning machinery of mass incarceration, and we are no safer as a result.

The Constitutional Framework

Any exploration of *Terry*'s failings must begin with the Constitution's restrictions on policing. Although there was nothing like the modern police force at the nation's founding, the Framers were well aware of the dangers of agents of the state going too far in their pursuit of law enforcement. The Constitution therefore provides a variety of protections for individual rights against police interference. The Fourth Amendment provides that "the right of the people to be secure in their persons, houses, papers, and effects, against unreasonable searches and seizures, shall not be violated, and no Warrants shall issue, but upon probable cause, supported by Oath or affirmation, and particularly describing the place to be searched, and the persons or things to be seized." The first clause of the Fourth Amendment, called the Reasonableness Clause, and the second, known as the Warrant Clause, had from the time of the nation's founding until 1968 been read in pari materia, or in tandem with each other. "The Warrant Clause's standard of 'probable cause' had been taken to define the 'reasonableness' of a search and seizure, even where obtaining a warrant was excused as impracticable."[34] Thus, whether a search or seizure was supported by a warrant or fell within an exception to the warrant requirement, law enforcement had to have probable cause of criminal activity. For most of the country's history, "probable cause" meant highly likely or more likely than not. It was satisfied if "the facts and circumstances within [officers'] knowledge and of which they had reasonably trustworthy information were sufficient in themselves to warrant a man of reasonable caution" to believe that a crime occurred or is being committed.[35] Though the Court later watered down the concept of probable cause with language like "substantial basis" or "fair probability," even that more relaxed standard requires far more to justify police action than reasonable suspicion.[36]

This is not only the most natural reading of the Fourth Amendment but the only sensible one. Why would the police have greater authority to act when they do not go to a magistrate for a warrant than when they do? If anything, the standard should be higher when the police act without a check in advance by a neutral magistrate because of a worry that the police will undervalue the individual liberty, privacy, and dignitary interests at stake and overvalue the law enforcement benefits.

What makes sense as a matter of textual interpretation and a commonsense reading of the two clauses is also supported by history. The Court often uses an originalist approach to interpreting the Constitution, and it has been especially committed to this methodology in recent decades when interpreting the Fourth Amendment.[37] There are, of course, numerous debates surrounding the Fourth Amendment's original meaning and how common law practices do or do not translate to modern policing and technologies. The common law approach used an accusatorial system driven by private citizens initiating arrests after they had been harmed, so it bears little in common with the world of today that relies on a professional force engaging in proactive policing and investigations.[38]

That said, the standard for seizures and searches is a question that is easily answered by looking to the common law, and it is an approach that translates well to modern times. A warrant, as the Fourth Amendment text makes clear, required probable cause. If the underlying crime was a misdemeanor, officers could make an arrest without a warrant only if they personally witnessed the person committing the crime. If the underlying crime was a felony, officers could make an arrest either if they personally witnessed its commission or if they had a sworn allegation that a crime in fact had been committed and had "probable cause" that the arrestee was the person who committed the offense. By 1827, English judges no longer required the sworn allegation and permitted arrests on the basis of probable cause alone. American judges quickly followed suit and also allowed warrantless felony arrests with a showing of probable cause.[39] As Barry Friedman reminds us in his comprehensive study of policing, there was "no evidence that the ratifying generation, many of whom were hysterical about government overreaching, thought something less [than probable cause] was appropriate" when the police acted without a warrant.[40]

Moreover, the overall landscape was even more protective of individual liberty because there were other operative checks on officers. For example, in the absence of a warrant, officers were liable in actions for trespass if an individual was acquitted after being arrested. Individuals often physically resisted arrests, so there was a threat to personal safety as well.[41] Thus, if anything, current policing practices should be held to a standard even greater than probable cause in the absence of these other checks operating. Certainly, there are no grounds for requiring a lesser standard.

Probable cause not only emerges as the minimum standard when one looks at the specific operation of the common law; it is also the appropriate standard if one considers the animating purpose of the Fourth Amendment and the underlying concerns that led to its ratification. The goal of the Fourth

Amendment was to cabin the discretionary authority of officers acting on behalf of the state because of the long history of abuse with general warrants in England and writs of assistance in the colonies. General warrants gave Crown officers broad powers to search and arrest, and writs of assistance gave colonial customs officers wide authority to search for smuggled goods.[42] In the infamous words of James Otis, these were instruments of "arbitrary power" that transformed "petty officer[s]" into "tyrants."[43] Preventing similar abuses was front and center in the Framers' minds when they drafted and adopted the Fourth Amendment. The warrant requirement allows a neutral magistrate to check law enforcement officers and make sure they have probable cause to pursue their targets. There is no reason for a lesser standard when officers act without a warrant because the same danger of arbitrary exercise of authority exists.

The constitutionality of stop-and-frisk is that rare Fourth Amendment question where text, the common law, the purpose of the Fourth Amendment, and a concern with liberty all squarely come to one answer. Both originalists and those who care about the current social justice implications of policing should readily agree that the Court got it utterly wrong in *Terry*. The text of the Fourth Amendment relies on probable cause, and the history behind that text makes it clear that it is the relevant standard for searches and seizures, with or without warrants. "There is scholarly consensus that eighteenth-century common law did not license warrantless investigatory stops based on reasonable suspicion," thus making *Terry* "a radical departure from the Fourth Amendment of the founding era." It is "indisputable that in every jurisdiction, what was not permitted was a seizure, no matter how brief, of an individual based on suspicion that an offense may have been committed."[44] This was the law of the land at the nation's founding when the Constitution was written. It was also the law when the Fourteenth Amendment was ratified. As a matter of the original meaning of the Fourth and Fourteenth Amendments, *Terry* finds zero support. The issue in *Terry* should thus be an easy one for anyone committed to originalism.

Requiring probable cause for all seizures and searches is also consistent with an unbroken line of Supreme Court cases—until *Terry*. No decision from the Court had, until Terry, suggested that a search or seizure could be permitted on anything less than probable cause.

The policy concerns underlying the Fourth Amendment strengthen the case for probable cause even more. As the NAACP Legal Defense and Education Fund (LDF) noted in its brief in *Terry*, the durability of the probable cause standard was "more than historical happenstance." It was an outgrowth of the Framers' concern with government abuses of discretion in law enforcement. "The unbounded discretion allowed under the general warrants and writs of assistance left government officers free to heed every urging of personal spite, paltry tyranny, arbitrariness and discrimination."[45] The Framers had seen firsthand the threat of government oppression and thus weighed that danger more heavily than the need to address crime.[46] They also understood that an oppressive and arbitrary government was an unstable one, inviting its own demise and presenting a risk far greater than any single crime. The Constitution embeds that same relative threat assessment. It guards against the short-term impulse to allow the government to address a crime panic with greater powers because of a concern that, over the longer term, governmental power will be the bigger threat to liberty and safety.

The potential for government abuse of stops based on anything less than probable cause is enormous. Giving the police such a tool is granting them license to harass minority communities. The Court once understood the need to check this kind of police power. "Power is a heady thing; and history shows that the police acting on their own cannot be trusted," the Court acknowledged in a 1948 case.[47] "The point of the Fourth Amendment," the Court said in another case, is to require factual review "by a neutral and detached magistrate instead of being judged by the officer engaged in the often competitive enterprise of ferreting out crime."[48]

Probable cause already strikes a balance between law enforcement interests and privacy because it does not require police to be correct in their estimate that a crime has been, is being, or will be committed. The police just need to have objective, particular facts that make criminal activity probable such that a neutral magistrate would agree when given those facts. As the Court stated in *Brinegar v. United States*, "requiring more would unduly hamper law enforcement," and requiring less "would be to leave law-abiding citizens at the mercy of the officers' whim or caprice."[49] Though the Court in *Terry* never defined reasonable suspicion, what it made clear is that it is a standard that requires less than probable cause—creating the danger of police whim and caprice that *Brinegar* warned about.

That the Court decided the balance needed to be tipped further in the direction of law enforcement in *Terry* is best understood not as a constitutional decision but as deference to law enforcement during a panic over crime and a desire to maintain order on the streets.

Terry v. Ohio and the Supreme Court's Capitulation to Law Enforcement Demands

The legal scholar William Stuntz described *Terry* as a case that "did not rest on legal principle or political ideology" but was instead a case "about political *necessity*."[50] Or at least what the Court perceived to be political necessity. In the throes of rising crime rates, civil unrest, and public opposition to some of its earlier criminal procedure decisions, the Court opted to side with law enforcement.

In some ways, it may seem surprising that a decision vesting so much discretion in the police would come from the Warren Court, which is often associated with being particularly vigilant in protecting individual rights in criminal cases. This was, after all, the same Court that produced *Miranda* and *Mapp*. It was also a Court attuned to racial discrimination and the need to combat it.

In many ways, though, it is precisely because of those earlier decisions that the Court reached the result it did in *Terry* and its companion cases. By the time *Terry* came to the Court, a backlash against the Court's decisions was underway. Homicide rates were spiking across the country, nearly doubling in the period between the Court's decision in *Mapp* and the time it considered *Terry*.[51] Urban riots and unrest dominated the headlines with racial tensions at their core. The Court came under attack in the 1964 presidential campaign when Barry Goldwater lashed out at its criminal procedure decisions, and Richard Nixon picked up the mantle in his campaign in 1968 while *Terry* was pending. His campaign focused on the crime and disorder sweeping the country, and he blamed the Court's criminal procedure decisions as one of the reasons for the violence. Other politicians and commentators did the same.

In the face of spiking homicide rates, increased violence, and a heroin epidemic, states turned to more aggressive forms of policing to try to deter crime. Policing started a shift in this direction a decade earlier, as the 1950s saw a theory of policing emerge that was more proactive and less reactive. Instead of waiting for victims to report a crime and then investigate it, some saw a more preventive role for the police.[52] By the 1960s, field interrogations—where police stopped people for questioning and frisked individuals who seemed like they were armed—were becoming more common.[53] Several states authorized these policing tactics, either by statute or case law, even when the police did not have probable cause. New York was one of those states, and cases posing constitutional challenges to the New York statute made their way to the Court alongside *Terry*.[54]

The targets of these stops were overwhelmingly poor people and people of color, creating enormous tension between those communities and the police. The Kerner Commission, which President Johnson charged with investigating the causes of urban riots in 1967, identified street stops as one of the practices contributing to the protests and riots. "In nearly every city surveyed, the Commission heard complaints of . . . the stopping of Negroes on foot or in cars without objective basis." These policing practices had the effect of "replac[ing] harassment by individual patrolmen with harassment by entire departments." Police departments instituted these practices "without weighing their tension-creating effects and the resulting relationship to civil disorder."[55]

Whether stops without probable cause could continue and inevitably expand, or whether they would be shut down, would all depend on the Supreme Court. This was the backdrop for the Court's consideration of *Terry* and companion cases raising questions about street stops and frisks. Terry was charged with carrying a concealed weapon, which was discovered after a police officer stopped and frisked him. In two other cases considered by the Court at the same time, the petitioners challenged New York's stop-and-frisk law. In all these cases, the Court was asked by law enforcement to abandon the traditional standard of probable cause and instead permit stops and frisks to take place if an officer simply had a reasonable suspicion.

The Court's decision on stop-and-frisk was "one of its most eagerly awaited opinions in years," and the opinion's release garnered front-page headlines.[56] Naturally, given the stakes, both law enforcement groups and civil rights groups took an interest. Numerous amicus briefs filed on behalf of law enforcement interests urged the Court to approve stop-and-frisk practices as necessary for public safety. Americans for Effective Law Enforcement, the National District Attorneys Association, the Attorney General for the State of New York, and the Solicitor General of the United States all filed briefs arguing that the Court should rule in favor of police discretion to stop and frisk without needing probable cause.

The New York and Ohio offices of the American Civil Liberties Union and NAACP's LDF filed briefs on the other side, urging the Court to hold that the Fourth Amendment required probable cause for both stops and frisks. The ACLU brief warned the Court that allowing stop-and-frisk on less than probable cause would be "inefficient as well as unconstitutional—it serves only to discredit the entire system of law enforcement in the eyes of the community which it serves and upon which it must ultimately depend to combat crime."[57] The LDF brief warned that a reasonable suspicion standard would result in deference to police hunches and intuitions—a dangerous enterprise given that police are predisposed to being suspicious given the nature of their work. The LDF further argued that those suspicions would be heightened in inner city minority communities because police officers had "little understanding of the way of life of the people" living there and "believe[] (with considerable justification)" the residents of those communities are hostile toward the police."[58]

The LDF requested argument time in the case, arguing that, "because of its long history representing Negroes—the allegedly prime victim of stop & frisk—it will provide assistance to the Court not otherwise available." It told the Court "its argument will be on behalf of a usually voiceless majority—those individuals who are illegally stopped and frisked by police and then let go because nothing incriminating is discovered." The Court was aware that argument time would go to Anthony Amsterdam, a well-regarded advocate who wrote the LDF amicus brief. When it first considered the motion, the Court voted unanimously to grant the request for argument time. Ultimately, however, the Court changed course and denied the LDF's motion.[59] The Court seemed to have decided that it did not want to highlight the racial justice issues inextricably linked to stop-and-frisk.[60]

That may also explain why the Court's recitation of the facts in *Terry* never mentions that the police officer in the case, Martin McFadden, was white, and the two men, John Terry and Richard Chilton, whom he observed standing on a Cleveland street corner in the middle of the day on October 31, 1963, were Black. The Court's opinion acknowledges that McFadden did not have much of an explanation for why he started watching the men in the first place. When he was asked in earlier court proceedings what drew his attention to the men, he said only that "they didn't look right to me at the time" and that he "didn't like them." McFadden, then a plainclothes detective, kept watching the men, and there was some uncertainty about exactly what happened next. The Court's opinion in *Terry* says the two men walked up and down the street "pausing to stare in the same store window roughly twenty-four times," arousing McFadden's suspicion. But when McFadden first filed the police report on the day the men were stopped, he wrote that the men walked up and back "about three times each." There are also discrepancies between the Court's opinion and the police report about what the men were looking at when they walked on the sidewalk. In his police report, McFadden said the men were looking at an airline ticket office—not exactly a prime target for a stickup for cash. Later, however, at the suppression hearing, McFadden said that it could have been either an airline ticket office or a jewelry store. Whatever they were looking at, McFadden did not stop the men at this point.

The stop came only later, after a third man, Carl Katz, came upon the scene. Katz started talking to Terry and Chilton while they were on the corner, and then Katz left. Terry and Chilton paced again after Katz left, and then they walked off together, following the same route that Katz took. McFadden followed them and saw them meet up again with Katz. It was at this point that McFadden walked over to them, identified himself as a police officer, and asked for their names. The opinion never mentions that Katz was white, but McFadden mentioned the race of all three in his testimony at the suppression hearing.[61] "Cleveland was a segregated city, and police lore had it that the only time whites and blacks congregated was to plan or commit a crime."[62] Race was clearly the unspoken—and in the Court's opinion, unwritten—story behind the stop.

McFadden's testimony was inconsistent about what happened after he asked for names. At one point, he said, "They gave it to me quick," but on other occasions, he said, "They mumbled something."[63] That was when McFadden, without any further questioning or conversation, suddenly grabbed Terry, patted down the outside of his clothing, and "felt something that seemed like a gun" in the breast pocket of Terry's coat. He ordered all three men inside a store, and while they entered, McFadden removed Terry's coat to allow him to take the weapon out of the pocket. He ordered all three men against a wall with their hands raised. He then frisked Chilton and Katz and found another weapon in Chilton's pocket but nothing on Katz. All three men were taken to the police station. Terry and Chilton were charged with carrying concealed weapons, and Katz was charged with the misdemeanor of "Being a Suspicious Person." The charge against Katz was dismissed, and he was released after two days. (The crime of Being a Suspicious Person was struck down as unconstitutionally vague a couple years later.) Terry and Chilton argued that the guns should be excluded as evidence against them because they were seized in violation of the Fourth Amendment. By the time the case reached the Supreme Court, Chilton had died in a shootout, so Terry was the lone challenger.

At the conference where they first discussed the case, the justices voted unanimously to uphold Terry's conviction. As Chief Justice Warren's law clerk at the time of *Terry* explained decades later, "individually, the Justices of the Supreme Court may have felt differing degrees of sympathy with the arguments of the police, but collectively they were unwilling to be—or to be perceived to be—the agents who tied the hands of the police in dealing with intensely dangerous and recurring situations on city streets."[64] It does not appear, however, that they gave much thought as to why the conviction should be upheld as a constitutional matter or how to cabin the sweeping authority they were prepared to give police. The Court's struggles are "plain on the face of the published opinions." The majority opinion "candid[ly]" reflects the way politics influenced the decision, stating at the outset the "great vigor on both sides of the public debate over the power of the police to 'stop and frisk.'"[65] The justices came out on the law enforcement side of that debate, but they did not have much of a constitutional basis to justify their votes.

Initially, it seemed like they agreed that the relevant legal standard to apply to the case was probable cause.[66] That was, after all, the standard always used for searches and seizures, and the Court made clear in the opinion that "whenever a police officer accosts an individual and restrains his freedom to walk away, he has 'seized' that person." To be sure, it was not entirely clear when that happened according to the facts of this case, but it certainly happened, at a minimum, when Officer McFadden grabbed Terry and spun him around. The Court also noted that it would be "nothing less than sheer torture of the English language to suggest that a careful exploration of the outer surfaces of a person's clothing all over his or her body in an attempt to find weapons is not a 'search.'"

The problem was that it was hard to see how probable cause was established on the facts.[67] As the trial court in *Terry* observed, "it would be stretching the facts beyond reasonable comprehension to find that Officer McFadden had probable cause to arrest."[68] He saw two men pacing and looking through a window several times and then talking to a third man. That is, to put it mildly, a far cry from probable cause. Nor was there anything in McFadden's background to indicate he had any special insight about what he was seeing. The Court in *Terry* emphasized that McFadden had patrolled that area of Cleveland for thirty years looking for shoplifters and pickpockets, but that was not what he was doing in Terry's case. The trial judge asked McFadden whether in his thirty-nine years as a police officer, "Have you ever had any experience in observing the activities of individuals in casing a place?" McFadden answered, "To be truthful with you, no."[69] During oral argument at the Supreme Court, Justice Marshall followed up on this issue, asking counsel where McFadden got his "expertise about somebody about to commit a robbery," and counsel responded that it came "by virtue of the fact he had been a member of the police department for forty years. . . . Even if by osmosis, some knowledge would have come to him of the various degrees of crimes."[70] The Supreme Court cautioned stops should not be based on "hunches," but this shows that *Terry* came down to osmosis.[71]

Apparently, though, the justices did not spend much time wrestling with the facts because they left the conference with Chief Justice Warren set to write an opinion upholding the conviction, maintaining probable cause as the relevant Fourth Amendment standard. Warren had initially hoped to "use the case to lay down hard rules for stop and frisk practices" and put forward something like a "model statute" on stop-and-frisk along the lines of what the Court did for police interrogation warnings in *Miranda*. He worried that "police would interpret a decision that did not spell out rules for proper stops and frisks as Supreme Court license to stop people at will." The other justices, however, did not seem to share that sentiment when they discussed the case at conference and rejected taking an approach similar to *Miranda*. Therefore, the first draft that Chief Justice Warren circulated to the Court argued that the frisk of the men was a search that required probable cause, a standard he said was satisfied because McFadden believed the men were armed and dangerous. In this draft, Warren sidestepped the question of whether there was probable cause for a stop.[72]

As Warren's law clerk later explained, the initial draft's attempt to uphold the conviction with a probable cause standard "foundered on the rather obvious fact that no one really suggested that Officer McFadden in *Terry* had 'probable cause' to believe much of anything." This draft circulated for "several weeks without collecting any votes." As a result, Justice Brennan decided a different approach was necessary to try to regain consensus. Brennan had his law clerk rework the draft to treat brief, investigative stops and frisks differently from more protracted seizures and searches and subject the former only to a "reasonableness" standard. He argued the Reasonableness Clause and the Warrant Clause should, for the first time, be treated as separate concepts. "The definition of a 'reasonable' search could and should be cut free from the standard of 'probable cause.'"[73] Thomas Davies, who has conducted extensive historical research on the Fourth Amendment, calls this move "a prochronistic fantasy" because "there is not so much as a hint" in the historical record supporting a reasonableness standard for warrantless arrests or searches.[74] Justice Brennan, however, was clearly not motivated by originalism, precedent, or any other traditional constitutional method of interpretation. He was seeking a pragmatic approach that would allow the police to use stops to maintain order on the street without having to meet the Constitution's requirement of probable cause. He shared with Chief Justice Warren a draft opinion setting out this framework, explaining that he thought sending along his thoughts via a draft opinion was "the best way for me to state them."[75] Brennan's approach became the blueprint for Chief Justice Warren's ultimate opinion in *Terry*.

One might well wonder at this point how it ended up that Justice Brennan was the key figure behind this unprecedented approach to the Fourth Amendment that would pave the way for such broad police authority. A note he wrote to Chief Justice Warren sheds some light on his thinking. Brennan was, in his words, "acutely concerned that the mere fact of our affirmance in *Terry* will be taken by the police all over the country as our license to them to carry on, indeed widely expand, present 'aggressive surveillance' techniques which the press tell us are being deliberately employed in Miami, Chicago, Detroit, [and] other ghetto cities." Brennan worried that "police will conjure up 'suspicious circumstances'" that will be credited by the courts. He feared this would, in turn, further stoke the "resentment" Black people have against the police, and ultimately "the Court will become the scapegoat."[76] He confessed that probable cause might do a better job holding police abuses in check.

Brennan seems to have endorsed the reasonableness standard because he thought that was the best option given the consensus of the Court, and Brennan clearly wanted a say in how the majority opinion was drafted. He told Chief Justice Warren that, "if we are to affirm *Terry* ... the tone of our opinion may be even more important than what we say." Brennan observed that the expansive use of police stops around the country was being done "in response to the 'crime in the streets' alarms being sounded in this election year in the Congress, the White House [and] every Governor's office." He was therefore well aware of the political environment in which the Court was writing. Neither Brennan nor the Court seemed able to ignore the political pressure. Brennan seemed to think reasonableness was the best way to balance the politics, law enforcement interests, and the other justices' views.

But Brennan concluded by noting he remained "truly worried." In light of how *Terry* has changed policing and fueled incarceration, he had good reason.

Brennan was certainly correct that the "tone" of the Court's opinion was important in such a closely watched case, but the Court ended up sending a pro-police message. Instead of requiring probable cause, as had always been the case for searches and seizures, the opinion held that stops and frisks "must be tested by the Fourth Amendment's general proscription against unreasonable searches and seizures."[77] For the first time in the country's history, the Court sanctioned a police officer, acting in the name of crime control, to seize or search a person without probable cause that the person had committed, was committing, or was about to commit a crime. The Court jettisoned precedents going back to the 1600s in abandoning probable cause.[78] The tone of that shift was unmistakable. Whatever reasonable suspicion means, it means the police would receive far more leeway than they had ever had before.

Because the facts supporting "reasonable suspicion" in *Terry* were, to put it charitably, thin, the opinion also sent the message to the police and lower courts that they, too, could support stops with weak evidence. The final majority opinion, like the first draft, conceded that stops and frisks were searches and seizures subject to the Fourth Amendment, though it still hedged somewhat on when the seizure occurred. It stated it was not clear from the record in *Terry* "whether any such 'seizure' took place here prior to Officer McFadden's initiation of physical contact for purposes of searching Terry for weapons, and we thus may assume that up to that point no intrusion upon constitutionally protected rights had occurred."[79] But consider the evidence McFadden had at the point when he grabbed Terry and turned him around to frisk him. All he saw were two men walking back and forth on the street, pausing to look in a window multiple times, and then meeting up with a third man. There was nothing in these facts giving rise to an assumption these men were armed. Affirming the conviction on those facts sent a message that the police were going to get the benefit of the doubt based on their supposed expertise. Moreover, that expertise did not require much proof. McFadden's relevant experience was paltry. He had amassed decades on the force, to be sure, but he had never seen anyone case a store. His police work was focused on pickpockets and shoplifters, so he had no experience or special expertise in identifying people who were armed. The claim was that he picked up that sense just by being on the force through "osmosis." The tone again was coming through loud and clear—the police were going to get the benefit of the doubt based on their intuition no matter what the Court said about requiring more than hunches.

The Court noted it was taking this path in part because it doubted whether requiring probable cause would end up deterring the police conduct at issue. The Court explained that probable cause comes into play when there is a motion to exclude discovered evidence in a criminal case against a defendant. The Court, however, thought that officers would continue to stop and frisk people even if they lacked probable cause because, in many instances, they would not care whether the evidence was ultimately excluded. They might stop some people for reasons "wholly unrelated to a desire to prosecute for crime," and in other instances they might be "willing to forgo successful prosecution in the interest of serving some other goal." Thus, the Court reasoned, "the wholesale harassment of certain elements of the police community, of which minority groups, particularly Negroes, frequently complain, will not be stopped by the exclusion of any evidence from any criminal trial." Moreover, on the other side of the ledger, the Court said that insisting on probable cause and therefore excluding evidence in some cases would "exact a high toll in human injury and frustration of efforts to prevent crime."[80]

Instead of using the opinion in *Terry* to send a message that police must adhere to the Fourth Amendment because of its importance, the Court decided to water down what the Fourth Amendment required. Brennan was right that tone mattered, but he and the rest of the justices in the majority did not do enough to signal limits on the police. Instead, the overwhelming signal being sent was the Court agreed with law enforcement that they needed wide discretion and more tools to fight crime.

The biggest hole in the Court's opinion is that it never explains why it thought the probable cause test, "with its long history and enshrinement in the Constitution," was not up to the task of balancing the privacy interest and the needs of law enforcement.[81] The Constitution had managed to do quite well on that score. Why did things suddenly change in 1968 after almost two centuries under a different model? (Four centuries if you include the common law.)[82] It is hard to reach a conclusion that does not come down to the Court feeling the pressures of the moment and the spike in urban violence around the country. They all voted to uphold Terry's conviction when they first voted in conference, presumably because they wanted officers to be able to act the way Officer McFadden did. The problem was that they needed some kind of path to get to that result, and probable cause was not going to suffice on those facts.

Thus, the Court invented a new standard that would allow stop-and-frisk to flourish. It adopted a reasonableness inquiry under the rationale that less invasive police intrusions require less justification. "In justifying the particular intrusion the police officer must be able to point to specific and articulable facts which, taken together with rational inferences from those facts, reasonably warrant that intrusion." To justify a stop, which is deemed less invasive than an arrest, the police must assert specific and articulable facts that lead to the reasonable inference that "criminal activity may be afoot." Similarly, because a frisk is less invasive than a full-blown search, the Court thought it should not require the same level of justification as a more intrusive search. Instead, to justify a frisk, an officer needs to show "he has reason to believe that he is dealing with an armed and dangerous individual, regardless of whether he has probable cause to arrest the individual for a crime."[83] The Court did not develop "the limitations which the Fourth Amendment places upon a protective seizure and search for weapons," leaving that task to other cases.[84]

All of the justices ultimately endorsed the basic reasonableness rubric set out in *Terry* except for Justice Douglas. While he was willing to go along with affirming the conviction under a probable cause framework, he opted to dissent when probable cause went on the chopping block. His dissenting opinion is as powerful as it is brief. As Douglas noted, "police officers up to today have been permitted to effect arrests or searches without warrants only when the facts within their personal knowledge would satisfy the constitutional standard of probable cause." He further recounted the importance of this standard to the Framers, who flatly rejected British practices that would allow a "strong reason to suspect" as grounds for arrest. He explained that what the Constitution means by "reasonable" is that there is probable cause. It makes no sense, he pointed out, to set a higher standard for getting a warrant than for a search or seizure that is conducted without one. Yet under the Court's decision, the police now "have a greater authority to make a 'seizure' and conduct a 'search' than a judge has to authorize such an action." Justice Douglas closed by observing that there had always been "hydraulic pressures" on the Court to "water down constitutional guarantees and give the police the upper hand." He noted the Court was facing those pressures like never before in *Terry* but urged a different outcome because "to give the police greater power than a magistrate is to take a long step down the totalitarian path."[85]

Justice Marshall later agreed that Justice Douglas was right. Four years after the Court decided *Terry*, he dissented in another Fourth Amendment case and observed that "it seems that the delicate balance that *Terry* struck was simply too delicate, too susceptible to the 'hydraulic pressures' of the day" and "is now heavily weighted in favor of the government." Justice Marshall had come to believe that the Court had "dealt a serious blow" to the Fourth Amendment and its ability to guard against "arbitrary and oppressive police action."[86]

Tracey Maclin, a Fourth Amendment expert, has observed that "a more confident Court would have surveyed the legal landscape, recognized that stop and frisk practices could not be reconciled with a robust Fourth Amendment, and begun the fight" to protect the poor and communities of color who would be the targets of the police. Instead, the actual collection of justices on the Court "succumbed to pressure to weaken constitutional principle when it was clear that many politicians, and a large segment of the public, had signaled their disapproval of the Court's effort to extend meaningful constitutional protection to those who needed it the most: Poor and minority persons suspected of criminal behavior."[87]

Admittedly, even if the Court insisted on probable cause for forcible stops and frisks, that would not have meant the end of stop-and-frisk by the police. Justice Brennan was likely right when he predicted that, if the Court had gone that way in the case, the police would probably still continue to frisk and "try to make a case that the frisk was incident to an arrest for public disturbances, vagrancy, loitering, breach of peace, etc." Stop-and-frisk, in other words, would not end. The police would find ways to stop people based on probable cause that they had committed minor crimes because there are so many such offenses to choose from.[88] But that is still a far more limited framework. Not all police officers will commit perjury to justify a stop, so many stops that occur under a reasonable suspicion framework would not occur if probable cause is required.[89] More fundamentally, it is hard to imagine departments adopting programmatic stop-and-frisk policies at the scale they did if they knew they depended on a showing of probable cause. The massive deployment of stop-and-frisk came about because it was so easy to have reasonable suspicion.

The Aftermath of *Terry*

The press applauded *Terry* and the Court after the opinion was released, viewing the case as a sign that the Court understood that it should not go further in curtailing the police at a time of high crime. The *Washington Post* argued that the decision should put an end to the "idea that the Supreme Court is unconcerned about the crime situation in the country and spends its time finding new ways to set criminals free."[90] The *New York Times* ran an editorial similarly observing that *Terry* would "help persuade policemen that the Court does not lie awake nights dreaming up ways to increase the hazards of their jobs."[91] The *Hartford Courant* called the decision "only common sense" and then added that, because "it has been a little harder to take the Court's practical sense for granted," the opinion "comes as both a pleasure and a surprise."[92] The Court thus achieved the short-term political validation it seemed to have been seeking with its compromise approach to stop-and-frisk.

The editorial writers reflected the sentiments of a majority of American society at the time. They showed a willingness to sacrifice individual liberty for the sake of fighting crime, particularly if the brunt of that liberty infringement would fall on poor people of color. The *Washington Post* editorial, for example, admitted that it is "a gross infringement on personal liberty to be stopped and searched" and called the "inevitably" disproportionate impact of that on poor people "particularly unpleasant." It nevertheless agreed with Chief Justice Warren's view that "the Court cannot stop the harassment of minority groups by some policemen" while vainly hoping that "some day, we can live in a society where crime is so small a problem that the demands of liberty can be safely elevated."[93] The editorial writers missed the point that enshrining liberties in the Constitution is to avoid just that sort of balancing based on immediate pressures. While it makes sense that newspapers might not appreciate that, the Court should have.

Terry's pragmatic attempt at balancing law enforcement interests with liberty under a reasonableness standard ultimately paved the way for virtually unchecked police discretion. This section first considers *Terry*'s effect on future court cases and then turns to *Terry*'s consequences on the streets.

Stop-and-Frisk in the Courts after *Terry*

Chief Justice Warren retired from the Supreme Court a year after *Terry* was decided, and the subsequent Burger, Rehnquist, and Roberts Courts all expanded its reach.[94] Because the Court did not spend time talking about when the stop occurred and focused on the moment Officer McFadden grabbed Terry to search him, subsequent cases filled in the definitional gap of what constitutes a stop and ultimately "narrow[ed] the definition of 'stop' to exclude most citizen-police encounters." A police officer basically has to use force of some kind or verbally command that the person stay still to trigger even the lax standard of *Terry*. Otherwise, courts find that a "reasonable person" would feel free to walk away and ignore officers who ask them questions or ask for identification. These cases are, of course, completely blind to the intimidation and power dynamics of these interactions.[95]

Things are little better when courts acknowledge a stop has taken place. While the majority opinion did not come out and say it was using a "reasonable suspicion" test, that is how Douglas characterized what it was doing, and that is how subsequent opinions have treated *Terry*. But the Court has never bothered to define reasonable suspicion, instead conceding it is an "abstract concept that cannot be reduced to a neat set of legal rules" and refusing to "impose a rigid structure" on its meaning.[96] Whatever its precise meaning, case law reveals that it requires very little to be satisfied. The Court has said it "requires a showing considerably less than preponderance of the evidence" and just a "minimal level of objective justification for making the stop."[97] It is based on "commonsense judgments and inferences about human behavior."[98] Furthermore, the Court allows a stop if an officer reasonably suspects *any* kind of criminal activity, including low-level offenses and traffic violations.[99] For some crimes, like drug trafficking, suspicious behavior includes "young men hanging out on street corners, talking with people as they walk by, maybe passing something between them and maybe not, sometimes talking with people in passing cars."[100] In other words, the kinds of activity that would make police suspicious of drug trafficking overlaps with normal activity in many urban spaces.

The Court has also failed to make clear that the police must at least have reasonable suspicion of a particular crime. *Terry* used the vague language that the police must suspect "criminal activity," and the Court has never taken an opportunity to clarify that means the police must articulate suspicion about a specific crime. Lower courts are in conflict, with some condoning stops on the basis of generalized suspicion without the police having to pinpoint a particular crime.[101]

The Court has exacerbated the risk young people of color will be stopped just for hanging outside together because it has held that the fact the activity takes place in a "high crime areas" is a relevant factor, as is whether a person takes evasive action to avoid the police. The Court held in *Illinois v. Wardlaw* that an individual trying to avoid the police in "an area known for heavy drug trafficking" is sufficient grounds for a stop. William Wardlaw, a young

Black man, was walking down a Chicago street in an area the police said was "known for heavy narcotics trafficking." When he noticed four unmarked police cars driving in a row, he "looked in their direction" before quickly turning to run the opposite way. That was when he was stopped by the police. He was frisked because, the officer said, "it was common for there to be weapons in the near vicinity of narcotics transactions." The Court said the stop was reasonable because Wardlaw's "unprovoked flight upon noticing the police" occurred in an area known for drug trafficking.[102] Effectively, the Court was saying that people in certain areas can be stopped solely because they do not want to interact with the police.[103] Areas labeled by the police as high-crime or known for drug trafficking are often minority neighborhoods, thus making people of color particularly likely to be stopped if they try to avoid the police. Yet innocent people in minority neighborhoods have multiple reasonable grounds for fearing contact with the police, including police brutality, racial bias, a desire to avoid a humiliating search, and abusive questions.[104] The Court's rulings thus foster a "vicious cycle": "Police use *Terry* stops aggressively in high-crime neighborhoods; as a result, African Americans and Hispanic Americans are subjected to a high number of stops and frisks. Feeling understandably harassed, they wish to avoid the police and act accordingly. This evasive behavior in (their own) high crime neighborhoods gives the police that much more power to stop and frisk."[105] Many of the reasons the Supreme Court and lower courts have cited as grounds for reasonable suspicion seem spurious. Lower courts have condoned stops when officers thought the subject seemed too nervous and when the subject seemed too calm. Sitting still for too long can be grounds for a stop, as can moving too much.[106] Courts have deferred to law enforcement agents claiming reasonable suspicion to stop someone pursuant to the drug courier profile even though that profile includes basically anyone. The drug courier profile includes people at airports who are among the first to deplane, the last to deplane, and those who deplane in the middle. It includes people who arrive at night and in the morning. You fit the profile if you have a one-way ticket or a round-trip ticket. If you travel alone, that is suspicious. It is also suspicious if you travel with a companion. You fit the profile with a coach ticket or a first-class ticket. It is suspicious to have no bags, a small bag, a medium bag, or two heavy suitcases. It should shock no one to learn that this "all-purpose checklist" gives law enforcement agents unbounded discretion and that they use it overwhelmingly to stop people of color.[107]

The drug courier profile puts the lie to the fact that the police have special expertise identifying suspicious people. What they have are suspicions generally, and they cast a wide net. If you cast any net wide enough, you pick up something. Yet the Supreme Court has blessed the idea that officers can satisfy the reasonable suspicion standard with otherwise innocuous facts based on the insights they have from their experience.[108] The Court seems to believe the police are "professional observers," seeing what others do not.[109] It believes that, "when used by trained law enforcement officers, objective facts, meaningless to the untrained, can be combined with permissible deductions from such fact to form a legitimate basis for suspicion."[110] Perhaps the courts have been so deferential to law enforcement agents because they only see the cases where the suspicions turned up evidence. The courts do not see the millions of stops that yield nothing. As a result, they overestimate police abilities and validate what seem to be correct "common sense judgments and inferences about human behavior."[111]

The reasonable suspicion standard is bad enough, but the Court has further licensed the police to stop just about anyone by "inflat[ing] the scope of 'reasonable suspicion' to include pretextual probable cause stops—often minor traffic violations—that open the door to investigations of other crimes."[112] In *Whren v. United States,* vice squad officers noticed two Black men inside a truck in a "high drug area" of the District of Columbia because the truck waited at a stop sign for "an unusually long time" that the officers estimated to be twenty seconds. The officers, who were in plainclothes and an unmarked car, followed the truck and then stopped it after it turned right without signaling and then took off at an "unreasonable" speed. The officers ordered the truck to stop and saw drugs inside. The occupants of the truck were charged with drug possession and filed a motion to exclude the evidence, arguing that the stop of the truck was pretextual so the officers could look for drugs.[113] In fact, the vice officers were prohibited from enforcing traffic laws as a matter of departmental policy, further buttressing the claims the stop was pretextual.[114] The defendants argued that, because there are so many traffic laws, "total compliance with traffic and safety rules is nearly impossible," thus the police "will almost invariably be able to catch any given motorist in a technical violation." They argued that the police are invariably tempted to use traffic stops to investigate other crimes and could use their wide discretion "to stop based on decidedly impermissible factors, such as the race of the car's occupants."[115]

The Court refused to consider a police officer's subjective motivations for stopping someone and said the stop of the truck was reasonable because the police had probable cause to believe a traffic violation had occurred. In other words, police do not even need to manufacture reasonable suspicion to stop a car if they have probable cause—or claim to have probable cause—that a traffic violation occurred. It is all too easy for the police to lie and say they saw a traffic violation that never happened. An investigation of New York City police officers in the 1990s found that "when officers unlawfully stop and search a vehicle because they believe it contains drugs or guns, officers will falsely claim in police reports and under oath that the car ran a red light (or committed some other traffic violation) and that they subsequently saw contraband in the car in plain view."[116] The alleged traffic violation opens the door for them to investigate the crime they really suspect is occurring. It is no wonder that the Drug Enforcement Agency estimated that 40 percent of all drug arrests nationwide are the result of a traffic stop.[117] According to Berkeley dean Erwin Chemerinsky, "no single decision was more responsible for expanding police power to stop individuals with impunity than *Whren*."[118] Moreover, when the police stop a car, they can order not only the driver out of the car but any passengers as well. The Supreme Court applied a balancing test to reach this result, reasoning that, even though there is no probable cause to believe the passenger committed a vehicular offense, "the additional intrusion on the passenger is minimal" as compared to the "weighty interest in officer safety."[119]

As with pedestrian stops, there are huge racial disparities in the targets of traffic stops. A study of police stops by Maryland state troopers patrolling Interstate 95 found that, although 17 percent of the drivers were Black or Hispanic, 70 percent of the people stopped were Black or Hispanic.[120] A case challenging stops on the New Jersey Turnpike revealed that, while Black and white drivers violated traffic laws at roughly the same rate, 46.2 percent of all stops were of Black drivers even though they were only 14 percent of all drivers on the turnpike. When stops were made on the basis of police discretion instead of radar, the percentage of Black people stopped doubled.[121] This path was hardly preordained. State supreme courts have held that pretextual stops are unlawful under the Fourth Amendment counterparts in their state constitutions.[122] The Court could have decided that officer motivation is relevant, as it has in other Fourth Amendment cases, and that to allow pretextual stops for traffic violations is tantamount to recreating the general warrant or writ of assistance because it permits the same arbitrary exercise of discretion that the Fourth Amendment was designed to guard against.[123] Indeed, one commentator has called the ability of the police to engage in traffic enforcement "the general warrant of the twentieth century."[124]

Whren and *Terry* give the police the power to stop just about anyone in a car or on foot. There is evidence, moreover, that the police view the two tactics interchangeably to achieve the same ends. In 2015, police in Chicago dramatically curtailed the number of their pedestrian stops in response to greater documentation requirements and a Department of Justice pattern-and-practice investigation. They reduced their pedestrian stops by 85 percent in a span of just five months. The researchers David Hausman and Dorothy Kronick analyzed the data and found "the Chicago Police switched from pedestrian to traffic stops," and this new spike in traffic stops was less likely to result in citations to the drivers and more likely to involve Black drivers.[125]

It is not just the power to stop that has grown beyond recognition. The ability to frisk seems to follow almost as a matter of course. Officers know they just need to allege that they feared a suspect was armed. Sometimes, they see a bulge; sometimes, the suspect makes a furtive movement. Courts are unfailingly deferential to their testimony.

Indeed, courts have made it even easier on officers by allowing them to frisk automatically if someone is suspected of engaging in crimes the courts think are sufficiently dangerous to justify an inference that someone might be armed.[126] Courts now allow frisks as a matter of course if someone is suspected of a drug crime—even if the crime suspected is just possession of narcotics. Indeed, if the police see someone in a neighborhood known for drug activity and that person tries to avoid them, the police will stop and frisk them as a matter of course.[127] The same is true of people suspected of burglaries or if they are in a gambling house. Courts allow automatic frisks of the companions of people arrested even if the companion poses no threat. They allow frisks if it is a "high-crime" area, if there are more suspects than police officers, or if it is dark.[128]

The nature of what the police can do as part of a stop-and-frisk has also expanded. Courts have allowed the police to draw their guns, use handcuffs, and force people to lie face down if the overall nature of the stop suggests that is necessary for officer safety. For example, if there are more suspects than officers or the person stopped does not obey all police orders, these more extreme measures can be part of a "stop" and still not considered an "arrest" that would trigger the probable cause standard.[129]

The most successful effort to limit stop-and-frisk through litigation came from a federal judge in New York. Judge Shira Scheindlin concluded that the NYPD stop-and-frisk program was unconstitutional under the Fourth and Fourteenth Amendments after finding that the NYPD had a policy of carrying out the stops without reasonable suspicion and based on empirical evidence of racial bias in the stops. Because higher-crime areas have more stops, and those areas are disproportionately populated by people of color, one would expect that people of color will be stopped more than others. This is the burden that comes from "the connection between race, place, and crime," as the legal scholar Tracey Meares puts it. However, a statistical analysis by the criminologist Jeffrey Fagan of the millions of stops conducted by the NYPD found that it was the racial composition of a given precinct, not the prevalence of crime in a precinct, that predicted stop patterns.[130] Within precincts, Black and Hispanic people were more likely to be stopped than white people, controlling for the racial composition of that precinct. The odds of a stop resulting in an arrest or summons were 8 percent lower if the person stopped was Black than if the person stopped was white, supporting the inference that Black people were being stopped on the basis of less reliable facts.[131] In addition to the statistical evidence, the court noted candid statements made by Ray Kelly, who was then the commissioner of the NYPD, to then state senator Eric Adams (now New York City mayor), at a meeting the two attended on a proposed stop-and-frisk law in 2010. Adams had raised concerns about the disproportionate number of people of color being stopped, and Kelly replied that the NYPD focused on people of color "to instill fear in them, every time they leave their home, they could be stopped by the police." Adams testified he was "amazed" that Kelly felt "comfortable enough to say that in the setting."[132]

It is not clear whether the decision would have survived on appeal. The New York City mayor at the time, Michael Bloomberg, was prepared to appeal the lower court decision, but when his term ended and Mayor Bill de Blasio was elected, the city settled the case. As part of that negotiated settlement, the city agreed to continue to have a court-appointed monitor oversee the NYPD to make sure it complies with the Fourth Amendment and does not engage in the same racially disparate patterns. The monitor's reports reflect progress but also show the limits to what even successful litigation can achieve. The number of stops has dropped from more than 500,000 in 2008, when the litigation started, to 190,000 in 2013, after the trial, to 15,000 in 2022.[133] The police have improved their reporting of articulable reasonable suspicion, but underreporting remains a significant problem, with 29 percent of stops still going unreported. Racial disparities in stops have been reduced, but the monitor remains concerned about compliance given the widespread underreporting by the police.[134]

Most critically, Judge Scheindlin's decision remains an outlier in post-*Terry* case law. It is the rare example where a court rejected a police department's stop-and-frisk practices, and it took smoking-gun evidence of bias and copious amounts of data to get there.[135] Most decisions have expanded *Terry*'s reach, and the Supreme Court has led the charge in that expansion. The Court's expansive grants of authority to the police have continued to come even as crime rates have fallen dramatically. The *Washington Post* may have expressed a hope in 1968 that "the demands of liberty can be safely elevated" when the high crime rates of the late 1960s got under control,[136] but the reality is that once the Court opens the door to inroads on liberty by diminishing a right, that door tends to open ever wider because the exceptional starts to seem normal. Crime rates become beside the point. *Terry* has been a malignant tumor on the Fourth Amendment—and it has metastasized. It is not the only Court case that flouted the Constitution and spurred mass incarceration. There are many. But *Terry* set the wheels in motion for a long line of such cases, and it is emblematic of how constitutional rights fade into the background when the Court believes public safety requires a different result than what adherence to the Constitution would demand.

Stop-and-Frisk on the Streets after *Terry*

The police took the Supreme Court's approval of stop-and-frisk in *Terry* as a signal to expand it. Stop-and-frisk is more than an occasional law enforcement tactic. It is now a bread-and-butter policing strategy. For many young men of color, being stopped by the police is a "fixture of everyday life."[137] Bob Herbert wrote in the *New York Times* in 1997 that "if you go into a predominantly black or Latino neighborhood, all you have to do is talk to young people at random. They will tell you how they are stopped, frisked, searched, threatened with arrest if they don't produce identification, cursed at, slapped around, spread-eagled on the ground, thrown against walls, run off streetcorners, threatened with weapons."[138] A study by the National Association for the Advancement of Colored People in 1995 found that police "rely on race as the primary indicator of both suspicious conduct and dangerousness."[139] Just as the LDF brief warned the Court, "the man likely to be stopped is not likely to be stopped once. He is likely to be stopped again and again, day in day out, and for the same reasons."[140]

Police departments throughout the United States use stop-and-frisk "systematically, deliberately, and with great frequency."[141] Departments like the NYPD have put pressure on officers to reach certain quotas and have implemented negative consequences if their stops and frisks do not meet the goals.[142] There is a "unanimous view among cops ... that the authority to stop, question and, where danger apparently exists, to frisk suspicious persons, is an indispensable part of their work."[143] Policing scholars like James Q. Wilson and Barbara Boland argued that stops and frisks could help fight crime by deterring would-be offenders who would fear being stopped and by increasing the detection of weapons.[144] Wilson conceded that "young black and Hispanic men will probably be stopped more often," but he viewed that as an acceptable trade-off for reduced crime.[145]

Accepting racial bias as the price for crime control is bad enough, but the police, policing scholars, and the Court were wrong in their estimated utility of stop-and-frisk as a law enforcement tactic. The legal scholar Aziz Huq summarizes the research on stop-and-frisk's effectiveness as a crime-fighting strategy as "surprisingly fragile." In contrast, the evidence for other policing strategies is more robust. For example, hot spot policing—targeting specific geographic areas known for high rates of crime for greater police interventions—has been shown to reduce crime. And critically, this strategy does not require forcible stops much less frisks. The increased police presence alone brings the crime-lowering benefits.[146] Police stops have abysmally low hit rates in terms of identifying danger. Jeffrey Fagan compared stops based on probable cause—what should be the constitutional floor—to stops based on *Terry*'s reasonable suspicion standard and found that probable cause stops helped reduce crime but that *Terry* stops "simply have no effect on local crime rates."[147] *Terry* stops "might appear indispensable to fighting crime, but it is just an appearance."[148]

Stop-and-frisk, moreover, takes up policing resources that could be used to solve more serious crimes and clogs the courts with low-level misdemeanor offenses. Clearance rates of serious crimes are shockingly low, with more than two-thirds of rapes and robberies nationwide going unsolved.[149] Instead of working to improve these rates and solve the most serious crimes that harm people and communities, police have turned to the much easier task of just running up their stop-and-frisk numbers. Scholars have lamented that communities most ravaged by crime thus suffer from both under- and overpolicing at the same time.[150] They are harassed by stops, but the most violent offenses go unsolved. When *Terry* lowered the standard for stop-and-frisk, police departments sent "officers on wild goose chases, without many wild geese to show for it."[151]

The police seem to be impervious to the low hit rates of stop-and-frisk because the empirical results do not seem to matter to them. That is because "many police and their bosses do not regard people who are stopped and released as innocent, but simply *not caught this time*."[152] If they are assuming the people stopped are guilty of something, that also explains why they do not care if community relations suffer. They are viewing entire communities as criminal and treating them as such.

Policymakers continue to turn to policing to address crime instead of addressing the structural root causes of crime because policing is a cheap, quick option compared to investments in education, employment opportunities, health care, transportation, and the infrastructure that makes communities strong, resilient, and safe. Governments turn to the brute force of proactive policing tactics because it is the easiest option, and it appeases the majority of the public. Few seem to notice it is not working.

However, the people most directly affected by stop-and-frisk policies have noticed. The data from the case against NYPD stop-and-frisk practices show that more than 80 percent of the people stopped by the NYPD were Black or Hispanic. By 1999, a survey of young Black and Latino men living in New York City reported that 81 percent had been stopped and frisked by the police at least once, with none of the stops resulting in an arrest.[153] Racial disparities in the use of stop-and-frisk are hardly unique to New York. This has been the pattern of stop-and-frisk everywhere it has been employed. Pretextual traffic stops follow the same model and overwhelmingly target people of color.[154] A meta study of vehicle stops from twenty-one states and thirty-five cities during the period from 2011 to 2018 found that Black drivers were stopped 43 percent more often than white drivers.[155] Studies of police departments around the country continually show that police disproportionately stop Black people in any public space, whether as pedestrians or drivers. After being stopped, Black people are also more likely to be searched. The stops and frisks of Black people, however, are less likely to yield contraband than the stops and frisks of white people.[156] It is no wonder that police legitimacy has plummeted in communities of color, and research shows that the more someone has been stopped by the police, the less likely that person is to view the police as legitimate. A study out of Chicago found that African

Americans who were subject to investigative stops were 45 percent less likely to trust the police than African Americans who did not have that experience.[157]

The Supreme Court in *Terry* noted that stops and frisks are "a serious intrusion upon the sanctity of the person, which may inflict great indignity and arouse strong resentment, and it is not to be undertaken lightly."[158] Judge Scheindlin in the case filed against the NYPD's practices similarly noted that stops are "demeaning and humiliating experience[s]" that leave people "justifiably troubled to be singled out."[159] Unfortunately, these stops are undertaken without much thought, and the indignity and trauma are even greater than the Court imagined.

Being unjustified targets of policing takes a toll on people and communities, and one of the costs is the effectiveness of law enforcement itself, which in turn fosters more crime and therefore more incarceration. "People alienated from the system are less likely to provide leads to the police, to testify as witnesses for the prosecution, to serve on juries when called, and to convict guilty defendants when they do serve."[160] People unjustly targeted are also less likely to respect the entire operation of law as legitimate and thus may be more likely to engage in criminal conduct as a result.[161] This happens both to the people stopped and to those who vicariously experience those stops.[162] *Terry*, then, not only steered more investments to policing as opposed to other crime prevention strategies. It made policing itself less effective.

> The sheer number of stops is actually ostracizing a huge number of people who live in these communities that are impacted by crime. It doesn't make sense that you're spending so many man hours, so much energy and resources, to stop so many innocent people and end up with very little output. The number of guns they found from the stops is extremely small. So it just doesn't seem effective.[163]

Many police stops do even more harm because they lead to escalating violence by the police. The brutal images of George Floyd, Elijah McClain, and countless others are indelibly marked in our brains. It is not unreasonable for any Black person to live in fear of a police stop and what it might mean. An analysis of stop data in New York City showed that the police were more likely to use force during a stop of Black and Hispanic people.

The LDF warned the Court how stops based on a standard less stringent than probable cause could lead to violence. Any police interaction with people of color is fraught with potential conflict. "But when the stop is based on the inarticulate, unregulated judgment of the cop on the beat, the potential is magnified." Giving the police "an inherently vague and standardless power to detain and search, especially where that power cannot effectively be regulated," reinforces the belief among communities of color "that police suspicion is mainly of suspicion of them, and police oppression their main lot in life."[164] It is throwing gas on an already explosive relationship between the police and these communities.

When these stops tragically escalate into police violence, the police typically face no consequences. The Court in *Terry* mistakenly thought that, in spite of the watered-down standard it created, courts would "retain their traditional responsibility to guard against police conduct which is overbearing or harassing."[165] Subsequent to *Terry*, however, the Supreme Court developed a doctrine of qualified immunity that effectively blocks any suit for damages against law enforcement officers. Officers are not liable for constitutional violations unless they violate "clearly established law." Under the Supreme Court's framework, unless the underlying facts of the police misconduct being challenged mirror precisely the facts of a previous court decision finding unconstitutional conduct, the police will win because courts will say the law was not "clearly established." This is far removed from the Framers' model, which assumed that the threat of a personal trespass action would keep officers in check.[166] Joanna Schwartz has extensively studied police misconduct and accountability, and she has documented many other obstacles that prevent successful lawsuits against the police, including the difficulty of finding lawyers willing to take cases, heightened pleading standards that often lead to the dismissal of cases because of an inability to get required evidence through discovery, jury sympathy to police officers, and the limited ability to obtain injunctions against unlawful police conduct given Supreme Court case law on the topic.[167] *Terry*'s reliance on other safeguards against the police was therefore misplaced.

The Court's approach to policing begs to be corrected, and it will require overturning more than one case. For example, given what we know about the substitutability of pedestrian and traffic stops, both *Terry* and *Whren* must be revisited to really make a dent on forcible police interactions that should not be occurring.

Terry, however, is the place to start. It is a constitutional abomination. It twisted the Fourth Amendment beyond recognition, and subsequent cases that followed its crooked path have gone even further astray. It also failed to bring the promised public safety trade-off that was supposed to make dispensing with people's rights worthwhile. People had intuitions and theories about its ability to lower crime or to maintain order, but when it was actually studied, stop-and-frisk as a policy, like stop-and-frisk so often does as a practice, came up empty. It does not lower crime, yet it fills up the country's prisons and jails. It tears at the fabric of our society, glaringly discriminates on the basis of race, shifts policing resources away from more important tasks, and too often leads to unnecessary violent confrontations and police killings of innocent lives. This was the worst of constitutional trades, and it is emblematic of many Supreme Court cases where the Court traded individual rights for what it thought was a needed public safety benefit. *Terry* is an epic failure no matter how you measure it.

CHAPTER SIX

OVERLOOKING PERVASIVE RACIAL BIAS

McCleskey v. Kemp

> The McCleskey decision was not really about the death penalty at all; rather, the Court's opinion was driven by a desire to immunize the entire criminal justice system from claims of racial bias. . . . Racial discrimination, the Court seemed to suggest, was something that simply must be tolerated in the criminal justice system, provided no one admits to racial bias.
>
> —MICHELLE ALEXANDER

If you visit any prison or jail in America, you will immediately notice the disproportionate number of people of color relative to their share of the overall population. Some of this can be explained by the fact that people of color are committing certain criminal offenses, like homicides and robberies, at disproportionately higher rates relative to their population size.[1] Their victimization rates for these offenses are likewise disproportionately higher. Pervasive and historical structural biases in America—in housing, education, employment opportunities, transportation, health care, inherited wealth, exposure to toxins, and just about everything else—account for these higher rates. Tackling this source of the disparity in prison and jail populations therefore requires one to look outside criminal law and punishment practices for solutions to these deep structural inequities.

Critically, though, disparities in offending rates do not come close to accounting for the gross disparities we see among the incarcerated population. A great deal of the disparity comes from racial bias in the enforcement and administration of criminal law and punishment itself. Racial bias infects every stage of the administration of criminal law and punishment in America, and it is a primary driver of the disproportionate number of people of color incarcerated. If we could eradicate bias in enforcement, we would make enormous progress in lessening the disparity we see in incarceration.

Start with policing. As the last chapter explained, racial bias permeates both traffic and pedestrian stops. One group of researchers studied 20 million traffic stops and found that Black people were twice as likely to be pulled over as white people, even though white people drive more on average.[2] Another study of 100 million traffic stops replicated those same findings and also found that the bias toward pulling over Black people dissipates after sunset, when it is more difficult for police officers to see the skin tone of a driver.[3] An ACLU study of police stops in Boston found that stops were "driven by a neighborhood's concentration of Black residents," not by crime rates.[4] Moreover, when white drivers are pulled over, it is more likely for noticeable traffic violations, such as driving at excessive speeds. Black drivers, in contrast, are more likely to be pulled over for record checks or alleged mechanical problems, and they are also more likely than other drivers not to receive any reason for their stop.[5] The same dynamics play out when Black people are walking instead of driving.[6]

It is not just that Black people are more likely to be stopped. They are also more likely to be searched after they are stopped. Black drivers are searched at a rate four times higher than white drivers. Black pedestrians are likewise more likely to be frisked after a stop than white pedestrians.[7] These searches, however, are not justified by actual contraband. The searches of Black people come up empty more often than searches of white people do.[8]

The police also disproportionately arrest people of color for offenses in which the police have discretion about whom to target for investigation and surveillance. These include lower-level offenses, such as trespass, loitering, and disorderly conduct, and more serious charges like drug offenses, where the police decide where to place their resources.[9] We know, for example, that Black and white people use and sell drugs at similar rates, yet Black people are arrested at much higher rates.[10]

Pretrial detention is another area with stark racial disparities. People of color are far more likely than white people to be detained pretrial after their arrest for similar crimes even when they have comparable criminal records. The bail amounts for people of color are twice as high as they are for white people.[11]

Prosecutorial charging and plea bargaining practices also result in glaring racial disparities. One summary of the research notes that people of color "receive disproportionately harsher treatment at each stage of the prosecutorial process."[12] In the case of misdemeanor charges, white defendants are 75 percent more likely than Black defendants to avoid incarceration because the charges against them are either reduced, dropped, or dismissed. In more serious cases, the disparity is not as extreme, but it is still significant, with white defendants being 25 percent more likely than Black defendants to have charges dismissed.[13] White defendants also receive more favorable plea offers in felony cases than Black defendants and are more likely to be given options other than incarceration.[14] Black defendants with prior convictions are more likely than white defendants with similar prior convictions to be charged as habitual offenders and face longer sentences as a result.[15] In the federal system, prosecutors are almost twice as likely to bring charges carrying a mandatory minimum sentence against a Black defendant than they are against a similarly situated white defendant.[16]

Prosecutorial bias also feeds into the fact that sentences vary dramatically for white people and people of color. For instance, prosecutors sought a life sentence under a Georgia law that allows it for a second drug offense sixteen times more often when the defendant was Black than when the defendant was white. A whopping 98.4 percent of the people who receive that life sentence are Black.[17] A study by the US Sentencing Commission found that Black men receive sentences 19 percent longer than white men, controlling for all relevant factors.[18] Researchers have found that, the darker a person's skin tone, the longer the sentence they receive. After controlling for the type of offense, researchers looking at first-time felony offenders in Georgia found that light-skinned Black men received sentences three and a half months longer on average than white men. Medium-skinned Black men received sentences a year longer than white men. Dark-skinned Black men received sentences that were a year and a half longer on average than white men.[19]

Racial bias permeates every aspect of the administration of criminal law. Black children are more likely to be transferred from juvenile court to adult court than white children. Black people wait longer than white people to get parole. Black people on probation are more likely to be revoked than white people. Black people are far less likely to receive clemency than white people.[20] Black people face worse treatment than white people while incarcerated. They are more likely to be held in solitary confinement and to face other forms of discipline.[21] Just about any aspect of criminal law's administration is characterized by these kinds of disparities.

All of this is an affront to the Equal Protection Clause of the Fourteenth Amendment. Passed in the aftermath of the Civil War and America's reckoning with slavery, the Equal Protection Clause was designed to prevent this kind of racial caste system in America. The Supreme Court, however, has made it almost impossible for anyone to successfully challenge racial bias in criminal enforcement.

It is admittedly hard to bring a claim of discrimination in any area of law in America because the Supreme Court requires individuals claiming equal protection violations to show the government purposefully discriminated against them. They cannot succeed solely by showing that an otherwise neutral law resulted in a racially disparate impact. In that sense, criminal law is just one casualty among many of the Court's high bar.

But it is noteworthy and not coincidental that the Supreme Court made discrimination claims much harder to succeed when it confronted a case raising overwhelming evidence of racial bias in the administration of criminal law and, specifically, in the imposition of capital punishment. The case that exposed that bias was *McCleskey v. Kemp*, and before *McCleskey* was decided, the Court's case law on proving purposeful discrimination emphasized that it was a contextual inquiry that required looking at the totality of the circumstances, including evidence of disparate impact. Up to that point, the Court had noted that disparate results "may for all practical purposes demonstrate unconstitutionality because in various circumstances the discrimination is very difficult to explain on nonracial grounds."[22] The Court's cases were not exactly friendly to discrimination claims before *McCleskey*, but there was an opening for the kind of empirical study that *McCleskey* provided to serve as the basis for a successful showing of discriminatory intent.

Indeed, one would think particularly powerful proof of discriminatory purpose would be a statistical study that uses multiple regression analysis to control for variables other than race so that one can be sure that race, as opposed to some other nonracial variable, is the reason for the disproportionate results. When researchers study racial bias in the operation and enforcement of criminal law discussed above, they do not just rely on raw data showing disparate impact, such as counting the number of people of each race stopped by police or charged for certain offenses. They use statistical tools to consider other possible explanations for the difference and rule those out in reaching their conclusions that race accounts for the differences and not some other factor. For example, the studies looking at police traffic stops account for crime rates in an area and driver behavior. The studies looking at charging and sentencing disparities control for the type of crime, criminal record, age, and other relevant factors. The idea is to rule out the possible explanations other than race to be sure that the disparity that one is seeing is actually because the decision is being made on the basis of race. It is the gold standard of social science.

An exemplary study along these lines made its way to the Supreme Court in *McCleskey*. An African American man, Warren McCleskey, killed a white police officer in Atlanta, Georgia, and received the death penalty. David Baldus and his colleagues carefully reviewed more than two thousand homicide cases in Georgia. The raw comparison of cases showed that the death sentencing rate for cases with white victims was 8.3 times higher than the rate for Black victim cases. Baldus and his colleagues then used multivariate analysis to see if nonracial factors explained the difference. After they controlled for 230 legitimate nonracial factors that could possibly explain the difference, they still found that defendants whose victims were white were more likely to get the death penalty than if their victims were Black. In the most explanatory model, they controlled for 39 legitimate factors and still found that, on average, a defendant who killed a white victim faced odds of getting a death sentence that were 4.3 times greater than similarly situated defendants whose victims were Black.[23] It is hard to know what more the Court could want to prove bias than this rigorous study.

The Supreme Court, however, viewed the Baldus study as essentially irrelevant because it could not prove that there was racial bias specifically in relation to McCleskey. This was not a result dictated by the Court's precedents. This was a new obstacle imposed by the Court in *McCleskey,* and a major reason the Court took such a hard line is that it was worried about opening the door to too many challenges to the operation of criminal law across a range of areas. The Court brazenly admitted as much, noting that, "if we accepted McCleskey's claim that racial bias has impermissibly tainted the capital sentencing decision, we would soon be faced with similar claims as to other types of penalty." It was aware that "studies already exist that allegedly demonstrate a racial disparity in the length of prison sentences." Instead of seeking to remedy all the forms of racial discrimination out there, the Court worried there would be too much of it, and "there is no limiting principle to the type of challenge brought by McCleskey."[24] Justice Brennan famously quipped in dissent that this was the majority's fear of "too much justice."[25]

The result of *McCleskey* is that the enforcement of criminal law in America is characterized by too little justice. Racial bias is its hallmark. *McCleskey*, in the words of *The New Jim Crow* author Michelle Alexander, "immunized the criminal justice system from judicial scrutiny for racial bias."[26] The kind of smoking gun evidence that *McCleskey* demands—a prosecutor or police officer or juror saying something making clear they are motivated by racial bias—rarely exists. In part, that is because people know better than to say the quiet part out loud. It is also because many of these biases are implicit and operate at an unconscious level. The harm, however, is no less because the bias was implicit rather than explicit. The bias that results should be intolerable for any society committed to equality.

The unwillingness in *McCleskey* to provide oversight against structural bias is all the more disturbing because of the many practices the Court has permitted, in contradiction to the Constitution's text and history, that exacerbate disparate treatment. As we saw in the previous chapters, time and again, the Court has been told that biased government action would result from its decisions, but the Court responded by noting that people could bring equal protection challenges to address any issues. The sad reality is that there is no such oversight. The Court condoned pretrial detention for dangerousness, coercive plea bargaining, excessive sentences, overcrowded prison conditions, and stop-and-frisk without probable cause knowing that, in each of these contexts, people of color would disproportionately suffer harm. The Court's equal protection doctrine means nothing will be done about it.

This unchecked racial bias is another key engine of mass incarceration. One of the reasons the bulk of American voters have tolerated our sky-high incarceration rates is that the bulk of the harm of that policy falls on communities of color, and the Court's decisions are a big part of the reason for the disparity.[27]

The Constitutional Framework

The Equal Protection Clause of the Fourteenth Amendment provides that no state shall deprive anyone within its jurisdiction the "equal protection of the laws."[28] Unlike some constitutional provisions, many of which were discussed in prior chapters, which are limited in applicability to criminal law enforcement, the Equal Protection Clause applies broadly, so any interpretation of "equal" must make sense in all the varied contexts in which it must be applied.

The text on its own does not answer what is meant by "equal." The history around the Fourteenth Amendment's ratification in 1868 provides some guidance. The Equal Protection Clause was designed to constitutionalize protections contained in the Civil Rights Act of 1866 and ensure they could not be easily overruled if legislators from insurrectionary states who supported slavery ended up with a majority in Congress.[29] The Civil Rights Act aimed to eradicate laws, known as the Black Codes, passed in Southern states in the wake of the Civil War.[30] Oftentimes, these laws created express racial classifications that denied Black people the same rights as white people and subjected Black people to harsher punishments than white people.[31] Sometimes, Southern laws were facially neutral, but they were applied in a discriminatory fashion. For example, the historical record shows that Congress viewed Southern vagrancy laws, which were neutral on their face, on par with laws that made express racial classifications because they were all "consciously conceived methods of resurrecting the incidents of slavery."[32] Section 2 of the Civil Rights Act "established criminal penalties for subjecting racial minorities 'to different punishment . . . by reason of . . . color or race, than is prescribed for the punishment of white persons.'"[33]

Just as the Civil Rights Act aimed to guard against such biased application of the law, so, too, does the Fourteenth Amendment. When Senator Jacob Howard introduced the Fourteenth Amendment to the Senate, he noted that it "abolishes all class legislation in the States and does away with the injustice of subjecting one caste of persons to a code not applicable to another." He went on to note that "it protects the black man in his fundamental rights as a citizen with the same shield which it throws over the white man."[34] He then asked rhetorically, "Ought not the time to be now passed when one measure of justice is meted out to a member of one caste while another and a different measure is meted out to the member of another caste, both castes being alike citizens of the United States?"[35] When the Equal Protection Clause was discussed in the House, Thaddeus Stevens similarly emphasized that the purpose of it was to assure "whatever law punishes a white man for a crime shall punish the black man precisely in the same way and to the same degree" and that "whatever law protects the white man shall afford 'equal' protection to the black man."[36] This history makes clear that equality in the context of criminal law enforcement and punishment was at the core of equal protection concerns.

The tougher question is whether the Equal Protection Clause also aims to prevent the use of a neutral law that has a racially discriminatory impact but where there is no evidence that the enforcement is the product of purposeful discrimination. This could include, for example, situations where there is unconscious bias or express bias and the disparate effects are dramatic, but there is no recorded evidence of an intent to discriminate. Justice Thurgood Marshall has explained that the goal of the Reconstruction Amendments (the Thirteenth, Fourteenth, and Fifteenth Amendments) was "to work a major revolution in the prevailing social order" and remove the "badges of slavery." That would require protection against not only "flagrant, intentional discrimination, but also against more subtle forms of discrimination which might successfully camouflage the intent to oppress through facially neutral policies."[37] At this level of generality, then, discriminatory racial effects would seem to be squarely within the prohibitions of the Equal Protection Clause. Professor Larry Tribe has argued as much, emphasizing that its goal was to protect those who are discriminated against "when the government is 'only' indifferent to their suffering or 'merely' blind to how prior official discrimination contributed to it and how current official acts will perpetuate it."[38]

However, many practices with discriminatory outcomes prevailed at the time the Reconstruction Amendments were adopted and in their wake. The Court condoned this inequality in *Plessy v. Ferguson* when it upheld a Louisiana law that mandated "equal but separate accommodations for the white and colored races."[39] *Plessy* signaled that "form, not substance, was the constitutional yardstick."[40] Until the Court decided *Brown v. Board of Education*, this acceptance of discriminatory practices prevailed. Thus, "whatever equality was intended to mean when the Amendments were drafted, from ratification until the *Brown* decision, the Amendments were not interpreted to be concerned with creating a commensurate quality of political and social life" for Black people.[41] The Court's decision in *Brown v. Board of Education* condemning segregated schools was a turning point, as the Court then applied *Brown*'s rationale in subsequent cases to cover all explicit state segregation practices.

After *Brown*, litigants also challenged government laws that did not explicitly treat people differently on the basis of race but that had the effect of doing so in practice. Until the 1970s, the Supreme Court treated allegations of racial bias in these contexts by using what the constitutional law scholar Ian Haney-López describes as "a holistic approach that gave weight to multiple sources of evidence, including the likely impact of the government's action, as well as the larger racial and social context." The Court "was not on the hunt for individual bigots" showing discriminatory intent and tended to be vague about what test it was applying. Instead, the Court took a totality-of-the-circumstances view and assessed each case with sensitivity to the context.[42]

The four Nixon appointments to the Supreme Court prompted a change in the Court's approach to equal protection challenges. What would ultimately be interpreted as the first step in the shift occurred in the 1976 decision in *Washington v. Davis*, in which the Court clarified that the touchstone of the equal protection inquiry is whether the government acted with a discriminatory purpose. *Davis* involved a challenge by two Black police officers to the promotion policies of the District of Columbia Metropolitan Police Department as racially discriminatory because the department used a written personnel exam that had a "highly discriminatory impact in screening out black candidates." The district court rejected their argument by noting that they were not alleging any purposeful discrimination and finding that the test was "reasonably and directly related to the requirements of the police recruit training program." The court of appeals reversed and used the disparate impact test from Title VII cases. It concluded that discriminatory intent was irrelevant and that the fact that Black people failed the test at a rate four times higher than white people was a disparate impact sufficient, standing alone, to establish a constitutional violation. The Supreme Court voted 7–2 to reverse. Justice White wrote the opinion. He started by clarifying that the standards for proving a statutory Title VII claim and a constitutional claim are not identical. "Our cases," he wrote, "have not embraced the proposition that a law or other official act, without regard to whether it reflects a racially discriminatory purpose, is unconstitutional solely because it has a racially disproportionate impact." The discriminatory purpose standard was designed to make sure courts were focusing on decisions that were being made on the basis of race as opposed to being made on the basis of some other classification (such as wealth) that simply correlated with race. The Court believed that a focus on intent would expose pretextual reasons when race was really the motivating factor, and then the decision would get strict scrutiny.[43]

The opinion then went on to clarify some important limits to its holding. Critically, it noted that disproportionate impact remains relevant because impact could be used to infer discriminatory purpose. It approvingly cited its many cases dealing with racial discrimination in jury selection and noted those cases recognized a prima facie case of discriminatory purpose because "the total or seriously disproportionate exclusion" of Black people was sufficiently unequal to show intentional discrimination. The burden of proof in those cases therefore appropriately shifted to the state to rebut the inference of unconstitutionality with a race-neutral reason that could explain the result. Even in contexts where disparate impact, standing alone, is not enough to infer discriminatory purpose, impact evidence remains relevant as part of the "totality of the relevant facts" to be considered. The problem with the court of appeals ruling, according to the Court, was that it held that disproportionate impact, standing alone, was sufficient to subject a law to strict scrutiny and to require the government to offer a compelling justification for the law to be upheld. The Court rejected that view because it "would be far-reaching and would raise serious questions about, and perhaps invalidate, a whole range of tax, welfare, public service, regulatory, and licensing statutes that may be more burdensome to the poor and to the average black than to the more affluent white." It additionally noted in a footnote a host of other laws that could fall, including bail schedules, minimum wage laws, utility rates, and bridge tolls.[44] The Court was thus clearly worried that, because of the relationship between wealth and income inequality and race, too many laws would fall based on disparate impact alone. The Court did not discuss the circumstances under which disparities alone could suffice to show discriminatory purpose; nor did it consider the role of studies that controlled for other variables, like income and wealth, to isolate the effects of race on outcomes.

Justice Stevens wrote a concurrence in *Davis* to emphasize some of these points. He noted that "frequently the most probative evidence of intent will be objective evidence of what actually happened rather than evidence describing the subjective state of mind of the actor" because "normally the actor is presumed to have intended the natural consequences of his deeds." He emphasized this was "particularly true in the case of government action which is frequently the product of compromise, of collective decision-making, and of mixed motivation." In those circumstances, he noted, it would be "unrealistic" to insist that the victim of discrimination "uncover the actual subjective intent of the decisionmaker." He wrote separately to highlight these points because "the line between discriminatory purpose and discriminatory impact is not nearly as bright, and perhaps not quite as critical, as the reader of the Court's opinion might assume." It is one thing to note that "a constitutional issue does not arise every time some disproportionate impact is shown." That is different than saying that evidence of disproportionate impact is never sufficient. He thus concluded by stating that he joined the Court's opinion "on the understanding that nothing which I have said is inconsistent with the Court's reasoning."[45]

While *Davis* emphasized discriminatory purpose as the driving question to answer in equal protection cases, the opinion did not alter the existing law to limit the ability of parties to bring successful equal protection challenges. *Davis* continued to endorse the contextually sensitive, totality-of-the-circumstances approach it had up to that point taken in its equal protection cases and even left room for impact evidence. That *Davis* itself was not a sea change cutting back on equal protection is demonstrated by the fact that none of the justices, including Justices Brennan and Marshall, who were the Court's civil rights stalwarts, objected to the Court's constitutional approach in *Davis*.[46]

Subsequent cases support the view of *Davis* as maintaining the status quo in the Court's equal protection approach. Shortly after *Davis* was decided, the Court accepted statistical evidence as sufficient to support an inference of a discriminatory purpose in a jury discrimination case. The Court in *Castaneda v. Partida* held that statistical evidence that a particular group is substantially underrepresented in a grand jury pool is sufficient to establish a prima facie case of discriminatory purpose that shifts the burden to the state to rebut. Notably, though, *Castaneda* was a 5–4 decision, and Justice Powell penned a dissent that expressed skepticism of the statistical evidence used in the case.[47] The margins were thus razor-thin in terms of where the doctrine would go, particularly if the composition of the Court changed.

A couple years after *Davis* was decided, in *Personnel Administrator of Massachusetts v. Feeney*, the Court rejected a challenge by female plaintiffs to a state hiring preference for veterans. The plaintiffs argued the law violated equal protection because the Massachusetts legislature was aware that most veterans are men and therefore its preference would produce large gender disparities. Under one definition of discriminatory intent, being aware of a substantial discriminatory effect and proceeding anyway could suffice. The Court in *Feeney*, however, rejected that approach and emphasized that a showing of discriminatory intent requires more than "awareness of consequences." The relevant decision-maker engaged in the challenged course of action must, according to the Court, act "at least in part 'because of,' not merely, 'in spite of,' its adverse effects upon an identifiable group." In other words, a litigant must show that the government was motivated in part by the prohibited factor. *Feeney* thus substantially narrowed the scope of what the Court would accept as discriminatory intent. *Feeney* made it almost impossible for people to successfully challenge racial inequalities.

There were, however, still some openings. Following the model it used in *Davis*, the Court clarified in a footnote in *Feeney* that foreseeability of consequences remains relevant as evidence and could be used to infer intent in some cases. It simply cautioned that "an inference is a working tool, not a synonym for proof." The inference did not "ripen into proof" in *Feeney* itself, according to the Court, because "the impact is essentially an unavoidable consequence of a legislative policy that has in itself always been deemed to be legitimate," and "the statutory history and all of the available evidence affirmatively demonstrate the opposite" of the inference.[48]

That the Court was not dismissing evidence of discriminatory impact as sufficient to establish purpose in some cases was made clear in a school discrimination case that came out shortly after *Feeney*, in which the Court upheld a lower court decision that relied on evidence of segregated schools. In that case, the Court said the lower court "correctly noted that actions having foreseeable and anticipated disparate impact are relevant evidence to prove the ultimate fact, forbidden purpose."[49] Justice Rehnquist dissented and was joined by Justice Powell. The dissenting opinion conceded that "the Court has not precisely defined the manner in which discriminatory purpose is to be proved" and could not provide "simple and precise rules for proving discriminatory purpose" given "the varied circumstances in which it might be at issue." It argued that the best evidence in that case would have been "a contemporaneous explanation of its action by the school board, or other less dramatic evidence of the board's actual purpose, which indicated that one objective was to separate the races." While the dissenting justices did not rule out the use of objective evidence to infer intent, they said it "must be carefully analyzed for it may otherwise reduce the 'discriminatory purpose' requirement to a 'discriminatory impact' test by another name." They noted that the objective evidence used to infer discriminatory intent "must be a reliable index of actual motivation for a governmental decision" and cited *Feeney*. While the foreseeability of a government action, according to the dissent, is permissible as one form of proof, it cannot be "the only type of proof."[50] That this view was expressed in a dissent and did not prevail shows that the Court was, at that point, still not ready to rule out evidence of disparate impact, standing alone, as sufficient to infer discriminatory intent in some contexts.

The Court's equal protection doctrine thus left open multiple, albeit exceedingly narrow, pathways for proving a prima facie case of a racially discriminatory governmental purpose when it heard *McCleskey v. Kemp*. As the number of conservative justices on the Court grew in number, it was only a matter of time before the Rehnquist/Powell view would prevail as a majority approach. Still, the Court's decision to shut the door on McCleskey's claim was not dictated by its precedent but rather by the majority's unwillingness to confront the full scope of racial bias in the operation of criminal law in America.

McCleskey v. Kemp and the Supreme Court's Fear of Too Much Justice

The case that tested the bounds of equal protection challenges was brought by Warren McCleskey, a Black man, who received a death sentence for killing a white police officer, Frank Schlatt, in the course of an armed robbery of the Dixie Furniture Store in Atlanta in 1978. In a statement to the police, McCleskey confessed to participating in the robbery along with three other men but denied he was the person who shot the officer. There were no eyewitnesses who could identify the shooter from among the four armed robbery participants, but the government introduced evidence at trial that the bullet that killed the officer matched the type of gun that McCleskey had previously stolen in a prior holdup and carried during the furniture store robbery. Additionally, two people—one of McCleskey's codefendants and one of his cellmates—testified that McCleskey admitted to them that he shot the officer. A jury with eleven white people and one Black person convicted McCleskey of murder. At the capital sentencing phase, the jury found two aggravating factors under Georgia's capital punishment law. One was that the murder was committed during the course of an armed robbery, and the other was that it was committed against a police officer performing his duties. McCleskey presented no mitigating evidence. The jury recommended a death sentence, and the court followed that recommendation.

After losing on direct appeal and in state habeas proceedings, McCleskey filed a petition in federal court for a writ of habeas corpus. In his federal habeas petition, McCleskey argued, among other challenges, that his death sentence was unconstitutional under the Eighth and Fourteenth Amendments because of systemic racial discrimination in Georgia's use of the death penalty. He relied on a statistical study conducted by Professors David Baldus, Charles Pulaski, and George Woodworth (the Baldus study mentioned above). The NAACP Legal Defense and Education Fund (LDF) obtained what was then the enormous sum of $250,000 from the Edna McConnell Clark Foundation to fund an empirical study of capital sentencing in a southern state to see if there was racial bias in its operation after states responded to the Court's decision striking down Georgia's death penalty in *Furman v. Georgia* in 1972. The Court in *Furman* held that Georgia's death penalty was imposed in an arbitrary and capricious manner without any rational way to predict which cases would result in capital punishment.[51] In the wake of *Furman*, several states, including Georgia, passed new capital punishment laws designed to check arbitrary punishment. The Supreme Court approved the new Georgia statute as constitutional in *Gregg v. Georgia* in 1976.[52] The LDF wanted to study these new statutes to see if they were still producing arbitrary and discriminatory outcomes, and they enlisted Professor Baldus, who was the coauthor of a well-regarded textbook on the use of statistics to prove discrimination and who had been conducting research with funding from the National Institute of Justice to examine capital cases in Georgia. Baldus told the LDF that "he did not believe he would find substantial discrimination by race" because of the various reforms that had been passed. LDF lawyers happily selected him anyhow, believing it was "far wiser to solicit data and analysis from a conscientious social scientist initially skeptical of the racial hypothesis than to retain someone predisposed to it from the outset." The LDF told Baldus he would be free to publish his findings if he found no discrimination, and Baldus agreed that, if he did find discrimination, he would share those findings with the LDF and testify for them in some capital cases.[53]

Baldus and his colleagues chose Georgia as the state to study, primarily because it had already assembled most of the relevant data. They then analyzed more than 2,400 murder cases in Georgia from 1974 to 1979, which covered the period after the Supreme Court struck down Georgia's previous capital punishment regime in *Furman* and Georgia put in place a new capital punishment law designed to remedy the flaws identified by the Court with the old regime. Of these cases, 128 resulted in death sentences.[54] The study was designed to test for discrimination at various stages of the capital decision-making process, including the prosecutor's decision to bring murder charges instead of lesser ones, the decision to pursue a capital murder charge, and the jury's vote whether to recommend a death sentence. The raw data showed that prosecutors sought the death penalty in 70 percent of the cases involving Black defendants and white victims, 32 percent of the cases involving white defendants and white victims, 15 percent of the cases involving Black defendants and Black victims, and 19 percent of the cases involving white defendants and Black victims. The Baldus study controlled for 230 possible variables that could have explained the differences on grounds other than race, including several variables designed to capture the strength of evidence in each case. The study found that the race of the victim and, to a lesser extent, the race of the defendant had a statistically significant effect on whether someone received a death sentence. After conducting a multiple regression analysis, Baldus found that defendants charged with killing white victims were 4.3 times as likely to receive a death sentence as defendants charged with killing Black victims. The race of the victim was as powerful a factor in explaining the imposition of a death sentence as aggravating factors like a defendant's prior conviction for murder or whether a defendant was the prime mover of a homicide.[55]

The LDF made the study available to capital defense lawyers working in Georgia, and McCleskey's lawyer, Robert Stroup, contacted them because his client's federal habeas petition had just been denied. The LDF lawyers helped him draft a motion to reopen the case on newly available evidence, and the district judge, J. Owen Forrester, granted the motion and agreed to hold a hearing.[56] At an evidentiary hearing in the district court, Baldus explained that the effects of bias were most pronounced in what he called mid-range cases. The study divided the 230-variable model into eight different ranges that were based on the estimated aggravation level of the offense. Baldus testified that "when the cases become tremendously aggravated so that everybody would agree that if we're going to have a death sentence, these are the cases that should get it, the race effects go away." In the mid-range cases, however, the race effects are pronounced. That is because those are the cases "where the decision makers have a real choice as to what to do. If there's room for the exercise of discretion, then the [racial] factors begin to play a role." The facts of McCleskey's case placed it in that midrange of cases.[57] Professor Baldus conducted additional regression analysis in response to concerns raised by the district court, and the additional analysis showed the same level of bias. Judge Forrester nevertheless still denied the writ with respect to the racial bias claims. His opinion "faulted nearly every aspect" of the Baldus study and concluded that it did not "capture every nuance of every issue." In Judge Forrester's opinion, "multivariate analysis is ill suited to provide the court with circumstantial evidence of the presence of discrimination, and it is incapable of providing the court with measures of qualitative difference in treatment which are necessary to a finding that a prima case has been established." The study, in the district court's view, thus did not "contribute anything of value" to the equal protection claim.[58] As the legal scholar Randall Kennedy observed, Judge Forrester's "objections [were] premised upon a wildly perfectionist standard that is impossible to satisfy" and renders all statistical evidence irrelevant.[59]

McCleskey appealed, and the Eleventh Circuit decided to take the appeal en banc "to consider the argument arising in numerous capital cases that statistical proof shows the Georgia capital sentencing law is being administered in an unconstitutionally discriminatory and arbitrary and capricious manner."[60] The oral argument focused on the validity of the study as well as the broader question of how to use a study like it in constitutional cases. Judge Robert Vance of Alabama expressed a concern that would later animate the Supreme Court's decision as well. He told McCleskey's lawyer, "You say there is racial discrimination in capital sentencing. Candidly, I think there's likely to be discrimination in *every* kind of criminal case. Just what are we supposed to do?"[61] What the Eleventh Circuit did was vote to affirm the district court's denial of habeas relief. The Eleventh Circuit assumed the validity of the study and its findings of bias based on the race of the victim and the defendant, but it still ruled against McCleskey. The court of appeals raised criticisms that would effectively mean no study could provide valid proof of discrimination because "countless" factors could be part of the decision. It then noted that the Baldus study did not consider "looks, age, personality, education, profession, job, clothes, demeanor, and remorse, just to name a few." Studies like the Baldus study, in the appellate court's view, were both "insufficient to demonstrate discriminatory intent or unconstitutional discrimination in the Fourteenth Amendment context" and "insufficient to show irrationality, arbitrariness, and capriciousness under any kind of Eighth Amendment analysis." The appeals court stated its view that "proof of disparate impact alone is insufficient to invalidate a capital sentencing scheme, unless the disparate impact is so great that it compels a conclusion that the system is unprincipled, irrational, arbitrary and capricious such that purposeful discrimination—i.e., race is intentionally being used as a factor in sentencing—can be presumed to permeate the system." The court concluded that "the marginal disparity based on the race of the victim" found in the study failed to meet that threshold and, in fact, "confirms rather than condemns the system," because it shows that reforms enacted since the Court struck down the previous death penalty regime in *Furman* were working. "In pre-*Furman* days, there was no rhyme or reason as to who got the death penalty and who did not." In contrast, according to the Eleventh Circuit opinion, "now, in the vast majority of cases, the reasons for a difference are well documented." In the appellate court's view, the fact that the study could not account for differences other than race "in a small percentage of the cases is no reason to declare the entire system unconstitutional."[62] While the Eleventh Circuit characterized the disparity as "marginal," the legal scholar Samuel Gross points out that the relationship shown by the Baldus study between race and capital punishment was stronger than the relationship between coronary heart disease and smoking, where smokers are 1.7 times more likely to die of coronary artery disease than nonsmokers. As he notes, it is generally accepted that cigarettes greatly increase the risk of heart disease, and yet it is "by a considerably smaller amount than the race-of-victim effect" that Baldus found.[63]

The Supreme Court agreed to hear the case, and the briefing and argument spent considerable time on the quality and the validity of the Baldus study as well as the implications of the study's findings, assuming they were valid. Lawyers for Georgia argued that the study was flawed in various respects, but McCleskey's lawyers persuasively refuted the various methodological challenges. For example, Georgia's legal team argued that Baldus and his team relied on incomplete information, but as McCleskey's brief explained, "Professor Baldus drew his information from an extraordinary range of official Georgia sources on each case, including the full trial transcripts, all appellate briefs, the files of the Georgia Department of Offender Rehabilitation, the files of the Georgia Bureau of Vital Statistics, and the files of the Parole Board."[64] The other main argument for the attorney general of Georgia and its amicus was that the quality of the study ultimately did not matter because, as the state of California put it in its amicus brief, "race discrimination can never be demonstrated through the use of a statistical study, no matter how sophisticated the methodology," because "each case is unique, involving its own quantum of variables, which are not comparable to any other set of variables."[65] The Georgia attorney general made the same point, claiming "it is simply impossible to quantify subjective factors which are properly considered both by the prosecutor and by the jury in reaching" their decisions.[66]

The Supreme Court ended up assuming the validity of the Baldus study and its findings but still voted 5–4 to affirm the lower courts and to reject McCleskey's argument that the Georgia capital punishment scheme violates the Equal Protection Clause. Justice Powell wrote the opinion for the majority. Justice Powell had previously expressed skepticism about the use of statistical evidence in his *Castaneda* dissent, and he had also previously cast doubt on the Baldus study in particular in a dissenting opinion from the

Court's grant of a stay of execution in another case from Georgia while the Eleventh Circuit was considering McCleskey's case en banc.[67] Chief Justice Rehnquist and Justices White, O'Connor, and Scalia joined his opinion.[68]

The opinion began by stating that, "to prevail under the Equal Protection Clause, McCleskey must prove that the decisionmakers in *his* case acted with discriminatory purpose." Because the Baldus study could not, as Baldus himself testified, "say to a moral certainty what it was that influenced the decision" in McCleskey's specific case, the Court said the equal protection challenge must fail.[69] It is hard to reconcile the Court's creation of this hurdle for McCleskey with its case law accepting statistical proof as sufficient for a prima facie case in other contexts, specifically cases involving claims of discrimination in jury selection and Title VII cases. The majority therefore had to explain why it required more of McCleskey, and its argument was, to put it charitably, weak.

The Court's main argument was that "the nature of the capital sentencing decision, and the relationship of the statistics to that decision, are fundamentally different" from the other contexts where it accepted statistical evidence because every jury that decides on capital sentencing is "unique in its composition" and its decision is necessarily individualized to the specifics of the case and the defendant. Statistical studies had to focus on "fewer entities" and "fewer variables" in the jury selection and Title VII contexts, according to the Court. The Court seemed to think there are only so many variables that go into a hiring decision or selecting a juror, whereas "a capital sentencing jury may consider *any* factor relevant to the defendant's background, character, and the offense."[70] The Court offered no support for these assumptions, and they are dubious. Employment decisions are often made based on personality and cultural fit in ways that are just as numerous as a capital sentencing jury's evaluation of a defendant. Jurors, too, are often picked based on a range of possible factors, particularly given the variation in case type. In the case law assessing racial bias claims in the use of peremptory challenges to jurors, courts have accepted explanations for juror strikes based on their clothing, weight, occupation, marital status, and "attitude."[71] As Justice Blackmun noted in dissent, "such decisions involve a multitude of factors, some rational, some irrational."[72] Even though he joined the opinion, Justice Scalia wrote a memo to the other justices stating he, too, "disagree[d] with the argument that the inferences that can be drawn from the Baldus study are weakened by the fact that each jury and each trial is unique, or by the large number of variables at issue."[73]

The Court's more persuasive point about the singularity of capital juries, however, was that trying to police their discretion is not possible in the same way one could police a hiring decision or jury selection. It pointed out that, in equal protection challenges to jury selection and employment decisions, the decision-maker would have an opportunity to rebut the claim and offer nonracial reasons for the statistical disparity. Capital jurors, in contrast, could not be asked to come in and testify as to the motives behind their collective decision-making process, likely many years after the fact, and explain why different juries may have decided their cases differently. One of the essential features of a jury, moreover, is the discretion to be lenient for whatever reason, even if it is tension with the letter of the law. That carries an inevitable risk of bias, but the trade-off is the jury's ability to bring needed flexibility and equity into the application of criminal law.

What the majority failed to do, however, was explain why prosecutorial decisions to seek the death penalty could not be challenged on equal protection grounds. It is true that jury sentencing might be regarded as distinct, given the changing nature of juries and their inherent discretion, but the Court treated the prosecutorial decision to seek capital punishment and the capital jury's decision to impose it as if they were both similarly distinguishable from the way prosecutors engage in jury selection. In fact, for purposes of raising an equal protection challenge, there is no meaningful difference between a prosecutor making racially biased jury selection decisions and a prosecutor making racially biased decisions about when to seek the death penalty. McCleskey's equal protection challenge to prosecutors in Georgia making racially biased decisions to seek the death penalty fits squarely within the Court's case law involving challenges to other prosecutorial decisions on equal protection grounds.

Moreover, while the Court is correct that it would be improper to ask jurors to testify about their motives, its claim that prosecutors should not have to explain capital charging decisions rested on the shakiest of foundations. The Court cited *Imbler v. Pachtman*, its decision giving prosecutors absolute immunity for their charging decisions when they are sued for damages under 42 U.S.C. §1983.[74] Scholars have shown that the Court exceeded its judicial role in creating this immunity out of whole cloth when Congress did not specify it in the statute or intend to create it.[75] Even if *Imbler* were correctly decided, however, it never suggested that prosecutors should be unaccountable for their decisions. Just the opposite, that case focused on the specific threat to prosecutorial independence from civil litigation for damages, while making clear that prosecutors would still be accountable in other ways for their decisions, including through professional disciplinary actions and criminal sanctions. Justice Blackmun made this point in his dissent in *McCleskey*, observing that, while "prosecutors undoubtedly need adequate discretion to allocate the resources of their offices and to fulfill their responsibilities to the public in deciding how best to enforce the law," that does not free them from "the constraints imposed on state action under the Fourteenth Amendment."

The Court has also required prosecutors to justify other decisions under the traditional burden-shifting equal protection framework since *Imbler* was decided. Just months before it granted the cert petition in *McCleskey*, the Court decided *Batson v. Kentucky*, which requires prosecutors to offer nondiscriminatory reasons for using peremptory challenges to strike jurors after the defendant has made a prima facie case of discrimination in jury selection. That prima facie case is based on the totality of the circumstances, and the Court has found it sufficient in some cases for it to be established with statistical evidence showing a pattern of exclusion based on someone's race.[76] The majority's claim that prosecutors cannot be held accountable for racially based decisions is thus, in the words of the Blackmun dissent, "completely inconsistent with the Court's longstanding precedents." The majority "nowhere explains" why McCleskey's challenge "does not require the same analysis that we apply in other cases involving equal protection challenges to the exercise of prosecutorial discretion."[77]

The majority ignored its prior approach to prosecutorial discretion and the Eighth Amendment by recasting McCleskey's claim as one challenging the state of Georgia's decision to pass and retain its capital punishment law despite its discriminatory application. The majority cited *Feeney* for the point that McCleskey would need to show the death penalty law was passed or maintained "because of, not merely in spite of," the discriminatory impact.[78] In the words of McCleskey's lawyer, this "erect[ed] all-but-insuperable future barriers against statistical proof of racial discrimination anywhere within the criminal justice system."[79]

Justice Scalia's internal memo to the Court disagreed that the case was really about proof. He candidly wrote, "It is my view that the unconscious operation of irrational sympathies and antipathies, including racial, upon jury decisions and (hence) prosecutorial decisions is real, acknowledged in the decisions of this court, and ineradicable." He then admitted, "I cannot honestly say that all I need is more proof." He thus accepted what McCleskey said as true, but he viewed such bias as inherent.[80] It is hard to shake the feeling that all the justices in the majority agreed with Justice Scalia and that the opinion avoided discussing prosecutorial discretion head-on so they would not have to admit it outright. John Charles Boger, McCleskey's lawyer in the Supreme Court, concluded as much, noting that "McCleskey is best understood as an act of Grand Racial Avoidance: a turning away from the reality of widespread racial discrimination in Georgia's capital sentencing system and an acquiescence to Scalia's cynical perspective."[81]

Justice Blackmun's dissent, by contrast, focused squarely on the prosecutorial decision to bring capital charges as the key Fourteenth Amendment problem and one squarely answered by the Court's "well-developed constitutional jurisprudence" setting out the requirements for equal protection claims.[82] He noted that "the Court treats the case as if it is limited to challenges to the actions of two specific decisionmaking bodies—the petit jury and the state legislature." Artificially restricting the parameters of the case in this way "enables the Court to distinguish this case from the venire-selection cases and cases under Title VII." But, as Justice Blackmun notes, McCleskey's claims are not so limited because he focused on the decision to seek the death penalty as well as the decision to impose it. That decision to seek capital punishment squarely rests with the prosecutor.

Justice Blackmun noted that policing racial bias in law enforcement was one of the main points of the Fourteenth Amendment. "Discriminatory enforcement of States' criminal laws was a matter of great concern for the drafters," who wrote in introductory remarks in their report on the Fourteenth Amendment that "deep-seated prejudice against color ... leads to acts of cruelty, oppression, and murder, which the local authorities are at no pains to prevent or punish."[83] Although Justice Blackmun did not quote him, it is noteworthy that when Senator Jacob Howard introduced the Fourteenth Amendment in the Senate, the first example he gave of what the Equal Protection Clause would prohibit is "the hanging of a black man for a crime for which the white man is not to be hanged."[84]

The Blackmun dissent then went on to document the overwhelming case of racial bias in the prosecutorial decision to seek the death penalty, "a step at which the evidence of the effect of the racial factors was especially strong." He cited the Baldus study's statewide findings and observed that data from Fulton County, where McCleskey's case took place, were comparable.[85]

Other evidence buttressed the statistical showing. McCleskey deposed Lewis R. Staton, who was then the district attorney of Fulton County and had served in that role for eighteen years. Staton explained that, "during his years in the office, there were no guidelines informing the Assistant District Attorneys who handled the cases how they should proceed at any particular stage of the process." They were given complete discretion whether to seek the death penalty and "informed Staton of their decisions as they saw fit." They "were not required to report to Staton the cases in which they decided not to seek the death penalty or the cases in which they did seek the death penalty."[86] Staton testified that his office followed the same approach in capital cases since 1965, when he took office, other than not seeking the death penalty in rape cases after the Court's decision striking down that option in *Coker v. Georgia*.[87] This same level of informality, with its lack of written or oral policies or guidelines, was typical of other counties in Georgia as well.[88] It is hard to imagine a better situation for racial bias to operate than within this unchecked authority in individual line prosecutors.

Thus, the Baldus study, the lack of any guidance to prosecutors in the process of selecting capital cases, and the evidence McCleskey provided of past discrimination in Georgia all combined to be, in the words of the Blackmun dissent, "of sufficient magnitude that, absent evidence to the contrary, one must conclude that racial factors entered into the decisionmaking process that yielded McCleskey's death sentence." Accordingly, the burden should have shifted to the state of Georgia to show that "legitimate racially neutral criteria and procedures yielded the racially skewed result."[89]

Justice Brennan's dissent focused on the Eighth Amendment.[90] Whereas the majority claimed McCleskey had to prove bias in his particular case, Justice Brennan argued that the Court's Eighth Amendment cases since *Furman v. Georgia* have focused on "the *risk* of the imposition of an arbitrary sentence." Justice Brennan wrote that the Baldus study's findings were "a powerful demonstration of the type of risk that our Eighth Amendment jurisprudence has consistently condemned." He went on to note that, while McCleskey could not rely "solely on the numbers themselves," there was much more than that because McCleskey's claim was "consonant with our understanding of history and human experience." The Brennan dissent recounted Georgia's long history with racially biased criminal laws. For example, the dissent noted that, at the time of the Civil War, the rape of a white female by a Black man was punishable by death, whereas the rape of a white woman by anyone else was punishable by a prison term of between two and twenty years. The rape of a Black woman was punishable by a fine and imprisonment at the discretion of the court. An enslaved person who wounded a white person could get the death penalty, but a person who willfully murdered an enslaved person was not punished until the second offense and even then would be responsible only for restitution to the slave owner. Justice Brennan cautioned that this history was not a "bill of indictment calling the State to account for pass transgressions" but was cited because "it would be unrealistic to ignore the influence of history in assessing the plausible implications of McCleskey's evidence." The "history and its continuing legacy thus buttress the probative force of McCleskey's statistics." He noted that "we cannot pretend that in three decades we have completely escaped the grip of a historical legacy spanning centuries."[91]

Both the Brennan and Blackmun dissents took particular issue with the Court's argument that "McCleskey's claim, taken to its logical conclusion, throws into serious question the principles that underlie our entire criminal justice system," and accepting it could therefore open the floodgates to further constitutional challenges to the exercise of discretion by governmental actors on the grounds of racial bias.[92] This is what sparked Justice Brennan to observe that the Court "seems to suggest a fear of too much justice." Justice Blackmun's dissent also highlighted this aspect of the majority's opinion as its "most disturbing aspect." Blackmun's dissent pointed out that, "if a grant of relief to [McCleskey] were to lead to a closer examination of the effects of racial considerations throughout the criminal justice system, the system, and hence, society, might benefit."[93] Justice Brennan observed that "the prospect that there may be more widespread abuse than McCleskey documents may be dismaying, but it does not justify complete abdication of our judicial role." The Court's role is to enforce the Constitution, and the Constitution, as Justice Brennan noted, "was framed fundamentally as a bulwark against governmental power."[94]

The Court's concerns about "too much justice," however, seemed to animate the entire ruling. The majority seemed to take to heart the warning of the Washington Legal Foundation in its amicus brief that a victory for McCleskey would mean "the jurisprudence of racial and ethnic proportionality will be carried to unprecedented extremes" and result in a "dangerous upheaval for the entire criminal sentencing process."[95] The Court did not want to perform the constitutional role of guaranteeing equal protection of the law because it knew that would mean wrestling with racial bias in many areas of criminal law's administration and fashioning an appropriate remedy across a range of contexts. That would be both time-consuming and challenging because discretion is pervasive in criminal law. Discretion is necessary because otherwise the application of the laws would be unduly harsh and ill fitting to some cases, so the Court would need to preserve the valuable function served by discretion while also finding ways to police against racial bias. The Court in *McCleskey* seemed to prefer to duck that thorny remedial question by denying there was a constitutional problem in the first place.[96]

One can sympathize with the Court's worries about remedies. However, while the question of how to remedy bias in the various circumstances in which it could arise would be difficult, it would not be impossible. The Court could find workable boundaries that balance both interests. In McCleskey's case, for example, Justice Stevens's dissent explained that could be done by limiting the eligibility of the death penalty to a narrower class of the most serious crimes that the Baldus data showed did not suffer from the same racial biases. Another possible solution would be to require standards for when prosecutors should pursue the death penalty.[97] Still, it is undeniable that the solution in each context where racial bias is demonstrated would not be obvious, and the Court would have to work with states to strike the right balance of limiting disparities while recognizing that some amount of unequal enforcement is inevitable when so many actors have discretion. It would be time-consuming, and it would be difficult. But it is a fair price to pay so that the Equal Protection Clause is not rendered a nullity.

That is not to say the solution will always be less punitive. In some instances, a solution might be to make things harsher for everyone. For example, to address the disparity finding in Georgia's administration of the death penalty, perhaps the state would make a greater effort to seek the death penalty in cases with Black victims. Nevertheless, while that may be a path states take in some instances, it seems unlikely that outcome would be the most common one. One reason mass incarceration persists is that its negative consequences fall on a disproportionately powerless group of people. Amping up enforcement or prosecution to get more white people ensnared would come at a political cost, and it would also involve the expenditure of more resources when budgets are limited. The more likely outcome would be that states would take greater care in how they target people and reduce the footprint of the criminal law.

The Court, however, preferred not to get involved in any of this and instead claimed that arguments like McCleskey's "are best presented to the legislative bodies."[98] This was "at a time when the political branches were engaged in a 'War on Crime,' incarceration rates were skyrocketing, and racial discrepancies in incarceration rates were in the headlines."[99] Handing these issues over to legislatures was thus tantamount to accepting racial bias, contrary to the role of the courts in the constitutional structure. It was the ultimate judicial cop-out. Crafting remedies might be difficult, but that is no excuse for not enforcing the Constitution. Yet that is what the Court has done in the case of the Equal Protection Clause.

The Aftermath of *McCleskey*

Justice Powell later told his biographer that his vote in *McCleskey* was the only one he regretted in his sixteen years on the Court, but not because he changed his mind on the use of the Baldus data. Instead, he ultimately decided capital punishment should be abolished.[100] If he came to that realization before the vote in *McCleskey*, McCleskey would have been spared execution—Georgia electrocuted him on September 25, 1991—and we potentially could have had a different framework for assessing racial bias claims. As things actually stand, "*McCleskey* effectively closed the book, not only on further racial challenges to capital sentencing but, far more broadly, on empirical racial challenges in other kinds of criminal cases."[101] Virtually every empirical study on the death penalty since *McCleskey* was decided has found, as Baldus and his colleagues did, significant racial disparities in capital charging and capital sentencing practices.[102] We have seen countless empirical studies documenting racial bias in policing, prosecution, sentencing, and corrections practices. This discrimination persists because the Supreme Court in *McCleskey* made it so hard to challenge, and lower courts have followed *McCleskey* "in cases challenging racial discrimination virtually anywhere in the criminal justice system."[103] Tony Amsterdam, one of the country's leading experts on the death penalty, points out that once you can accept racial bias in the operation of the death penalty, it makes it easier to accept it in other contexts where the stakes are not as high. "Accept *McCleskey*," he argues, "and race discrimination in matters less momentous than life or death can be shrugged off."[104]

McCleskey demands evidence of particular "bad actors with specific discriminatory intent that caused the discrimination in question."[105] Even mountains of reliable, peer-reviewed empirical evidence of wholesale discrimination is insufficient. People raising equal protection challenges need evidence of retail discrimination in a particular case. They essentially need a smoking gun, where a police officer, prosecutor, juror, or some other participant in their case makes a racist statement. As the legal scholar William Stuntz observed, "the system as a whole may discriminate massively, but if no single decisionmaker is responsible for more than a small fraction of the discrimination, the law holds no one accountable for it."[106]

Most racial bias that occurs in the operation of criminal law today is the kind of bias that operates implicitly or unconsciously, where the people making the decisions have no conscious awareness that they are making distinctions between people of different races even though they are, in fact, doing so.[107] Proving unconscious bias is a far different matter than proving express bias. Because a person exhibiting unconscious bias honestly does not intend to treat people differently on the basis of race, there will likely be no direct evidence of an intent to discriminate in a particular case.[108] Instead, implicit bias is best demonstrated by the kind of empirical evidence Baldus assembled. The Court's decision in *McCleskey* thus effectively takes these biased decisions outside the purview of constitutional scrutiny because the Court demands an individual actor showing bias in a particular case.

It is impossible to top Amsterdam's summary of the flawed reasoning of *McCleskey* on this score:

> *McCleskey* assumes and declares that we need to worry about a denial of the Equal Protection of the Laws only in the short-lived situation where some individual decisionmaker, temporarily invested with the powers of government, is prompted by overt racial prejudice to act discriminatorily, and that we need not be concerned about any denial of Equal Protection in those long-continuing, culturally impacted situations where hundreds upon hundreds of publicly empowered actors—police, prosecutors, jurors, and judges—with no need for collusion and usually with no awareness of their own racial biases, march in lockstep to produce a pattern of color-coded results that reflect the powerful prejudices of an entire population.
>
> This is wrong as a matter of fact; it is ignorant as a matter of ethnology; it is ass-backward as a matter of political science; and it is pure perversity as a matter of constitutional law.[109]

McCleskey's blindness to unconscious racial discrimination explains why it has been likened to *Dred Scott*.[110] A decision might be morally more repugnant when it is the result of conscious rather than unconscious racism, but the lack of impartiality and the harmful effect on those who have to live with the decision are the same in both contexts. As the legal scholar Angela Davis notes, "the Court, by focusing on intent rather than harm, has refused to recognize, much less provide a remedy for, this most common and widespread form of racism."[111]

The Discovery Hurdle of *United States v. Armstrong*

Even when there is explicit bias, it will be hard to get the kind of smoking-gun evidence the Court demands. For starters, most people do not verbalize racist sentiments, even if they harbor them, because they know the consequences.[112] Ian Haney-López wrote in 2012 that since the Court adopted the "because of, not in spite of," racial discrimination test in *Feeney*, in 1979, "it has bever been met—not even once."[113]

In the rare case where evidence of bias exists, it will be difficult for a criminal defendant to find it. In the context of claims of discriminatory law enforcement practices, the relevant information lies with the government, as only the government knows who was targeted for investigation and who was arrested and released. The Supreme Court, however, has made it almost impossible to get discovery from the government to pursue a selective prosecution claim.[114] In *United States v. Armstrong*, five Black men were charged by the US Attorney for the Central District of California in 1992 with distributing crack cocaine, illegal possession of handguns, and conspiracy in violation of federal law. The defendants raised a selective prosecution claim that Black crack offenders were being charged in federal court, with its higher penalties, while white crack offenders were being charged in state court.[115] The *Armstrong* defendants were not the only ones raising a challenge to enforcement patterns in federal crack cases. Defendants were bringing cases around the country challenging federal crack prosecutions as racially biased.[116] These challenges emerged because the punishment difference between federal and state charges for crack cocaine charges was dramatic. For example, one of the *Armstrong* defendants faced a mandatory life term if convicted in federal court given his prior convictions, but he would serve as little as six years under California state law.[117] Another defendant faced a sentence of three to nine years in state court compared to fifty-five years to life in federal court.

Harsh federal penalties for crack cocaine use and distribution were falling almost exclusively on Black people. Although they made up only 12 percent of the population, they were 92.6 percent of the people sentenced to federal prison for crack offenses. White defendants in the federal system were more likely to be charged with powder cocaine offenses, thus receiving the less serious punishments associated with that form of the drug. Huge disparities existed in arrests as well. Between 1986 and 1991, arrests of people of color for drug offenses increased at a rate almost ten times that of arrests of white people.[118] The year before *Armstrong* was briefed and argued in the Supreme Court, the Sentencing Commission proposed sentencing guidelines to equalize federal sentences for crack and powder cocaine because the disparity in sentencing, in which a defendant had to distribute one hundred times the quantity of powder cocaine as crack cocaine to trigger the same sentence, was creating extreme racial disparities, and the disproportionate impact was "creating a perception of unfairness."[119] The two forms of the drug were pharmacologically the same, so there was no reason to treat them so differently. These facts did not matter given the crazed politics of the time, which was in favor of ever harsher drug sentences and seemingly insensitive to the racial disparities in punishment. Congress passed a law overriding the Sentencing Commission's proposed changes to equalize crack and powder penalties, and President Bill Clinton signed it.

To support their selective prosecution claim and request for discovery from the government, the defendants in *Armstrong* submitted a study by the Office of the Federal Public Defender in the Central District of California, supported by an affidavit from a paralegal there, stating that all twenty-four cases closed by that office in 1991 involved Black defendants. The study also looked at cases from 1992 and 1993 and found that in 1992, twelve of the fourteen defendants were Black and the other two were Latino, and in 1993, twelve of the fifteen defendants were Black and the other three were Latino. In a three-year period, not a single case out of the fifty-three handled by the federal defender in Los Angeles involved a white defendant.[120] On the basis of this evidence, Armstrong and his codefendants filed a motion for discovery seeking information on the race of people charged and arrested for crack offenses and the standards the US Attorney's Office used in deciding whether to bring a federal case. The *Armstrong* defendants also informed the district court at the hearing on the motion that they had tried unsuccessfully to get comparable information about the race of people prosecuted in state prosecutions. The district court granted the defendants' motion for discovery on this basis. District Judge Consuelo Marshall noted that, "what the Court wants to know is whether or not there is any criteria in deciding which of these cases will be filed in state court versus Federal court and if so, what is the criteria ... and if it is not based on race what is it based on?"[121]

The government did not answer that question or comply with the discovery order but instead moved for reconsideration, arguing that the federal defender study was explained in part by "a tendency of blacks to predominate in the sale of crack."[122] The government also submitted affidavits from prosecutors and law enforcement officers arguing that race was not the reason they brought the case against the *Armstrong* defendants.[123] The lead police officers and Bureau of Alcohol, Tobacco, and Firearms agents on the case claimed they did not even know the race of the individuals involved when they began their investigation of the suspected crack ring in Inglewood that ensnared the defendants. As Armstrong and some of his codefendants pointed out in their brief to the Supreme Court, the district court judge used her twelve years of experience on the federal bench and "familiarity with local circumstances" to help her assess these claims, as "any judge in Los Angeles . . . would understand that law enforcement officials would know full well that an investigation targeted at Inglewood, rather, for example, than at the Hispanic community in Van Nuys, or the white suburb of Simi Valley, would lead to the arrest of black suspects."[124]

In opposing the government's motion for reconsideration, the defendants submitted an affidavit from a defense lawyer who alleged "that an intake coordinator at a drug treatment center had told her that there are 'an equal number of caucasian users and dealers to minority users and dealers.'" The defendants also submitted an affidavit from Armstrong's defense lawyer, who had practiced in both the Central District of California and in Los Angeles County courts, alleging that he could not recall a single crack case involving a non-Black defendant in federal court and "alleging that in his experience many nonblacks are prosecuted in state court for crack offenses."[125] The government identified only eleven people who were not Black who were prosecuted in federal court over a three-year period. Moreover, as the defendants pointed out, all eleven people listed were people of color, and not a single person was white.[126]

The district court denied the government's motion for reconsideration, and when the government indicated it would not comply with the discovery order, the district court dismissed the indictments but stayed that order pending appeal. A divided Ninth Circuit appeals panel reversed, and then the full Ninth Circuit affirmed the district court after hearing the case en banc.[127]

The Supreme Court reversed in an 8–1 vote and held, in an opinion by Chief Justice Rehnquist, that in order to obtain discovery in a selective prosecution case, a defendant must offer "some evidence that similarly situated defendants of other races could have been prosecuted, but were not." The Court deliberately set out to make discovery difficult, noting that "the showing necessary to obtain discovery should itself be a significant barrier to the litigation of insubstantial claims." Armstrong had presented some evidence, but the Court did not find that sufficient because it dismissed the affidavits as "hearsay" and based on "anecdotal evidence."[128] Justice Stevens noted in dissent that Armstrong's lawyer's affidavit was "based on his own extensive experience in both federal and state courts," so it is hard to imagine what more the Court could have wanted. Justice Stevens further observed that the district could draw adverse inferences from the fact that the government did not provide a single example of a white defendant charged with a crack offense.[129] In rejecting this type of information as sufficient to get discovery, the Court places defendants in a catch-22: they need information regarding similarly situated people of other races who were not prosecuted to get discovery, but if they had that information, they would not need discovery in the first place. Moreover, by the time the Supreme Court heard the case, a study of Los Angeles state court prosecutions showed that more than two hundred white crack dealers had been prosecuted in state court during the period from 1990 to 1992, a period when the US Attorney's Office in the Central District did not bring a single case against a white person. This study was cited in briefs before the Court, so the Supreme Court knew that the affidavits filed in the district court were, in fact, accurate.[130]

Anticipating that its standard might be viewed as "impossible to prove," the Court cited a single case, *Yick Wo v. Hopkins,* as an example of a case where the challengers were able to meet that burden. In that case, which was decided in 1886, the defendants successfully challenged on equal protection grounds the enforcement of an ordinance prohibiting the operation of a laundry in a wood structure without first obtaining a permit. The authorities had denied all two hundred permit applications submitted by Chinese people and granted all but one of the applications submitted by white people. The Court in *Yick Wo* concluded that there was "no reason" for the permit denials "except hostility to the race and nationality to which the petitioners belong, and which in the eye of the law is not justified."[131] *Yick Wo* was decided when racism was more likely to be overtly displayed, and it presented the unusual case where it was easy to identify similarly situated people treated differently.[132] *Yick Wo* shows only that, according to the criminal law scholar Richard McAdams, "before the equal protection clause or norms of social equality created any incentive for governmental officials to conceal their racist intentions or actions, it was possible for someone to gather evidence needed to prove selective prosecution." Today, however, he notes, "racist decisions are much more likely to be shrouded in plausible non-racial rationalizations than they were in 1886."[133] Angela Davis similarly criticized the Court's reliance on *Yick Wo* as the lone example of the ability of people to satisfy the *Armstrong* test in an article written in 1998, noting that "the fact that no civil plaintiff or criminal defendant in a race-based selective prosecution case has prevailed in the Supreme Court in 112 years suggests the scant likelihood of satisfying the 'similarly situated' requirement."[134] It has been twenty-five additional years since Davis wrote that, and the record has not changed. The same dismal record exists in the lower courts, with only one published case in either state or federal courts dismissing a criminal charge because a defendant raised a racially selective prosecution claim.[135]

Armstrong is important not only because of the high bar for discovery it imposes but also because of the window it provides on the Court's thinking. The Court criticized the Ninth Circuit's declaration that "we must start with the presumption that people of all races commit *all* types of crimes—not with the premise that any type of crime is the exclusive province of any particular racial or ethnic group."[136] The Court did not believe that presumption was justified and in support of its view cited Sentencing Commission data showing that "more than 90% of the persons sentenced in 1994 for crack cocaine trafficking were black" and that "93.4% of convicted LSD dealers" and "91% of those convicted for pornography or prostitution" were white. The Court claimed that the Ninth Circuit's presumption was "at war with [these] presumably reliable statistics."[137] As Justice Stevens noted in dissent, these data do not disprove the Ninth Circuit's claim because these are sentencing data, not data that directly measure who commits these crimes. These numbers could reflect biased policing and charging practices—the very claim being made by Armstrong and his codefendants. These numbers are, as Justice Stevens noted, therefore "entirely consistent with the allegation of selective prosecution."[138] Moreover, a joint amicus brief filed by the LDF and the ACLU informed the Court of numerous state and federal judicial task force findings that "race continues to exercise influence wherever discretion is exercised, whether it be at the arrest, charging, bail, jury selection, or sentencing stage," and that "state and federal task forces consistently identified that differences in prosecutorial charging decisions could only be accounted for by race."[139] Eight justices were nevertheless comfortable using the Sentencing Commission data to buttress their claim that there are racial differences in offending and did not pause to consider that they could be the result of biased enforcement patterns by police and prosecutors. The constitutional law scholar Pam Karlan observed that she could not "think of a single other area of current equal protection doctrine in which the Court is prepared to assume, based on ambiguous statistics, that blacks and whites differ in a legally cognizable way."[140]

The Court also seemed reluctant to allow selective enforcement claims to be easily brought because of its dislike of a remedy that could mean dismissal of an otherwise valid case. Justice Scalia admitted as much during the oral argument in *Armstrong*, noting, "I'm very resistant to the notion that because you have one bad egg in the Federal prosecutor's office we punish him by letting somebody who's been duly convicted of a crime walk away."[141] Justice Scalia called the equal protection challenge an "extraneous issue" and argued that "by and large our criminal trials ought to be about whether the defendant is guilty of what he's charged with having done," thus justifying a "fairly high threshold" for bringing an equal protection claim.[142] Karlan suggests the concern with a remedy of dismissing a case or giving too great a benefit to a guilty defendant explains much of the Court's approach to equal protection in the criminal sphere.[143]

The Court thus strikes the balance the way the public might: putting a thumb on the scale of perceived public safety instead of enforcing a bedrock constitutional value. If the Court were serious about the Constitution's commitment to equal protection, it would recognize that policing implicit racial bias is just as critical as policing explicit bias and adjust the doctrinal test for bringing an equal protection claim accordingly. The dissents by Justices Brennan and Blackmun in *McCleskey* both recognized the way unconscious bias affects decision-making. Just because it is "more subtle" does not make it "less real or pernicious."[144] Using evidence like the Baldus study helps unearth those biases. The dissent therefore viewed the data, coupled with the fact there were no guidelines for prosecutorial decisions to seek the death penalty or any clear oversight, as sufficient to establish a prima facie case. If a majority of the Court had done so, it would set the stage for this kind of evidence to be used in many other contexts to prove discrimination. By rejecting this option, the Court turned the Equal Protection Clause into a virtual dead letter in the operation of criminal law, an area where it is so urgently needed.

The World Where Data Does Not Matter

The Court's lackluster approach to equal protection and rejection of empirical evidence is all the more egregious given the governmental policies it has condoned that were discussed in previous chapters. The Court not only ignored the Constitution's text, history, and its case law to give the government greater powers; it also knew it was enabling the government to act in ways that would disproportionately negatively affect people of color.

The Court, for example, knew full well when it decided *Terry* that the stop-and-frisk regime it condoned would disproportionately target people of color. It nevertheless created out of whole cloth a more lenient standard to allow stop-and-frisk in spite of the Constitution's demands. Paul Butler notes this is part of a pattern by the Court. It repeatedly receives warning that particular policing practices will have harmful and disparate effects, and yet the Court goes ahead and stretches the law to allow them anyway.[145] In *Whren v. United States,* the Court allowed pretextual stops, and in response to the argument that these stops were likely to be racially motivated, the Court said those claims could be brought under the Equal Protection Clause.[146] But those equal protection challenges are likely to go nowhere given the Court's almost impossible-to-meet evidentiary burden. The Court was well aware of this when it decided *Whren,* as the decision came out within a month of *Armstrong.* The Court had to know challengers would struggle to get past the discovery barrier it created. It is unlikely, to say the least, that someone challenging stops as racially biased will be able to get the needed evidence about similarly situated people who are not being stopped to qualify for discovery.

Even when lower courts have recognized this difficulty and have allowed evidence of disparate impact to substitute for the evidence of those similarly situated not being stopped, discovery is unlikely to yield helpful information because department data collection practices are inconsistent and their records are usually woefully incomplete.[147] Moreover, on the merits, there remains the challenge of bearing the burden of showing discriminatory intent in particular cases. Statistical evidence standing alone satisfies this burden only if it is on par with the overwhelming evidence in *Yick Wo v. Hopkins.* Unless a person challenging law enforcement has statistical evidence of that magnitude, they need evidence of discriminatory intent in their specific case. This, as one article said in summarizing the state of the law, "has doomed the vast majority of cases" raising claims of police discrimination.[148]

A few courts have found statistical evidence of bias to be sufficient to establish a prima facie case, either ignoring *McCleskey* or finding a way to distinguish it, such as when the evidence relates to an individual decision-maker, such as a single county police department or officer.[149] Typically, though, to be successful, a litigant needs to supplement any statistical evidence with nonstatistical evidence of discriminatory intent. The plaintiffs' successful equal protection challenge to the New York Police Department's use of stop-and-frisk shows just how hard it is to succeed in these cases. The plaintiffs' statistical study required access to mountains of data, which only occurred because of prior years of arduous litigation. In many contexts, litigants will never get the data they need. If the challenge is based on charging or sentencing, they will need information from the prosecutor's office, and they will run up against the *Armstrong* threshold. Access to the data, moreover, is just the first step. The data need to be coded, sorted, and analyzed, which takes time and money.

The decision in *McCleskey* means that still is not enough, so the plaintiffs in the NYPD case also had to find the smoking-gun evidence of purpose, and that was the rare case where they struck gold. The department urged officers to focus their stops on "the right people, the right time, the right location." The highest-ranking uniformed member of the NYPD admitted that "the right people would be young black and Hispanic youths 14 to 20." The court heard testimony that then commissioner Kelly of the NYPD admitted that he stopped a disproportionate number of people of color "to instill fear in them."[150] Even with all this evidence, it was unclear whether the ruling would have been upheld on appeal had the case not settled without further appellate review.[151]

This same dynamic plays out in the context of claims of discrimination related to prosecution practices. The Supreme Court has made it clear that disproportionate impact is insufficient to show discriminatory intent in prosecution, and *Armstrong* makes it virtually impossible to get evidence of intent were it even to exist.[152]

Prosecutorial and judicial pretrial detention practices also avoid equal protection oversight. This is another area where the Court should have been well aware of the disproportionate impact that pretrial detention for dangerousness would have on people of color. An amicus brief filed by the ALCU pointed out that detention based on dangerousness would amount to "a hunting license for the government to incarcerate those who are undefinably 'bad,' providing no advance warning of what sort of future 'badness' a person should avoid and little basis on which any individual might defend himself against the amorphous accusation."[153] The Court would certainly know that people of color would be targeted disproportionately, but the Court nevertheless forged ahead, just as it did in *Terry*.

The Court's Eighth Amendment case law is similarly that much worse in light of *McCleskey*'s high bar for showing racial disparity. Many of the Court's other Eighth Amendment capital cases, such as *Furman,* focused on how capital sentencing operates at a systemic level, so one would think systemic issues with racial bias should be scrutinized under the Eighth Amendment as well. The Court's insistence that racial bias be shown in the individual case under review, however, prevents systemic analysis. As the judges who dissented in the Eleventh Circuit in *McCleskey* observed, this means "arbitrariness based on race will be more difficult to eradicate than any other sort of arbitrariness in the sentencing system."[154] It is bad enough that the Court ignores the ample evidence of racial bias, but it is even worse that it also does not perform proportionality review. That means racial bias is not just resulting in leniency for people who are white but that it leads to excessive sentences for people of color because no mechanism is in place to review the biased severity. The Court in *McCleskey* and *Harmelin* punted these issues to the legislature, even though legislative inattention to disparities and predilection to severity motivated the Framers to put limits on legislatures by including the Eighth and Fourteenth Amendments in the Constitution. The Court's unwillingness to provide any oversight of punishment is not proper deference to the legislature but an improper abdication of its constitutional duties.

The picture is bleak, and absent a change in the Court and its doctrine, it is likely to remain so. Successful challenges for racial bias in criminal cases are few and far between in the wake of *McCleskey*. It is no wonder we see rampant, unchecked bias throughout the country in the administration of criminal law and punishment given this high bar for striking it down. The Court's reliance on legislatures to address these issues has predictably proved to be disappointing.

In the capital context, little has been done to address the glaring racial disparities. Kentucky is a rare bright spot. It passed its Racial Justice Act in 1998, which allows challenges in capital cases on the basis of evidence "that death sentences were sought significantly more frequently ... upon persons of one race than upon persons of another race." The law specifically allows "statistical evidence" as proof of discrimination.[155] Defendants must raise their claims prior to trial and show discrimination by clear and convincing evidence, so they still face a high hurdle in succeeding. Nevertheless, there is some evidence that defendants received better plea offers after requesting statistical information from prosecutors.[156] North Carolina passed a similar law in 2009, and it led to numerous successful legal challenges. That success ultimately led to the law's repeal in 2013 when the state legislature flipped to Republican control and there were enough votes to strike down the law, thanks in part to the lobbying efforts of the state's district attorneys, who were nearly unanimous in arguing that the law went too far in limiting the use of the death penalty.[157]

Little progress been made on the legislative front to address racial disparities outside the capital context. California passed its Racial Justice Act in 2020, and it not only addresses bias in capital cases but also allows challenges to any conviction or sentence made on the basis of race.[158] Five states (Connecticut, Iowa, Minnesota, New Jersey, and Oregon) have required racial impact statements to be considered before the passage of more general criminal law legislation. The idea is that showing legislators the predicted disparate effects from a law might motivate them to consider alternatives or at least explain why they nevertheless decided to adopt the law despite its disproportionate impact on communities of color.[159] For example, Iowa legislators abandoned plans to increase sentences for cocaine offenses after a racial impact statement demonstrated the law would have a disproportionate effect on Black people.[160]

Unfortunately, though, these are rare exceptions. If racial impact is left to the political process, the outcome is likely to produce exactly what we see now. The majority of the public appears willing to accept disparity. Indeed, some studies suggest that white people are even more supportive of a harsh policy if they find it will disproportionately affect Black people.[161] This acceptance of disparity feeds mass incarceration and makes it that much harder to dismantle.

Racial bias in the operation of criminal law contributes to mass incarceration in a second, less obvious way. There is a wealth of research by scholars like Tom Tyler, Tracey Meares, and others documenting how communities who view the operation of law as procedurally unfair come to see the law as less legitimate, which in turn makes them less likely to comply with it.[162] Nothing delegitimizes respect for the law more than biased enforcement based on race.[163] People who lose respect for the law are not only less likely to comply with it, but they are also less likely to cooperate with the police to solve crimes, which undermines the deterrent effect of the law because punishment becomes less likely. That, in turn, may fuel the demand for ever harsher sentences in a vain attempt to buttress deterrence in another way.

It does not have to be this way. The Supreme Court of Washington offers a model of what happens when a state court is willing to consider empirical evidence of racial bias. It struck down that state's death penalty regime on the basis of an empirical study showing that it was being applied arbitrarily and in a racially disparate manner where Black defendants were four and a half times more likely to be sentenced to death than similarly situated white defendants.[164] The court was not concerned with the 11 percent statistical chance that the relationship found between race and the death penalty was the result of "random chance rather than true association." The court noted that "indisputably true social science" is not required and "given the evidence before this court and our judicial notice of implicit and overt racial bias against black defendants in this state, we are confident that the association between race and the death penalty is not attributed to random chance."[165] A criminal legal system can survive without a death penalty, so the court's decision to strike down the state's capital punishment regime did not present the remedial difficulties that findings of bias create in other contexts. The Washington State Supreme Court has not yet wrestled with tough remedial questions based on statistical evidence in other contexts. But it is willing to do so because it recognizes the reality of how bias is proven. It may not always get the remedy right, but it is at least prepared to acknowledge what the empirical evidence and so much lived experience makes clear and to try to mitigate discriminatory practices.

Racial bias could and should be checked. It is what the Equal Protection Clause demands. Remedies might not be easy to craft, but they are not impossible, and certainly some improvements could be made even if the solutions are not perfect. Unfortunately, though, it is not something the Supreme Court appears interested in pursuing. It would rather ignore the constitutional violations than wrestle with how best to address them.

CONCLUSION

> Justices continue to think and change.... I am ever hopeful that if the Court has a blind spot today, its eyes will be open tomorrow.
> —RUTH BADER GINSBURG

It is a familiar story that America's tough-on-crime politics has led to excessive punishment and mass incarceration. While critics have pointed to the role of politicians, voters, the media, prosecutors, police, and racial and social dynamics, one institution that has largely escaped scrutiny has been the Supreme Court.

The Supreme Court's role in fostering mass incarceration has been pivotal. The six cases showcased in this book reveal a constitutional core that should have prevented mass incarceration from ever taking shape. The Constitution prohibits incarceration based on predicted dangerousness and instead requires proof beyond a reasonable doubt that a crime has been committed before someone can be locked away. The Constitution enshrines the jury trial as a bulwark against government efforts to strip someone's liberty and prohibits the government from coercing people into giving up that valuable protection by pleading guilty. The Framers knew full well the dangers of disproportionate punishments, and the Eighth Amendment's function is to guard against both excessively long sentences and inhumane conditions of confinement. The Fourth Amendment does not permit police seizures and searches without probable cause, which limits the number of arrests that puts the criminal process into motion. The Constitution also demands equal protection of the law, which means racial bias should have no place in its operation. With these bedrocks in place, we would not have the scope of incarceration we have today. Not even close.

What happened instead is the Court authorized the government to detain people deemed dangerous based on nothing more than the charges against them, without a trial, and permitted judges to set bail amounts based on danger instead of flight risk. Almost a quarter of the people incarcerated in America are behind bars without having been convicted, and most of them would not be there if the Court had protected the presumption of innocence and due process.

The Court's decisions also account for the huge population that is incarcerated after conviction. Plea bargaining is the engine driving the machine, because people have to give up their right to a trial or risk sentences even more disproportionate than the ones being offered by the prosecution. This leads to many more convictions than would ever be obtained if the government had to first prove its case in a trial. If the Court policed these plea offers to make sure they were not coercive, in the same way it polices the terms of government conditions on other constitutional rights as part of the unconstitutional conditions doctrine, we would have many more trials and far fewer people sent to prison. The Court has largely written off the Eighth Amendment, so there are effectively no limits on the amount of incarceration that can be threatened or imposed, which means sentences are far longer than the Constitution condones. People are jammed into overcrowded and deplorable facilities that fail to live up to constitutional standards, giving jurisdictions what is in effect a huge constitutional discount on the use of incarceration as a form of punishment. Nothing about this process or these conditions is acceptable under the Constitution, yet the Court has normalized it to the point that people can hardly see a different approach.

The Court's policing decisions also feed into mass incarceration. When the Court gave the greenlight to stop and frisk in *Terry*, the police took that to mean they could embark on a strategy of massive numbers of stops, which brought hundreds of thousands of people into the police's purview, typically to be charged with the most minor of offenses. This paved the way for an entirely new vision of policing, and subsequent Court decisions exacerbated the harms and further led to excess policing.

And all of this—every stage—is tainted by racial disparities because the Court has failed to police the Equal Protection Clause. The Fourteenth Amendment's core is about making sure people do not live under two different systems of justice based on race, and yet no one who looks at America's criminal processes can come away with anything but disgust about how much racial bias exists. It did not need to be this way, but the Court took an artificially narrow view of discrimination precisely to avoid giving the operation of criminal law and punishment close scrutiny. The justices did, indeed, fear too much justice because they knew what they would find, and they knew remedies would be difficult to fashion.

The Constitution is no better than the people who defend it, and the Supreme Court has shown it has not been up to the task of protecting constitutional rights in the face of government claims that they must yield in the interest of public safety. The Court should have been on the front lines defending the Constitution against the relentless attempts at excessive governmental powers and severity. Its failure to fulfill its central constitutional role in this context is both tragic and indefensible. By refusing to uphold key constitutional protections, the Court paved the way for the mass incarceration we see today.

Despite its pivotal role, the Supreme Court has largely escaped scrutiny of its contribution to mass incarceration. The Warren Court's protection of criminal defendants' rights in well-known cases like *Mapp* and *Miranda* may have created the impression that the Court has been fighting against popular efforts to get tough on crime at the expense of individual liberty. But those blockbuster cases mask the reality that, in lesser-known but monumentally important contexts, the Court has been an eager partner in the effort to strip away constitutional rights in the name of public safety. Not coincidentally, blowback from *Mapp* and *Miranda* is one of the reasons for the Court's subsequent actions. *Terry* came in the midst of a presidential election where the Supreme Court was very much on the ballot as criticism of the Warren Court's criminal procedure decisions was a central campaign issue. The pressure may have felt like too much for the Court, and it caved.

The political backlash to the Court's pro-defendant rulings amid rising crime also changed the composition of the Court and shaped it for decades. After the 1968 election, President Nixon filled four Supreme Court vacancies, and he deliberately selected nominees known or thought to be hostile to the Warren Court's pro-defendant rulings.[1] Those selections put a pro-carceral Court in full swing, and it has never swung back. These justices were also skeptical of civil rights and led the way in making racial discrimination claims in criminal cases almost impossible to prove. Nixon's pick for chief justice, Warren Burger, was so vigorously tough on crime that he gave a speech to the American Bar Association in 1981 to decry the way "crime and the fear of crime have permeated the fabric of American life" and then asked whether the constitutional balance was too favorable to criminal defendants by "provid[ing] massive safeguards for accused persons" but "fail[ing] to provide elementary protection for its law abiding citizens." In rhetoric more fitting for someone running for office than for a judge, he asked, "Must we be hostages within the borders of our own self-styled, enlightened, civilized country?" He argued that governments "exist chiefly to protect people," and if they do not, "they are not excused or redeemed by showing that they have established the most perfect systems to protect the claims of defendants in criminal cases." He argued police forces should be larger, that pretrial release statutes should allow for the detention of those deemed dangerous because "bail crime" causes "internal terrorism," and that America should be prepared to "spend[] more money than we ever have before devoted to law enforcement."[2] It should surprise no one that a justice willing to give a speech as nakedly political as that one failed to uphold constitutional ideals protecting the individual liberty interests of those accused of crimes.

Chief Justice Burger may have been an outlier in his willingness to vocalize his opinions on crime policy, but most of the other justices who have been on the Court in the past five decades seem to have shared his views. Mass incarceration came to dominate America's punishment landscape because the Court has not had a majority in place that has cared enough to enforce the key constitutional provisions that should have stopped mass incarceration in its tracks. The last time the Court had a majority of justices appointed by a Democratic president was 1969. Sixteen of the last twenty-one justices were Republican presidential picks, and even some of the selections made by Democratic presidents have been deferential to the government on crime issues.[3] President Clinton's selection of Justice Stephen Breyer, for example, put another longtime government lawyer on the Court, and he often sided with the government in criminal cases.[4] While Justice Ruth Bader Ginsburg had an illustrious career as a public interest lawyer, she had little experience with criminal law issues, and her votes on the Court reflected as much. She did not take much of an interest in those issues and often sided with the government.[5]

It is important to identify the Supreme Court's role in perpetuating mass incarceration, not only to have an accurate and full account of its rise but also because it presents a possible path of correction. There are two strategies to changing course at the Court. The first is to focus on who sits on the Supreme Court with an eye to what the appointment means for criminal justice issues. Abortion has long been a litmus test for justices because advocates who care about that issue have understood the Court's central role. Criminal justice advocates need to come to that same realization. The Court is an enormously important lever for mass incarceration. Anyone who cares about reducing it must pay close attention to who gets on the Court. That has not been the practice to this point. Rarely has anyone brought up whether a justice will be sufficiently protective of the rights of the accused. To the extent the rights of defendants have come up, it has been by senators seeking to tank a nominee for being too soft on crime. Those who care about curbing mass incarceration and racial justice need to reshape the nomination narrative to bring the importance of criminal justice issues at the Court into focus.

One reason we have seen decades of government deference is that most Supreme Court justices have spent careers as government-side attorneys. To the extent they have worked on criminal justice issues or thought about them, it has been with the perspective of the government front and center in their minds. They are therefore just as likely to be susceptible to crime panics and government requests for greater authority and discretion as the public—indeed, maybe more so.

Reversing course will require a shift in thinking about who gets appointed to the Court. Picking justices with different personal and professional backgrounds could help break the spell of government infallibility and bring needed skepticism to claims that constitutional rights must be discarded in the name of public safety. Although Justice Sonia Sotomayor served as an assistant district attorney in Manhattan, she seems to have gleaned from that experience, along with her background as a trial judge and growing up in the Bronx, a more realistic picture of the harms of excessive policing and mass incarceration.[6] She has therefore been sensitive to the costs of the tough-on-crime agenda and not simply a knee-jerk defender of government positions. Justice Ketanji Brown Jackson worked in a public defender's office. Both Justice Sotomayor and Justice Jackson have thus far been reliable and powerful voices seeking to correct the harms of mass incarceration. The Court would need more appointments along these lines for the needed shift to occur, and those who care about criminal justice issues need to make sure those concerns are front and center in the selection of future nominees.

But even if the Court's personnel does not change, or does not change soon enough, there is a second strategy for shifting course. Litigants in criminal justice cases should be presenting arguments to the Court right now to overrule or chip away at the decisions that form the foundation of mass incarceration discussed in Chapters 1–6. We have a Court that has shown itself eager to overturn precedent if it believes it is "egregiously wrong from the start," has "exceptionally weak" reasoning, and "the decision has had damaging consequences."[7] The Court has also emphasized a willingness to strike cases even four and five decades old if they are "not a continuation of a long line of decisions but a break from them."[8]

As Chapters 1–6 outlined, the decisions discussed meet that standard. Five of them were egregiously wrong from the start, employing all the major constitutional interpretive methodologies. Originalists should reject *Salerno, Bordenkircher, Harmelin, Rhodes,* and *Terry* as inconsistent with the Constitution's original meaning. Non-originalists should likewise see how these decisions fail under even more dynamic interpretations designed to expand liberty interests because all of them undermined individual rights instead of advancing them. These cases rested on fundamentally flawed reasoning that boiled down to acquiescence to government claims that the Constitution had to yield to public safety and administrative convenience. But the government's claims of public safety necessity have been proved false, and each case has caused incalculable damage because of the many harms from mass incarceration. These cases broke from long lines of precedent that did not recognize anything like the government incursions the Court ultimately approved in these flawed decisions. These cases should not be viewed as settled law under any measure or approach to the Constitution.

The most difficult case for reconsideration is *McCleskey* because the historical meaning of equal protection is less clearly defined, so some originalists might balk at second-guessing it because the historical record is not sufficiently clear. Others, however, would see how *McCleskey* undermines the central point of the Equal Protection Clause. The argument for overturning *McCleskey* becomes even stronger when one considers that the Court previously recognized a more contextual inquiry of bias before that decision and that disallowing statistical evidence essentially shields the operation of criminal law and punishment from any scrutiny for racial bias. This, moreover, is an area of law where the Court has not been as wedded to originalist claims and history. The Court has been more than willing to change its equal protection approach over time, as its rejection of affirmative action makes clear, and bias in the operation of criminal law cries out for reconsideration and correction.

Some advocates may be uncomfortable with a litigation strategy that seeks to get these cases reconsidered by highlighting their inconsistencies with the Constitution's original meaning because they do not want to legitimate an approach they believe produces outcomes they do not like in other contexts.

But the current Court has made clear it is interested in these arguments, so it would be self-defeating not to employ this methodology to show these cases were flawed at their inception for those who care about original meaning. Fights over methodology can continue to be waged, but in the battle against mass incarceration, it makes no sense not to employ this valuable weapon. We currently have a Court with a majority of justices who self-identify as committed to the Framers' design, and most of these justices have likewise taken a flexible view of stare decisis that allows overturning cases when they conflict with the Constitution's original meaning.[9] The cases discussed in Chapters 1–6 rest on shaky foundations if one is committed to originalism, and when they were originally argued, that history was not sufficiently unearthed. They are ideal candidates for reconsideration on these grounds.

Admittedly, one would have to be naive to assume that the same justices who show a commitment to originalism or a willingness to abandon precedent would do so in an area like criminal justice that may not align with their policy preferences. It is one thing for a justice who is anti-choice to overturn *Roe v. Wade* and quite another for a justice who leans toward "law and order" to rethink plea bargaining. Scholars have pointed out that the Court is not exactly consistent in its commitment to originalism across all areas.[10]

That said, there is reason to believe five votes can be obtained to overrule some of these cases. Justices Sotomayor and Jackson, as noted, have been strongly protective of constitutional rights for criminal defendants, and the arguments presented here should be powerful enough to convince them that these precedents should be overruled or dramatically limited. They could be persuaded by originalist arguments or by a showing of how valuable rights were needlessly decimated by the Court's holdings. Justice Gorsuch has proved to be a more reliable originalist than his conservative colleagues and has already shown his receptivity to protecting the rights of criminal defendants and putting what he sees as a flawed jurisprudential path on the right course.[11] It is too soon to tell where Justice Barrett's jurisprudence will take her, but given her stated alliance with Justice Scalia's approach, the arguments presented here should be persuasive if she sticks with her methodological commitments. Others, like Chief Justice Roberts, Justice Kagan, and Justice Kavanaugh, seem less wedded to any methodology, and their more flexible approach to cases may make them more likely to continue to favor government-side arguments and supporting these precedents. They, too, however, might be persuaded to shift course given that these cases are not critical for public safety and rest on such weak constitutional footing no matter what one's preferred interpretive approach. Justice Thomas has several notable decisions where he has voted with criminal defendants because an originalist methodology required a broad reading of the jury guarantee.[12] That same view should lead him to see the flaws with *Bordenkircher*, and he may be a possible vote to overturn other cases as well given the strength of the originalist arguments.[13] Only Justice Alito seems impossible to get, as he consistently rules for the government in criminal cases no matter how strong the textual, originalist, or precedential arguments are on the other side.

The key to persuading five justices may depend on who is presenting the arguments. Undoubtedly the government will oppose reconsidering any of them, so it is critical that outside groups make clear that the government's public safety claims are as flawed as the constitutional arguments. There should be a broad coalition of people on the left and right of the political spectrum to urge reconsideration of the cases that form the foundation of mass incarceration. If organizations whose views the justices trust press the argument that these cases need to be overruled, it is possible that majorities will form even on the current Court to overrule them or at least limit their scope.

It may not be an easy or a quick path to get the Supreme Court to roll back these cases, but it is a necessary journey. We are no safer as a result of the failed war on crime and the mass incarceration it produced, and we have lost fundamental protections against government overreach in the process. The Court made this bad bargain, trading away constitutional guarantees for illusory claims of public safety, and it is the Court that must fix it. That means we need either new justices willing to enforce constitutional rights even when they are unpopular and the government claims they are dangerous, or current justices willing to stand up for what is right and admit that the Court has taken far too many wrong turns when it comes to the administration of criminal law and punishment.

Advocates can and should continue to fight mass incarceration in legislatures and seek to change public opinion. They can and should continue to fight in state courts that might be more progressive. But those efforts will necessarily be piecemeal and unsuccessful in large parts of the country. The Constitution anticipated the danger of a government committed to mass incarceration, and it stands at the ready to stop it across the nation. We just need a Supreme Court willing to enforce it and not one content to leave justice abandoned.

NOTES

Introduction

1. Peter Wagner and Wanda Bertram, "What Percent of the U.S. Is Incarcerated? (And Other Ways to Measure Mass Incarceration)," *Prison Policy Initiative*, January 16, 2020, https://www.prisonpolicy.org/blog/2020/01/16/percent-incarcerated; Wendy Sawyer and Peter Wagner, "Mass Incarceration: The Whole Pie 2022," press release, *Prison Policy Initiative*, March 14, 2022, https://www.prisonpolicy.org/reports/pie2022.html; "Highest-to-Lowest Prison Population Rate," World Prison Brief, accessed November 1, 2021, https://www.prisonstudies.org/highest-to-lowest/prison_population_rate?field_region_taxonomy_tid=All; Danielle Kaeble and Mary Cowhig, "Correctional Populations in the United States, 2016," Table 4, pub. no. NCJ 251211, Bureau of Justice Statistics, U.S. Department of Justice, April 2018, https://bjs.ojp.gov/content/pub/pdf/cpus16.pdf.
2. Franklin E. Zimring, *The Insidious Momentum of American Mass Incarceration* (New York: Oxford University Press, 2020), 3–6.
3. Rachel E. Barkow, *Prisoners of Politics: Breaking the Cycle of Mass Incarceration* (Cambridge, MA: Harvard University Press, 2019); David Garland, *The Culture of Control: Crime and Social Order in Contemporary Society* (Chicago: University of Chicago Press, 2001); William J. Stuntz, *The Collapse of American Criminal Justice* (Cambridge, MA: Harvard University Press, 2011); James Forman, Jr., *Locking Up Our Own: Crime and Punishment in Black America* (New York: Farrar, Straus and Giroux, 2017).
4. President George Washington, "First Inaugural Address," April 30, 1789.
5. Patrick Henry, "Speech at the Virginia Ratifying Convention," June 5, 1788.
6. Samuel Adams, "Letter," *Boston Gazette*, October 28, 1771.
7. While the Framers may not have had an inclusive vision of *who* should be protected from government excess and therefore that concept needed to evolve over time, their ideas of *what* needed to be protected was comprehensive.
8. Alexander Hamilton, "The Federalist No. 74," in *The Federalist Papers*, ed. Ian Shapiro (New Haven: Yale University Press, 2009), 376; Steven Wilf, *Law's*

Imagined Republic: Popular Politics and Criminal Justice in Revolutionary America (Cambridge: Cambridge University Press, 2010), 140.
9. Rachel E. Barkow, "Separation of Powers and the Criminal Law," *Stanford Law Review* 58 (2006): 989–1054.
10. For a discussion of how the policies of mass incarceration backfire as a matter of public safety, see Barkow, *Prisoners of Politics*. Thus, even if one endorses a purely pragmatic theory of constitutional interpretation, these cases fail because they did not achieve their pragmatic goal of public safety but made things worse on that score.
11. The rate, while still high, has been declining. While "33% of Black men born in 1981 could expect to go to prison by their late 30s," researchers estimate that for the group of Black men born in 2001, their risk of incarceration by the age of 38 has dropped to 18.3 percent. Jason P. Robey, Michael Massoglia, and Michael T. Light, "A Generational Shift: Race and the Declining Lifetime Risk of Imprisonment," *Demography* 60, no. 4 (2023): 977–1003. These researchers caution, however, that "trends in decarceration are reversible," so there is no guarantee that rates will continue to fall. "A Generational Shift," 1000.
12. David Garland, "The Meaning of Mass Imprisonment," *Punishment & Society* 3, no. 1 (2001): 5–7, 6.

1. Lowering the Bar for Pretrial Detention

Epigraph: United States v. Salerno, 481 U.S. 739, 767 (1987) (Marshall, J., dissenting).
1. Nick Pinto, "The Bail Trap," *New York Times*, August 13, 2015.
2. Robert Lewis, "Waiting for Justice," *CalMatters*, March 31, 2021, https://calmatters.org/justice/2021/03/waiting.for.justice/.
3. ACLU, "LA County Jails," n.d., https://www.aclu.org/issues/prisoners-rights/cruel-inhuman-and-degrading-conditions/la-county-jails; Sharon Dolovich, "Two Models of the Prison: Accidental Humanity and Hypermasculinity in the L.A. County Jail," *Journal of Criminal Law & Criminology* 102, no. 4 (2012): 965–1117, 992–994.
4. Jennifer Gonnerman, "Kalief Browder, 1993–2015," *New Yorker*, June 7, 2015.
5. Caleb Foote, "The Coming Constitutional Crisis in Bail: II," *University of Pennsylvania Law Review* 113, no. 8 (1965): 1125–1185, 1132. A more recent examination in Maryland found that 7 percent of defendants jailed pretrial subsequently had all charges dropped. Colin Starger, "The Argument that Cries *Wolfish*," *MIT Computational Law Report*, August 14, 2020, https://law.mit.edu/pub/theargumentcrieswolfish/release/2.
6. Human Rights Watch, "The Price of Freedom: Bail and Pretrial Detention of Nonfelony Low-Income Defendants in New York City," December 2010, 2, https://www.hrw.org/sites/default/files/reports/us1210webwcover_0.pdf.
7. Caleb Foote, "The Coming Constitutional Crisis in Bail: I," *University of Pennsylvania Law Review* 113, no. 7 (1965): 959–999, 960.

8. Laura I. Appleman, "Justice in the Shadowlands: Pretrial Detention, Punishment, and the Sixth Amendment," *Washington & Lee Law Review* 69, no. 3 (2012): 1297–1369, 1312–1321; Alison Siegler, "Freedom Denied: How the Culture of Detention Created a Federal Jailing Crisis," Federal Criminal Justice Clinic, University of Chicago Law School, October 2022, 63–66.
9. Will Dobbie, Jacob Goldin, and Crystal S. Yang, "The Effects of Pre-trial Detention on Conviction, Future Crime, and Employment: Evidence from Randomly Assigned Judges," *American Economic Review* 108, no. 2 (2018): 201–240, 201; Paul Heaton, Sandra Mayson, and Megan Stevenson, "The Downstream Consequences of Misdemeanor Pretrial Detention," *Stanford Law Review* 69, no. 3 (2017): 711–794, 711; Christopher T. Lowenkamp, Marie VanNostrand, and Alexander Holsinger, "The Hidden Costs of Pretrial Detention," Laura & John Arnold Foundation, November 2013.
10. Brief of Amicus Curiae Public Defender Service for the District of Columbia in Support of Respondents, United States v. Salerno, 481 U.S. 739 (1987) (No. 86-87), 12–13.
11. United States v. Edwards, 430 A.2d 1321, 1355 (1981) (Ferren, J., concurring in part and dissenting in part).
12. Christopher T. Lowenkamp, Marie VanNostrand, and Alexander Holsinger, "Investigating the Impact of Pretrial Detention on Sentencing Outcomes," Laura & John Arnold Foundation, November 2013.
13. Siegler, "Freedom Denied," 68.
14. Alison Siegler and Erica Zunkel, "Rethinking Federal Bail Advocacy to Change the Culture of Detention," *The Champion* 44 (July 2020): 47.
15. Léon Digard and Elizabeth Swavola, "Justice Denied: The Harmful and Lasting Effects of Pretrial Detention," evidence brief, Vera Institute of Justice, April 2019, https://www.vera.org/downloads/publications/Justice-Denied-Evidence-Brief.pdf.
16. Shima Baradaran, "Restoring the Presumption of Innocence," *Ohio State Law Journal* 72, no. 4 (2011): 723–776, 725.
17. Matthew G. Rowland, "The Rising Federal Pretrial Detention Rate, in Context," *Federal Probation* 82, no. 2 (2018): 13–56, https://www.uscourts.gov/sites/default/files/82_2_2_0.pdf.
18. For those who posed a risk of flight, the law focused on release conditions as the first best option, and for bond to be used sparingly. The law made clear that preventive detention was not appropriate because "under American criminal jurisprudence pretrial bail may not be used as a device to protect society from the possible commission of additional crimes by the accused." Daniel Richman, "United States v. Salerno: The Constitutionality of Regulatory Detention," *Criminal Procedure Stories*, ed. Carol Steiker (New York: Foundation Press/St Paul, MN: Thomson/West, 2006), 416–417 (citing legislative history). The law also expanded factors judges could consider in making bail and release decisions, including the weight of evidence against the defendant. 18 U.S.C. § 3142(g)(2). In its defense of the law, the Department of Justice argued that the presumption of innocence had no applicability pretrial and this consideration

was appropriate. While the DOJ's stance had the effect of justifying a greater number of releases pursuant to the 1966 legislation, that same stance would later be used in support of arguments that more people should be detained pretrial because they were dangerous and that doing so did not undercut the presumption of innocence because it did not apply to pretrial detention. The law also explicitly allowed defendants to be held based on a dangerousness finding in capital cases. Although capital cases had historically been treated differently, that was because those defendants were presumed to be a flight risk. This law instead shifted the rationale to one of dangerousness—an idea that would ultimately come to dominate. John Logan Koepke and David G. Robinson, "Danger Ahead: Risk Assessment and the Future of Bail Reform," *Washington Law Review* 93, no. 4 (2018): 1725–1807, 1726, 1736–1737.

19. U.S. House of Representatives, Report No. 1541, 89th Cong., 2nd sess., 5–6, reprinted in *1996 U.S. Code Congressional and Administrative News*, 2296.
20. Appleman, "Justice in the Shadowlands," 1330.
21. Baradaran, "Restoring the Presumption," 741 and n.99.
22. "Presidential Statement to Congress: Nixon's D.C. Proposals," *CQ Almanac 1969*, 25th ed., 30-A32-A (Washington, DC: Congressional Quarterly, 1970).
23. Koepke and Robinson, "Danger Ahead," at 1740.
24. U.S. Senate, Report No. 225, 98th Cong., 2nd sess., 6, reprinted in *1984 U.S. Code Congressional and Administrative News*, 3188.
25. See, for example, Don Stemen and David Olson, "Is Bail Reform Causing an Increase in Crime?" HFG Research and Policy in Brief, Harry Frank Guggenheim Foundation, January 2023, https://www.hfg.org/wp-content/uploads/2023/01/Bail-Reform-and-Crime.pdf (finding no pattern between bail reform efforts and crime rates); Sishi Wu and David McDowall, "Does Bail Reform Increase Crime in New York State: Evidence from Interrupted Time-Series Analyses and Synthetic Control Methods," *Justice Quarterly* 41, no. 3 (2024): 371–399, 393, (finding that "the effect of bail reform on crime rate increase is negligible"); James Austin and Wendy Naro-Ware, "Why Bail Reform Is Safe and Effective: The Case of Cook County," JFA Institute, Denver CO, April 2020, 12, available at https://dx.doi.org/10.2139/ssrn.3599410 (finding that implementation of judicial order on pretrial release "resulted in over 3,000 people each year who no longer are needlessly jailed because they can't afford bail. . . . And crime rates have dropped. By any reasonable measures, bail reform in Cook County works and is safe to use."); Criminal Justice Reform, Report to the Governor and the Legislature, Jan. 1–Dec. 31, 2018, New Jersey Courts, April 2019, 5, https://web.archive.org/web/20200229165900/https://www.njcourts.gov/courts/assets/criminal/2018cjrannual.pdf?c=taP (finding that "statistics show that predictions of an increase in crime under CJR did not materialize").
26. "The Real Impact of Bail Reform on Public Safety," John Jay College of Criminal Justice, news release, March 8, 2023, https://new.jjay.cuny.edu/news-events/news/real-impact-bail-reform-public-safety.
27. U.S. Constitution, amends. V & XIV.

28. U.S. Constitution, amend. VIII.
29. United States v. Melendez-Carrion, 790 F.2d 984, 998 (2nd Cir. 1986).
30. Baradaran, "Restoring the Presumption," 730. According to Blackstone, all felonies were bailable "[b]y the ancient common law, before and since the conquest . . . till murder was excepted by statute." William Blackstone, *Commentaries on the Laws of England*, vol. 4, *A Facsimile of the First Edition of 1765–1769* (Chicago: University of Chicago Press, 1979), 295.
31. Stack v. Boyle, 342 U.S. 1, 4 (1951).
32. Matthew J. Hegreness, "America's Fundamental and Vanishing Right to Bail," *Arizona Law Review* 55, no. 4 (2013): 909–996, 914.
33. Baradaran, "Restoring the Presumption," 729.
34. United States v. Melendez-Carrion, 790 F.2d 984, 997 (2nd Cir. 1986) (citing State v. Konigsberg, 164 A.2d 740, 743 (N.J. 1960)).
35. Donald B. Verrilli, Jr., "The Eighth Amendment and the Right to Bail: Historical Perspectives," *Columbia Law Review* 82, no. 2 (1982): 328–362, 349.
36. Laurence H. Tribe, "An Ounce of Detention: Preventive Justice in the World of John Mitchell," *Virginia Law Review* 56, no. 3 (1970): 371–407, 377.
37. Gerstein v. Pugh, 420 US. 103 (1975).
38. United States v. Salerno, 73.
39. 790 F.2d at 1001.
40. Hudson v. Parker, 156 U.S. 277, 285 (1895).
41. Baradaran, "Restoring the Presumption," 735–736.
42. Foote, "The Coming Constitutional Crisis in Bail: I," 968.
43. Baradaran, "Restoring the Presumption," 727.
44. Foote, "The Coming Constitutional Crisis in Bail: I," at 974 (noting that "the English statutory pattern was in force in at least some of the colonies," and observing that New York included a bail right "taken almost verbatim from the English Habeas Corpus Act").
45. The bedrock importance of pretrial release may explain why the Excessive Bail Clause garnered little debate or discussion. There was no mention of it in the Senate and only one short mention in the House, where one representative did not object to the fact that the clause "seems to express a great deal of humanity" but asked "[w]hat is meant by the terms excessive bail?" and "[w]ho are to be the judges?" 1 Annals of Cong. 754 (1789–91). This did, not, however, spark any debate or further discussion. The amendment passed with broad approval. The Framers also drafted the First Judiciary Act, which provided a right to bail in all cases other than capital offenses, where judges would have discretion to set bail. It provided that "all persons shall be bailable, unless for capital offences, where the proof shall be evident, or the presumption great." 1 Stat. 91, § 33 (1789).
46. William F. Duker, "The Right to Bail: A Historical Inquiry," *Albany Law Review* 42, no. 1 (1977): 33–120, 69.
47. United States v. Melendez-Carrion, 998.
48. Tribe, "An Ounce of Detention," 400–401 (citing A. Highmore, A Digest of the Doctrine of Bail; in Civil and Criminal Cases (1783)).

49. Verrilli, "The Eighth Amendment and the Right to Bail," 357.
50. Verrilli, "The Eighth Amendment and the Right to Bail," 351. The exceptions were Hawaii and West Virginia.
51. Hegreness, "America's Fundamental and Vanishing Right to Bail," 956.
52. Baradaran, "Restoring the Presumption," 727–731.
53. Foote, "The Coming Constitutional Crisis in Bail: I," 980–982.
54. Sandra G. Mayson, "Dangerous Defendants," *Yale Law Journal* 127, no. 3 (2018): 490–568, 490, 503.
55. Hegreness, "America's Fundamental and Vanishing Right to Bail," 968.
56. Bearden v. Georgia, 461 U.S. 660, 672 (1983) (noting in the context of revocation proceedings that if someone is indigent "the court must consider alternate measures" and "[o]nly if alternate measures are not adequate" can imprisonment result); Pugh v. Rainwater, 572 F.2d 1053, 1058 (5th Cir. 1978) (en banc) ("We have no doubt that in the case of an indigent, whose appearance at trial could reasonably be assured by one of the alternate forms of release, pretrial confinement for inability to post money bail would constitute imposition of an excessive restraint."). See also Kellen R. Funk, "The Present Crisis in American Bail," *Yale Law Journal Forum* 128 (April 22, 2019): 1098–1125, 1107 (arguing that due process requires that "[t]he government must engage in sufficient process to carefully determine whether there is any other alternative to detention for failure to pay bail"); Sandra G. Mayson, "Detention by Any Other Name," *Duke Law Journal* 69 (2020): 1643–1680, 1670 (arguing that orders imposing unaffordable bail should be treated as denials and subject to the same level of process and checks).
57. Kansas v. Crane, 534 U.S. 407, 413 (2002).
58. Christopher Slobogin, "A Jurisprudence of Dangerousness," *Northwestern University Law Review* 98, no. 1 (2003): 1–62.
59. See, for example, 18 U.S.C. § 3148.
60. United States v. Melendez-Carrion, 790 F.2d at 1003.
61. Until 1966, federal defendants in non-capital cases could be released if they could post sufficient bail. The Bail Reform Act of 1966 tried to shift the model away from one that relied so heavily on a defendant's resources by "restricting the use of financial bonds in favor of pretrial release conditions." The 1966 legislation also authorized pretrial detention on the grounds of dangerousness in capital cases. Amaryllis Austin, "The Presumption of Detention Statute's Relationship to Release Rates," *Federal Probation* 81, no. 2 (September 2017): 52–63, 53.
62. Presidential Report, *Congressional Quarterly Weekly Report* 27 (February 7, 1969): 237–239, 238.
63. John N. Mitchell, "Bail Reform and the Constitutionality of Pretrial Detention," *Virginia Law Review* 55, no. 7 (1969): 1223–1242, 1225. Mitchell also argued that the Excessive Fines Clause sets no limits on what Congress itself can do. Tribe decimated this reading as well, pointing out that it "would render the Excessive Bail Clause superfluous, since the Due Process Clause standing alone would forbid the judicial imprisonment of a man

specifically entitled to release" under federal law. Tribe, "An Ounce of Detention," 400. The Eighth Amendment does more than that and limits legislative abuse and unjust limits on pretrial release. The Eighth Amendment limits Congress in all the contexts it covers—sentencing, bail, and fines. And the states are similarly limited by the incorporation of the clause through the Fourteenth Amendment.
64. United States v. Melendez-Carrion, 790 F.2d at 998.
65. Mitchell, "Bail Reform and the Constitutionality of Pretrial Detention," 1231. Then-Justice Rehnquist repeated this argument in his opinion for the Court in Bell v. Wolfish, 441 U.S. 520, 533 (1979), arguing without any support that the presumption of innocence "has no application to a determination of the rights of a pretrial detainee during confinement before his trial has even begun." The Court in *Wolfish* used the argument to permit onerous conditions on individuals who were detained pretrial, including double-bunking them in spaces designed for one person, condoning intrusive body cavity searches of detainees, and prohibiting them from receiving food and personal items from sources outside the institution.
66. Tribe, "An Ounce of Detention," at 373–374.
67. Tribe, "An Ounce of Detention," 371, 381, 390, 393.
68. D.C. Code Ann. §§ 23-1321-1332.
69. Richman, "United States v. Salerno: The Constitutionality of Regulatory Detention," 417.
70. Samuel Wiseman, "Discrimination, Coercion, and the Bail Reform Act of 1984: The Loss of the Core Constitutional Protections of the Excessive Bail Clause," *Fordham Urban Law Journal* 36, no. 1 (2009): 121–158, 143.
71. 18 U.S.C. § 3142(e)(3).
72. Austin, "The Presumption of Detention," 58, 60.
73. Senate Report No. 225, 98th Cong., 1st Sess., 6–7 (1983).
74. Richman, "United States v. Salerno: The Constitutionality of Regulatory Detention," 434.
75. Rowland, "The Rising Federal Detention Rate, in Context," 17 (internal quotations and citation omitted).
76. D.C. Code Ann. § 23-1322(d).
77. The Speedy Trial Act provides for a trial within 100 days of arrest, 18 U.S.C. §§ 3161(b), (c)(1), but it also has a list of specific exclusions as well as a catch-all exception to extend the limit if "the ends of justice served" by granting continuances "outweigh the best interest of the public and the defendant in a speedy trial." 18 U.S.C. § 3161(h)(7)(A).
78. United States v. Melendez-Carrion, 790 F.2d 984, 996 (1986) (quoting legislative history).
79. United States v. Melendez-Carrion, 996.
80. Austin, "The Presumption of Detention," 53, 60.
81. Marc Miller and Martin Guggenheim, "Pretrial Detention and Punishment," *Minnesota Law Review* 75, no. 2 (1990): 335–426, 347–348.
82. House Report 1419, 94th Cong., 2nd Sess., 4 (1976).

83. Albert W. Alschuler, "Preventive Pretrial Detention and the Failure of Interest-Balancing Approaches to Due Process," *Michigan Law Review* 85, no. 3 (1986): 510–569, 519.
84. S. Rep. No. 225, 98th Cong., 2d Sess. 4, reprinted in 1984 U.S. Code Cong & Admin News 3182, 3185.
85. Miller and Guggenheim, "Pretrial Detention and Punishment," 400–404.
86. United States v. Salerno, 631 F. Supp. 1364, 1375 (S.D.N.Y. 1986).
87. 18 U.S.C. § 3143(b)(1).
88. United States v. Salerno, 481 U.S. 739, 756 n.1 (1987) (Marshall, J., dissenting).
89. United States v. Salerno, 757 (Marshall, J., dissenting).
90. United States v. Salerno, 769 n.2 (Stevens, J., dissenting).
91. Alschuler, "Preventive Pretrial Detention," 512 n.3; Hegreness, "America's Fundamental and Vanishing Right to Bail," 959.
92. Hegreness, "America's Fundamental and Vanishing Right to Bail," at 961.
93. United States v. Brown, 381 U.S. 437, 458 (1965).
94. The Colonial Laws of Massachusetts § 18, at 37 (W. Whitmore ed. 1889).
95. Hudson v. Parker, 156 U.S. 277, 285 (1895) (emphasis added).
96. Stack v. Boyle, 341 U.S. 1, 8 (1951) (Jackson, J.).
97. United States v. Salerno, 747 ("The legislative history of the Bail Reform Act clearly indicates that Congress did not formulate the pretrial detention provisions as punishment for dangerous individuals.").
98. United States v. Salerno, 747.
99. 18 U.S.C. § 3142(i)(2).
100. Bail Reform Act Hearings on Oversight and H.R. 1098, H.R. 3005, and H.R. 3491: Hearing Before the H. Subcomm. on Courts, Civil Liberties, and the Admin. of Justice of the H. Comm. on the Judiciary, 98th Cong. 230 (1984) (statement of Congressman Romano Mazzoli, Member, H. Subcomm. on Courts, Civil Liberties, and the Admin. of Justice).
101. Mitchell, "Bail Reform and the Constitutionality of Pretrial Detention," at 1236.
102. New York Post Editorial Board, "Change the Bail Laws to Punish Fentanyl Killers—NOW," *New York Post*, March 2023.
103. Chris Rosato, "State Representative Wants Stiffer Bail for Violent Crime," *WAFB*, April 7, 2023, https://www.wafb.com/2023/04/07/state-representative-wants-stiffer-bail-violent-crime/.
104. Amicus Curiae Brief of the American Civil Liberties Union, New York Civil Liberties Union and ACLU Foundation of Southern California in Support of Respondents, U.S. v. Salerno, 481 U.S. 739 (1987) (No. 86-87) [hereinafter ACLU Brief].
105. State v. Konigsberg, 33 N.J. 367, 375 (1960).
106. United States v. Salerno, 749–50.
107. ACLU Brief, 32.
108. Brief for the United States, Salerno v. United States, 17.
109. Samuel Issacharoff and Richard H. Pildes, "Emergency Contexts without Emergency Powers: The United States' Constitutional Approach to Rights

during Wartime," *International Journal of Constitutional Law* 2, no. 2 (2004): 296–333, 311.
110. Trump v. Hawaii, 138 S.Ct. 2392, 2423 (2018) (quoting Korematsu v. United States, 323 U.S. 214, 248 (1944) (Jackson, J., dissenting)).
111. Interestingly enough, the Supreme Court's opinion, unlike the SG's brief, does not cite *Korematsu* directly when it makes this claim, perhaps recognizing, even in 1987, that *Korematsu* was not exactly a standard to rely on. But *Salerno* relies on the same framework, and *Korematsu* is certainly a cautionary tale that liberty should not be ignored in the face of momentary panic.
112. The Court mentioned other lines of authority, but those are also easily distinguishable. One involved non-citizens, another involved those with mental illnesses, and a third involved people detained in order to preserve the ability for a trial to go forward. The power to detain aliens falls into a different category because they "possess less than the full breadth of constitutional protection." Those with mental illnesses are distinguishable because the "ordinary restraint of law is unavailable" precisely because of how their mental illness operates on their decision-making. And the power to detain people incident to arrest or to protect witnesses is to ensure a fair trial. Miller and Guggenheim, "Pretrial Detention and Punishment," 361–365.
113. Schall v. Martin, 467 U.S. 253, 255 (1984).
114. Congress passed the Bail Reform Act within a few months of the release of the opinion in *Schall*, and some commentators believe it felt "emboldened" to do so as a result. Baradaran, "Restoring the Presumption," 747.
115. Schall v. Martin, 265.
116. Miller and Guggenheim, "Pretrial Detention and Punishment," 349.
117. Schall v. Martin, 305–306 (Marshall, J., dissenting).
118. Schall v. Martin, at 295 n.21 (Marshall, J., dissenting).
119. Miller and Guggenheim, "Pretrial Detention and Punishment," 353–354, 361.
120. Schall v. Martin, 290 (Marshall, J., dissenting).
121. Schall v. Martin, at 271.
122. Stack v. Boyle, 342 U.S. 1, 4 (1951).
123. United States v. Salerno, 755 (Marshall, J., dissenting).
124. United States v. Salerno, 755 (Marshall, J., dissenting).
125. United States v. Salerno, 760–761 (Marshall, J., dissenting).
126. United States v. Salerno, 763–764 (Marshall, J., dissenting). Justice Brennan joined Justice Marshall's opinion. Justice Stevens wrote a separate dissent to note "a pending indictment may not be given any weight in evaluating an individual's risk to the community or the need for immediate detention." In his view, "[i]f the evidence of imminent danger is strong enough to warrant emergency detention, it should support that preventive measure regardless of whether the person has been charged, convicted, or acquitted of some other offense." United States v. Salerno, 768–769 (Stevens, J., dissenting).
127. Baradaran, "Restoring the Presumption," 751.
128. Hegreness, "America's Fundamental and Vanishing Right to Bail," 964.

129. Shima Baradaran and Frank McIntyre, "Predicting Violence," *Texas Law Review* 90, no. 3 (2012): 497–570, 507.
130. Grace Ashford and Johan E. Bromwich, "New York's Bail Laws, Reconsidered: 5 Things to Know," *New York Times*, March 29, 2022.
131. Scott W. Howe, "The Implications of Incorporating the Eighth Amendment Prohibition on Excessive Bail," *Hofstra Law Review* 43, no. 4 (2015): 1039–1085, 1041.
132. Digard and Swavola, "Justice Denied: The Harmful and Lasting Effects of Pretrial Detention."
133. United States v. Salerno, 747 n.4.
134. United States v. Salerno, 750.
135. Mitchell, "Bail Reform and the Constitutionality of Pretrial Detention," at 1237.
136. United States v. Salerno, 755.
137. Rowland, "The Rising Federal Detention Rate, in Context." This is up from 60 percent in 2006, and 38 percent in 1992. Baradaran, "Restoring the Presumption," 725. In 1985, 19 percent of defendants were detained pretrial and 10 percent were held for failure to make bail. Stephen Kennedy and Kenneth E. Carlson, "Pretrial Release and Detention: The Bail Reform Act of 1984," special report, NCJ 109929, Bureau of Justice Statistics, February 1988, 2, Table 1, https://bjs.ojp.gov/content/pub/pdf/prd-bra84.pdf. The 1983 statistic is from Siegler, "Freedom Denied," 22, fig. 1.
138. Austin, "The Presumption of Detention," 55.
139. Siegler, "Freedom Denied," 16, 40.
140. United States v. Salerno, 747.
141. Siegler, "Freedom Denied," 23.
142. See, for example, Rivera v. United States, 511 U.S. 1011 (No. 93-1095) (March 28, 1994) (denying cert where question presented was whether a two-year period of pretrial detention violated the Due Process Clause); Pappas v. United States, 520 U.S. 1198 (No. 96-1543) (April 28, 1997) (denying cert where petitioner charged with fraud challenged more than 20-month period of pretrial detention).
143. Petition, Boese v. United States, 1992 WL 12073445 (1992); Boese v. United States, 507 U.S. 916 (No. 92-1059) (Feb. 22, 1993) (cert denied).
144. Siegler, "Freedom Denied," 32.
145. Tribe, "An Ounce of Detention," 375.
146. Foote, "The Coming Constitutional Crisis in Bail: II," 1172.
147. Shima Baradaran, "Race, Prediction, and Discretion," *George Washington Law Review* 81, no. 1 (2013): 157–222, 161–162.
148. Besiki Kutateladze, Whitney Tymas, and Mary Crowley, "Race and Prosecution in Manhattan," research summary, Vera Institute of Justice, July 2014, 5, https://www.vera.org/downloads/publications/race-and-prosecution-manhattan-summary.pdf. See also Dobbie, Goldin, and Yang, "The Effects of Pretrial Detention on Conviction, Future Crime, and Employment," 214

(Black defendants and defendants from zip codes with below median incomes in Miami-Dade County in Florida and Philadelphia County in Pennsylvania were more likely to be detained pretrial than other defendants).

149. Shawn D. Bushway and Jonah B. Gelbach, "Testing for Racial Discrimination in Bail Setting Using Nonparametric Estimation of a Parametric Model," unpublished ms, August 20, 2011, 10, available at https://papers.ssrn.com/sol3/papers.cfm?abstract_id=1990324.
150. Stephen Demuth, "Racial and Ethnic Differences in Pretrial Release Decisions and Outcomes: A Comparison of Hispanic, Black, and White Felony Arrestees," *Criminology* 41, no. 3 (2003): 873–908, 895–897.
151. Siegler, "Freedom Denied," 33, 58.
152. Brief for Americans for Effective Law Enforcement, et al. as Amici Curiae Supporting Petitioner, United States v. Salerno, No. 86–87, (1987), 13.
153. Alwyn Scott and Suzanne Barlyn, "U.S. Bail-bond Insurers Spend Big to Keep Defendants Paying," Reuters, March 26, 2021, https://www.reuters.com/article/us-usa-insurance-bail-jails-insight/u-s-bail-bond-insurers-spend-big-to-keep-defendants-paying-idUSKBN2BI1BP; Amanda Gullings, "The Commercial Bail Industry: Profit or Public Safety?" Center on Juvenile and Criminal Justice, May 2012, 7, https://www.cjcj.org/media/import/documents/profit_or_public_safety.pdf.
154. "For Better or For Profit: How the Bail Bonding Industry Stands in the Way of Fair and Effective Pretrial Justice," Justice Policy Institute, Washington, DC, September 2012, 27, https://justicepolicy.org/wp-content/uploads/justicepolicy/documents/_for_better_or_for_profit_.pdf.
155. Scott and Barlyn, "U.S. Bail-bond Insurers Spend Big."
156. Siegler, "Freedom Denied," 47.
157. Brian A. Reaves, "Felony Defendants in Large Urban Counties, 2009—Statistical Tables," NCJ 243777, Bureau of Justice Statistics, U.S. Department of Justice, 15, https://bjs.ojp.gov/content/pub/pdf/fdluc09.pdf.
158. Samuel R. Wiseman, "Fixing Bail," *George Washington Law Review* 84, no. 2 (2016): 417–479, 429–430.
159. Appleman, "Justice in the Shadowlands," 1311.
160. United States v. Salerno, 755.
161. American Bar Association Project on Minimum Standards for Criminal Justice, *Standards Relating to Pretrial Release* (New York: Institute on Judicial Administration, 1968).
162. S. Rep. No. 225, 98th Cong., 2d. Sess., 11 reprinted in *1984 U.S. Code Cong. & Admin. News,* at 3194. See also Brief for Americans for Effective Law Enforcement, 11–12.
163. Lauryn P. Gouldin, "Disentangling Flight Risk from Dangerousness," *Brigham Young University Law Review* 2016, no. 3 (2016): 837–898, 837, 863.
164. Koepke and Robinson, "Danger Ahead," at 1786.
165. 342 U.S. at 10 (Jackson, J., concurring).

166. Siegler, "Freedom Denied," 24–26, 47.
167. Funk, "The Present Crisis in American Bail," 1114.
168. Arpit Gupta, Christopher Hansman, and Ethan Frenchman, "The Heavy Costs of High Bail: Evidence from Judge Randomization," *Journal of Legal Studies* 45, no. 2 (2016): 471–505, 475.
169. Between 1990 and 2004, the average bail amount in felony cases increased more than 40 percent. Carissa Byrne Hessick, *Punishment without Trial: Why Plea Bargaining Is a Bad Deal* (New York: Abrams Press, 2021), 70.
170. Brief for Americans for Effective Law Enforcement, 13.
171. Lowenkamp, VanNostrand, and Holsinger, "Hidden Costs of Pretrial Detention," 19; Charles E. Loeffler and Daniel S. Nagin, "The Impact of Incarceration on Recidivism," *American Review of Criminology* 5, no. 1 (2021): 133–152, 143, 149; Emily Leslie and Nolan G. Pope, "The Unintended Impact of Pretrial Detention on Case Outcomes: Evidence from New York City Arraignments," *Journal of Law and Economics* 60, no. 3 (2017): 529–557, 529.
172. Siegler, "Freedom Denied," 70–71.
173. Siegler, "Freedom Denied," 23.
174. United States v. Salerno, 767 (Marshall, J., dissenting).

2. Normalizing Coercive Plea Bargaining

Epigraph: William Blackstone, *Commentaries on the Laws of England*, vol. 4, *A Facsimile of the First Edition of 1765–1769* (Chicago: University of Chicago Press, 1979), 350.

1. Josh Bowers, "Plea Bargaining's Baselines," *William & Mary Law Review* 57, no. 4 (2016): 1083–1145, 1109; "Clarence Aaron," Families for Justice Reform (FAMM), May 2, 2018, https://web.archive.org/web/20240303224315/https://famm.org/stories/clarence-aaron/.
2. United States v. Angelos 345 F.Supp.2d 1227, 1230 (2004). Angelos served only 13 years because of widespread advocacy on his behalf.
3. Jeffrey Abramson, *We, The Jury* (New York: Basic Books, 1994), 28.
4. Bordenkircher v. Hayes, 434 U.S. 357 (1978).
5. Rachel E. Barkow, "The Court of Mass Incarceration," *Cato Supreme Court Review* (2022): 11.
6. Santobello v. New York, 404 U.S. 257 (1971).
7. N. Pipeline Constr. Co. v. Marathon Pipe Line Co., 458 US. 50, 58 (1982).
8. United States ex rel. McCann v. Adams, 126 F.2d 774, 775–776 (2d Cir.), rev'd on other grounds, 317 U.S. 269 (1942).
9. Abramson, *We, The Jury*, 87.
10. U.S. Constitution, art. III, § 2, cl. 3.
11. Jon P. McClanahan, "The 'True' Right to Trial by Jury: The Founders' Formulation and Its Demise," *West Virginia Law Review* 111, no. 3 (2009): 791–830, 793.

12. Rachel E. Barkow, "Recharging the Jury: The Criminal Jury's Constitutional Role in an Era of Mandatory Sentencing," *University of Pennsylvania Law Review* 152, no. 1 (2003): 33–127, 54.
13. Alexander Hamilton, "The Federalist No. 83," in *The Federalist Papers* (New York: New American Library, 1961), 499.
14. Thomas Jefferson to the Abbé Arnoux, July 17, 1789, in *The Papers of Thomas Jefferson*, vol. 15, *27 March to 30 November 1789*, ed. Julian P. Boyd and William H. Gaines, Jr. (Princeton, NJ: Princeton University Press, 1958), 282, 283.
15. United States ex rel. Toth v. Quarles, 350 U.S. 11, 18–19 (1955).
16. Sir Patrick Devlin, *Trial by Jury* (London: Hamlyn, 1966), 160.
17. George Fisher, *Plea Bargaining's Triumph: A History of Plea Bargaining in America* (Stanford, CA: Stanford University Press, 2004). For other excellent histories of plea bargaining, see Albert W. Alschuler, "Plea Bargaining and Its History," *Columbia Law Review* 79, no. 1 (1979): 1–43, 1; Lawrence M. Friedman, "Plea Bargaining in Historical Perspective," *Law & Society Review* 13, no. 2 (1979): 247–259; John H. Langbein, "Understanding the Short History of Plea Bargaining," *Law and Society Review* 13, no. 2 (1979): 261–272.
18. Nancy Jean King, "Priceless Process, Nonnegotiable Features of Criminal Litigation," *UCLA Law Review* 47, no. 1 (1999): 113–181, 125.
19. William Ortman, "When Plea Bargaining Became Normal," *Boston University Law Review* 100, no. 4 (2020): 1435–1499, 1437–1466 and Table 1.
20. Ortman, "When Plea Bargaining Became Normal," at 1476–1477 (citation omitted).
21. Albert W. Alschuler, "Plea Bargaining and Mass Incarceration," *NYU Annual Survey of American Law* 76 (2021): 205–234, 213.
22. President's Commission on Law Enforcement and Administration of Justice, *The Challenge of Crime in a Free Society* (Washington, DC: US GPO, 1967), 134–135.
23. American Bar Association Project on Minimum Standards for Criminal Justice, *Standards Relating to Pleas of Guilty*, Tentative Draft (Chicago: American Bar Association, Feb. 1967), 49–51. The ABA tried to couch this as consistent with the purposes of punishment because it stated that, "in localities with a significant court congestion problem," guilty pleas can help facilitate prompt and certain punishment for more people, which furthers the "rehabilitative, preventive, and deterrent objectives of the criminal law."
24. President's Commission on Law Enforcement and Administration of Justice, *The Challenge of Crime in a Free Society* (Washington, DC: U.S. GPO, February 1967), 135.
25. Koontz v. St. John's River Water Mgmt. District, 570 U.S. 595, 604 (2013) (internal quotations and citations omitted).
26. Thomas R. McCoy and Michael J. Mirra, "Plea Bargaining as Due Process in Determining Guilt," *Stanford Law Review* 32, no. 5 (1980): 887–941, 887–888.

27. Howard E. Abrams, "Systemic Coercion: Unconstitutional Conditions in the Criminal Law," *Journal of Criminal Law & Criminology* 72, no. 1 (1981): 128–164.
28. "Another Look at Unconstitutional Conditions," *University of Pennsylvania Law Review* 117, no. 1 (1968): 144–182, 174.
29. John H. Langbein, "On the Myth of Written Constitutions: The Disappearance of Criminal Jury Trial," *Harvard Journal of Law & Public Policy* 15, no. 1 (1992): 119–127, 124.
30. Jason Mazzone, "The Waiver Paradox," *Northwestern University Law Review* 97, no. 2 (2003): 801–878, 802.
31. Koontz v. St. John's River Water Mgmt. District, 608.
32. Frost v. Railroad Comm'n of California, 271 U.S. 583, 593–594 (1926).
33. Mazzone, "The Waiver Paradox," 802–803. Kay L. Levine, Jonathan Remy Nash, and Robert Schapiro, "The Unconstitutional Conditions Vacuum in Criminal Procedure," *Yale Law Journal* 133, no. 5 (2024), (noting that criminal procedure rights more generally have been improperly ignored under the unconstitutional conditions framework).
34. In 1957, a Fifth Circuit panel decision followed the unconstitutional conditions framework to its logical conclusion and concluded that a guilty plea obtained by a promise of leniency was not voluntary, noting that "[j]ustice and liberty are not the subjects of bargaining and barter." Shelton v. United States, 242 F.2d 1010, 113 (5th Cir. 1957). The Fifth Circuit sitting en banc reversed, 246 F.2d 571 (5th Cir. 1957). The Solicitor General seemed to want to avoid Supreme Court review of the issue at that point and confessed error, conceding that the trial court did not do conduct a sufficient inquiry before accepting the plea. William Ortman, "When Plea Bargaining Became Normal," *Boston University Law Review* 100, no. 4 (2020): 1435–1499, 1494.
35. William E. Nelson, *Americanization of the Common Law: The Impact of Legal Change on Massachusetts Society, 1760–1830* (Cambridge, MA: Harvard University Press, 1994), 96.
36. For a discussion of coercion in the unconstitutional conditions framework, see Kathleen M. Sullivan, "Unconstitutional Conditions," *Harvard Law Review* 102, no. 7 (1989): 1413–1506, 1428–1442.
37. Mazzone, "The Waiver Paradox," 832.
38. Rachel E. Barkow, "Separation of Powers and the Criminal Law," *Stanford Law Review* 58, no. 4 (2006): 989–1054, 1037.
39. Sparf v. United States, 156 U.S. 51 (1895).
40. Akhil Reed Amar, *The Bill of Rights: Creation and Reconstruction* (New Haven, CT: Yale University Press, 1998), 108; Patton v. United States, 281 U.S. 276 (1930). The Court has not permitted defendants to waive a jury trial in favor of a bench trial when the government opposes. Singer v. United States, 380 U.S. 24 (1965).
41. Rachel E. Barkow, "The Ascent of the Administrative State and the Demise of Mercy," *Harvard Law Review* 121, no. 5 (2008): 1332–1365.

42. Rebecca Love Kourlis, "Not Jury Nullification; Not a Call for Ethical Reform; But Rather a Case for Judicial Control," *University of Colorado Law Review* 67, no. 4 (1996): 1109–1120, 1111–1112.
43. Abramson, *We, The Jury*, 3–4.
44. Kate Stith-Cabranes, "The Criminal Jury in Our Time," *Virginia Journal of Social Policy & Law* 3, no. 1 (1995): 133–146, 143.
45. Barkow, "Recharging the Jury," 84 (citing ABA study).
46. John Gramlich, "Jury Duty Is Rare, but Most Americans See It as Part of Good Citizenship," Pew Research Center, August 24, 2017, https://www.pewresearch.org/fact-tank/2017/08/24/jury-duty-is-rare-but-most-americans-see-it-as-part-of-good-citizenship/.
47. Loftus E. Becker, Jr., "Plea Bargaining and the Supreme Court," *Loyola of Los Angeles Law Review* 21, no. 3 (1988): 757–841, 830.
48. "The Unconstitutionality of Plea Bargaining," *Harvard Law Review* 83, no. 6 (1970): 1387–1411, 1399–1401.
49. Garrity v. New Jersey, 385 U.S. 493, 500 (1967).
50. Indeed, plea bargaining at the federal level could be ruled unconstitutional as a violation of separation of powers even without applying the doctrine of unconstitutional conditions. For a discussion of this separation of powers argument, see Barkow, "Separation of Powers and the Criminal Law," 1044–1050.
51. "The Unconstitutionality of Plea Bargaining," 1398.
52. "The Unconstitutionality of Plea Bargaining," 1405.
53. "Another Look at Unconstitutional Conditions," *University of Pennsylvania Law Review* 117 (1968): 174–180.
54. United States v. Jackson, 390 U.S. 570, 581 (1968).
55. American Bar Association, *Standards Relating to Pleas of Guilty*, 41–48.
56. McCoy and Mirra, "Plea Bargaining as Due Process in Determining Guilt," 905 and n. 91.
57. McCoy and Mirra, "Plea Bargaining as Due Process in Determining Guilt," 894, 905 and nn.36, 91–92. See also Ryan C. Williams, "Unconstitutional Conditions and the Constitutional Text," *University of Pennsylvania Law Review* 172, no. 3 (2024): 788–794.
58. Williams, "Unconstitutional Conditions and the Constitutional Text," 790.
59. Koontz v. St. John's River Water Mgmt. District, 605–606; Levine, Nash, and Schapiro, "The Unconstitutional Conditions Vacuum," 56.
60. Mitchell N. Berman, "Coercion Without Baselines: Unconstitutional Conditions in Three Dimensions," *Georgetown Law Journal* 90, no. 1 (2001): 1–112, 102–103.
61. John H. Langbein, "Torture and Plea Bargaining," *University of Chicago Law Review* 46, no. 1 (1978): 3–22, 12.
62. National Federal of Independent Business v. Sebelius, 567 U.S. 519, 681 (2012) (Scalia, J., dissenting). Justice Scalia went on to state his view that courts should therefore not strike down legislation on this basis "unless the coercive

nature of an offer is unmistakably clear." He concluded that was met in the Affordable Care Act case based on congressional intent, thus presumably it would be just as clear in a case like *Bordenkircher* given the prosecutor's clear statement of intent. Bowers, "Plea Bargaining's Baselines," 1139 and n.314.
63. Levine, Nash, and Schapiro, "The Unconstitutional Conditions Vacuum," 56–57 (noting that the Court's incorporation cases emphasize the importance of the jury "to an ordered system of justice").
64. American Bar Association, Criminal Justice Section, *Plea Bargain Task Force Report*, August 2023, 25, https://www.americanbar.org/content/dam/aba/publications/criminaljustice/plea-bargain-tf-report.pdf.
65. Becker, "Plea Bargaining and the Supreme Court," 788. Indeed, this was the "heyday" of the doctrine. See also n.172.
66. In 1959, Robert Brady had been charged under a federal kidnapping law that provided for the death penalty if a jury found that the victim had "not been liberated unharmed, and if the verdict of the jury shall so recommend." A trial before a judge would preclude the death penalty as an option, but the trial judge in Brady's case refused to hear the case without a jury. Brady initially pleaded not guilty, but he changed his mind after learning that his codefendant pleaded guilty and was available to testify against him. At that point, Brady pleaded guilty. He later filed a habeas petition challenging his plea as involuntary. Brady relied on *United States v. Jackson*, 390 U.S. 570 (1968), decided after his conviction, and in which the Supreme Court found the federal kidnapping statute under which he was charged to be unconstitutional because it "needlessly penalize[d] the assertion of a constitutional right." The Supreme Court, however, rejected Brady's argument that *Jackson* required the invalidation of his plea as coerced. It found that Brady changed his plea from not guilty to guilty because his codefendant became available to serve as a witness against him if he went to trial, not because a decision to go to trial would mean he could get the death penalty. The Court added, however, that "even if we assume that Brady would not have pleaded guilty except for the death penalty provision" of the statute, that "does not necessarily prove that the plea was coerced and invalid as an involuntary act." Brady v. United States, 397 U.S. 742, 750 (1970).
67. Chief Justice Warren Earl Burger, "The State of the Judiciary—1970," *American Bar Association Journal* 56, no. 10 (1970): 929–934, 931.
68. Santobello v. New York, 260–261.
69. Blackledge v. Allison, 431 U.S. 63, 71 (1977).
70. Brady v. United States, 751 n.8.
71. In a concurrence in *Brady*, Justice Brennan noted that "the term 'involuntary' has traditionally been applied to situations in which an individual, while perfectly capable of rational choice, has been confronted with factors that the government may not constitutionally inject into the decision-making process." Brady v. United States, 802 (Brennan, J. concurring). Justice Brennan then cited one of the unconstitutional conditions cases, *Garrity v. New Jersey*, 385 U.S. 493 (1967), in which the Court held that police officers did not validly waive the privilege against self-incrimination when they were told they would

be fired if they did not confess. The door thus remained open for the Court to view prosecutorial threats of more serious charges or sentences to obtain pleas as unconstitutional conditions on the jury trial right. Justice Douglas's concurring opinion in *Santobello* echoed this reading of the cases, as he pointed out that the Court had not yet "spelled out what sorts of promises by prosecutors tend to be coercive." Santobello v. New York, 266 (Douglas, J., concurring).
72. Bordenkircher v. Hayes, 434 U.S. 357, 358 n.1 (1978).
73. William J. Stuntz, "Bordenkircher v. Hayes: Plea Bargaining and the Decline of the Rule of Law," in *Criminal Procedure Stories*, ed. Carol Steiker (New York: Foundation Press/St Paul, MN: Thomson/West, 2006), 352–356.
74. Brief Amicus Curiae on Behalf of Jimmy Harris, Mitchell Ray Rodgers and Other Texas Prison Inmates Similarly Situated Urging Affirmance, Bordenkircher v. Hayes, No. 76-1334, 1977 WL 189706 (Aug. 15, 1977).
75. Brief of Amicus Curiae State of Texas in Support of Petitioner, Bordenkircher v. Hayes, No. 76-1334, 1977 WL 189708, 4, 6 (July 21, 1977).
76. Brief of the Office of the California State Public Defender, the California Public Defenders Association, and the California Attorneys for Criminal Justice as Amici Curiae in Support of the Respondent, Bordenkircher v. Hayes, No. 76-1334, 1977 WL 189704, 3 (Aug. 12, 1977).
77. 434 U.S. at 363.
78. 434 U.S. at 363, 365.
79. Albert W. Alschuler, "Lafler and Frye: Two Small Band-Aids for a Festering Wound," *Duquesne Law Review* 51, no. 3 (2013): 673–707, 686.
80. Clarissa Byrne Hessick, *Punishment Without Trial: Why Plea Bargaining Is a Bad Deal* (New York: Abrams Press, 2021), 47.
81. Albert Alschuler, "The Supreme Court, the Defense Attorney, and the Guilty Plea," *University of Colorado Law Review* 47 (1975): 1–71, 55.
82. Brady v. United States, 758.
83. "Innocents Who Plead Guilty," National Registry of Exonerations, University of Michigan Law School, November 24, 2015, 1, http://www.law.umich.edu/special/exoneration/Documents/NRE.Guilty.Plea.Article1.pdf.
84. Samuel Dash, "Cracks in the Foundation of Criminal Justice," *Illinois Law Review* 46, no. 3 (1951): 385–406, 401.
85. American Bar Association, *Plea Bargain Task Force Report*, 20; McCoy and Mirra, "Plea Bargaining as Due Process in Determining Guilt," 928.
86. Bordenkircher v. Hayes, 364.
87. United States v. Goodwin, 457 U.S. 368, 378 (1982).
88. Brady v. United States, 751 n.8.
89. Kaley v. United States, 571 U.S. 320, 338 (2014).
90. Bordenkircher v. Hayes, 364 n.8.
91. William Ortman, "Probable Cause Revisited," *Stanford Law Review* 68, no. 3 (2016): 511–568.
92. Bordenkircher v. Hayes, 367 (Blackmun, J., dissenting) (internal quotation omitted).

93. Bordenkircher v. Hayes, 360–361.
94. Bordenkircher v. Hayes, 367, 368 (Blackmun, J., dissenting).
95. Doug Lieb, "Vindicating Vindictiveness: Prosecutorial Discretion and Plea Bargaining, Past and Future," *Yale Law Journal* 123, no. 4 (2014): 1014–1069, 1023–1024 (citing Letter from Justice Lewis Powell to Justice Potter Stewart, Dec. 28, 1977).
96. Bordenkircher v. Hayes, 372 (Powell, J., dissenting).
97. Mazzone, "The Waiver Paradox," 846, 849.
98. McCoy and Mirra, "Plea Bargaining as Due Process in Determining Guilt," 914.
99. Bowers, "Plea Bargaining's Baselines," 1090.
100. Stuntz, "Bordenkircher v. Hayes," 363–364, 375–377.
101. Angela J. Davis, "The American Prosecutor: Independence, Power, and the Threat of Tyranny," *Iowa Law Review* 86 (2001): 393–465, 413.
102. American Bar Association, *Plea Bargain Task Force Report*, 17.
103. Alschuler, "Plea Bargaining and Mass Incarceration," 226–228, 233.
104. American Bar Association, *Plea Bargain Task Force Report*, 14.
105. G. K. Chesterton, *Tremendous Trifles* (New York: Dodd, Mead,, 1909), 86. While Chesterton was referring specifically to judges, not prosecutors, his point applies equally to prosecutors.
106. Gerard E. Lynch, "Our Administrative System of Criminal Justice," *Fordham Law Review* 66, no. 6 (1998): 2117–2151, 2122.
107. Hessick, *Punishment Without Trial*, 169, 171–75.
108. McNabb v. United States, 318 U.S. 332, 343 (1943).
109. Alschuler, "Plea Bargaining and Mass Incarceration," 219–220.
110. Missouri v. Frye, 566 U.S. 134, 144 (2012) (quoting Barkow, "Separation of Powers and the Criminal Law," 1034).
111. William J. Stuntz, "Plea Bargaining and Criminal Law's Disappearing Shadow," *Harvard Law Review* 117, no. 8 (2004): 2548–2569, 2554.
112. Rachel E. Barkow, "Administering Crime," *UCLA Law Review* 52 (2005): 715–814, 728 and n.25; Shon Hopwood, "The Misplaced Trust in the DOJ's Expertise on Criminal Justice Policy," *Michigan Law Review* 118, no. 6 (2020): 1181–1203.
113. Federal Cocaine Sentencing Policy, Hearing Before the Subcomm. on Crime and Drugs of the Senate Comm. on the Judiciary, 107th Cong., May 22, 2002 (statement of Roscoe C. Howard, U.S. Attorney for the District of Columbia), https://www.govinfo.gov/content/pkg/CHRG-107shrg86452/html/CHRG-107shrg86452.htm.
114. Drug Mandatory Minimums: Are They Working? Hearing Before the Subcomm. on Criminal Justice, Drug Policy, and Human Resources of the House Comm. on Government Reform, 106th Cong., May 11, 2000 (statement of John Roth, Chief, Narcotic and Dangerous Drug Section, Criminal Division, Dept. of Justice), https://www.govinfo.gov/content/pkg/CHRG-106hhrg70887/html/CHRG-106hhrg70887.htm.

115. William J. Stuntz, "The Pathological Politics of Criminal Law," *Michigan Law Review* 100, no. 3 (2001): 505–600; Rachel E. Barkow, "Institutional Design and the Policing of Prosecutors," *Stanford Law Review* 61, no. 4 (2009): 869–921, 880.
116. Stephanos Bibas, "Regulating the Plea-Bargaining Market: From Caveat Emptor to Consumer Protection," *California Law Review* 99, no. 4 (2011): 1117–1161, 1138.
117. Alschuler, "Plea Bargaining and Mass Incarceration," 209.
118. Alschuler, "Plea Bargaining and Mass Incarceration," 210–211.
119. Stephen J. Schulhofer, "Plea Bargaining as Disaster," *Yale Law Journal* 101, no. 8 (1992): 1979–2009, 1993.
120. 161 Congressional Record S955-02, S963 (daily ed. Feb. 12, 2015).
121. Barkow, "Separation of Powers and the Criminal Law," 1034 n.249.
122. United States v. Docampo, 573 F.3d 1091, 1101 (11th Cir. 2009).
123. United States v. Cano-Flores, 796 F.3d 83, 90 (D.C. Cir. 2015); Keri A. Gould, "Turning Rat and Doing Time for Uncharged, Dismissed, or Acquitted Crimes: Do the Federal Sentencing Guidelines Promote Respect for the Law?" *New York Law School Journal of Human Rights* 10, no. 3 (1993): 835–875, 871–872; George C. Harris, "Testimony for Sale: The Law and Ethics of Snitches and Experts," *Pepperdine Law Review* 28, no. 1 (2000): 49–58; Mona Lynch, "Prosecutorial Discretion, Drug Case Selection, and Inequality in Federal Court," *Justice Quarterly* 35, no. 7 (2018): 1309–1336.
124. Missouri v. Frye, 566 U.S. 134, 144 (2012).
125. United States v. Mezzanatto, 513 U.S. 196, 210 (1995).
126. Becker, "Plea Bargaining and the Supreme Court," 835.
127. Petition for Writ of Certiorari at 26–29, United States v. Pollard, 929 F.2d 1011 (D.C. Cir. 1992) (No. 92-17), 1992 WL 12074306.
128. Petition for Writ of Certiorari, at 9–14, Spilmon v. United States, 2006 WL 2966559.
129. "Why Do Wrongful Convictions Happen?" Korey Wise Innocence Project, University of Colorado School of Law, n.d., https://www.colorado.edu/outreach/korey-wise-innocence-project/our-work/why-do-wrongful-convictions-happen#perjury.
130. Lafler v. Cooper, 566 U.S. 156 (2012); Missouri v. Frye, 566 U.S. 134 (2012).
131. Bowers, "Plea Bargaining's Baselines," 1144.
132. Becker, "Plea Bargaining and the Supreme Court," 823.
133. Jeffrey Bellin, "Plea Bargaining's Uncertainty Problem," *Texas Law Review* 101 (2023): 539–586, 575–576.
134. Buffey v. Ballard, 236 W.Va. 509, 521 (W. Va. 2015).

3. Upholding Disproportionate Sentences

1. Brief for the Appellant, Riggs v. Fairman, No. 02-55185, Riggs v. Warden, 2003 WL 22670704, June 26, 2003.

2. Eric Slater, "Pizza Thief Receives Sentence of 25 Years to Life in Prison," *Los Angeles Times*, March 3, 1995.
3. Ed Pilkington, "Over 3,000 US Prisoners Serving Life without Parole for Non-violent Crimes," *The Guardian*, November 13, 2013; Jennifer Turner, "A Living Death: Life without Parole for Nonviolent Offenses," American Civil Liberties Union (ACLU), November 12, 2013, https://www.aclu.org/wp-content/uploads/legal-documents/111813-lwop-complete-report.pdf.
4. Turner, "A Living Death," 109–110.
5. Hannigan v. State, 84 So. 3d 450 (Fla. Dist. Ct. App. 2012) (Evander, J., concurring).
6. George served 17 years before President Obama commuted her sentence. Carrie Johnson and Marisa Peñaloza, "After 17 Years Behind Bars, Coming Home to a Different Life," *NPR*, December 16, 2014, https://www.npr.org/2014/12/16/371007232/after-17-years-behind-bars-coming-home-to-a-different-life. Hers is the rare example of a sentence being corrected by executive clemency.
7. Alexander Hamilton, "The Federalist No. 74," in *The Federalist Papers*, ed. Ian Shapiro (New Haven: Yale University Press, 2009).
8. Rachel E. Barkow, "Recharging the Jury: The Criminal Jury's Constitutional Role in an Era of Mandatory Sentencing," *University of Pennsylvania Law Review* 152, no. 1 (2003): 33–127.
9. Rachel E. Barkow, "The Court of Life and Death: The Two Tracks of Constitutional Sentencing Law and the Case for Uniformity," *Michigan Law Review* 107, no. 7 (2009): 1145–1205.
10. National Research Council, *The Growth of Incarceration in the United States: Exploring Causes and Consequences* (Washington: National Academies Press, 2014), 33, 53, 70.
11. John F. Stinneford, "The Original Meaning of 'Cruel,'" *Georgetown Law Journal* 105, no. 2 (2017): 441–506, 472.
12. John F. Stinneford, "The Original Meaning of 'Unusual': The Eighth Amendment as a Bar to Cruel Innovation," *Northwestern University Law Review* 102, no. 4 (2008): 1739–1825, 1748.
13. Henry De Bracton, *On the Laws and Customs of England*, trans. Samuel E. Thorne, vol. 2 (Cambridge, MA: Belknap Press of Harvard University Press, 1968), 299–300.
14. Solem v. Helm, 463 U.S. 277, 285 (1983) (internal quotations and citations omitted). See also Anthony F. Granucci, "'Nor Cruel and Unusual Punishments Inflicted': The Original Meaning," *California Law Review* 57, no. 4 (1969): 839–865, 846–847 (citing English sources supporting the argument that by 1400, it was clear in English law that punishment should not be "greatly disproportionate to the offense charged").
15. Rummel v. Estelle, 445 U.S. 263, 289 (1980) (Powell, J., dissenting).
16. John F. Stinneford, "Rethinking Proportionality Under the Cruel and Unusual Punishments Clause," *University of Virginia Law Review* 97, no. 4 (2011): 899–978, 935.

17. Stinneford, "The Original Meaning of 'Cruel,'" 472–473.
18. Stinneford, "The Original Meaning of 'Cruel,'" 464.
19. Other states did as well. While most used the "cruel and unusual" formulation, others used the disjunctive "cruel or unusual" and some just used "cruel." Stinneford explains they all mean the same thing. "The word 'cruel' stated the abstract moral principle, and the word 'unusual' provided a concrete reference point for determining whether that punishment had been violated." Stinneford, "The Original Meaning of 'Unusual,'" 1799.
20. Stinneford, "The Original Meaning of 'Cruel,'" 474.
21. Furman v. Georgia, 408 U.S. 238, 320–321 (Marshall, J., concurring) (quoting debates).
22. Stinneford, "Rethinking Proportionality," 939–942, 944–951.
23. Ian P. Farrell, "Gilbert & Sullivan and Scalia: Philosophy, Proportionality, and the Eighth Amendment," *Villanova Law Review* 55, no. 2 (2010): 321–368, 366–367.
24. Pervear v. Massachusetts, 72 U.S. 475 (1866).
25. O'Neill v. Vermont, 144 U.S. 323, 370–371 (1892) (Harlan, J., dissenting).
26. O'Neill v. Vermont, 338–340, 364–365 (Field, J., dissenting).
27. Weems v. United States, 217 U.S. 349, 368–380 (1910).
28. Weems v. United States, 217 U.S. 349, 385, 390, 395 (White, J., dissenting).
29. Granucci, "'Nor Cruel and Unusual Punishments Inflicted,'" 846–847; Stinneford, "The Original Meaning of 'Cruel,'" 472–473.
30. Weems v. United States, 398 (White, J., dissenting).
31. Trop v. Dulles, 356 U.S. 86, 99–101 (1958).
32. Robinson v. California, 370 U.S. 660, 667 (1962).
33. Robinson v. California, 370 U.S. 660, 676 (Douglas, J., concurring).
34. Coker v. Georgia, 433 U.S. 584 (1977); Enmund v. Florida, 458 U.S. 782 (1982); Kennedy v. Louisiana, 554 U.S. 407 (2008). The Court later cut back on its ruling in *Enmund* and held that individuals can receive the death penalty for felony murder if they are major participants in the felony and show a reckless indifference to human life. Tison v. Arizona, 481 U.S. 137 (1988).
35. Atkins v. Virginia, 536 U.S. 304 (2002); Roper v. Simmons, 543 U.S. 551 (2005).
36. Ford v. Wainwright, 477 U.S. 399 (1986).
37. Barkow, "The Court of Life and Death," 1179.
38. Barkow, "The Court of Life and Death," 1160.
39. Rummel v. Estelle, 273–274. Justice White's dissent in *Weems* points out that the punishment imposed there was not actually unique. He observed that hard and painful labor was a "well known" feature of prison life and the use of chains "is commonly applied in this country, as a means of preventing the escape of prisoners." Weems v. United States, 411–412 (White, J., dissenting). The civil consequences of Weems' conviction, such as property loss and the loss of parental rights, are also, sadly, quite common even today.
40. Rummel v. Estelle, 293, 307 (Powell, J., dissenting).

41. Hutto v. Davis, 454 U.S. 370, 373–375 (1982). Justice Brennan wrote a dissent, joined by Justices Marshall and Stevens, that criticized the Court for deciding the case summarily and disagreeing with the outcome on the merits.
42. Solem v. Helms, 284–290.
43. Solem v. Helms, 292.
44. 463 U.S. at 304–308 (Burger, C.J., dissenting).
45. 463 U.S. (quoting Henry Friendly, Federal Jurisdiction: A General View 36 (1973)).
46. Harmelin v. Michigan, 501 U.S. at 965.
47. Harmelin v. Michigan, at 985.
48. Stinneford, "The Original Meaning of 'Unusual,'" 1764.
49. Stinneford, "The Original Meaning of 'Unusual,'" 1819–1821.
50. Harmelin v. Michigan, 1010 (White, J., dissenting).
51. Stinneford, "The Original Meaning of 'Unusual,'" 1813, 1820. Stinneford, "The Original Meaning of 'Cruel,'" 476. Justice Scalia suggested these punishments could not have been seen as disproportionate to the killing of 15 people, seeing Oates's crime as more than perjury. This, however, is not how proportionality is assessed because it is measured against the crime of conviction, not what a judge thinks might have really happened beyond that. Stinneford, "The Original Meaning of 'Unusual,'" 1820 n. 475.
52. Tom Stacy, "Cleaning Up the Eighth Amendment Mess," *William & Mary Bill of Rights Journal* 14, no. 2 (2005): 475–553, 510.
53. Roper v. Simmons, 608 (Scalia, J., dissenting) (internal citations omitted).
54. Atkins v. Virginia, 338 (Scalia, J., dissenting).
55. Harmelin v. Michigan, 1018 (White, J., dissenting).
56. Brief for the United States as Amicus Curiae Supporting Respondent at 7–10, Harmelin v. Michigan, No. 89-7272, 1990 WL 10012671, Oct Term, 1990 (claiming "the Court has embraced a set of principles" including the primacy of the legislature, that states may select different theories of punishment, the inherent nature of federalism, and that objective factors should govern).
57. 501 U.S. at 998, 1001 (Kennedy, J., concurring in part and concurring in the judgment).
58. Barkow, "The Court of Life and Death," 1157.
59. Brief Amicus Curiae of the National District Attorneys Association in Support of the Respondent 5–6, Harmelin v. Michigan, No. 89-7272, 1990 WL 10012670, Oct. Term, 1990.
60. Brief for the United States as Amicus Curiae Supporting Respondent at 2, 5, Harmelin v. Michigan, No. 89-7272, 1990 WL 10012671, Oct Term, 1990.
61. Brief of Amici Curiae the Washington Legal Foundation, Citizens for Law and Order, Families and Friends of Missing Persons and Violent Crime Victims, the Maryland Coalition against Crime, the Parents Association to Neutralize Drug and Alcohol Abuse, and the Stephanie Roper Committee, Inc. in Support of Respondent at 10–12, Harmelin v. Michigan, No. 89-7272, 1990 WL 10012674.

62. Harmelin v. Michigan, 1003.
63. Justice White's dissent, joined by Justices Blackmun and Stevens, exposed the flaws in Justice Scalia's discussion of text, history, and precedent, and then set its sights on the Kennedy alternative. The threshold test created by Justice Kennedy, the dissent noted, essentially overrules *Solem*. Justice White argued that the Court's precedents require a proportionality analysis to include consideration of the historical development of the punishment being reviewed and intrajurisdictional and interjurisdictional comparisons. Justice Marshall wrote a separate dissent to note he believed capital punishment is unconstitutional and "especially restricted by the Eighth Amendment," but emphasized that he also believes the Eighth Amendment imposes a proportionality requirement in noncapital cases. 501 U.S. at 1027–1028 (Marshall, J., dissenting). Justice Stevens also filed a dissenting opinion, joined by Justice Blackmun, to emphasize his view that capital punishment is not in the same category as life without parole, but to note that they share in common a rejection of any change of rehabilitation of the perpetrator. Justice Stevens thought it "irrational" for Michigan to use a mandatory penalty and make that assumption about every drug offender. 501 U.S. at 1028 (Stevens, J., dissenting).
64. House Legislative Analysis March 23, 1988, Brief of Petitioner, Harmelin v. Michigan, No. 89-7272, 1990 WL 10012669, Appendix 12a-15a.
65. Petitioner Brief, 43 n.8.
66. It actually derived from a Michigan case decided almost a decade before *Solem*, but it employed the same measures of comparison.
67. Michigan v. Bullock, 440 Mich. 15, 37–40 (1992).
68. This is because there is a general rule that treats the narrowest ground supporting a judgment as the holding of a case when the justices are fragmented and no position gets five votes. United States v. Marks, 430 U.S. 188, 193 (1977).
69. John Clark, James Austin, and D. Alan Henry, "'Three Strikes and You're Out': A Review of State Legislation," research brief, National Institute of Justice, September 1997, https://www.ojp.gov/pdffiles/165369.pdf.
70. Sara Sun Beale, "The Story of Ewing: Three Strikes Laws and the Limits of the Eighth Amendment Proportionality Review," in *Criminal Law Stories*, ed. Donna Coker and Robert Weisberg (New York: Foundation Press/Thomson Reuters, 2013), 430.
71. The three-strikes ballot initiative could be changed only by subsequent ballot initiatives or a two-thirds vote of the legislature. Beale, "The Story of Ewing," 433–434. In 2004, California Ballot Proposition 66 sought to reform the three-strikes law to require serious or violent third strikes instead of any felony. The California District Attorneys Association fought against reforming the law, and the corrections union in the state also opposed it, spending $700,000 to defeat it. Then Governor Arnold Schwarzenegger also opposed changing the law and the Governor's California Recovery Team

donated $1 million to the opposition advertising campaign. Beale, "The Story of Ewing," 453–454. Proposition 66 was defeated in the 2004 election by a margin of 52.68 percent to 47.32 percent. Beale, "The Story of Ewing," 454. Notably, polling data of the almost 12 million voters who participated in the election "suggested that 1.5 million voters changed their minds in the last ten days of the campaign, which was the fastest reversal of public opinion in decades." Beale, "The Story of Ewing," 454 (citing Jennifer E. Walsh, *Three Strikes Laws* (Westport, CT: Greenwood Press, 2007), 4–9). California's three-strike law wasn't modified until 2012, when California voters passed Proposition 36. Prop 36 limits the application of third-strike sentences to new "serious or violent" felonies and allows individuals incarcerated prior to 2012 under the three-strikes law to request resentencing if their third strike was neither violent nor serious and a court determines they don't "pose an unreasonable risk of danger to public safety." Mia Bird et al., "Three Strikes in California," California Policy Lab, Institute for Research on Labor and Employment, University of California, Berkeley, August 2022, 9, 16. As of 2022, approximately 3,200 people have been released as a result of resentencing (16).
72. "Three Strikes Basics," Three Strikes Project, Stanford Law School, n.d., https://law.stanford.edu/three-strikes-project/three-strikes-basics/; Brief of Amici Curiae Families to Amend California's Three Strikes and Congress of California Seniors in Support of Respondent at 5–8, Lockyer v. Andrade, No. 01-1127, 2002 WL 1626166, July 17, 2002.
73. Beale, "The Story of Ewing," 439.
74. People v. Romero, 917 P.2d 628 (Cal. 1996).
75. Brief for Families Against Mandatory Minimums as Amicus Curiae in Support of Petitioner, at 18, Ewing v. California, No. 01-6978, 2002 WL 1467405, July 1, 2002.
76. Ewing v. California, 31–32 (Scalia, J., concurring in the judgment). See also 32 (Thomas, J., concurring in the judgment).
77. Harmelin v. Michigan, 999 (Kennedy, J., concurring in part and concurring in the judgment).
78. Ewing v. California, 538 U.S. 11, 23–25 (2003).
79. Stinneford, "The Original Meaning of 'Unusual,'" 1824.
80. Oral Argument, Ewing v. California, 2002 WL 31525401, at 39.
81. Youngjae Lee, "The Constitutional Right Against Excessive Punishment," *Virginia Law Review* 91, no. 3 (2005): 677–745, 706–708.
82. 538 U.S. at 33 (Stevens, J., dissenting).
83. Brief for Petitioner at 10, Ewing v. California, No. 01-6978, 2002 WL 1769930, July 28, 2002.
84. Barkow, "The Court of Life and Death," 1158. It was from Nevada, where a defendant with three prior felonies, including armed robbery, and nine prior misdemeanors, received a life without parole sentence for stealing a purse and wallet containing $476. 538 U.S. at 43–47 (Breyer, J., dissenting).

85. See, for example, Continental Trend Resources, Inc. v. OXY USA, Inc., 101 F.3d 634, 639 (10th Cir. 1996).
86. Brief of Respondent at 22, Lockyer v. Andrade, No. 01-1127, 2002 WL 1987633, July 15, 2002.
87. Lockyer v. Andrade, 538 U.S. 63, 72 (2003).
88. Jay Schweikert, "Qualified Immunity: A Legal, Practical, and Moral Failure," Policy Analysis no. 101, Cato Institute, September 14, 2020, https://www.cato.org/policy-analysis/qualified-immunity-legal-practical-moral-failure#.
89. City & Cnty. of San Francisco v. Sheehan, 575 U.S. 600, 613 (2015).
90. Joanna C. Schwartz, "The Case against Qualified Immunity," *Notre Dame Law Review* 93, no. 5 (2018): 1797–1851, 1798.
91. Lockyer v. Andrade, 538 U.S. 63, 78–83 (Souter, J., dissenting).
92. Brief on the Merits of Amicus Curiae California District Attorneys Association at 28, Ewing v. California, No. 01-6978, 2002 WL 1885468, August 1, 2002.
93. Brief on the Merits of Amicus Curiae California District Attorneys Association at 6–7 and n.8, 29, Lockyer v. Andrade, No. 01-1127, 2002 WL 1378856, June 17, 2002. The SG's brief agreed with the DAs' presentation of property crimes as dangerous. Property crimes—or "[s]o called property crimes," as the United States put it in their brief—"pose a risk of confrontation and injury." Brief for the United States as Amicus Curiae Supporting Respondent at 18, n.8, Ewing v. California, No. 01-6978, 2002 WL 1798896, July 31, 2002. Thus, just as any drug crime inevitably leads to violence in their view, so, too, does any property offense, and the government should therefore be free to address the danger.
94. Transcript of Oral Argument at 11, 13, 15, Ewing v. California, 538 U.S. 11 (2003) (No. 01-6978).
95. Rummel v. Estelle, 276.
96. Solem v. Helms, 290.
97. Woodson v. North Carolina, 428 U.S. 280, 304 (1976) (plurality opinion).
98. Atkins v. Virginia, 306.
99. Roper v. Simmons, 570.
100. 560 U.S. 48 (2010).
101. Miller v. Alabama, 567 U.S. 460 (2012).
102. Ohio v. Moore, No. 16-1167 (Oct. 2, 2017). The Ohio Supreme Court upheld this categorical Eighth Amendment challenge in direct conflict with holdings from the 5th and 6th Circuit in US v. Walton, 537 Fed. Appx. 430 (5th Cir. 2013) and State v. Bunch, 685 F.3d 546 (6th Cir. 2012).
103. Nelson v. Minnesota, No. 20-1155 (Apr. 19, 2021); Veal v. Georgia, 139 S. Ct. 320 (2018).
104. Oral Argument, Ewing v. California, 2002 WL 31525401, 55.
105. Solem v. Helm, 315 (Burger, C.J., dissenting).
106. Rummel v. Estelle, 275–276.

107. Anthony M. Kennedy, "An Address by Anthony M. Kennedy, Associate Justice, Supreme Court of the United States," Speech at the American Bar Association Annual Meeting, August 9, 2003, https://www.supremecourt.gov/publicinfo/speeches/sp_08-09-03.html.
108. Carol S. Steiker and Jordan M. Steiker, "Opening a Window or Building a Wall? The Effect of Eighth Amendment Death Penalty Law and Advocacy on Criminal Justice More Broadly," *University of Pennsylvania Journal of Constitutional Law* 11, no. 1 (2009): 155–205, 189.
109. Barkow, "The Court of Life and Death," 1148, 1197; see also James S. Liebman, "Slow Dancing with Death: The Supreme Court and Capital Punishment, 1963–2007," *Columbia Law Review* 107, no. 1 (2007): 1–130, 106–107.
110. United States v. Bajakajian, 524 U.S. 321, 334 (1998).
111. David Pozen, *The Constitution of the War on Drugs* (New York: Oxford University Press 2024), 112.
112. BMW of North America, Inc. v. Gore, 517 U.S. 559, 575–576 and n.24 (1996).
113. State Farm Mut. Auto. Ins. Co. v. Campbell, 538 U.S. 408, 419 (2003).
114. State Farm Mut. Auto. Ins. Co. v. Campbell, 423.
115. Erwin Chemerinsky, "The Constitution and Punishment," *Stanford Law Review* 56, no. 5 (2004): 1049–1080, 1063.
116. Adam M. Gershowitz, "The Supreme Court's Backwards Proportionality Jurisprudence: Comparing Judicial Review of Excessive Criminal Punishments and Excessive Punitive Damages Awards," *Virginia Law Review* 86, no. 6 (2000): 1249–1302, 1252.
117. Gershowitz, "The Supreme Court's Backwards Proportionality Jurisprudence," 1276–1285.
118. Ewing v. California, 33 (Stevens, J., dissenting).
119. Stacy, "Cleaning Up the Eighth Amendment Mess," 526; Gershowitz, "The Supreme Court's Backwards Proportionality Jurisprudence," 1253–1255.
120. Stinneford, "The Original Meaning of 'Unusual,'" 1817.
121. Paul H. Robinson and John M. Darley, *Justice, Liability, and Blame: Community Views and the Criminal Law* (Boulder, CO: Westview Press, 1995), 223–273.
122. Atkins v. Virginia, 312 (citing Penry v. Lynaugh, 492 U.S. 302 (1989)).
123. Reply Brief for Petitioner at 3, Ewing v. California, No. 01-6978, 2002 WL 31120962, Sept. 4, 2002.
124. Ashley Nellis, "No End in Sight: America's Enduring Reliance on Life Sentences," The Sentencing Project, Washington, DC, February 17, 2021, https://www.sentencingproject.org/app/uploads/2022/08/No-End-in-Sight-Americas-Enduring-Reliance-on-Life-Imprisonment.pdf. In 2021, 200,000 people in US prisons were serving a life sentence, which it defines as either a life sentence with parole, a life sentence without parole, or a "virtual/de facto" life sentence of 50 years or more.

125. Ashley Nellis, "Still Life: America's Increasing Use of Life and Long-Term Sentences," The Sentencing Project, Washington, DC, 2017, 12, https://www.sentencingproject.org/app/uploads/2022/10/Still-Life.pdf.
126. "Federal Drug Sentencing Laws Bring High Cost, Low Return," brief, The Pew Charitable Trusts, August 2015, https://www.pewtrusts.org/-/media/assets/2015/08/federal_drug_sentencing_laws_bring_high_cost_low_return.pdf.
127. Hamedah Hasan, "A Letter from Behind Bars on President's Day," American Civil Liberties Union (ACLU), February 15, 2010, https://www.aclu.org/news/smart-justice/letter-behind-bars-presidents-day.
128. State v. Carter, 773 So. 2d 268 (4th Cir. 2000).
129. German Lopez, "Mass Incarceration in America, Explained in 22 Maps and Charts," Vox, October 11, 2016, tbl. 13.
130. See, for example, Richard Frase, "Excessive Prison Sentences, Punishment Goals, and the Eighth Amendment: 'Proportionality' Relative to What?" *Minnesota Law Review* 89 (2005): 571–651, 605–606; Gregory Schneider, "Sentencing Proportionality in the States," *Arizona Law Review* 54, no. 1 (2012): 241–275; William W. Berry III, "Cruel and Unusual Non-Capital Punishments," *American Criminal Law Review* 58, no. 4 (2021): 1627–1658, 1637–1655.
131. Woodson v. North Carolina, 304 (plurality opinion).
132. Barkow, "The Court of Life and Death," 1176–78.

4. Tolerating Overcrowded Prisons

Epigraph: Bryan Stevenson, *Just Mercy: A Story of Justice and Redemption* (New York: Spiegel & Grau, 2014), 17.
1. Matthew L. Myers, "12 Years after James v. Wallace," National Prison Project Journal, American Civil Liberties Union (ACLU), Fall 1987, 8–9, https://www.prisonlegalnews.org/media/publications/journal%2013.pdf.
2. United States v. Alabama, Civil No. 2:20-cv-01971-RDP (N.D. AL, May 19, 2021), available at https://www.alreporter.com/wp-content/uploads/2021/05/Amended_DOJ_Complaint.pdf.
3. Kay Ivey, "An Alabama Solution to an Alabama Problem: Rebuilding the Alabama Corrections System," CBS42 (Birmingham, AL), February 12, 2019, https://www.cbs42.com/news/gov-ivey-writes-op-ed-on-alabamas-prison-plan/.
4. Josh Moon, "DOJ Provides Court with Specific Details of Abuse, Unconstitutional Conditions in Alabama Prisons," *Alabama Political Reporter*, November 23, 2021, https://www.alreporter.com/2021/11/23/doj-provides-court-with-specific-details-of-abuse-unconstitutional-conditions-in-alabama-prisons/.
5. Newt Gingrich, *To Renew America* (New York: HarperCollins, 1995), 205.
6. "Joe Arpaio," *Ballotpedia*, https://ballotpedia.org/Joe_Arpaio.

7. Fernanda Santos, "Outdoor Jail, a Vestige of Joe Arpaio's Tenure, Is Closing," *New York Times*, April 4, 2017.
8. Christopher Zoukis, "Use of Nutraloaf on the Decline in U.S. Prisons," *Prison Legal News*, March 31, 2016, https://www.prisonlegalnews.org/news/2016/mar/31/use-nutraloaf-decline-us-prisons/#:~:text=The%20prison%20systems%20in%20California,nutraloaf%20as%20a%20disciplinary%20tool.
9. Maurice Chammah, "American Sheriff," *The Marshall Project*, May 4, 2016, https://www.themarshallproject.org/2016/05/04/american-sheriff.
10. Rachel E. Barkow, *Prisoners of Politics: Breaking the Cycle of Mass Incarceration* (Cambridge, MA: Harvard University Press, 2019), 19–32.
11. Ariana Garcia, "Advocates, Legal Experts Decry Gov. Greg Abbott Diverting $4M in State Prisons Funding for Election Audits," *Chron*, November 23, 2021, https://www.chron.com/politics/article/Texas-election-audit-Greg-Abbott-Trump-16645026.php.
12. Rachel E. Barkow, "Federalism and the Politics of Sentencing," *Columbia Law Review* 105, no. 4 (2005): 1276–1314, 1290.
13. Judith Resnik, "(Un)constitutional Punishments: Eighth Amendment Silos, Penological Purposes, and People's 'Ruin,'" *Yale Law Journal Forum* 129 (2020): 365–415, 389–391.
14. Malcolm M. Feeley and Edward L. Rubin, *Judicial Policy Making and the Modern State: How the Court's Reformed America's Prisons* (Cambridge: Cambridge University Press, 1998), 19.
15. Weems v. United States, 217 U.S. 249, 366, 377–378 (1910). A parallel is a sentence of death. The Court has determined that the mode of execution is relevant to the Eighth Amendment inquiry. Not all sentences of death are equivalent.
16. Farmer v. Brennan, 511 U.S. 825, 832 (1994) (quoting Helling v. McKinney, 509 U.S. 25, 31 (1993)). The exception is Justice Thomas, who has expressed a view that the Eighth Amendment does not apply to prison conditions at all because he believes those are not "punishment" under the Eighth Amendment unless they are imposed as part of a sentence. Farmer, 511 U.S. at 859 (Thomas, J., concurring in the judgment); Helling v. McKinney, 509 U.S. 25, 40 (1993) (Thomas, J., dissenting). For a refutation of this position, see Sharon Dolovich, "Cruelty, Prison Conditions, and the Eighth Amendment," *NYU Law Review* 84, no. 4 (2009): 881–979, 900–909. Dolovich notes that public (as opposed to private) punishment is not the result of individual decisions by officials but is the result of a complex set of decisions by institutions—legislatures, courts, prisons. The resulting conditions and circumstances of incarceration are thus all part of the sentence and punishment imposed by the state.
17. DeShaney v. Winnebago County Department of Social Services, 489 U.S. 189, 199–200 (1989). Sharon Dolovich refers to this as the state's carceral burden. Dolovich, "Cruelty, Prison Conditions, and the Eighth Amendment," 911–923.

18. Malcolm M. Feeley and Edward L. Rubin, *Judicial Policy Making and the Modern State: How the Court's Reformed America's Prisons* (Cambridge: Cambridge University Press, 1998), 31–34.
19. Margo Schlanger, "The Constitutional Law of Incarceration, Reconfigured," *Cornell Law Review* 103, no. 2 (2018): 357–436, 367–368; see also Feeley and Rubin, *Judicial Policy Making and the Modern State*, 35.
20. Robinson v. California, 370 U.S. 660 (1962); Cooper v. Pate, 378 U.S. 546 (1964). For a discussion of the range of legal changes, see Resnik, "(Un)constitutional Punishments," 370–371, 383.
21. Judith Resnik et al., "Punishment in Prison: Constituting the 'Normal' and the 'Atypical' in Solitary and Other Forms of Confinement," *Northwestern University Law Review* 115, no. 1 (2020): 45–157, 68.
22. Claudia Angelos and James B. Jacobs, "Prison Overcrowding and the Law," *Annals of the American Academy of Political and Social Science* 478, no. 1 (March 1985): 100–112, 102.
23. Judith Resnik, "The Puzzles of Prisoners and Rights: An Essay in Honor of Frank Johnson," *Alabama Law Review* 71 (2020): 665–722, 671; Feeley and Rubin, *Judicial Policy Making and the Modern State*, 37.
24. Lee v. Washington, 390 U.S. 333 (1968).
25. 418 U.S. 539, 555–556 (1974).
26. Feeley and Rubin, *Judicial Policy Making and the Modern State*, 43.
27. Pugh v. Locke, 406 F. Supp. 318 (M.D. Ala. 1976).
28. Feeley and Rubin, *Judicial Policy Making and the Modern State*, 39–40. It is not a coincidence that Southern states dominated the early litigation, as many ran their prisons along the model of slave plantations, some even occupying the very same land as former slave plantations, using incarcerated people to work it for profit, and deploying corporal punishment as a mode of discipline (150–158).
29. Terence P. Thornberry et al., "Overcrowding in American Prisons: Policy Implications of Double-Bunking Single Cells," July 1982, 1, https://www.ojp.gov/pdffiles1/Digitization/85969NCJRS.pdf.
30. Palmigiano v. Garrahy, 443 F. Supp. 956, 979 (1977).
31. Resnik, "(Un)constitutional Punishments," 404.
32. Schlanger, "The Constitutional Law of Incarceration, Reconfigured," 369–370.
33. Feeley and Rubin, *Judicial Policy Making and the Modern State*, 206–207, 328.
34. Nancy Dubler, "Medical Care: Past and Future," National Prison Project Journal, American Civil Liberties Union (ACLU), Fall 1987, 29, https://www.prisonlegalnews.org/media/publications/journal%2013.pdf.
35. Dubler, "Medical Care: Past and Future," 29.
36. Estelle v. Gamble, 429 U.S. 97, 102 (1976) (quoting Jackson v. Bishop, 404 F.2d 571, 579 (8th Cir. 1968).
37. Estelle v. Gamble, 102–103, 107.
38. Estelle v. Gamble, 116–117 (Stevens, J., dissenting).

39. John F. Stinneford, "The Original Meaning of 'Cruel,'" *Georgetown Law Journal* 105, no. 2 (2017): 441–506, 493.
40. Wilson v. Seiter, 501 U.S. 294, 302 (1991).
41. Feeley and Rubin, *Judicial Policy Making and the Modern State*, 39.
42. Hutto v. Finney, 437 U.S. 678, 680–685 (1978).
43. Hutto v. Finney, 711 (Rehnquist, J., dissenting).
44. Thornberry, "Overcrowding in American Prisons," 20–21 and Table 6.
45. United States v. Wolfish, 428 F. Supp. 333, 339 (1977).
46. Wolfish v. Levi, 573 F.2d 118, 124 (2nd Cir. 1978) (internal quotation and citation omitted).
47. Bell v. Wolfish, 441 U.S. 520, 533 (1979).
48. Bell v. Wolfish, 552 n.11 (Stevens, J., dissenting).
49. Bell v. Wolfish, 538, 542, 562.
50. Bell v. Wolfish, 568 n.5 (Marshall, J., dissenting).
51. Bell v. Wolfish, 542–543. Justice Marshall wrote a dissent rejecting the majority's narrow test for punishment, raising some of the same points he would reiterate in *Salerno*. He would have used a test that weighed the government's interest against deprivation suffered by the individual. Because the district court decided the double bunking issue on cross-motions for summary judgment and did not engage in sufficient factfinding to conduct that balancing test, Justice Marshall would have remanded the case on the double bunking issue for the lower courts to more fully consider the psychological and physical harms from overcrowding. Bell v. Wolfish, 571–572 (Marshall, J., dissenting). Justice Stevens wrote a separate dissent, joined by Justice Brennan, disagreeing with the majority's test for punishment as too permissive to the government. He noted that "if the standard is to afford any meaningful protection for the citizen's liberty, it must require something more than either an explicit statement by the administrator that his rule is designed to inflict punishment, or a sanction that is so arbitrary that it would be invalid even if it were not punitive." He believed there was enough evidence to infer double-bunking was punitive under a current version of that test, and he would have remanded to the district court to conduct that inquiry. Bell v. Wolfish, 598–599 (Stevens, J., dissenting).
52. Feeley and Rubin, *Judicial Policy Making and the Modern State*, 300.
53. Thornberry et al., "Overcrowding in American Prisons," 50.
54. Thornberry et al., "Overcrowding in American Prisons," 51–52.
55. Brief of Petitioners at 20, Rhodes v. Chapman, No. 80-332, Dec. 22, 1980, 1980 WL 339863.
56. Chapman v. Rhodes, 434 F. Supp. 10007, 1009 (S.D. Ohio 1977).
57. Brief of Respondents at 9, Rhodes v. Chapman, No. 80-332, 1980 WL 339864.
58. Chapman v. Rhodes, 1017 (S.D. Ohio 1977).
59. Brief of Respondents at 34–37.
60. Brief of Respondents at 10–11, 14.

61. Brief of Respondents at 13, 22.
62. Chapman v. Rhodes, 1021 (S.D. Ohio 1977).
63. Brief of Respondents at 20.
64. Chapman v. Rhodes, 1020–22 (S.D. Ohio 1977).
65. Chapman v. Rhodes, 624 F.2d 1099 (6th Cir. 1980).
66. Brief of the American Medical Association and the American Public Health Association at 8, 12, 16–19, 21, Rhodes v. Chapman, No. 80-332, 1980 WL 339867.
67. Brief of the State Public Defender of California in Support of Respondents at 1720–21, Rhodes v. Chapman, No. 80-332, 1980 WL 339866.
68. Memorandum for the United States as Amicus Curiae at 2, 4, Rhodes v. Chapman, No. 80-332, January 1981, 1981 WL 390389.
69. Brief of the States at 16–18, Rhodes v. Chapman, No. 80-332, December 18, 1980, 1980 WL 339866.
70. *Bell v. Wolfish*, as noted, was a case involving pretrial detainees, and the Court decided their confinement did not amount to punishment. Those questions were squarely raised by the conditions at SOCF. Interestingly, both SOCF and the facility at issue in *Bell* were new and "did not reflect the physical reality of the majority of jails" and prisons. Elizabeth Alexander, "Prisoners' Lawyers Face Critical Issues," National Prison Project Journal, American Civil Liberties Union (ACLU), Fall 1987, 22–23, https://www.prisonlegalnews.org/media/publications/journal%2013.pdf.
71. Rhodes v. Chapman, 344, 352 (1981).
72. Rhodes v. Chapman, 351 n.16.
73. Jonathan Simon, "The New Overcrowding," *Connecticut Law Review* 48, no. 4 (2016): 1191–1216, 1202.
74. Rhodes v. Chapman, 347, 349, 352 (1981).
75. Rhodes v. Chapman, 348 n.13.
76. Rhodes v. Chapman, 352–353 (Brennan, J., concurring in the judgment).
77. Rhodes v. Chapman, 353–354.
78. Rhodes v. Chapman, 354–362.
79. Rhodes v. Chapman, 362–364.
80. Rhodes v. Chapman, 367 and n.15. A 1978 study found that 35 percent of all incarcerated people shared a cell with someone else. Thornberry et al., "Overcrowding in American Prisons," viii.
81. Sharon Dolovich, "Forms of Deference in Prison Law," *Federal Sentencing Reporter* 24, no. 4 (2012): 245–259, 249.
82. 452 U.S. at 367–368.
83. Angelos and Jacobs, "Prison Overcrowding," 105.
84. 452 U.S. at 370 (Marshall, J., dissenting).
85. 452 U.S. at 371 and n.3.
86. 452 U.S. at 374 (quoting district court decision).
87. 452 U.S. at 375.
88. 452 U.S. at 375–377.

89. Sharon Dolovich, "The Coherence of Prison Law," *Harvard Law Review Forum* 135 (2022): 301–342, 303. The conditions at the Indiana Reformatory at Pendleton give a flavor of the kind of facts it took to succeed after *Rhodes*. Individuals there were double-bunked and had approximately 24 square feet per person. The ceilings were so low, the individual in the top bunk could not sit up. Almost half the incarcerated people who were double-bunked spent 20–23 hours per day together in their cell. Cells had no running water, no heat in the winter, and were stifling in the summer. The facility was filthy, poorly lit, and had only one full-time doctor on staff to treat the 200 requests for medical care each day. It was on these grounds that the Seventh Circuit was able to distinguish *Rhodes*. French v. Owens, 777 F.2d 1250 (7th Cir. 1985).
90. Sharon Dolovich, "Evading the Eighth Amendment: Prison Conditions and the Courts," in *The Eighth Amendment and Its Future in a New Age of Punishment*, ed. Meghan J. Ryan and William W. Berry III (Cambridge: Cambridge University Press, 2020), 148.
91. Vincent Nathan, "Lawsuits Fundamental to Prison Reform," National Prison Project Journal, American Civil Liberties Union (ACLU), Fall 1987, 16–17, https://www.prisonlegalnews.org/media/publications/journal%2013.pdf.
92. Nathan James, "The Federal Prison Population Buildup: Options for Congress," Congressional Research Service, May 20, 2016, App. Table A-1, https://sgp.fas.org/crs/misc/R42937.pdf.
93. James, "The Federal Prison Population Buildup," 1.
94. Feeley and Rubin, *Judicial Policy Making and the Modern State*, 48.
95. Justin Driver and Emma Kaufman, "The Incoherence of Prison Law," *Harvard Law Review* 135, no. 2 (2021): 515–584, 546.
96. Simon, "The New Overcrowding," 1198, 1208.
97. Resnik, "(Un)constitutional Punishments," 399.
98. Simon, "The New Overcrowding," 1202–1203.
99. Feeley and Rubin, *Judicial Policy Making and the Modern State*, 379.
100. Feeley and Rubin, *Judicial Policy Making and the Modern State*, 379.
101. Simon, "The New Overcrowding," 1195–1998, 1209–1210, 1212.
102. Jones v. N.C. Prisoners' Union, Inc., 433 U.S. 119, 128 (1977) (noting that courts "ordinarily defer" to prison officials when it comes to questions of "security and order"); Bell v. Wolfish, 546–547 (emphasizing need for "institutional security and preserving internal order" as reason for deference to jail officials regulating pretrial detainees).
103. See, for example, Heather Schoenfeld, "Mass Incarceration and the Paradox of Prison Conditions Litigation," *Law & Society Review* 44, no. 3/4 (2010): 731–767, 740 (noting that the director of Florida's Department of Corrections "embraced" a lawsuit challenging overcrowded conditions and "welcomed the chance to use the court as leverage with state legislators"); Feeley and Rubin, *Judicial Policy Making and the Modern State*, 61 (noting cooperation of Arkansas's state commissioner of corrections likely helped the plaintiffs draft their complaint challenging prison conditions in the state);

noting that the commissioner of corrections in Colorado cooperated with litigants to reach a settlement because it could mean an increase in his department's budget (101); noting the cooperation of the sheriff in the lawsuit challenging conditions in the Santa Clara County jail (116).
104. Thornberry et al., "Overcrowding in American Prisons," 88–89.
105. Thornberry et al., "Overcrowding in American Prisons," 67–70.
106. Resnik et al., "Punishment in Prison," 50, 87.
107. In California prisons, for example, there were 449 lockdowns in 2006 lasting an average of 12 days, with 20 lockdowns lasting 60 days or longer. Brown v. Plata, 563 U.S. 493, 521 (2011).
108. Staughton Lynd, *Lucasville: The Untold Story of a Prison Uprising* (Philadelphia: Temple University Press, 2004), 17–21.
109. "Prison Riot, U.S.A.," *Captive*, Lightbox, aired December 9, 2016.
110. Lynd, *Lucasville: The Untold Story of a Prison Uprising*, 196–199.
111. Jo Ingles, Daniel Konik, and Karen Kasler, "Lucasville Legacy: A Historic, Deadly Prison Riot Prompted Changes in Ohio's Lockups," *Statehouse News Bureau*, April 28, 2023, https://www.statenews.org/government-politics/2023-04-28/lucasville-legacy-a-historic-deadly-prison-riot-prompted-changes-in-ohios-lockups.
112. "Ohio's Statehouse-to-Prison Pipeline," 134th General Assembly 2021–2022, ACLU of Ohio, March 2023, https://www.acluohio.org/sites/default/files/ohiosstatehousetoprisonpipeline-134thgeneralassembly2021-2022_web_2023_0307.pdf.
113. Linda Dailey Paulson, "Attica Correctional Facility," *Britannica*, June 13, 2013, https://www.britannica.com/topic/Attica-Correctional-Facility.
114. See Paulson, "Attica Correctional Facility"; Nick Manos, "Attica Prison Riot (1971)," *Black Past*, November 18, 2017, https://www.blackpast.org/african-american-history/attica-prison-riot-1971-2/.
115. Manos, "Attica Prison Riot (1971)."
116. "California Prison Erupts, Hundreds Hurt in Riot, Multiple Causes Cited," *Prison Legal News*, March 15, 2010, https://www.prisonlegalnews.org/news/2010/mar/15/california-prison-erupts-hundreds-hurt-in-riot-multiple-causes-cited/.
117. Pamela M. Rosenblatt, "The Dilemma of Overcrowding in the Nation's Prisons: What Are Constitutional Conditions and What Can be Done?" *New York Law School Journal of Human Rights* 8, no. 2 (1991): 489–521, 490–493.
118. Thornberry et al., "Overcrowding in American Prisons," 78.
119. Simon, "The New Overcrowding," 1210–1211.
120. Simon, "The New Overcrowding," 1215.
121. Schlanger, "The Constitutional Law of Incarceration, Reconfigured," 381. As noted, a subjective requirement is not consistent with the original meaning of cruel as elaborated by John Stinneford. See Stinneford, "The Original Meaning of 'Cruel,'" 493.
122. 501 U.S. 294, 306, 309–311 (1991) (White, J., concurring in the judgment). Justice White was right to worry. Prison officials have successfully used lack

of resources as a defense in §1983 actions. Peralta v. Dillard, 744 F.3d 1076 (9th Cir. 2014).
123. 441 U.S. 520, 567 (Marshall, J., dissenting).
124. 511 U.S. 825, 837 (1994).
125. 511 U.S. 825, 854–856 (Blackmun, J., concurring). Justice Stevens also concurred to note his continued disagreement with a subjective standard and to reiterate his view "that a state official may inflict cruel and unusual punishment without any improper subjective motivation." 511 U.S. 825, 858 (Stevens, J., concurring). Justice Thomas wrote separately to repeat his view that prison conditions are not imposed as part of a sentence and are therefore not subject to Eighth Amendment oversight. 511 U.S. 825, 859 (Thomas, J., concurring in the judgment). He further noted he would be willing to overrule *Estelle*. 511 U.S. at 861 (Thomas, J., concurring in the judgment).
126. Mary D. Fan, "Beyond Budget-Cut Criminal Justice: The Future of Penal Law," *North Carolina Law Review* 90, no. 3 (2012): 581–653, 611.
127. Lauren Salins and Shepard Simpson, "Efforts to Fix a Broken System: Brown v. Plata and the Prison Overcrowding Epidemic," *Loyola University Chicago Law Journal* 44, no. 4 (2013): 1153–1200, 1158–1160.
128. Arnold Schwarzenegger, "Prison Overcrowding State of Emergency Proclamation," Office of the Governor, October 4, 2006, 1, https://www.library.ca.gov/wp-content/uploads/GovernmentPublications/executive-order-proclamation/38-Proc-2006-93.pdf.
129. Coleman v. Wilson, 912 F. Supp. 1282, 1306, 1316 (E.D. Cal. 1995).
130. Brown v. Plata, 563 U.S. 493, 507–509 (2011).
131. The PLRA requires both findings before an order to reduce the population can issue.
132. Fan, "Beyond Budget-Cut Criminal Justice," 614.
133. Fan, "Beyond Budget-Cut Criminal Justice," 517.
134. Fan, "Beyond Budget-Cut Criminal Justice," 503 n.1.
135. Fan, "Beyond Budget-Cut Criminal Justice," 502–506 and 519 n.4.
136. Fan, "Beyond Budget-Cut Criminal Justice," 529–530.
137. Calling "preposterous" a theory of the Eighth Amendment that would allow the class to include patients "in a system that has systemic weaknesses" without each showing "an individualized showing of mistreatment." Brown v. Plata, 553 (Scalia, J., dissenting).
138. 511 U.S. at 828, 842. Justice Scalia himself joined the opinion for the Court in *Farmer v. Brennan*, which held that deliberate indifference to "a substantial risk of serious harm" violates the Eighth Amendment and is grounds for an injunction. The Court has reiterated this as the relevant standard in challenges to the method of execution in capital cases. See, for example, Glossip v. Gross, 576 U.S. 863, 877 (2015); Bucklew v. Precythe, 139 S.Ct. 1112, 1119 (2019).
139. Brown v. Plata, 550 (Scalia, J., dissenting).
140. Brown v. Plata, 551–554 (Scalia, J., dissenting).
141. Brown v. Plata, 555.
142. Brown v. Plata, 561.

143. Brown v. Plata, 566, 581 (Alito, J., dissenting).
144. Brown v. Plata, 536.
145. Brown v. Plata, 578 (Alito, J., dissenting).
146. Dolovich, "Forms of Deference in Prison Law," 251.
147. Brown v. Plata, 581 (Alito, J., dissenting).
148. "Public Safety Realignment Act of 2011 Implementation Plan," Community Corrections Partnership, Alameda County, CA, 2012, https://www.bscc.ca.gov/wp-content/uploads/Alameda_County_2011-2012.pdf.
149. "Public Safety Realignment Act of 2011 Implementation Plan."
150. Angie Wootton, "AB 109 and Its Impact on Prison Overcrowding and Recidivism: A Policy Analysis," *Themis: Research Journal of Justice Studies and Forensic Science* 4, no. 1 (2016): 99–112, 104.
151. Jody Sundt, "Clarifying the Effect of California Realignment on Motor Vehicle Theft: Results of an Interrupted Time Series," *Journal of Experimental Criminology* (2022), https://doi.org/10.1007/s11292-022-09545-7.
152. Magnus Lofstrom and Brandon Martin, "Public Safety Realignment: Impacts So Far," Public Policy Institute of California, September 2015, https://www.ppic.org/wp-content/uploads/content/pubs/report/R_915MLR.pdf.
153. Ruth Wilson Gilmore, *Golden Gulag: Prisons, Surplus, Crisis, and Opposition in Globalizing California* (Berkeley: University of California Press, 2007).
154. "31 States Reform Criminal Justice Policies through Justice Reinvestment," fact sheet, The Pew Charitable Trusts, January 2016, https://www.pewtrusts.org/-/media/assets/2016/01/pspp_jrireformmatrixoverview.pdf; "Mississippi's 2014 Corrections and Criminal Justice Reform: Legislation to Improve Public Safety, Ensure Certainty in Sentencing, and Control Corrective Costs," brief, The Pew Charitable Trusts, May 2014, https://www.pewtrusts.org/~/media/assets/2014/09/pspp_mississippi_2014_corrections_justice_reform.pdf; "South Carolina's Public Safety Reform," issue brief, The Pew Charitable Trusts, June 2010, https://www.pewtrusts.org/-/media/assets/2010/06/10/pspp_south_carolina_brief.pdf; Rachel E. Barkow, "Federalism and the Politics of Sentencing," *Columbia Law Review* 105, no. 4 (2005): 1276–1314, 1285–90.
155. See, for example, Feeley and Rubin, *Judicial Policy Making and the Modern State*, 93, 379–380; Stephen D. Gottfredson, "Institutional Responses to Prison Crowding," *NYU Review of Law and Social Change* 12, no. 1 (1984): 259–274, 268.
156. Feeley and Rubin, *Judicial Policy Making and the Modern State*, 375–376.
157. Schoenfeld, "Mass Incarceration and the Paradox of Prison Conditions Litigation," 749.

5. Greenlighting Stop-and-Frisk

Epigraph: Utah v. Strieff, 579 U.S. 232, 254 (2016) (Sotomayor, J., dissenting).
1. John F. Stinneford, "Punishment Without Culpability," *Journal of Criminal Law and Criminology* 102, no. 3 (2012): 653–723.

2. Atwater v. City of Lago Vista, 532 U.S. 318 (2001).
3. Whren v. United States, 517 U.S. 806 (1996).
4. Schneckloth v. Bustamonte, 412 U.S. 218 (1973).
5. For that reason, the relationship between policing, the Supreme Court, and mass incarceration is a complicated topic that deserves its own book-length treatment. Two excellent places to start are Barry Friedman, *Unwarranted: Policing Without Permission* (New York: Farrar, Straus and Giroux, 2017); and Erwin Chemerinsky, *Presumed Guilty: How the Supreme Court Empowered the Police and Subverted Civil Rights* (New York: Liveright, 2021).
6. 392 U.S. 1 (1968).
7. Brinegar v. United States, 338 U.S. 160, 175 (1949) (internal quotations and citations omitted).
8. David Rudovsky and David A. Harris, "*Terry* Stops-and-Frisks: The Troubling Use of Common Sense in a World of Empirical Data," *Ohio State Law Journal* 79 (2018): 501–546, 511–512.
9. Sarah A. Seo, "The Originalist Road Not Taken in *Kansas v. Glover*," American Constitution Society *Supreme Court Review 2019–2020*, ed. Steven D. Schwinn, 4th ed., 143–165, https://www.acslaw.org/the-originalist-road-not-taken-in-kansas-v-glover/.
10. 367 U.S. 643 (1961).
11. Wayne R. LaFave, "'Street Encounters' and the Constitution: *Terry, Sibron, Peters*, and Beyond," *Michigan Law Review* 67, no. 1 (1968): 39–126, 43, n.15 (discussing the Uniform Arrest Act and the states in which it was still in force by the 1960s).
12. United States. Sokolow, 490 U.S. 1, 7 (1989).
13. Aziz Z. Huq, "The Consequences of Disparate Policing: Evaluating Stop and Frisk as a Modality of Urban Policing," *Minnesota Law Review* 101 (2017): 2398–2400, 2411–2412.
14. David Hausman and Dorothy Kronick, "The Illusory End of Stop and Frisk in Chicago?" *Science Advances* 9 (September 29, 2023): eadh3017, 2.
15. Floyd v. City of New York, 573; Rudovsky and Harris, "Terry Stops-and-Frisks," 511–512.
16. Rudovsky and Harris, "*Terry* Stops-and-Frisks," 513 n.58, 536–541.
17. Rudovsky and Harris, "*Terry* Stops-and-Frisks," 512 n.56.
18. Alexandra Natapoff, *Punishment without Crime: How Our Massive Misdemeanor System Traps the Innocent and Makes America More Unequal* (New York: Basic, 2018); "Local Jails: The Real Scandal Is the Churn," Prison Policy Initiative, n.d., https://www.prisonpolicy.org/graphs/pie2022_jail_churn.html.
19. Huq, "The Consequences of Disparate Policing," 2418, 2422–2423; Jeffrey Fagan, "*Terry's* Original Sin," *University of Chicago Legal Forum* 2016 (2016): 43–97, 46; Ames Grawert, "Stop and Frisk's Effect on Crime in New York City," fact sheet, Brennan Center for Justice, October 7, 2016, https://www.brennancenter.org/our-work/research-reports/fact-sheet-stop-and-frisks-effect-crime-new-york-city; Jonathan Tebes and Jeffrey Fagan, "Stopped by

the Police: The End of 'Stop-and-Frisk' on Neighborhood Crime and High School Dropout Rates," unpublished ms., December 2022.
20. "Crime Falls as New York Abandons Stop-and-Frisk," Equal Justice Initiative, January 19, 2018, https://eji.org/news/new-york-crime-falls-as-police-end-stop-and-frisk/.
21. Robert Hunter, "We Know That Stop-and-Frisk Is All Kinds of Horrible: So Why Is It Expanding Nationwide?" ACLU, September 24, 2013, https://www.aclu.org/news/smart-justice/we-know-stop-and-frisk-all-kinds-horrible-so-why-it-expanding.
22. Joseph Goldstein, "Judge Rejects New York's Stop-and-Frisk Policy," *New York Times*, August 12, 2013.
23. Huq, "The Consequences of Disparate Policing," 2412.
24. These three stops were all discussed in Floyd v. City of New York, 959 F.Supp.2d 540, 625–626, 630–632, 640–642 (S.D.N.Y. 2013).
25. Center for Constitutional Rights, *Stop and Frisk: The Human Impact*, July 2012, 5–6, 9, https://ccrjustice.org/stop-and-frisk-human-impact.
26. Brief for the NAACP Legal Defense and Educational Fund, Inc., as Amicus Curiae, *Sibron v. New York*, 1967 WL 113672, at 62–63 (Aug. 31, 1967) (internal quotations and citations omitted).
27. The President's Commission on Law Enforcement and the Administration of Justice issued a report in 1967 that was cited in the briefs and the Court's opinion, and a report by the Kerner Commission was released three months before the Court's decision.
28. 392 U.S. at 14 and n.11; Adina Schwartz, "'Just Take Away Their Guns': The Hidden Racism of *Terry v. Ohio*," *Fordham Urban Law Journal* 23 (1996): 317–375, 322–328.
29. Tracey Maclin, "*Terry v. Ohio*'s Fourth Amendment Legacy: Black Men and Police Discretion," *St. John's Law Review* 72, no. 3/4 (1998): 1271–1321, 1317 (citing Fred P. Graham, *The Self-Inflicted Wound* (New York: Macmillan, 1970), 10, 15).
30. Graham, *The Self-Inflicted Wound*, 8–9.
31. Corinna Barrett Lain, "Countermajoritarian Hero or Zero," *University of Pennsylvania Law Review* 152, no. 4 (2004): 1361–1452, 1374 (observing that "scholars have long regarded *Mapp* as one of the two most unpopular criminal procedure decisions in Supreme Court history").
32. Lewis R. Katz, "*Terry v. Ohio* at Thirty-Five: A Revisionist View," *Mississippi Law Journal* 74 (2004): 423–500, 437–440.
33. For an argument in favor of the *Terry* Court's "pragmatic framework" along these lines, see Stephen J. Schulhofer, *More Essential Than Ever: The Fourth Amendment in the Twenty First Century* (New York: Oxford University Press, 2012), 74–77.
34. Earl C. Dudley, Jr., "*Terry v. Ohio*, The Warren Court, and the Fourth Amendment: A Law Clerk's Perspective," *St. John's Law Review* 72, no. 3/4 (1998): 891–903, 894. See also Thomas Y. Davies, "The Fictional Character of

Law-and-Order Originalism: A Case Study of the Distortions and Evasions of Framing-Era Arrest Doctrine in *Atwater v. Lago Vista*," *Wake Forest Law Review* 37, no. 2 (2002): 239–438, 389–398.
35. Carroll v. United States, 267 U.S. 132, 162 (1925).
36. Illinois v. Gates, 462 U.S. 213, 246 (1983); Davies, "The Fictional Character of Law-and-Order Originalism," 249, 379–382. Empirical studies show that judges translate probable cause as demanding a higher numerical probability than reasonable suspicion. See Richard Seltzer et al., "Legal Standards by the Numbers," *Judicature* 100, no. 1 (2016): 56–66, Table 1.
37. David A. Sklansky, "The Fourth Amendment and Common Law," *Columbia Law Review* 100, no. 7 (2000): 1739–1814.
38. George C. Thomas III, "Time Travel, Hovercrafts, and the Framers: James Madison Sees the Future and Requires the Fourth Amendment," *Notre Dame Law Review* 80, no. 4 (2005): 1451–1518, 1462, 1472–1474.
39. Thomas Y. Davies, "The Supreme Court Giveth and the Supreme Court Taketh Away: The Century of Fourth Amendment 'Search and Seizure' Doctrine," *Journal of Criminal Law & Criminology* 100, no. 3 (2010): 933–1042, 943–944, 946–947, 950.
40. Friedman, *Unwarranted*, 156.
41. Thomas, "Time Travel," 1462, 1472–1474.
42. William J. Cuddihy, *The Fourth Amendment: Origins and Original Meaning, 602–1791* (Oxford: Oxford University Press, 2009).
43. Davies, "The Fictional Character of Law-and-Order Originalism," 399.
44. Seo, "The Originalist Road," 11.
45. NAACP Legal Defense Brief, *Sibron v. New York*, 20, 23.
46. Davies, "The Fictional Character of Law-and-Order Originalism," 428.
47. McDonald v. United States, 335 U.S. 451, 456 (1948).
48. Johnson v. United States, 333 U.S. 10, 13–14 (1948).
49. 338 U.S. 160. 176 (1949). See also Scott E. Sundby, "An Ode to Probable Cause: A Brief Response to Professors Amar and Slobogin," *St. John's Law Review* 72, no. 3 (1998): 1133–1139, 1138 ("Probable cause embodies the idea of reciprocal citizen-government trust: The citizenry is obligated to obey the government's laws, but the government may engage in intrusive activities to ensure compliance only once the citizen's behavior gives rise to an objective belief that the trust has been violated.").
50. William J. Stuntz, "*Bordenkircher v. Hayes*: Plea Bargaining and the Decline of the Rule of Law," in *Criminal Procedure Stories*, ed. Carol Steiker (New York: Foundation Press/St Paul, MN: Thomson/West, 2006), 362; Barry Friedman, *The Will of the People: How Public Opinion Has Influenced the Supreme Court and Shaped the Meaning of the Constitution* (New York: Farrar, Straus and Giroux, 2009), 277.
51. Jeffrey Fagan, "*Terry's* Original Sin," *University of Chicago Legal Forum* 2016 (2016): 43–97.

52. Tracey L. Meares, "Programming Errors: Understanding the Constitutionality of Stop-and-Frisk as a Program, Not an Incident," *University of Chicago Law Review* 82, no. 1 (2015): 159–179, 166–167.
53. National Center on Police and Community Relations, *A National Survey of Police and Community Relations* (Washington, DC: U.S. Government Printing Office, 1967), 328.
54. The New York law authorizes stops when an officer "reasonably suspects" the person "is committing or is about to commit" a felony or other offenses specified. It allows a frisk when the officer "reasonably suspects that he is in danger of life or limb." N.Y. Code Crim. Proc. § 180-a.
55. Report of the National Advisory Commission on Civil Disorders (1968), 157–160.
56. David A. Harris, "Frisking Every Suspect: The Withering of *Terry*," *U.C. Davis Law Review* 28, no. 1 (1994): 1–52, 1–10.
57. Brief of American Civil Liberties Union, American Civil Liberties Union of Ohio, and New York Civil Liberties Union, Amici Curiae, 1967 WL 113689, at 3 (Sept. 29, 1967).
58. NAACP Legal Defense Brief, *Sibron v. New York*, 42–44.
59. John Q. Barrett, "Deciding the Stop and Frisk Cases: A Look Inside the Supreme Court's Conference," *St. John's Law Review* 72, no. 3/4 (1998): 749–844, 771.
60. This echoes the Court's decision not to talk about the link between coerced confessions and police brutality in interrogations and racial bias. Tracey Maclin, "Comprehensive Analysis of the History of Interrogation Law, with Some Shots Directed at *Miranda v. Arizona*," *Boston University Law Review* 95, no. 4 (2015): 1387–1423, 1396–1397.
61. Hon. Louis Stokes, "Representing John W. Terry," *St. John's Law Review* 72, no. 3/4 (1998): 727–731, 729–730.
62. Katz, "*Terry v. Ohio* at Thirty-Five," 430–433.
63. Brief for Petitioner, Terry v. Ohio, 1967 WL 113684, at 5 (Oct. 18, 1967).
64. Dudley, "Terry v. Ohio," 893.
65. Terry v. Ohio, 9–10.
66. Barrett, "Deciding the Stop and Frisk Cases," 791, 838.
67. This is especially so given that the probable cause standard was more robust in 1968, before the Court watered it down in *Illinois v. Gates*, 462 U.S. 213 (1983).
68. 392 U.S. at 7–8 (internal quotations omitted).
69. Maclin, "*Terry v. Ohio*'s Fourth Amendment Legacy," 1300 (quoting the trial transcript).
70. Maclin, "*Terry v. Ohio*'s Fourth Amendment Legacy," 1301 (quoting The Oyez Project).
71. Terry v. Ohio, 22.
72. Barrett, "Deciding the Stop and Frisk Cases," 790, 794, 797 (internal quotation and citation omitted). Warren's law clerk wrote a memo spelling

out the strategic thinking behind avoiding the stop argument. He worried that giving the police broad leeway to stop would mean they would have broad leeway to engage in frisks, too. Focusing on the frisk, he thought, would make it easier to explain that the police needed to show they were afraid for their safety to justify it. The clerk was also worried that a decision approving stops would risk allowing the police to stop people based on political views. He thought it was better to wait for a better vehicle to address the stop issue that would "more clearly expose[] the larger values that were at stake." Barrett, "Deciding the Stop and Frisk Cases," 817–818. When Justice Brennan read the draft along these lines, however, he urged Chief Justice Warren to confront the stop issue directly.

73. Dudley, "Terry v. Ohio," 894.
74. Davies, "The Supreme Court Giveth," 952.
75. Barrett, "Deciding the Stop and Frisk Cases," 825.
76. Barrett, "Deciding the Stop and Frisk Cases," 825–826 (quoting the letter from Justice Brennan to Chief Justice Warren).
77. Terry v. Ohio, 20.
78. Friedman, *Unwarranted*, 147.
79. Terry v. Ohio, 19 n.16.
80. Terry v. Ohio, 13–15.
81. Chemerinsky, *Presumed Guilty*, 112.
82. Friedman, *Unwarranted*, 143. Justice Scalia criticized *Terry* for making "no serious attempt to determine compliance with traditional standards." He posited that, if the Court had done so, it might have found a common-law antecedent for stops in "so-called nightwalker statutes," which allowed individuals engaged in suspicious activities at night to be detained, though he could find no support for the frisk authorization. Minnesota v. Dickerson, 508 U.S. 366, 380–381 (1993) (Scalia, J., concurring). Scalia did not give this a close look, however—or if he did, he made a mistake. As it turns out, there was no support for the stop portion of the opinion, either, because although the nightwalker statutes allowed officials or private persons to detain suspicious people found on the streets in the evening, "there is little indication that the standard for arrest under the nightwalker statutes was any less stringent than the standard governing any other kind of arrest." Lawrence Rosenthal, "Pragmatism, Originalism, Race, and the Case Against Terry v. Ohio," *Texas Tech Law Review* 43 (2010): 299–356, 331. See also Sklansky, "The Fourth Amendment and Common Law," 1804 (noting that the detention of nightwalkers "typically lasted all night and was treated as an arrest"). By the time the Fourteenth Amendment was ratified, moreover, the nightwalker statutes became an even more spurious basis for allowing stops. The Supreme Court struck down the vagrancy laws that were the modern versions of the nightwalker statutes because they led to arbitrary and discriminatory enforcement in violation of the Fourteenth Amendment.
83. Terry v. Ohio, 21, 27, 30.

84. It attempted to provide some limits of when and how an officer could frisk someone—over the clothing, not inside pockets—in the companion case of *Sibron v. New York*, which was decided the same day as *Terry*. In that case, a Brooklyn police officer, Anthony Martin, watched Nelson Sibron over the course of eight hours on March 9, 1965, talk to numerous people whom Martin "knew from past experience to be narcotics addicts." Martin never saw Sibron hand drugs or anything else to any of these people. Around midnight, Sibron went inside a restaurant, spoke to three more people known by Martin to be addicts, and then sat down for some pie and coffee. That was when Martin reached his limit. He told Sibron to join him outside the restaurant and then said to him, "You know what I am after." Martin claims Sibron "mumbled something and reached into his pocket." At the same time, Martin reached into the same pocket and pulled out several glassine envelopes containing heroin. Sibron was charged with unlawful possession of heroin. The Supreme Court overturned Sibron's conviction because Martin did not claim he searched Sibron because he feared he was armed and dangerous. When he said, "[y]ou know what I am after," to Sibron, he was clearly alluding to drugs, and that is what he was eager to obtain from Sibron's pocket. It would, however, take monumental faith in the honesty of police officers to think that, after *Sibron* and *Terry*, officers would not alter their testimony to make sure they fell within the Court's rubric to at least get the ability to do the pat down outside of clothing. It is hard to imagine Officer Martin facing the same scenario today and not arguing he was afraid Sibron was armed because he was trafficking drugs and drug traffickers are usually armed.
85. Terry v. Ohio, 35–39 (Douglas, J., dissenting).
86. Adams v. Williams, 407 U.S. 143, 162 (1972) (Marshall, J., joined by Douglas, J., dissenting).
87. Maclin, "*Terry v. Ohio*'s Fourth Amendment Legacy," 1287.
88. Sherry F. Colb, "The Qualitative Dimension of Fourth Amendment 'Reasonableness,'" *Columbia Law Review* 98, no. 7 (1998): 1642–1725, 1660.
89. The Court cut back on the scope of vagrancy laws in *Papachristou* four years after *Terry* because they gave police too much discretion. Papachristou v. Jacksonville, 405 U.S.156 (1972). As William Stuntz pointed it, it was only when "loitering and vagrancy laws started to fall to vagueness challenges" in the late 1960s in state court decisions that "ordinary police-citizen encounters on the street became a serious Fourth Amendment issue." Until then, the police could claim probable cause that those laws were being violated when they stopped someone. William J. Stuntz, "*Terry*'s Impossibility," *St. John's Law Review* 72, no. 3/4 (1998): 1213–1229, 1215–1216.
90. "Balancing Order with Liberty," *Washington Post*, June 12, 1968, 1.
91. "'Unreasonable' Still Stands," *New York Times*, June 12, 1968, 46.
92. "The High-Court Allows Stop-and-Frisking," *Hartford Courant*, June 11, 1968, 24.
93. "Balancing Order with Liberty," 1.

94. Chemerinsky, *Presumed Guilty*, 116.
95. Katz, "*Terry v. Ohio* at Thirty-Five," 481–483.
96. Kansas v. Glover, 140 S.Ct. 1183, 1190 (2020).
97. United States v. Sokolow, 490 U.S. 1, 7 (1989).
98. Illinois v. Wardlaw, 528 U.S. 119, 125 (2000).
99. Rudovsky and Harris, "*Terry* Stops-and-Frisks," 506.
100. William J. Stuntz, "*Terry* and Substantive Law," *St. John's Law Review* 72, no. 3/4 (1998): 1362–1366, 1364.
101. Lauryn P. Gouldin, "Crimes of Suspicion," *Emory Law Journal* 72, no. 6 (2023): 1429–1484, 1432–1433, 1458, 1471, 1478.
102. 528 U.S. 119, 121–124 (2000).
103. Chief Justice Warren, who wrote *Terry*, discussed this issue with his fellow justices at their conference after argument in the cases. One reason he thought stops should be treated differently for Fourth Amendment purposes is that people questioned by the police are under no obligation to answer and can "'walk away,' which would leave the officer with 'no probable cause' to do anything further." Barrett, "Deciding the Stop and Frisk Cases," 785 (internal citations omitted). *Wardlaw* turns this rationale on its head, making flight a valid reason for the police to stop someone.
104. Paul Butler, "The White Fourth Amendment," *Texas Tech Law Review* 43 (2010): 245–254, 251.
105. David A. Harris, "Factors for Reasonable Suspicion: When Black and Poor Mean Stopped and Frisked," *Indiana Law Journal* 69, no. 3 (1994): 659–688, 681.
106. Rudovsky and Harris, "*Terry* Stops-and-Frisks," 508, n.36.
107. David Cole, "Discretion and Discrimination Reconsidered: A Response to the New Criminal Justice Scholarship," *Georgetown Law Journal* 87, no. 5 (1999): 1059–1093, 1077–1079.
108. See, for example, Ornelas v. United States, 517 U.S. 690, 700 (1996).
109. Harris, "Factors for Reasonable Suspicion," 666.
110. United States v. Cortez, 449 U.S. 411, 419 (1981).
111. Illinois v. Wardlaw, 528 U.S. 119, 124–125 (2000).
112. Fagan, "*Terry*'s Original Sin," 44.
113. 517 U.S. 806, 808–809 (1996).
114. David A. Sklansky, "Traffic Stops, Minority Motorists, and the Future of the Fourth Amendment," *Supreme Court Review* (1997): 271–329, 278.
115. Whren v. United States, 810.
116. The City of New York Commission to Investigate Allegations of Police Corruption and the Anti-Corruption Procedures of the Police Department, *Commission Report* (1994), 38.
117. Sklansky, "Traffic Stops," 299.
118. Chemerinsky, *Presumed Guilty*, 220.
119. Maryland v. Wilson, 519 U.S. 408, 412–415 (1997). The Court later compounded the negative effects of *Whren* even further when it held that an officer can arrest and take into custody the person stopped for the traffic

violation even if state law expressly forbids an arrest for a traffic violation. Atwater v. Lago Vista, 532 U.S. 318 (2001). For a persuasive account that *Atwater* was inconsistent with framing era arrest doctrine, see Davies, "The Fictional Character of Law-and-Order Originalism."
120. Cole, "Discretion and Discrimination Reconsidered," 1076.
121. Rudovksy and Harris, "*Terry* Stops-and-Frisks," 531–532.
122. State v. Sullivan, 74 S.W.3d 215 (Ark. 2002); State v. Ladson, 979 P.2d. 833 (Wash. 1999).
123. Sklansky, "Traffic Stops," 284–286.
124. Barbara C. Salken, "The General Warrant of the Twentieth Century? A Fourth Amendment Solution to Unchecked Discretion to Arrest for Traffic Offenses," *Temple Law Review* 62, no. 1 (1989): 221–275.
125. Hausman and Kronick, "The Illusory End of Stop and Frisk in Chicago?" 1.
126. These courts are thus taking up the suggestion Justice Harlan made in his concurrence that "the right to frisk is automatic when an officer lawfully stops a person suspected of a crime whose nature creates a substantial likelihood that he is armed." Sibron v. New York, 74 (Harlan, J., concurring).
127. Harris, "Factors for Reasonable Suspicion," 676, 680–681.
128. Harris, "Frisking Every Suspect," 22–32.
129. Omar Saleem, "The Age of Unreason: The Impact of Reasonableness, Increased Police Force, and Colorblindness on *Terry* 'Stop and Frisk,'" *Oklahoma Law Review* 50, no. 4 (1997): 451–493, 466.
130. Meares, "Programming Errors," 173–174.
131. Floyd v. City of New York, 589.
132. Floyd v. City of New York, 606.
133. Stop and Frisk Data, NYCLU, ACLU of NYC, March 14, 2019, https://www.nyclu.org/en/stop-and-frisk-data; "Floyd, et al. v. City of New York, et al.," What We Do: Active Cases, Center for Constitutional Rights, n.d., https://ccrjustice.org/home/what-we-do/our-cases/floyd-et-al-v-city-new-york-et-al.
134. "Sixteenth Report of the Independent Monitor: General Compliance Report," NYPD Monitor Reports, May 6, 2022, 9, 26–27, https://www.nypdmonitor.org/wp-content/uploads/2022/09/16-Sixteenth-Report-.pdf.
135. The data were available only because of a settlement agreement in an earlier lawsuit alleging racial profiling in stop-and-frisk in New York that required the NYPD to turn over data. Center for Constitutional Rights, *Stop and Frisk: The Human Impact*, 3.
136. "Balancing Order with Liberty," at 1.
137. Robert Vargas et al., "Capitalizing on Crisis: Chicago Policy Responses to Homicide Waves, 1920–2016," *University of Chicago Law Review* 89, no. 2 (2022): 405–439, 423.
138. Bob Herbert, "The Police Bullies," *New York Times*, March 7, 1997.
139. Charles J. Ogletree et al., *Beyond the Rodney King Story: An Investigation of Police Conduct in Minority Communities* (Boston: Northeastern University Press, 1995), 23.

140. NAACP Legal Defense Brief, *Sibron v. New York*, 35.
141. Meares, "Programming Errors," 164.
142. Floyd v. City of New York, 596.
143. James J. Fyfe, "*Terry*: A[n Ex-]Cop's View," *St. John's Law Review* 72, no. 3/4 (1998): 1231–1248.
144. Meares, "Programming Errors," 171–172.
145. James Q. Wilson, "Just Take Away Their Guns," *New York Times Magazine*, March 20, 1994, 46–47.
146. Huq, "The Consequences of Disparate Policing," 2418, 2422–2423.
147. Fagan, "*Terry's* Original Sin," 46. Aggressive stop-and-frisk policies likewise failed to stem the tide of rising homicides in Chicago. Vargas et al., "Capitalizing on Crisis," 423.
148. Seo, "The Originalist Road," 15.
149. "Offenses Cleared," *Crime in the United States, 2019*, FBI Uniform Crime Reporting, https://ucr.fbi.gov/crime-in-the-u.s/2019/crime-in-the-u.s.-2019/topic-pages/clearances.
150. Alexandra Natapoff, "Underenforcement," *Fordham Law Review* 75, no. 3 (2006): 1715–1776, 1718–1719.
151. Friedman, *Unwarranted*, 157.
152. Fyfe, "*Terry*," 1238.
153. Tovah Renee Calderon, "Race-Based Policing from *Terry* to *Wardlow*: Steps Down the Totalitarian Path," *Howard Law Journal* 44, no. 1 (2000): 73–105, 79–80.
154. David Cole, *No Equal Justice: Race and Class in the American Criminal Justice System* (New York: New Press, 1999), 36–40.
155. Chemerinsky, *Presumed Guilty*, 114.
156. Michael Tonry, *Punishing Race: A Continuing American Dilemma* (Oxford: Oxford University Press, 2011), 50–73; Rory Kramer and Brianna Remster, "Stop, Frisk, and Assault: Racial Disparities in Police Use of Force during Investigatory Stops," *Law & Society Review* 52, no. 4 (2018): 960–993, 981.
157. Huq, "The Consequences of Disparate Policing," 2434.
158. 392 U.S. at 16–17.
159. 959 F.Supp.2d. at 557.
160. Cole, "Discretion and Discrimination Reconsidered," 1091.
161. Tom R. Tyler, Jeffrey Fagan, and Amanda Geller, "Street Stops and Police Legitimacy: Teachable Moments in Young Urban Men's Legal Socialization," *Journal of Empirical Legal Studies* 11, no. 4 (2014): 751–785; Tom R. Tyler and Jeffrey Fagan, "Legitimacy and Cooperation: Why Do People Help the Police Fight Crime in Their Communities," *Ohio State Journal of Criminal Law* 6 (2008): 231–275.
162. Fagan, "*Terry's* Original Sin," 91.
163. Center for Constitutional Rights, *Stop and Frisk: The Human Impact*, 15.
164. NAACP Legal Defense Brief, *Sibron v. New York*, 68–69.

165. Terry v. Ohio, 15.
166. Davies, "The Fictional Character of Law-and-Order Originalism," 403; William Baude, "Is Qualified Immunity Unlawful?" *California Law Review* 106, no. 1 (2018): 45–90.
167. Joanna Schwartz, *Shielded: How the Police Became Untouchable* (New York: Viking, 2023).

6. Overlooking Pervasive Racial Bias

Epigraph: Michelle Alexander, *The New Jim Crow: Mass Incarceration in an Age of Colorblindness* (New York: New Press, 2010), 111.

1. "Arrests by Race and Ethnicity," Crime in the U.S. 2019, Uniform Crime Reporting, FBI, Table 43, https://ucr.fbi.gov/crime-in-the-u.s/2019/crime-in-the-u.s.-2019/tables/table-43.
2. Frank R. Baumgartner, Derek A. Epp, and Kelsey Shoub, *Suspect Citizens: What 20 Million Traffic Stops Tell Us about Policing and Race* (Cambridge: Cambridge University Press, 2018).
3. Simoiu Pierson et al., "A Large-Scale Analysis of Racial Disparities in Police Stops across the United States," *Nature Human Behaviour* 4, no. 7 (2020): 736–745.
4. "Black, Brown and Targeted: A Report on Boston Police Department Street Encounters from 2007–2010," American Civil Liberties Union (ACLU), October 2014.
5. Lynn Langton and Matthew Durose, "Police Behavior during Traffic and Street Stops, 2011," NCJ 242937, Special Report, U.S. Department of Justice, September 2013, rev. October 27, 2016.
6. Topher Sanders, Kate Rabinowitz, and Benjamin Conarck, "Walking While Black," *ProPublica*, November 16, 2017, https://features.propublica.org/walking-while-black/jacksonville-pedestrian-violations-racial-profiling/. Jeffrey Fagan, "No Runs, Few Hits, and Many Errors: Street Stops, Bias, and Proactive Policing," *UCLA Law Review* 68, no. 6 (2022): 1584–1676.
7. Philip J. Levchak, "Stop-and-Frisk in New York City: Estimating Racial Disparities in Post-Stop Outcomes," *Journal of Criminal Justice* 73 (2021): 101784, 7.
8. Baumgartner, Epp, and Shoub, *Suspect Citizens*, 87–88.
9. Devon W. Carbado, "Predatory Policing," *UMKC Law Review* 85, no. 3 (2017): 545–566, 553–554; Becca Cadoff, Kristyn Jones, Preeti Chauhan and Michael Rempel, "Lower-Level Enforcement, Racial Disparities, & Alternatives to Arrest: A Review of Research and Practice from 1970 to 2021," Data Collaborative for Justice, John Jay College of Criminal Justice, February 2023, https://datacollaborativeforjustice.org/wp-content/uploads/2023/02/A2AReport.pdf.

10. "Rates of Drug Use and Sales, by Race; Rates of Drug Related Criminal Justice Measures by Race," chart, The Hamilton Project, Brookings Institution, October 21, 2016, https://www.hamiltonproject.org/data/rates-of-drug-use-and-sales-by-race-rates-of-drug-related-criminal-justice-measures-by-race.
11. Wendy Sawyer, "How Race Impacts Who Is Detained Pretrial," briefing, Prison Policy Initiative, October 9, 2019. David Arnold, Will Dobbie and Crystal S. Yang, "Racial Bias in Bail Decisions," *Quarterly Journal of Economics* 133, no. 4 (2018): 1885–1932; Stephen Demuth, "Racial and Ethnic Differences in Pretrial Release Decisions and Outcomes: A Comparison of Hispanic, Black, and White Felony Arrestees," *Criminology* 41, no. 3 (2003): 873–908, 890–895.
12. "Developments in the Law: Race and the Criminal Process," *Harvard Law Review* 101, no. 7 (1988): 1472–1641, 1525.
13. Carlos Berdejó, "Criminalizing Race: Racial Disparities in Plea Bargaining," *Boston College Law Review* 59, no. 4 (2018): 1188–1249, 1191, 1216.
14. Ram Subramanian et al., "In the Shadows: A Review of the Research on Plea Bargaining," Vera Institute of Justice, September 2020, https://www.vera.org/downloads/publications/in-the-shadows-plea-bargaining.pdf.
15. Matthew S. Crow and Katherine A. Johnson, "Race, Ethnicity, and Habitual-Offender Sentencing: A Multi-level Analysis of Individual and Contextual Threat," *Criminal Justice Policy Review* 19, no. 1 (2008): 63–83, 72–73.
16. Sonja B. Starr and M. Marit Rehavi, "Mandatory Sentencing and Racial Disparity: Assessing the Role of Prosecutors and the Effects of *Booker*," *Yale Law Journal* 123, no. 1 (2013): 2–80, 28–29.
17. Paul Butler, "One Hundred Years of Race and Crime," *Journal of Criminal Law & Criminology* 100, no. 3 (2010): 1043–1060, 1049.
18. U.S. Sentencing Commission, "Demographic Differences in Sentencing: An Update to the 2012 *Booker* Report," November 2017, 6, https://www.ussc.gov/sites/default/files/pdf/research-and-publications/research-publications/2017/20171114_Demographics.pdf.
19. Jennifer L. Hochschild and Vesla Weaver, "The Skin Color Paradox and the American Racial Order," *Social Forces* 86, no. 2 (2007): 643–670, 649. Other studies have found similar results. Traci Burch, "Skin Color and the Criminal Justice System: Beyond Black-White Disparities in Sentencing," *Journal of Empirical Legal Studies* 12, no. 3 (2015): 395–420, 408.
20. Radley Balko, "There's Overwhelming Evidence That the Criminal Justice System Is Racist. Here's the Proof," *Washington Post*, June 10, 2020; Jeree Michele Thomas and Mel Wilson, "The Color of Youth Transferred to the Adult Criminal Justice System: Policy & Practice Recommendations," Social Justice Brief, National Association of Social Workers, 2017, rev. September 18, 2018, 1, http://www.campaignforyouthjustice.org/images/pdf/Social_Justice_Brief_Youth_Transfers.Revised_copy_09-18-2018.pdf.
21. Juleyka Lantigua-Williams, "The Link between Race and Solitary Confinement," *The Atlantic*, December 5, 2016; Hannah Pullen-Blasnik, Jessica T. Simes, and Bruce Western, "The Population Prevalence of Solitary Confine-

ment," *Science Advances* 7 (November 26, 2021) eabj1928; Katie Michaela Becker, "Race and Prison Discipline: A Study of North Carolina Prisons," *North Carolina Central Law Review* 43, no. 2 (2021): 175–225; Grace Ashford, "Widespread Racial Disparities in Discipline Found at N.Y. Prisons," *New York Times*, December 1, 2022.
22. Washington v. Davis, 426 U.S. 229, 242 (1976).
23. This model was considered the best by the Baldus team. Even though one might intuitively think more variables are better, that is not always true. "After a certain point, additional independent variables become correlated with variables already being considered and distort or suppress their influence. The most accurate models strike an appropriate balance between the risk of committing a significant factor and the risk of multicollinearity." McCleskey v. Kemp, 753 F.2d 877, 916 (11th Cir. 1985) (en banc) (Johnson, J., dissenting in part and concurring in part).
24. McCleskey v. Kemp, 481 U.S. 279, 315, 318 (1987).
25. McCleskey v. Kemp, 481 U.S. 279, 339 (Brennan, J., dissenting).
26. "Bill Moyers Journal," with Bryan Stevenson and Michelle Alexander, transcript, April 2, 2010, https://www.pbs.org/moyers/journal/04022010/transcript3.html.
27. Heather Schoenfeld, *Building the Prison State: Race and the Politics of Mass Incarceration* (Chicago: University of Chicago Press, 2018).
28. Although the Fourteenth Amendment applies only to the states, the Supreme Court has concluded that there is an equal protection guarantee as part of the Fifth Amendment's Due Process Clause, so that equal protection applies to the federal government as well as to the states. Bolling v. Sharpe, 347 U.S. 497 (1954).
29. During the debate over the Fourteenth Amendment, Representative James Garfield explained: "The civil rights bill is now a part of the law of the land. But every gentleman knows that it will cease to be a part of the law whenever the sad moment arrives when [the Democratic] party comes into power. It is precisely for that reason that we propose to life that great and good law above the reach of political strife, beyond the reach of the plots and machinations of any party, and fix it in the serene sky, in the eternal firmament of the Constitution, where no storm of passion can shake it and no cloud can obscure it." Cong. Globe, 39th Cong., 1st Sess. 2462 (May 8, 1866). See also 2459 (Thaddeus Stevens) (noting that the civil rights law "is repealable by a majority" and then adding "I need hardly say that the first time that the South with their copperhead allies obtain the command of Congress it will be repealed"); Kurt T. Lash, "Enforcing the Rights of Due Process: The Original Relationship between the Fourteenth Amendment and the 1866 Civil Rights Act," *Georgetown Law Journal* 106, no. 5 (2018): 1389–1467, 1447.
30. Eric Foner, *Reconstruction: America's Unfinished Revolution, 1863–1877* (New York: Harper & Row, 1988), 199–204.
31. General Bldg. Contractors Ass'n, Inc. v. Pennsylvania, 458 U.S. 375, 386–387 (1982).

32. General Bldg. Contractors Ass'n, Inc. v. Pennsylvania, 387; id. at 410 (Marshall, J., dissenting); see also Lash, "Enforcing the Rights of Due Process," 1404, 1463 (noting that laws protecting freedmen "were often unenforced or unequally enforced").
33. Students for Fair Admissions, Inc. v. President and Fellows of Harvard College, 143 S.Ct. 2141, 2229 (Sotomayor, J., dissenting).
34. Cong. Globe, 39th Cong., 1st Sess. 2766 (May 23, 1866).
35. Cong. Globe, 39th Cong., 1st Sess. 2766 (May 23, 1866).
36. Cong. Globe, 39th Cong., 1st Sess. 2459 (May 8, 1866).
37. General Bldg. Contractors Ass'n, 412 (Marshall, J., dissenting).
38. Laurence H. Tribe, *American Constitutional Law*, 2nd ed. (Mineola, NY: Foundation Press, 1988), 1519.
39. 163 U.S. 537, 540 (1896).
40. William J. Stuntz, *The Collapse of American Criminal Justice* (Cambridge, MA: Harvard University Press, 2011), 118.
41. Mario L. Barnes and Erwin Chemerinsky, "The Once and Future Equal Protection Doctrine?" *Connecticut Law Review* 43, no. 4 (2011): 1059–1088, 1070.
42. Ian Haney-López, "Intentional Blindness," *NYU Law Review* 87, no. 6 (2012): 1779–1877, 1790, 1798.
43. Daniel R. Ortiz, "The Myth of Intent in Equal Protection," *Stanford Law Review* 41, no. 5 (1989): 1105–1151, 1139.
44. Washington v. Davis, 241–242, 248 and n.14.
45. Washington v. Davis, 253–254, 256 (1976) (Stevens, J., concurring).
46. Justice Brennan's dissent, joined by Justice Marshall, focused on the statutory decision in the case and would have ruled for the officers pursuant to Title VII. Justices Brennan and Marshall did not take issue with the general approach outlined by the majority, which Ian Haney-López explains is consistent with viewing *Davis* as "consolidating contextual intent," which was the approach used by the Court all along. Haney-López, "Intentional Blindness," 1803, 1806.
47. Castaneda v. Partida, 430 U.S. 482, 494–495 (1977). The Court's decision in *Village of Arlington Heights v. Metropolitan Housing Development Corp.*, 429 U.S. 252, 265–267 (1977), also reiterated the contextual approach that should be taken in equal protection cases and emphasized that litigants need only prove that race was "a motivating factor" not the sole or primary one.
48. 442 U.S. 256, 279 and n.25 (1979).
49. Columbus Board of Education v. Penick, 443 U.S. 449, 464 (1979).
50. Columbus Board of Education v. Penick, 509–510, 513 (Rehnquist, J., dissenting).
51. Furman v. Georgia, 408 U.S. 238 (1972).
52. 428 U.S. 153 (1976). The Court approved similar capital statutes passed in Florida and Texas that used a guided discretion approach. Proffitt v. Florida, 428 U.S. 242 (1976); Jurek v. Texas, 428 U.S. 262 (1976). It rejected capital

statutes from North Carolina and Louisiana that made the death penalty mandatory in some cases. Woodson v. North Carolina, 428 U.S. 280 (1976); Roberts v. Louisiana, 428 U.S. 325 (1976).
53. John Charles Boger, "*McCleskey v. Kemp*: Field Notes from 1977–1991," *Northwestern University Law Review* 112, no. 6 (2018): 1637–1688, 1657–1658.
54. McCleskey v. Kemp, 920 (11th Cir. 1985) (Clark, J., dissenting in part and concurring in part).
55. It was more important than whether a defendant was the prime mover in a homicide and almost as important as whether a defendant had a prior conviction for a capital crime. McCleskey v. Kemp, 355 and n. 9–10.
56. Boger, "*McCleskey v. Kemp*," 1660.
57. McCleskey v. Kemp, 287 n.5.
58. Brief for Petitioner, McCleskey v. Kemp, No. 84-6811, 1986 WL 727359 (Sept. 3, 1986).
59. Randall L. Kennedy, "*McCleskey v. Kemp*: Race, Capital Punishment, and the Supreme Court," *Harvard Law Review* 101, no. 7 (1988): 1388–1483, 1400.
60. McCleskey v. Kemp, 881 (11th Cir. 1985).
61. Boger, "*McCleskey v. Kemp*," 1663.
62. McCleskey v. Kemp, 892, 894, 899 (11th Cir. 1985).
63. Samuel R. Gross, "Race and Death: The Judicial Evaluation of Evidence of Discrimination in Capital Sentencing," *UC Davis Law Review* 18 (1985): 1275–1325, 1307.
64. Petitioner's Reply Brief, McCleskey v. Kemp, No. 84-6811, 1986 WL 727363, at 17 (Oct. 4, 1986).
65. Brief of Amici Curiae State of California in Support of Respondent, McCleskey v. Kemp, No. 84-6811, 1986 WL 727362, at 11 (Sept. 22, 1986).
66. Brief for Respondent, McCleskey v. Kemp, No. 84-6811, 1986 WL 727361, at 14 (Sept. 22, 1986).
67. Justice Powell wrote in that dissent that, "[i]f the Baldus study is similar to" other studies filed in capital cases, it failed to offer the kind of particularized evidence necessary to prove intentional racial discrimination, and "such arguments cannot be taken seriously under statutes approved in *Gregg*." Stephens v. Kemp, 464 U.S. 1027, 1030 n.2 (1984) (Powell, J., dissenting).
68. While Justice White voted with the majority in *Castaneda*, he joined Justice Powell's opinion in *McCleskey*. A note he sent to Justice Powell indicates he did so because he agreed with the district court's skepticism about the Baldus study's validity. McCleskey v. Kemp Supreme Court Case Files Collection, box 132, Powell Papers, Lewis F. Powell Jr. Archives, Washington and Lee School of Law, Lexington, VA, available at https://scholarlycommons.law.wlu.edu/cgi/viewcontent.cgi?article=1168&context=casefiles. Chief Justice Burger and Justice Stewart also agreed with Justice Powell in *Castaneda*, but the new Justices on the Court, Justices O'Connor and Scalia, provided the additional votes in support of Powell's position. Professor Haney-López describes Powell's dissent in *Castaneda* as "anticipat[ing] a looming

epistemological opposition to social science, history, and local context." Haney-López, "Intentional Blindness," 1823.
69. McCleskey v. Kemp, 292 and n.29.
70. McCleskey v. Kemp, 292–297 and n.14.
71. Pamela S. Karlan, "Race, Rights, and Remedies in Criminal Adjudication," *Michigan Law Review* 96, no. 7 (1998): 2001–2030, 2021.
72. McCleskey v. Kemp, 362 (Blackmun, J., dissenting).
73. Boger, "*McCleskey v. Kemp*," 1680 (quoting the Memorandum from Antonin Scalia, Assoc. Justice, Supreme Court of the United States, to the Conference (Jan. 6, 1987)).
74. 424 U.S. 409 (1976).
75. Margaret Z. Johns, "Unsupportable and Unjustified: A Critique of Absolute Prosecutorial Immunity," *Fordham Law Review* 80, no. 2 (2011): 509–535, 521; Karen McDonald Henning, "The Failed Legacy of Absolute Immunity under Imbler: Providing a Compromise Approach to Claims of Prosecutorial Misconduct," *Gonzaga Law Review* 48 (2012): 219–278, 238–239.
76. Batson v. Kentucky, 476 U.S. 79 (1986).
77. McCleskey v. Kemp, 350 n.3 and 363 (Blackmun, J., dissenting).
78. McCleskey v. Kemp, 298.
79. Boger, "*McCleskey v. Kemp*," 1638.
80. He wrote that he expected to make those points in a separate opinion "but not until I see the dissent." Boger, "*McCleskey v. Kemp*," 1680.
81. Boger, "*McCleskey v. Kemp*," 1680.
82. Justices Marshall and Stevens joined his dissent in full, whereas Justice Brennan joined all but the last section, which argued that acceptance of McCleskey's claim would not require striking down capital punishment in Georgia, but rather would allow a narrower version that focused on the extremely aggravated murders where Baldus did not find the same evidence of racial bias.
83. McCleskey v. Kemp, 346 (Blackmun, J., dissenting).
84. Cong. Globe, 39th Cong., 1st Sess. 2766 (May 23, 1866).
85. McCleskey v. Kemp, 345, 350–351, 356 (Blackmun, J., dissenting).
86. McCleskey v. Kemp, 356–358 (Blackmun, J., dissenting).
87. 433 U.S. 584 (1977).
88. Brief for Petitioner, McCleskey v. Kemp, No. 84-6811, 1986 WL 727359, at 59 (Sept. 3, 1986).
89. McCleskey v. Kemp, 359.
90. Justice Marshall joined Justice Brennan's dissent in full. Justices Blackmun and Stevens joined all of it except the portion where Justice Brennan stated his position that the death penalty is cruel and unusual and unconstitutional in all circumstances.
91. McCleskey v. Kemp, 322, 328–330, 334, 344 and n.8 (Brennan, J., dissenting).
92. McCleskey v. Kemp, 314–315.
93. McCleskey v. Kemp, 365 (Blackmun, J., dissenting).
94. McCleskey v. Kemp, 339 (Brennan, J., dissenting).

95. Brief Amicus Curiae of the Washington Legal Foundation and the Allied Educational Foundation in Support of Respondent, McCleskey v. Kemp, No. 84-6811, 1986 WL 727360, at 2–3 (Sept. 19, 1986).
96. Kennedy, "*McCleskey v. Kemp*," 1414.
97. Stephen B. Bright and James Kwak, *The Fear of Too Much Justice: Race, Poverty, and the Persistence of Inequality in the Criminal Courts* (New York: New Press, 2023), 21.
98. McCleskey v. Kemp, 319.
99. Reva B. Siegel, "Blind Justice: Why the Court Refused to Accept Statistical Evidence of Discriminatory Purpose in *McCleskey v. Kemp*—and Some Pathways for Change," *Northwestern University Law Review* 112, no. 6 (2018): 1269–1291, 1285–86.
100. John C. Jeffries Jr., *Justice Lewis F. Powell, Jr.: A Biography* (New York: Charles Scribner's Sons, 1994), 451.
101. Boger, "*McCleskey v. Kemp*," 1678.
102. Steven F. Shatz & Terry Dalton, "Challenging the Death Penalty with Statistics: Furman, McCleskey, and a Single County Case Study," *Cardozo Law Review* 34 (2013): 1227–1282, 1246. For a discussion of factors that lead to these disparities, including police practices and the political pressure on district attorneys in cases involving white victims, see Bright and Kwak, *The Fear of Too Much Justice*, 226.
103. Sharad Goel, Maya Perelman, Ravi Shroff, and David Alan Sklansky, "Combatting Police Discrimination in the Age of Big Data," *New Criminal Law Review* 20, no. 2 (2017): 181–232, 186.
104. Anthony G. Amsterdam, "Opening Remarks: Race and the Death Penalty Before and After *McCleskey*," *Columbia Human Rights Law Review* 39 (2007): 47.
105. Destiny Peery & Osagie K. Obasogie, "Equal Protection and the Social Sciences Thirty Years after *McCleskey v. Kemp*," *Northwestern University Law Review* 112, no. 6 (2018): 1261–1268, 1263.
106. Stuntz, *The Collapse of American Criminal Justice*, 120.
107. Sheri Lynn Johnson, "Unconscious Racism and the Criminal Law," *Cornell Law Review* 73, no. 5 (1988): 1016–1037; Angela J. Davis, "Prosecution and Race: The Power and Privilege of Discretion," *Fordham Law Review* 67, no. 1 (1998): 13–67; Charles R. Lawrence III, "The Id, the Ego, and Equal Protection: Reckoning with Unconscious Racism," *Stanford Law Review* 39, no. 2 (1987): 317–388; David A. Sklansky, "Cocaine, Race, and Equal Protection," *Stanford Law Review* 47 (1995): 1283–1322, 1307–1308.
108. Lawrence, "The Id, the Ego, and Equal Protection," 355.
109. Amsterdam, "Opening Remarks," 55–56.
110. Amsterdam, "Opening Remarks," 47; Kennedy, "*McCleskey v. Kemp*," 1388–89.
111. Davis, "Prosecution and Race," 34.

112. Richard H. McAdams, "Race and Selective Prosecution: Discovering the Pitfalls of *Armstrong*," *Chicago-Kent Law Review* 73 (1998): 605–667, 605, 646.
113. Haney-López, "Intentional Blindness," 1783.
114. Some lower courts have used the same difficult standard for selective law enforcement claims against the police, but others have recently made discovery easier for claims of discrimination involving the police in fake stash house cases, where the police approach people to induce them to agree to rob a nonexistent drug stash house. In some of these cases, courts have recognized that it would be impossible to identify people who had no contact with the police, so they have allowed statistical evidence of disparities in targets to suffice for obtaining discovery on the criteria the police use to identify their targets. Alison Siegler and William Admussen, "Discovering Racial Discrimination by the Police," *Northwestern University Law Review* 115, no. 4 (2021): 987–1054.
115. United States v. Armstrong, 517 U.S. 456, 458–59 (1996).
116. Brief for the National Association of Criminal Defense Lawyers as Amicus Curiae in Support of Respondent, United States v. Armstrong, No. 95-157, 1996 WL 17133, at 19–20 (Jan. 9, 1996). Many defendants tried to challenge the Anti-Drug Abuse Act of 1986, which punished crack cocaine offenses far more harshly than powder cocaine offenses, as violating the Equal Protection Clause. The discussion around the passage of that law, which passed one week before November midterm elections, certainly had racial overtones, but the litigants challenging the law universally failed under the Court's doctrine and the lack of proof of discriminatory intent on the basis of race. Sklansky, "Cocaine, Race, and Equal Protection," 1303. The Armstrong defendants, as well as other defendants, made the different claim that the federal crack law was being selectively enforced against Black people and that white crack offenders were getting prosecuted under more lenient state laws.
117. United States v. Armstrong, 479 and n.5 (Stevens, J., dissenting).
118. Brief Amicus Curiae of Former Law Enforcement Officials & Police Organizations, et al. in Support of Respondents, United States v. Armstrong, No. 95-157, 1996 WL 17132, at 13 (Jan. 16, 1996).
119. Brief for Respondent Robert Rozelle, United States v. Armstrong, No. 95-137, 1996 WL 14112, at 33–35 (Jan. 8, 1996).
120. Brief Amicus Curiae of Former Law Enforcement Officials & Police Organizations, et al. in Support of Respondents, United States v. Armstrong, No. 95-157, 1996 WL 17132, at 2–3 (Jan. 16, 1996).
121. Brief for Respondent Robert Rozelle, United States v. Armstrong, No. 95-137, 1996 WL 14112, at 26–27 (Jan. 8, 1996).
122. Brief for Respondents Shelton Auntwan Martin, Aaron Hampton, Christopher Lee Armstrong, and Freddie Mack, United States v. Armstrong, No. 95-157, 1996 WL 17111, at 2, 4, 7 (Jan. 9, 1996).

123. Brief for Respondent Robert Rozelle, 27.
124. Brief for Respondent Robert Rozelle, 55.
125. United States v. Armstrong, 460; id. at 481 (Stevens, J., dissenting).
126. Brief for Respondents Martin et al., 8.
127. While the case was pending on appeal, a study conducted as part of a selective prosecution challenge to crack prosecutions in another case in the Central District of California found that 42 percent of people arrested for crack distribution were non-Black and that 47 percent of the state charges for crack sales were against people who were not Black. Brief for Respondents Martin et al., 12.
128. United States v. Armstrong, 464, 469–470. The government, it is worth noting, did not object to the admissions of these declarations in the district court. Brief of Former Law Enforcement Officials, at 23.
129. United States v. Armstrong, 481 and n.6 (Stevens, J., dissenting).
130. Brief of NAACP Legal Defense & Educational Fund, Inc., and American Civil Liberties Union as Amicus Curiae in Support of Respondents, United States v. Armstrong, No. 95-157, 1996 WL 17149, at 17 (Jan. 16, 1996) (citing Richard Berk, "Preliminary Data on Race and Crack Charging Practices in Los Angeles," *Federal Sentencing Reporter* 6 (1993): 36).
131. Yick Wo v. Hopkins, 118 U.S. 356, 359, 368, 374 (1886).
132. Anne Bowen Poulin, "Prosecutorial Discretion and Selective Prosecution: Enforcing Protection after United States v. Armstrong," *American Criminal Law Review* 34 (1997): 1071–1125, 1099 and n.128.
133. McAdams, "Race and Selective Prosecution," 615.
134. Davis, "Prosecution and Race," 45.
135. McAdams, "Race and Selective Prosecution," 615–616.
136. United States v. Armstrong, 48 F.3d 1508, 1516–1517 (9th Cir. 1995) (en banc).
137. United States v. Armstrong, 469–470 (1996).
138. United States v. Armstrong, 482 (Stevens, J., dissenting).
139. Brief of NAACP Legal Defense & Educational Fund, Inc., and American Civil Liberties Union as Amicus Curiae in Support of Respondents, United States v. Armstrong, No. 95-157, 1996 WL 17149, at 5–7 (Jan. 16, 1996).
140. Karlan, "Race, Rights, and Remedies in Criminal Adjudication," 2025.
141. Oral Argument, United States v. Armstrong, No. 95-157, 1996 WL 88550, at 24 (February 26, 1996).
142. Oral Argument, United States v. Armstrong, 42.
143. Oral Argument, United States v. Armstrong, 2027–2030.
144. McCleskey v. Kemp, 333–334 (Brennan, J., dissenting); McCleskey v. Kemp, 364 (Blackmun, J., dissenting).
145. Paul Butler, "Equal Protection and White Supremacy," *Northwestern University Law Review* 112, no. 6 (2018): 1457–1464, 1459.
146. Whren v. United States, 517 U.S. 806, 813 (1996).
147. Goel et al., "Combatting Police Discrimination in the Age of Big Data," 206–207.

148. Goel et al., "Combatting Police Discrimination in the Age of Big Data, 198–199.
149. Siegel, "Blind Justice," 1288.
150. Floyd v. City of New York, 959 F. Supp. 2d 540, 603, 606 (S.D.N.Y. 2013).
151. Michael B. Mukasey, "New York's Stop-And-Frisk Ruling Is Ripe for Appeal," *Wall Street Journal*, August 19, 2013; The Constitutionality of Stop-and-Frisk in New York City, 162 U. Pa. L. Rev. Online 117 (2013–2014).
152. Wayte v. United States, 470 U.S. 598 (1985). It is hard to square the Court's acceptance of plea bargaining in *Bordenkircher* with *McCleskey*'s paean to the need for juries. The Court in *McCleskey* praised the jury and its "function to make the difficult and uniquely human judgments that defy codification" and bring needed equity and flexibility into the administration of criminal law, a sentiment that is completely at odds with its willingness to let prosecutors make defendants pay for exercising their jury trial right with harsher sentences. McCleskey v. Kemp, 311. If it is important enough to preserve the jury's discretion, even if it leads to racial bias, it is hard to see how it can be permissible for prosecutors to coerce defendants into giving up that constitutional protection.
153. Amicus Curiae Brief of the American Civil Liberties Union, New York Civil Liberties Union, and ACLU Foundation of Southern California in Support of Respondents at 6, United States v. Salerno, 481 U.S. 739 (1987) (No. 86-87).
154. McCleskey v. Kemp, 910–911 (11th Cir. 1985) (Johnson, J., dissenting in part and concurring in part).
155. Ky. Rev. Stat. Ann. § 532.300 (West 2021).
156. Rees Alexander, "A Model State Racial Justice Act: Fighting Racial Bias without Killing the Death Penalty," *George Mason University Civil Rights Law Journal* 24, no. 2 (2014): 113–157, 126.
157. Matt Smith, "'Racial Justice Act' Repealed in North Carolina," *CNN*, June 21, 2013, https://www.cnn.com/2013/06/20/justice/north-carolina-death-penalty/index.html.
158. "Racial Justice Acts of North Carolina and California," sidebar, in "Race and the Jury" report, 81–84, Equal Justice Initiative, Montgomery, AL, 2021, https://eji.org/report/race-and-the-jury/what-needs-to-happen/sidebar/racial-justice-acts-of-north-carolina-and-california/.
159. Ifeoma Ajunwa and Angela Onwuachi-Willig, "Combating Discrimination against the Formerly Incarcerated in the Labor Market," *Northwestern University Law Review* 112, no. 6 (2018): 1385–1415, 1404; Catherine London, "Racial Impact Statements: A Proactive Approach to Addressing Racial Disparities in Prison Populations," *Law & Inequality* 29, no. 1 (2011): 211–248, 227; Kevin R. Reitz, "Demographic Impact Statements, O'Connor's Warning, and the Mysteries of Prison Release: Topics from a Sentencing Reform Agenda," *Florida Law Review* 61, no. 4 (2009): 683–707, 691–692.
160. Ajunwa and Onwuachi-Willig, "Combating Discrimination against the Formerly Incarcerated," 1405.

161. Rebecca C. Hetey and Jennifer L. Eberhardt, "Racial Disparities in Incarceration Increase Acceptance of Punitive Policies," *Psychological Science* 25, no. 10 (2014): 1949–1954, 1950–1951 (finding that "the Blacker the prison population, the less willing registered voters were to take steps to reduce the severity of a law they acknowledged to be overly harsh").
162. Tom R. Tyler, *Why People Obey the Law* (New Haven: Yale University Press, 1990); Aziz Z. Huq, Tom R. Tyler, and Stephen J. Schulhofer, "Why Does the Public Cooperate with Law Enforcement?" *Psychology, Public Policy, and Law* 17, no. 3 (2011): 419–450; Tracey Meares, "Broken Windows, Neighborhoods, and the Legitimacy of Law Enforcement or Why I Fell In and Out of Love with Zimbardo," *Journal of Research in Crime and Delinquency* 52, no. 4 (2015): 609–625; Tracey Meares, "The Legitimacy of Police among Young African-American Men," *Marquette Law Review* 92, no. 4 (2009): 651–666.
163. United States v. Berrios, 501 F.2d 1207, 1209 (2d Cir. 1974).
164. State v. Gregory, 427 P.3d 621, 630, 633 (Wash. 2018).
165. State v. Gregory, 634–635.

Conclusion

Epigraph: Tessa Berenson, "Ruth Bader Ginsburg: Male Justices Have 'Blind Spot' about Women," *Time*, July 31, 2014.

1. Chief Justice Burger was a vocal opponent of the exclusionary rule and favored the government in criminal cases in his time on the D.C. Circuit, frequently disagreeing with his more liberal colleagues on that court. Justice Lewis Powell spoke "vigorously and emphatically" in favor of crime control. Justice Rehnquist served in the Nixon Administration and was a key architect of its tough-on-crime agenda before joining the Court and then upholding those same policies when they were challenged. Chief Justice Burger vouched for Justice Blackmun as being in the same camp, though it turned out he was a less reliable pro-government vote. Thomas Y. Davies, "The Supreme Court Giveth and the Supreme Court Taketh Away: The Century of Fourth Amendment 'Search and Seizure' Doctrine," *Journal of Criminal Law & Criminology* 100, no. 3 (2010): 933–1042, 993–494.
2. Warren E. Burger, "Annual Report to the American Bar Association by the Chief Justice of the United States," *American Bar Association Journal* 67, no. 3 (1981): 290–292.
3. "Table of Supreme Court Justices," *Constitution Annotated*, accessed June 22, 2023, https://constitution.congress.gov/resources/supreme-court-justices/.
4. Rachel E. Barkow, "Originalists, Politics, and Criminal Law on the Rehnquist Court," *George Washington Law Review* 74 (2006): 1061–62.
5. "RBG's Mixed Record on Race and Criminal Justice," *The Marshall Project*, September 23, 2020, https://www.themarshallproject.org/2020/09/23/rbg-s-mixed-record-on-race-and-criminal-justice.

6. Rachel E. Barkow, "Justice Sotomayor and Criminal Justice in the Real World," *Yale Law Journal Forum*, March 24, 2014, https://www.yalelawjournal.org/forum/justice-sotomayor-and-criminal-justice-in-the-real-world.
7. Dobbs v. Jackson Women's Health Org., 142 S.Ct. 2228, 2243 (2022).
8. Loper Bright Enterprises v. Raimondo (Gorsuch, J., concurring), slip op. at 17 (June 28, 2024).
9. "Confirmation Hearing on the Nomination of Amy Coney Barrett to the U.S. Supreme Court: Questions for the Record," "Questions from Senator Coons," October 16, 2020, 10, https://www.judiciary.senate.gov/imo/media/doc/Barrett%20Responses%20to%20QFRs.pdf; "Confirmation Hearing on the Nomination of the Hon. Brett M. Kavanaugh to be an Associate Justice of the Supreme Court of The United States: Hearing Before the Senate Committee on the Judiciary," 115th Cong., 196 (2018), https://www.govinfo.gov/content/pkg/CHRG-115shrg32765/pdf/CHRG-115shrg32765.pdf; Neil Gorsuch, *A Republic, If You Can Keep It* (New York: Crown Publishing Group, 2019); "A Conversation with Justice Clarence Thomas," *Pepperdine Law Review* 37, no. 5 (2009): 7–32, 20; Confirmation Hearing on the Nomination of Ketanji Brown Jackson to be an Associate Justice of the Supreme Court of the United States: Questions for the Record," "Questions from Senator Chuck Grassley," March 21, 2022, 1, https://www.judiciary.senate.gov/imo/media/doc/Judge%20Ketanji%20Brown%20Jackson%20Written%20Responses%20to%20Questions%20for%20the%20Record.pdf. Justice Alito has hedged his commitment to originalism, claiming he is a so-called "practical originalist." Matthew Walther, "Sam Alito: A Civil Man," *The American Spectator*, April 21, 2014. Chief Justice Roberts has similarly disavowed having "an overarching judicial philosophy," even though he has stated his view that "the Framers' intent is the guiding principle that should apply." "Confirmation Hearing on the Nomination of John G. Roberts, Jr. to be Chief Justice of the United States: Hearing Before the S. Comm. on the Judiciary," 109th Cong. (2005): 159, 182, https://www.judiciary.senate.gov/imo/media/doc/GPO-CHRG-ROBERTS.pdf (statement of John G. Roberts, Jr., Nominee, Chief Justice of the United States Supreme Court).
10. Erwin Chemerinsky, *Worse than Nothing: The Dangerous Fallacy of Originalism* (New Haven, CT: Yale University Press, 2022), 139–165; Richard H. Fallon, Jr., "Selective Originalism and Judicial Role Morality," *Texas Law Review* 102, no. 2 (2023): 221–304.
11. See, for example, Sessions v. Dimaya, 138 S. Ct. 1204, 1209–10, 1223–33 (2018) (Gorsuch, J., concurring in part and concurring in the judgment) (joining the Court's opinion that the residual clause of the Immigration and Nationality Act's definition of 'crime of violence' was unconstitutionally vague, emphasizing the importance of fair notice to defendants); Carpenter v. United States, 138 S. Ct. 2206, 1261–72 (2018) (Gorsuch, J., dissenting) (advocating a reevaluation of the third-party doctrine in the digital age and

endorsing a property-based approach to Fourth Amendment rights, potentially fortifying privacy protections for individuals' digital data); United States v. Davis, 139 S. Ct. 2319, 1223–36 (2019) (Gorsuch, J., writing for the majority) (holding that the statute imposing enhanced penalties for certain robberies and extortions is unconstitutionally vague); McGirt v. Oklahoma, 140 S. Ct. 2452, 2459–82 (2020) (Gorsuch, J., writing for the majority) (affirming the treaty rights of the Muscogee (Creek) Nation and protecting the jurisdictional boundaries against state encroachment, impacting the criminal jurisdiction over Native Americans); Ramos v. Louisiana, 140 S. Ct. 1390, 1391–97 (2020) (Gorsuch, J., writing for the majority) (holding that unanimous jury verdicts are required in state criminal trials in light of the original meaning of the Sixth Amendment).

12. See, for example, Apprendi v. New Jersey, 530 U.S. 466, 500–523 (2000) (Thomas, J., concurring) (writing separately to explain how the original understanding of the jury-trial requirement supports the Court's ruling that every fact increasing a penalty beyond the statutory maximum must be submitted to a jury and proven beyond a reasonable doubt); Ring v. Arizona, 536 U.S. 584, 610–12 (2002) (Thomas, J., concurring) (emphasizing the jury's role in death penalty eligibility, arguing against judge-only capital sentencing determinations); Blakely v. Washington, 542 U.S. 296, 303–304 (2004) (Thomas, J., joining the majority) (challenging sentencing guidelines that mandate sentence enhancements based on judicial fact-finding as a violation of the jury guarantee); Cunningham v. California, 549 U.S. 270, 290–293 (2007) (Thomas, J., joining the majority) (opposing diminished jury role in sentencing enhancements); Southern Union Co. v. United States, 567 U.S. 343, 360 (2012) (Thomas, J., joining the majority) (applying *Apprendi* to criminal fines); Alleyne v. United States, 570 U.S. 99, 108 (2013) (Thomas, J., writing for the majority) (extending *Apprendi* to mandatory minimums); United States v. Booker, 543 U.S. 220, 313 (2005) (Thomas, J., dissenting in part) (upholding jury trial rights in sentencing and offering a differing view on severability); Harris v. United States, 536 U.S. 545, 560–61 (2002) (Thomas, J., dissenting) (arguing that mandatory minimums not determined by a jury violate the Sixth Amendment); Ice v. Oregon, 555 U.S. 160, 168–169 (2009) (Thomas, J., dissenting) (maintaining the necessity of jury findings for facts increasing sentences beyond the maximum); and Hurst v. Florida, 577 U.S. 92, 102–103 (2016) (Thomas, J., joining the majority) (rejecting judge-only fact-finding in capital sentencing).

13. Given his stated views of the Eighth Amendment, however, Justice Thomas would not support proportionality review or oversight of prison conditions. He also seems unlikely to support a rollback of *McCleskey*. He could, however, possibly be convinced that *Salerno* and *Terry* were wrongly decided because the originalist arguments against both decisions are so strong.

ACKNOWLEDGMENTS

I first presented a version of the book's thesis in my B. Kenneth Simon Lecture for Constitution Day at the Cato Institute, and arguments from the lecture have been included throughout this book. The lecture was published as Rachel E. Barkow, The Court of Mass Incarceration, Cato Supreme Court Review 11 (2021–2022). I am grateful to the Cato Institute, and especially Clark Neily, for inviting me to give the lecture that sparked the central idea for this book.

It is impossible for me to give adequate thanks to my amazing colleagues who read the entire first draft of the book and offered invaluable feedback. Daryl Levinson remains the best framer of arguments in the business, and I owe him a huge thanks for being the first reader of the manuscript in its entirety and helping me see my own arguments in their best light. Erin Murphy is my partner in crime, or at least criminal law, and her gift with words helped make every chapter better. Barry Friedman always had the key questions to ask about each chapter, and his comments were invaluable. David Pozen helped me sharpen the framing of how the cases fall short under different modalities of constitutional interpretation.

I am also thankful for colleagues who took a close look at individual chapters to offer feedback. My interest in the Supreme Court's role in shaping criminal law and punishment in America can be traced to Tracey Maclin's class at Harvard Law School when I was a 3L, and it has never abated. He was and is a spectacular teacher, and I am so grateful he opened my eyes to these issues all those years ago and was willing, thirty years later, to offer helpful feedback on the *Terry* chapter. Steve Schulhofer and David Rudovsky also provided helpful pushback on that chapter, and I owe them a huge thanks for their views on *Terry*, which helped me to clarify my own presentation of the case. Terry Maroney also offered excellent suggestions on the *Terry* chapter, and she more than deserves getting the chapter named in her honor. John Meixner Jr. provided terrific feedback on the *Bordenkircher* chapter, for which I am grateful. Emma Kaufman and Sharon Dolovich know more about prison law than just about anyone, and they were both kind enough to offer helpful feedback on the *Rhodes* chapter and the overall framing of the book.

The students at NYU are the best, and I was fortunate to have an A-team of research assistants help with the book. Scott Baker, Jordan Battle, Gaelin Bernstein, Aimee Campbell, Connor Crinion, Ben Healy, Christopher Kim, Madison Leahy, Cleo Nevakivi-Callanan, Miriam Raffel-Smith, Gabriel Rosenblum, Walker Schulte Schneider, and Brooks Weinberger all contributed to the book by finding sources and providing wonderful feedback and edits.

I am also hugely grateful to Christine George, an amazing librarian who helped me track down sources, and my superstar assistant, Lara Maraziti, who helped proofread and format the manuscript.

I have worked at NYU under three deans, Ricky Revesz, Trevor Morrison, and Troy McKenzie, all of whom have fostered the collegial and intellectual climate that makes NYU the best place to work on a project like this one.

My husband, Tony Barkow, read the first draft of the book and offered helpful comments that made every chapter better. I am grateful I married someone who is as smart as he is kind. Everyone should have an in-house editor.

I had a yearlong sabbatical to write this book, and my son, Nate, made endless jokes about how I was getting paid to do nothing. His sense of humor and good nature always lift my spirits, and his ribbing was the best motivator because I knew I had to finish this book on time to prove to him that I was, in fact, researching and writing what would become a real book. The Post-it notes he left on my desk saying he was proud of me are among my most prized treasures. He will always be my greatest contribution to the world, intellectual and otherwise.

While I was writing this book, both my mother, Judi Selinfreund, and my brother, Mike Selinfreund, passed away. They did not follow my work closely because neither was particularly interested in the field I research, but both of them would always tell me they were proud of me. I hope they would be proud of this book. I miss them, and wish I could mail them a copy with an inscription letting them know how much I love them. I am grateful I will at least get the chance to do that for the rest of my family and friends.

INDEX

Aaron, Clarence, 48
Abbott, Greg, 125
Adams, Eric, 192
Adams, Sam, 3
Alexander, Michelle, 204
Alito, Samuel, 158–159, 160, 243
Alschuler, Al, 70, 77
American Bar Association (ABA): Burger's speech to, 65, 66, 238; Kennedy's speech to, 115–116, 118; on preventive detention, 43; Project on Minimum Standards for Criminal Justice, 60; report on jury trials, 75; report on plea bargaining, 55, 78, 257n23; Standards Relating to Pleading Guilty, 60
American Civil Liberties Union (ACLU): National Prison Project, 129; study of police stops in Boston, 200; *Terry v. Ohio* and, 176–177; *United States v. Armstrong* and, 229; *United States v. Salerno* and, 33
American Civil War, 202, 205, 220
American Medical Association, 131, 139
American Public Health Association, 139
Amsterdam, Anthony, 177, 223, 224
Andrade, Leandro, 110–113. *See also Lockyer v. Andrade*
Angelos, Claudia, 129
Angelos, Weldon, 48
Arpaio, Joe, 124

Article II of US Constitution, 84
Article III of US Constitution, 51–52, 84
Attica Prison Riot, 150. *See also* prison riots and uprisings

Bagby, Glen, 67–69, 70, 71, 72–73, 74. *See also Bordenkircher v. Hayes*
bail, right to, 18–19, 21, 31, 37, 249n45
Bail Reform Act (1966), 16, 17, 25–28, 30, 32, 34, 36, 39–41, 43, 250n61. *See also United States v. Salerno*
Baldus, David, 203, 211–213
Baldus study, 203, 211–216, 219, 220, 222, 223, 224, 230
Batson v. Kentucky, 218
Bell v. Wolfish, 135–137, 152, 251n65
Bill of Rights, English (1689), 20, 86–87, 90–91, 92, 96, 100–102
Bill of Rights, US, 43, 84, 87, 100–102, 128
Black Codes, 205
Blackmun, Harry: *Bordenkircher v. Hayes* and, 72–73; *Estelle v. Gamble* and, 130, 131; *Farmer v. Brenan* and, 153; *McCleskey v. Kemp* and, 216, 218–221, 230; *Solem v. Helm* and, 96; *Terry v. Ohio* and, 142; *Wilson v. Seiter* and, 152
Bloody Code, 3, 100
Bloomberg, Michael, 192
BMW of North America, Inc. v. Gore, 117, 118

Boger, Charles, 219
Boland, Barbara, 194
Bordenkircher v. Hayes, 6, 49; aftermath and impact, 74–81; case background, 67–69; decision and argument, 69–74; dissent, 72–73; originalism and, 241. *See also* plea bargaining
Bowers, Josh, 74
Brady v. United States, 64–65, 66–67, 71–72, 74, 260n66
Brennan, William J., Jr., 142
Brewer, David J., 88
Breyer, Stephen, 110, 156, 239
Brinegar v. United States, 174
Browder, Kalief, 14
Brown v. Board of Education, 129, 169–170, 206
Brown v. Plata, 153–162
Burger, Warren, 65–66, 97, 115, 141, 186, 238, 239

cadena temporal, 89, 94, 128
Cafaro, Vincent, 28–30. *See also United States v. Salerno*
California Correctional Peace Officers Association, 155
capital sentences, 84–85, 91–93, 203, 211, 214, 216, 219, 223
Carcetti, Gil, 109
Carter, Paul, 120
Castaneda v. Partida, 209, 215
Chemerinsky, Erwin, 190
Chertoff, Michael, 115
Chesterton, G. K., 75
Chilton, Richard, 177, 178. *See also Terry v. Ohio*
civil commitment, 22, 23, 44
Civil Rights Act (1866), 205
Clark, Charles, 54
Clarke, David, 124–125
clemency, 84, 105, 118, 201
Clinton, Bill, 226, 239
coercive plea bargaining. *See* plea bargaining
Coker v. Georgia, 220
common law, 86, 87, 101, 172–173

Cooper v. Pate, 129
COVID-19 pandemic, 151
Cruel and Unusual Punishment Clause, 6, 88, 91–92, 95, 99, 101, 109–112, 117, 129, 134

Davies, Thomas, 180–181
Davis, Angela, 74, 224, 228–229
Davis, Cynthia, 150
Davis, Richard Allen, 107–108
de Blasio, Bill, 192
De Bracton, Henry, 86
defamation, 19
Deitch, Michele, 125
disproportionate sentences: Constitutional framework, 85–93; cruel and unusual punishment and, 84–102, 109–112, 116–117, 121; Eighth Amendment and, 84–104, 109–110, 114–119, 121; examples of, 82–83; normalizing, 85. *See also Harmelin v. Michigan*
District of Columbia Court Reform and Criminal Procedure Act (1970), 16, 25–27
DNA evidence, 71
double bunking and double celling, 7, 126, 135–141, 144, 145–146, 148, 149, 150, 151, 161. *See also* overcrowded prisons
Douglas, William O., 91, 184–185, 187, 261n71
Draper Correctional Center (Alabama), 122–123
Dred Scott v. Sandford, 224
Driver, Justin, 148

Eighth Amendment, 5–6, 20, 236; Cruel and Unusual Punishment Clause, 6, 88, 91–92, 95, 99, 101, 109–112, 117, 129, 134; disproportionate sentencing and, 84–104, 109–110, 114–119, 121; Excessive Bail Clause, 18, 20, 21, 30, 37, 38; overcrowded prisons and, 125–135, 141, 143–144, 146, 152–159, 162; pretrial detention and, 37–38;

proportionality test, 103–107; racial bias and, 214, 218, 220, 232
Equal Protection Clause, 202, 204–205, 215, 222–223, 230, 231, 237–238, 241
Estelle v. Gamble, 130–134
Ewing v. California, 108–110, 112–115, 120
Excessive Fines Clause, 116–117, 250–251n63
Ex Post Facto Clause, 51

Fagan, Jeffrey, 192, 194
false self-condemnation, 69, 71
Farmer v. Brenan, 153
Federalist Papers, 53, 84
Federal Standards for Prisons and Jails, 140
Feeley, Malcolm, 127, 148
Field, Stephen Johnson, 88–89
Fifteenth Amendment, 206
Fifth Amendment, 61, 74
First Amendment, 74, 129
Fisher, George, 54
flight risk, 19, 21–23, 26, 31, 44, 248n18
Floyd, George, 196
Forrester, J. Owen, 213–214
Fourteenth Amendment, 84, 93, 173, 192, 202, 204, 205–206, 218–219. *See also* Equal Protection Clause
Fourth Amendment, 76, 164, 165, 171–174, 176, 178; Reasonableness Clause, 171, 180; Warrant Clause, 171, 180
Frankel, Marvin, 135
Frankfurter, Felix, 76
Friedman, Barry, 172
Furman v. Georgia, 212, 214, 220, 232

Gamble, J. W. *See Estelle v. Gamble*
Garland, David, 8–9
George, Stephanie, 83
Gingrich, Newt, 124
Ginsburg, Ruth Bader, 110, 156, 239
Goldwater, Barry, 175
Graham v. Florida, 114
Grassley, Charles, 78

Gregg v. Georgia, 212
Gross, Samuel, 215

Habeas Corpus Act (1679), 20
habitual offender laws, 68, 107, 120
Hamilton, Alexander, 53, 84
Hand, Learned, 51, 52–53
Haney-López, Ian, 206–207, 225
Hannigan, Todd, 83
Harlan, John Marshall, 88, 287n126
Harmelin v. Michigan, 6; aftermath and impact, 107–121; case background, 98; decision and argument, 98–99, 102, 103; dissent, 110, 112; historical context, 94–97; originalism and, 241; proportionality test for, 103–107. *See also* disproportionate sentences
Harris, Jimmy, 68
Hasan, Hamedah, 120
Hausman, David, 191
Hayes, Paul Lewis, 67–69, 70, 73. *See also Bordenkircher v. Hayes*
Helm, Jerry, 96. *See also Solem v. Helm*
Henry, Patrick, 3, 87
Herbert, Bob, 193
Hessick, Carissa Byrne, 70
Hogan, Timothy Sylvester, 138, 139
Holman Maximum Security Facility (Alabama), 122–123
Howard, Jacob, 205, 219
Hudson v. Parker, 31
Hutto v. Davis, 95, 103
Hutto v. Finney, 133, 134

Illinois v. Wardlaw, 187–188
Imbler v. Pachtman, 217–218
industrialization, 2
Ivey, Kay, 124

Jackson, Ketanji Brown, 240, 242
Jackson, Robert, 31, 44
Jackson, Timothy, 83
Jacobs, Jim, 129
Jefferson, Thomas, 53
Jimenez, Victor, 13–14
job displacement, 2

Johnson, Frank, 143
Johnson, Lyndon, 55, 176
Judiciary Act (1789), 18–19, 249n45
juvenile detention, 35–37

Kagan, Elena, 156, 242
Karlan, Pam, 229–230
Katzenbach Commission, 54–55
Kaufman, Emma, 148
Kavanaugh, Brett, 242
Kelly, Ray, 192, 232
Kennedy, Anthony, 6, 98, 103–107, 109, 114–119, 151, 156, 267n63
Kennedy, Randall, 213–214
Kennedy, Robert, 170
Kentucky Habitual Criminal Act, 67–68
Kerner Commission, 176
King, Martin Luther, Jr., 170
Klaas, Polly, 107–108
Korematsu v. United States, 34–35, 253n111
Kronick, Dorothy, 191

Langbein, John, 62
life without parole (LWOP), 48, 104, 114
Lima State Hospital for the Criminally Insane, 138
Lockyer v. Andrade, 110–113, 115
Lynch, Gerard, 76

Maclin, Tracey, 185
mafia, 28–29
Magna Carta, 86
mandatory minimum sentences, 6, 48, 77–78, 81, 84, 114, 115, 120, 153, 210
Mapp v. Ohio, 165, 169–170, 175, 238
Marshall, Consuelo, 226
Marshall, Thurgood: *Estelle v. Gamble* and, 130–131; *Rhodes v. Chapman* and, 145–147; *United States v. Salerno* and, 29–30, 35–36, 37, 38–39, 46, 253n126, 274n51
Mason, George, 87
Mazzoli, Romano, 32–33
McAdams, Richard, 228
McClain, Elijah, 196

McCleskey v. Kemp: aftermath and impact, 204, 223–224; Baldus study and, 203, 211–216, 219, 220, 222, 223, 224, 230; case history, 211–215; decision and argument, 215–218; dissent, 216, 218–222. *See also* racial bias and disparities
McFadden, Martin, 177–180, 182, 183, 186. *See also Terry v. Ohio*
McKenna, Joseph, 90
Meares, Tracey, 192, 234
Metropolitan Correctional Center (MCC), 135
Michigan State Supreme Court, 106–107
Michigan v. Bullock, 106
Miranda v. Arizona, 169–170, 175, 180, 238
Mitchell, John, 24–25, 30, 33, 39–40, 250–251n63
Morris, Gouverneur, 52

NAACP Legal Defense Fund, 129, 169, 173–174, 176–177, 193, 196, 211–213, 229
National District Attorneys Association, 104, 176
National Prison Project, 129
National Rifle Association, 107
Nelson, Bill, 56–57
New Jersey State Supreme Court, 33–34
Newman, Jon, 20
Nixon, Richard: appointments to Supreme Court, 207, 238; criticism of Supreme Court's criminal procedure decisions, 169, 175; DC Court Reform and Criminal Procedure Act, 16, 25–27; pretrial detention policies, 16, 24, 25, 28

Oates, Titus, 101, 266n51
O'Connor, Sandra Day, 97, 98, 109, 111–112, 114, 117, 151, 216
O'Neill v. Vermont, 88–89
organized crime, 28–29
Ortman, William, 72

INDEX

Otis, James, 173
overcrowded prisons: Constitutional framework, 127–134; Eighth Amendment and, 125–135, 141, 143–144, 146, 152–159, 162; examples of, 122–123; history of, 134–135; lower court constitutional challenges, 127–130; statistics, 147, 153; Supreme Court constitutional challenges, 130–134. *See also* double bunking and double celling; *Rhodes v. Chapman*

pedestrian stops, 190–191, 200
Personnel Administrator of Massachusetts v. Feeney, 209–210, 218, 225
Petition of Right (1628), 20
plea bargaining, 6, 9; ABA report, 55, 78, 257n23; acceptance of coercive plea bargaining, 64–74; bias and disparities in, 75, 78; *Brady v. United States*, 64–65, 66–67, 71–72, 74, 260n66; Constitutional framework, 50–64; doctrine of unconstitutional conditions and, 55–64, 65, 74; examples of, 48; history of, 47–50; racial disparities and, 201; right to trial by jury and, 50–55; statistics, 74–75. *See also Bordenkircher v. Hayes*
Plessy v. Ferguson, 206
police violence, 196–197
Pollard, Jonathan, 79
Powell, Lewis F., 73, 96–97, 141–142, 209, 215, 223
Pozen, David, 117
presumption of innocence, 5, 19–21, 25, 27, 43, 72, 135–136, 159, 198, 237
pretrial detention: acceptable reasons for, 21–23; average period for federal defendants, 27; civil commitment and, 22, 23, 44; Constitutional framework, 17–24; costs and impact of, 14–15, 31–32; Due Process Clause and, 18–19, 21, 30–31, 32, 34, 37, 38; examples of, 12–14; Excessive Bail Clause and, 18, 20, 21, 30, 37, 38; flight risk and, 19, 21–23, 26, 31, 44, 248n18; history of, 15–16; physical conditions of, 14; racial disparities and, 41–42, 44, 200, 232; statistics, 15–16, 27–28, 40, 42, 44–45; surveillance and, 22–23, 34; witness tampering and, 22, 23. *See also* bail; Bail Reform Act; *United States v. Salerno*
preventive detention, 16, 17, 30, 33–37, 39–40, 42–45, 247n18. *See also* pretrial detention
Prison Litigation Reform Act (PLRA), 154–155, 158–159
prison lockdowns, 149, 154
Prison Overcrowding State of Emergency Proclamation (California), 153–154
Prison Release Reoffender Law (Florida), 83
prison riots and uprisings, 129, 135, 139, 140, 149–151
probable cause, 9, 72, 164–165, 168–177, 179–185, 189–191, 194
profiling, 188–189
Pulaski, Charles, 211. *See also* Baldus study

racial bias and disparities, 9, 199–204; Constitutional framework, 204–211; Eighth Amendment and, 214, 218, 220, 232; plea bargaining and, 78, 201; policing and, 200; pretrial detention and, 41–42, 44, 200, 232; prosecutorial charging and, 201; sentencing and, 201; stop-and-frisk and, 192, 194; traffic stops and, 200, 203. *See also McCleskey v. Kemp*
racial impact statements, 234
Racial Justice Act (California), 234
Racial Justice Act (Kentucky), 233
racism, 2, 223–225, 228–229. *See also* racial bias and disparities
Racketeer Influenced and Corrupt Organizations (RICO) Act, 28
Reconstruction Amendments, 206. *See also* Fourteenth Amendment

Rehnquist, William: *Bell v. Wolfish* and, 135–136; *Harmelin v. Michigan* and, 109, 113; *Hutto v. Finney* and, 134; *McCleskey v. Kemp* and, 216; *Personnel Administrator of Massachusetts v. Feeney* and, 210; pretrial detention and, 30, 34, 35, 36; *Rummel v. Estelle* and, 94–95, 97–99; *State Farm Mutual Automobile Insurance Co. v. Campbell* and, 117; *Terry v. Ohio* and, 141; *United States v. Armstrong* and, 227
Resnik, Judith, 148
Reynolds, Mike, 107–108
Rhodes v. Chapman, 7; aftermath and impact, 126, 127, 147–162; case background, 126; historical context, 134–135; originalism and, 241. *See also* overcrowded prisons
Richman, Dan, 26
Riggs, Michael, 82
Rikers Island, 13–14
riots. *See* prison riots and uprisings; urban riots
Robinson v. California, 91, 93, 129
Rodgers, Mitchell Ray, 68
Rubin, Ed, 127, 148
Rummel v. Estelle, 94–99, 103, 113, 115, 119

Salerno, Anthony, 28–30. *See also United States v. Salerno*
Saltzman, Lance, 83
Santobello v. New York, 65–66, 80, 97, 261n71
Scalia, Antonin, 98, 230, 242; *Brown v. Plata* and, 157–158; *Harmelin v. Michigan* and, 98–103; *McCleskey v. Kemp* and, 216, 218–219; originalism of, 99–102; *Wilson v. Seiter* and, 151
Schall v. Martin, 35–37, 38
Scheindlin, Shira, 192, 193, 196
Schlanger, Margo, 128
Schlatt, Frank, 211. *See also McCleskey v. Kemp*
Schwartz, Joanna, 197
Schwarzenegger, Arnold, 153–154

Sentencing Commission, US, 201, 225–226, 229
Sentencing Project, 120, 121
Seo, Sarah, 164–165
Silva, Duane, 83
Simon, Jonathan, 141, 148
Solem v. Helm, 96, 97–98, 103, 106, 112–113, 115, 117, 129
Sotomayor, Sonia, 156, 163, 240, 242
Souter, David, 98, 110, 112, 151
Southern Ohio Correctional Facility (SOCF), 137–139, 142, 145, 146, 149–151
Speedy Trial Act, 26, 40, 251n77
Spilmon, Bryan, 79
Stack v. Boyle, 18–19
Starr, Kenneth, 104
State Farm Mutual Automobile Insurance Co. v. Campbell, 117
Staton, Lewis R., 219–220
Stevens, John Paul: *Bell v. Wolfish* and, 136; *Estelle v. Gamble* and, 132–133; *Harmelin v. Michigan* and, 110; on proportionality review, 118; *Terry v. Ohio* and, 142; *United States v. Salerno* and, 30; *Weems v. United States* and, 95
Stevens, Thaddeus, 205
Stewart, Potter, 69, 91, 141
stop-and-frisk: background and examples, 163–170; Constitutional framework, 171–174; probable cause and, 9, 72, 164–165, 168–177, 179–185, 189–191, 194. *See also Terry v. Ohio*
Story, Joseph, 90
Stroup, Robert, 213
Stuntz, William, 175, 223–224
suicide, 14, 139, 151, 155
Summer, George, 140
surveillance: aggressive surveillance techniques, 181; *cadena temporal* and, 89; pretrial detention and, 22–23, 34; racial bias and, 200

Terry v. Ohio, 8, 164–165, 169–170; aftermath and impact, 165, 169,

185–198; case background, 175–178; decision and argument, 179–185; dissent, 184–185; media coverage of, 185–186; originalism and, 241; probable cause and, 164–165, 168–185, 189–191, 194; stop-and-frisk in the courts after, 186–192; stop-and-frisk on the streets after, 192–198. *See also* stop-and-frisk
Thirteenth Amendment, 206
Thomas, Clarence, 109, 116, 157, 243
three-strikes laws: California, 82–83, 107–115; Kentucky, 67
Thurmond, Strom, 26
Title VII cases, 207, 216, 219
Tomlin, Tyrone, 12–13, 14
tough-on-crime policies: costs and impact of, 1, 6–7, 236; legislators and, 77; politicians and, 16, 125; Rehnquist and, 299n1; Sotomayor and, 240; Supreme Court and, 9–10, 38, 93. *See also* pretrial detention
traffic stops, 189–191, 195, 197, 200, 203
Tribe, Larry, 25, 41, 206
Trop v. Dulles, 91, 92, 113–114
Trump, Donald, 34
Tyler, Tom, 234

unconstitutional conditions, doctrine of, 55–64, 65, 74
United States v. Armstrong, 225–230, 232
United States v. Bajakajian, 116–117
United States v. Jackson, 260n66
United States v. Salerno, 5; aftermath and impact, 39–46; amicus brief by police and prosecutors, 42, 45, 229; case background, 28–30; decision and argument, 30–38, 43, 112, 135–136; dissent, 29–30, 35–36, 37, 38–39, 46, 253n126, 274n51; historical context, 24–28; *Korematsu* and, 253n111; originalism and, 30, 33, 38, 241. *See also* pretrial detention
urban riots, 169–170, 175, 176

Vance, Robert, 214
Vermont Supreme Court, 88, 89
Verrilli, Don, 21
Vietnam War protests, 170
Virginia Declaration of Rights, 87

Walker, John, 28–29
Wardlaw, William. *See Illinois v. Wardlaw*
war on drugs, 91, 104, 106
Warren, Earl, 169–170, 175, 179–181, 186, 203, 211, 238
Washington, George, 3
Washington Legal Foundation, 221
Washington State Supreme Court, 234–235
Washington v. Davis, 207–210
Weems v. United States, 89–91, 94–95, 128, 265n39
White, Byron, 90–91, 97, 100, 103, 129, 141, 152, 207, 216, 267n63
Whren v. United States, 189–191, 197, 231
Williams, Jerry DeWayne, 82
Wilson, James Q., 194
Wilson, Pete, 108
Wilson v. Seiter, 151–153
witness tampering, 22, 23
Wolff v. McDonnell, 129
Woodworth, George, 211. *See also* Baldus study

Yick Wo v. Hopkins, 228, 231

Zenger, John Peter, 52–53